CRIMINAL JUSTICE, LAW ENFORCEMENT AND CORRECTIONS SERIES

DELINQUENCY: CAUSES, REDUCTION AND PREVENTION

Criminal Justice, Law Enforcement and Corrections Series

Homicide Investigations
Allan B. Smythe (Editor)
2009 ISBN 978-1-60692-258-3

Mass Incarceration and Offender Reentry in the United States
Russell D. Javitze (Editor)
2009 ISBN 978-1-60692-657-4

Batterer Intervention: Program Approaches and Criminal Justice Strategies
Kerry Healey, Christine Smith and Chris O'Sullivan
2009 ISBN 978-1-60876-537-9

Digital Surveillance: Laws, Security and Related Issues
Joseph G. Massingale (Editor)
2009 ISBN 978-1-60692-312-2

Incarceration and the Family: Issues, Effects and Approaches to Successful Reentry
U.S. Dept. of Health and Human Services
2009 ISBN 978-1-60692-933-9

Policing the Police: Knowledge Management in Law Enforcement
Petter Gottschalk
2009 ISBN: 978-1-60741-765-1

Policing the Police: Knowledge Management in Law Enforcement
Petter Gottschalk
2009. ISBN 978-1-60876-653-6
Online Book

Gun Ownership and the Second amendment
Pjeter D. Baldrige (Editor)
2009 ISBN: 978-1-60692-226-2

Batterer Intervention: Program Approaches and Criminal Justice Strategies
Kerry Healey, Christine Smith, and Chris O'Sullivan
2009. ISBN: 978-1-60692-934-6

Homicide: Trends, Causes and Prevention
Randal B. Toliver and Ulrich R. Coyne (Editors)
2009. ISBN: 978-1-60741-625-8

Delinquency: Causes, Reduction and Prevention
Ozan Sahin and Joseph Maier (Editor)
2009 ISBN: 978-1-60741-558-9

CRIMINAL JUSTICE, LAW ENFORCEMENT AND CORRECTIONS SERIES

DELINQUENCY: CAUSES, REDUCTION AND PREVENTION

OZAN SAHIN
AND
JOSEPH MAIER
EDITORS

Nova Science Publishers, Inc.
New York

For permission to use material from this book please contact us:
Telephone 631-231-7269; Fax 631-231-8175
Web Site: http://www.novapublishers.com

LIBRARY OF CONGRESS CATALOGING-IN-PUBLICATION DATA

Deliquency causes, reduction and prevention / [edited by] Ozan Sahin and Joseph Maier.
p. cm.
Includes index.
ISBN 978-1-60741-558-9 (hardcover)
1. Juvenile delinquency. 2. Juvenile delinquency--Prevention. I. Sahin, Ozan. II. Maier, Joseph, 1964-
HV9069.D47 2009
364.36--dc22

2009024602

Published by Nova Science Publishers, Inc. ✝ New York

CONTENTS

PREFACE

Delinquency is an antisocial misdeed in violation of the law by a minor. This book examines the correlation between family environment and juvenile delinquency and criminality. Also discussed are the social factors that influence delinquent behavior. The unresolved and contentious issue of different explanatory "types" or "etiological patterns" among delinquents and the conflict this creates for advocates of "general theory" in delinquency are also addressed. Additional chapters look at adolescent religiosity as a factor for delinquency, psychopathic tendencies and causes of delinquency from a biosocial criminological perspective.

Chapter 1 - Theoretical approaches in delinquency have prioritized the search for a "general" global theory with the assumption that a single unified theory underlies all delinquency (e.g. strain theory, social control, social learning, low self-control, etc).

Recent theorists have also attempted to integrate various elements of these diverse theories into a unified general model (e.g. Farrington 2003, Elliot et al 1985, Sampson and Laub 2005). In contrast, the taxonomic approach adopts a theoretical pluralism that denies the existence of a single unified explanation. It aims to unravel delinquency populations into multiple categories or sub-types that may represent diverse causal processes. Moffitt (1993), Lykken (1995) and others, offer such proposals.

The theoretical stakes are high with advocates on both sides. The Authors will address several issues central to this debate including: Can diverse types of delinquents be reliably identified? Are the boundaries between types distinct? What kind of taxonomic structure exists in this population? The Authors then report on a large scale (N = 3070) replication and refinement of a previously published delinquent taxonomy using the Youth COMPAS assessment system (Brennan, Breitenbach and Dieterich 2008).

Multiple validation methods were used. Substantially the same results emerged, with evidence of stable taxonomic structure in which six out of seven replicated types emerged; these were again nested within five more super-ordinate clusters. These types had multiple matches in the prior literature on explanatory delinquent typologies. The authors finally explore the implications of our findings for the debate over the general theory paradigm.

Chapter 2 - There are nearly as many supposed causes of juvenile delinquency as authors writing on the subject! While a consistent sociological literature has been produced on the sociological mechanisms of the aetiology of juvenile delinquency, and while an equally consistent psychosociological literature has also been produced about peer group influence on the same topic, much less has been published on the influence of family environment.

Though, not all poor children become delinquent! The authors present here a review about what they have learnt from developmental psychopathology works concerning this question.

Chapter 3 - Involvement in delinquent behavior is quite common during adolescence, and many authors consider it to be a transient phenomenon. However, the prevalence of mental disorders in juvenile delinquents appears to be relevant. It has been proposed that emotional disturbances are frequently associated with neuropsychological dysfunction as a result of a common biological, mainly genetic origin. Among cognitive dysfunctioning, impairment in executive cognitive functions (ECF) may be related especially to mental disorders, to failures in personality development, and to conduct and personality disorders. ECF include cognitive flexibility, hypothesis generation, abstract reasoning, problem solving, selective attention, inhibitory control and ability to organize and use information contained in working memory, all fundamental in social cognition and social behaviors. High prevalence rates (up to 80%) of ECF deficits have been reported in juvenile criminals. ECF and other neuropsychological and cognitive impairments, such as lower IQ and verbal deficits, have been associated with the pattern of antisocial and delinquent behavior starting in childhood (early-onset), but not with late-onset antisocial behavior. Based on this background, their purpose was to evaluate ECF in a sample of adolescents and young adults, with a pattern of late-onset delinquent behavior and no antecedents of conduct disorder, referred to the Social Services of the Department of Juvenile Justice of the city of Messina (Italy). The hypothesis tested with this design was that late-onset delinquent adolescents and young adults differ from nonantisocial controls matched for age and educational level on neuropsychological measures sensitive to ECF dysfunction (Stroop Color-Word task, or Stroop task; AB-AC; Raven's Standard Progressive Matrices (SPM); Verbal Fluency, both Phonemic and Semantic; and Winsconsin Card Sorting Test). Results showed significant differences between late-onset offenders and control groups on the following tasks: Stroop ($t = 3.570$; $p = < 0.0001$), SPM ($t = -7.174$; $p = < 0.0001$), and Phonemic Fluency ($t = -10.743$; $p = < 0.0001$). Chi-square analysis showed that a significantly greater number of late-onset offending participants scored in the clinical range on several ECF measures. Current findings add to the growing literature comparing juvenile offenders to other adolescent populations. These results imply that executive cognitive impairment, even subtle and subclinical, may be a contributing factor in the development and persistence of antisocial behaviors displayed by late-onset adolescent delinquents. The findings also suggest the need for additional research aimed to assess a broader range of cognitive abilities and specific vulnerability and risk factors for late-onset adolescent offenders.

Chapter 4 - Reputation enhancement theory is a dominant theory in the juvenile delinquency literature. It has clearly established that a delinquent identity requires public proof of a deviant disposition and that deviant acts are committed not alone, but in the company of others. Therefore, self-image is fostered by the visibility of actions to others, and perceptions and descriptions of oneself and others. If these are key elements on which the psychology of reputation is built, how then does this apply to adolescents who commit delinquent acts, but alone? Very little is known about the delinquent activities and reputational orientations of adolescent loners, yet recent research by the authors clearly shows the unique profiles of these individuals. In this chapter, the authors present the findings from a series of studies which they believe to be the only ones to date pertaining to the delinquent activities and reputational orientations of loners.

First, the instruments we have developed over time to measure these aspects of adolescents' behavior are briefly described along with their psychometric properties. Following this, the authors present empirical evidence from our research in which the authors employed various statistical analyses to compare the self-report delinquency and reputational orientations of adolescent loners and nonloners.

Chapter 5 - This chapter presents an investigation of the patterns of offending and antisocial behaviour amongst young people from the age of 11-16 years who are categoried as high risk or vulnerable to delinquency and antisocial behaviour. The chapter will draw upon findings from the first five datasweeps of the Belfast Youth Development Study (BYDS), a longitudinal study of the onset and development of adolescent problem behaviour. Through a detailed exploration of the onset and development of delinquency and antisocial behaviour from the age of 11-16 years it will provide insights for targeting and development of appropriate interventions for school aged high risk young people who do not attend mainstream school in adolescence. The findings will form the empirical base for a discussion of the key issues around appropriate interventions and the development of conclusions in relation to young people who have received comparatively less attention in the delinquency literature but who are considered more likely to offend during adolescence.

Chapter 6 - The first section of this chapter reviews evidence showing that although greater religiosity has been associated with less involvement in delinquent and analogous behaviors, the mechanisms and processes through which religiosity is linked to delinquent behavior are not well understood. In the second section of the chapter, a conceptual framework and theory for studying the religion-delinquency association will be presented. The framework adapts and builds on Gottfredson and Hirschi's (1990) General Theory of Crime. The third section of the chapter presents results of the initial study guided by the framework. Data are drawn from a longitudinal study of development during the transition from middle childhood to adolescence. Participants (n = 181) completed standard self-report assessments. Results provide initial evidence that the link between religiosity and delinquent behavior problems can be explained by the reduced opportunities and dispositions to engage in delinquent behavior more common among highly religious than less highly religious adolescents.

Chapter 7 - New instrumentation measuring psychopathic-like-traits and aggression in children and adolescents suspended from mainstream school were developed. One hundred and seventeen psychopathy related items and 63 aggression items were generated from reviews of current instrumentation and interviews with school personnel, psychologists, and detention centre officers.

These were subsequently reduced to 56 and 20, respectively. Data from one pilot study and the preliminary analysis of data from a larger scale study analyzed using item affectivity and discrimination resulted in 43 psychopathy items and 20 aggression items being retained. Maximum likelihood factor analyses of data from 137 suspended mainstream school students revealed four factors for psychopathy (Callous/Unemotional, Narcissism, Thrill- Seeking, and Moral Detachment of Self) and three for aggression (Physical Aggression, Reactive Verbal Aggression and Proactive Verbal Aggression). Cronbach's alpha revealed high internal consistency.

Chapter 8 - Violent offending by young people is a visibly growing problem for both society and the particular individuals involved. Recent research conducted in the United Kingdom revealed that over 20% of 10 to 25 year olds report having committed a crime, 59%

of which were violent offences (Wilson, Sharp and Patterson, 2006). Prior research has examined particular factors that make children and adolescents more inclined to criminal activities and whether these factors are controllable. This study looks at the interaction of risk factors at the family, social and community levels by testing a causal model in a sample composed of 2528 participants aged 10-16 who were drawn from the 2005 Offending, Crime and Justice Survey dataset.

To begin with, the authors review some data on the prevalence of violent offending among young people in different countries, and continue by discussing some of the main family, school and community factors that have been related to involvement in violent offending and delinquent behaviours in adolescence. Family variables include quality of children-parent relationships and parenting skills such as family communication. School variables refer to attitude to school and whether the child has been suspended or expelled from school. Finally, community variables include the existence of problem behaviours in the local area and degree of trust in local police.

Following this review, the authors analyse the role played by two other direct antecedents of offending that have been highlighted in the scientific literature, namely antisocial behaviour and victimization. Finally, a causal model is tested to examine the interactions among all the aforementioned variables and their joint contribution to the explanation of youth offending. The model tested explained 22% of the variance in violent offending by the young people in the sample. Victimization and anti-social behaviour independently contributed to the amount of variance, while family, community and school contexts had differential effects on these two proximal causes. By jointly considering the influence of the most important social contexts in adolescence, this study provides a fuller picture and clearer understanding of the risks for violent adolescent offending. Implications and future areas of research are discussed.

Chapter 9 - This study aimed to examine the relation between childhood social behaviors and later delinquency. To assess this relation, we used ratings of the level of difficultness and aggression exhibited by 90 5-year-old children during their interactions with an unfamiliar peer and assessed parent ratings of delinquency at age 5 and parent and self-ratings of delinquent activities five to ten years later. Early social behaviors were related to concurrent parent ratings of delinquency but they were not predictive of later delinquency. However, adolescent peers' delinquent behaviors were correlated with adolescent delinquency. Additionally, there was preliminary evidence that youth who began exhibiting delinquent behaviors as young as age 5 were more likely to show interpersonal difficult behaviors at age 5, whereas those who did not report delinquent behaviors until adolescence did not show preschool difficult behaviors but were equally as likely as the early starters to report having delinquent peers. Thus, although early difficult interactions with peers are related to delinquent activities at the same age, peer play behaviors during childhood are neither necessary nor sufficient causes to account for association with deviant peers or engaging in delinquent activities during adolescence.

Chapter 10 - The discipline of criminology has a long history of focusing narrowly on the environmental correlates to antisocial behaviors, while simultaneously ignoring the possibility that genetic factors are important. With the mapping of the human genome and with the advent of complex brain imaging machines, researchers have been able to study the genetic basis to all types of human behaviors. The results of these studies have unequivocally shown that virtually all antisocial outcomes are the result of genetic *and* environmental factors working independently and interactively. An emerging perspective—known as biosocial criminology—has recently been advanced as a way of incorporating these findings from the biological sciences into criminology. In the current chapter, the authors provide an overview of the biosocial criminological perspective. In doing so, the authors pay particular attention to explaining gene X environment interactions, gene X environment correlations, and epigenetic processes, and how they affect the development of antisocial behaviors.

Chapter 11 - This research work focuses on twenty-five male adolescents who have been placed in a children's French community home. The authors have developed a theoretical model to deal with the specific identity disorders of adolescents by developing *the concept of narcissistic identity vulnerability* and making it operational. The clinical protocol used and more particularly the hypothetic-deductive methodology applied to case studies constitute a *clinical evaluation method* of narcissistic identity vulnerability that can be transposed, in situations of clinical practice, to problem adolescents with a view to assessing and guiding personalized projects. This concept enables us to offer a *dynamic-economic analysis of maladjusted behaviour* in adolescents.

The authors suggest a clinical battery of investigation that can be applied to clinical practice. This battery including *Wechsler's Intelligence Test, Rorschach's Projective Test, Life Line and Genogram, The Family Test « FAST »* (developed by Gehring and Debry in Belgium), enables us to analyse the adolescent's representation of his family and to grasp the intra-family dynamics and an adaptation to an analysis of adolescents' representation of the institution *The institutional FAST.*

As concerns the suggested model, its results confirm the clinical interest of the concept of narcissistic identity vulnerability which is operational, particularly as we can integrate the physical, cognitive and behavioural dimensions, making it possible to take *the complexity of the bio-psychosocial functioning of the subject* into account.

As for the suggested clinical evaluation method; its results reveal that no index is pertinent in itself and that only a dynamic reading which links the various indicators is meaningful.

The progressive hypothetic-deductive approach used for case studies constitutes *a clinical method* that can be applied in clinical practice.

The etiological, structural and risk diagnosis opens up interesting possibilities for *clinical expertise* which could be *an interesting tool for magistrates* when they have to make decisions as to the socio-judicial answers to be found as concerns notably *juvenile offenders.*

Chapter 12 - Premeditation in homicide is defined as the clear intention to kill someone preceding the act. There is little research on the personal and social context and the psychological and pathological variables associated with premeditation.

Our study compares two groups of inmates, all convicted of homicide, through 210 penal and prison files of the male homicide inmates of the Muret Detention Centre (South West region of France).

The groups were constituted on the basis of the penal conviction label: 94 were labelled "premeditated murder" (group 1) and 116 "unpremeditated murder" (group 2).

The results revealed socio-demographic, psychiatric and forensic differences between the groups.

In the logistic regression model, a higher risk of committing a first degree murder (*vs.* second degree) was related to being socially isolated during the days preceding the homicide

(OR 2.86). Furthermore, jealousy motives (OR 5.80) and revenge motives (OR 8.33) were the most significant risk factors in committing premeditated murder.

Finally, we discuss these results and propose two distinct criminological profiles for the individuals in the two groups.

Chapter 13 - The search for the origins of antisocial and delinquent behavior has a long and rich history in the fields of personality and abnormal psychology. Current thinking suggests that a combination of two orthogonal personality traits, shyness *and* sociability, may play an important role in understanding antisocial and delinquent behavior. The author argues that an interaction of these two traits results in a "socially conflicted" personality style. Socially conflicted individuals exhibit distinct patterns of brain and autonomic activity at rest and in response to social challenge and are at risk for antisocial and delinquent behaviors. These individuals may engage in risky and antisocial behaviors as a means of coping with their conflict.

In: Delinquency: Causes, Reduction and Prevention
Editor: Ozan Sahin and Joseph Maier
ISBN 978-1-60741-558-9

Chapter 1

THE TAXONOMIC CHALLENGE TO GENERAL THEORIES OF DELINQUENCY: LINKING TAXONOMY DEVELOPMENT TO DELINQUENCY THEORY

Tim Brennan* and Markus Breitenbach
Northpointe Institute, 101 Pat Mell Drive,
Peachtree City, Ga 30269, U.S.A.

ABSTRACT

Theoretical approaches in delinquency have prioritized the search for a "general" global theory with the assumption that a single unified theory underlies all delinquency (e.g. strain theory, social control, social learning, low self-control, etc).

Recent theorists have also attempted to integrate various elements of these diverse theories into a unified general model (e.g. Farrington 2003, Elliot et al 1985, Sampson and Laub 2005). In contrast, the taxonomic approach adopts a theoretical pluralism that denies the existence of a single unified explanation. It aims to unravel delinquency populations into multiple categories or sub-types that may represent diverse causal processes. Moffitt (1993), Lykken (1995) and others, offer such proposals.

The theoretical stakes are high with advocates on both sides. We will address several issues central to this debate including: Can diverse types of delinquents be reliably identified? Are the boundaries between types distinct? What kind of taxonomic structure exists in this population? We then report on a large scale (N = 3070) replication and refinement of a previously published delinquent taxonomy using the Youth COMPAS assessment system (Brennan, Breitenbach and Dieterich 2008).

Multiple validation methods were used. Substantially the same results emerged, with evidence of stable taxonomic structure in which six out of seven replicated types emerged; these were again nested within five more super-ordinate clusters. These types had multiple matches in the prior literature on explanatory delinquent typologies. We

* E-mail: tbrennan@npipm.com

finally explore the implications of our findings for the debate over the general theory paradigm.

INTRODUCTION

This chapter addresses the unresolved and contentious issue of different explanatory "types" or "etiological patterns" among delinquents and the conflict this creates for advocates of "general theory" in delinquency. We also explore the on-going development and validation of a previously published taxonomy of delinquent youth (Brennan, Breitenbach and Dieterich et al 2008). This taxonomy is subjected to several new tests of replication and we examine the degree to which it generalizes on a large new sample. In this paper we focus on a male only sample. An analogous taxonomy for female delinquents has been separately presented (Brennan 2008). The examination of males only was motivated by the possibility that different pathways may exist for boys and girls driven by the differential importance of certain factors (e.g. sexual abuse, relationship issues, parental supervision etc) and the possibility of heterogeneous interactions leading to different patterns of explanatory factors by gender. Thus, this paper aims to achieve more precise, homogeneous and explanatory profiles for boys. Finally, an overall theme of this chapter is to explore some of the theoretical implications of typological analysis for delinquency research.

The chapter is structured as follows. First, several contentious but critical issues are examined regarding whether "types" exist, given the anti-typological views of many prominent delinquency theorists. Second, we briefly review the prior literature on explanatory typologies of male delinquents and we identify several recurring types in this body of research. We then conduct a replication of our earlier taxonomic analysis on delinquents (Brennan, Breitenbach and Dieterich 2008). This examines the degree to which the types generalize on a new sample (N = 3070) and the similarity between original and replicated types. We incorporate the McIntyre-Blashfield (1980) replication test to examine both cross sample and within-sample robustness of this typology. All seven types from the earlier taxonomy re-appear in the validation sample, however one small cluster from the original taxonomy was unstable and did not recur in the new taxonomic analysis of the validation sample. We then assess whether the present types replicate or match any of the type profiles identified in prior published research on delinquent types (Warren 1971, Rubenfeld 1976, Harris and Jones 1999 and others). To conclude we discuss some theoretical implications of our taxonomic findings. In the debate on the "existence" of delinquent types the present findings offer additional evidence of the reality of these types. In this spirit we invoke Salmon's (1984) well known maxim that it is a "damn strange coincidence" when highly similar empirical data structures re-emerge across diverse mathematical approaches, different falsification tests and different samples (Meehl 1992).

GOALS

The goals of this chapter are as follows.

1. In the first section we discuss several issues pertaining to the theoretical debate between advocates of a "general theory" of delinquency as opposed to the typological approaches and theoretical pluralism.
2. In the main empirical section we replicate and further develop a previously published taxonomy of delinquent youth.
3. We will examine the structural evidence that may support or detract from the conjecture that taxonomic or categorical structure exists in the explanatory causal domain of delinquency.
4. We contextualize our typological findings by examining the congruency of the new type patterns against prior published explanatory typologies of delinquency in the social-psychological explanatory domain. Since the classic integrative studies of Rubenfeld (1967) and Warren (1971) an increasing number of studies have aimed to build taxonomies on a broad range of social and psychological domains (e.g. Stefurak and Calhoun 2004, Harris and Jones 1999). This literature remains scattered and poorly integrated.

THEORETICAL ISSUES AND TAXONOMIC RESEARCH

The theoretical importance of the present study would best be explicated by examining the reciprocal links between taxonomy and theory development. However, this topic is large and complex so that a full presentation is beyond the scope of this chapter (see Enc 1972, Thagard 1992, Murphy 2006). However, we comment on several issues that seem particularly pertinent to the current situation in criminological theory:

1. The dominance of the General Theory Paradigm: The dominant paradigm in delinquency theory denies the existence of types both in regard to criminal specialization and in terms of differentiated explanatory patterns. Instead, many prominent criminologists prioritize the development of a unified or global explanatory theory of delinquent behavior (e.g. Gottfredson and Hirschi 1990; Jessor et al. 1991; Sampson and Laub 2005, Thornberry 2005, and others). This paradigm assumes that a single causal explanatory process underlies all forms of delinquency and that distinct etiological types do not exist. Such omnibus general explanations include the General Theory of Crime of Gottfredson and Hirschi (1990), Sampson and Laub's General Age-Graded Theory of social-control (1993), Agnew's General Strain Theory (1997), Cohen and Felson's (1979), Routine Activities Theory, and several "integrated" unified theories (Catalano and Hawkins, 1996; Farrington, 2003; Thornberry 1987; Elliott, Ageton and Cantor, 1984, and others).

The "anti-typological" stance among criminologists is shown in several ways. It is reflected in a tendency to deny or ignore the existence of types. Hirschi and Gottfredson (1994) starkly dismiss taxonomic heterogeneity ascribing most criminal behavior to a single "persistent underlying trait." Sampson and Laub (1993, 2004) reject the typological approach partly for it's methodological difficulties and the belief that the fundamental causes of delinquency are the same for everyone. They also claim that typological results are unreliable and that the groups often discussed in this literature are "tenuous". David Farrington (2003) underlined the on-going dominance of the global theory paradigm in a presidential address to the American Society of Criminology, noting that most recent theoretical developments, with the exception of Moffitt's (1993) taxonomic theory, do not support the idea of types. Osgood (2005) explicitly states his preference for general theories and the "dimensional" data structures assumed to underlie the causal reality of general theories of delinquency.

However, it is worth noting that in spite of decades of research to test, refine and compare such omnibus theories none of them has achieved general acceptance among criminologists. Additionally, most remain only partially supported, and numerous studies show only modest empirical support for any of these theories (e.g. Mak, 1990, LaGrange and Silverman 1999; Longshore et al 2004; Longshore and Turner 1998; Hay and Forrest 2008, and others). The contents of any recent annual meeting of the American Society of Criminology (ASC) will show that most of the general theories remain in contention.

2. The lack of analytical categories in delinquency as a basis for theoretical development: However, from the perspective of theory development a key role of taxonomic research in any science including criminology is to produce analytical categories and causally homogeneous types that can identify and demarcate some natural classes or coherent process. These categories - often known as scientific objects (Daston 2000) – can then become starting points for more focused explanatory or theoretical questions to clarify, define and progressively explicate the causal structures underlying the identified category or process (Bryant 2000, Thagard 1992). In this regard, Belnap (2006) has argued that we have not yet established appropriate analytical categories for delinquency explanations of either boys or girls. Belnap also argues that much theorizing in delinquency is premature since the preliminary taxonomic work of establishing basic categories of delinquency has been neglected. More than two decades ago Cernkovich and Giordano (1979) complained about criminological theorists rushing into print with causal models of delinquency before knowing what it is they are explaining.

This typical scientific sequence appears to have been ignored in the field of delinquency research as theory development was quickly prioritized leading to a tendency to leapfrog or ignore basic taxonomic tasks. Sadly, this lack of clear coherent categories of delinquents continues to the present and remains widespread. Tremblay (2003), for example, in a broad review of the current status of causal analysis and delinquency taxonomies - whether of behavioral phenotypes, criminal careers or explanatory taxonomies – asserted that this field still does not yet have clear, agreed upon or consensus categories to support effective causal and theoretical research. Thus, a consistent hazard for delinquency research and theory development is that even the dependent variable (e.g. delinquency, variously defined) or the delinquent population or target group being studied, is often a hodge-podge of diverse latent classes that does not represent any clear category or pattern (Richters 1997). This is reflected in Tremblay's conclusions following his review of behavioral and explanatory taxonomies in delinquency:

> "Considering its prevalence….its social relevance….one would expect a well established taxonomy. Unfortunately, this is not the case" (p.186).

Thus, the substantial failure in criminology and delinquency to address the critical task of descriptive taxonomy is still largely unaddressed. It appears that we still need to discover or demarcate suitable "scientific objects" for further study (Daston 2000). Such taxonomic progressions can then reciprocally interact with on-going theory development to refine and clarify the causal mechanisms that may produce and underlie the taxonomic patterns. In this way there is a complex interaction between refinements of both the initial taxonomy and evolving theory related to the relevant taxonomic categories (Enc 1972; Hey 2001).

The damage to criminology and delinquency research of ignoring basic taxonomic work is perhaps enormous. In the absence of identification such scientific objects or categories cannot be accurately described, experimentally manipulated, and compared with appropriate contrast categories to build new knowledge and theories. The fields of psychopathology and personality theory are aware of this typical scientific sequence of tasks. For example, Cattell (1940) emphatically stated that: "nosology precedes etiology". Biologists are also emphatic of the need to carefully establish basic pre-theoretical descriptive classifications and patterns prior to theoretical and explanatory work (Brady 1994). (added linebreak)

In delinquency this disinterest in basic taxonomic research and the prioritization of general theory continues, paralleled by a fairly strong anti-taxonomic attitude among several major theorists. The present study thus runs counter to this tendency by tackling two early tasks of taxonomic research i.e. discovery (identification) of patterns/homogeneous categories and their empirical description.

TAXONOMIES AND THEORETICAL PLURALISM

Taxonomic research has a different set of assumptions from the general theory paradigm. It rejects the idea of a unified global theory and the assumed causal homogeneity that purports to explain all forms crime and delinquency. It embraces an explanatory model that assumes theoretical pluralism and the existence of heterogeneous or differentiated offender categories (types) representing multiple causal processes or pathways to criminal behavior. It asserts that the dominant paradigm mistakenly tries to "force" all forms of delinquency and delinquents into a single promethean structure. Several difficult and unresolved theoretical and empirical issues are involved in this controversy:

Causal homogeneity vs. Heterogeneity: Does theoretical pluralism occur in criminology? Theoretical pluralism is usually understood as describing a situation where no single explanation or theory is sufficient for a given domain. In this approach several different theories or explanatory processes may apply within diverse categories and/or different phases or processes within a given domain. Such pluralism is compatible with the taxonomic approach and is prevalent in most scientific fields e.g. biology, ecology, genetics, medical diseases, psychopathology, and so on (Beatty 1994, Richters 2001).

The explanatory taxonomy that has emerged for medical diseases (Thagard 1999) may be instructive to criminology in its delineation of several broad "generic" explanatory categories with several disease sub-types nested within each broad causal category. This explanatory schema has four broad disease "genera" or causal categories. The clarification of these different explanatory categories was instrumental in the development of different treatment approaches to each category. These explanatory categories of medical diseases are as follows:

1. Nutritional diseases – These diseases result from the body being deprived of some critical nutrients (e.g. scurvy, beriberi). Explanatory analogues in delinquency causation may include theories emphasizing social deprivation, strain and low human and social capital (Lykken 1995; Walsh 2002).

2. Infectious diseases – This category has several subtypes based on different sub-classes of infectious agent e.g. bacteria, viruses, fungi and the recently discovered infectious agent named prions (Creutzfeldt-Jakob disease). Theoretical analogues in delinquency may include models that emphasize social learning theory and the learning of anti-social attitudes, excuses and neutralizations, skills, motives, etc.
3. Molecular-Genetic diseases – This more recently recognized category has two broad sub-categories. Mendelian diseases, (e.g. cystic fibrosis) are caused by an inherited mutation in a single gene. Its sub-categories emerge from mutations arising from any of the five Mendelian inheritance processes. The second broad molecular-genetic category includes Multi-factorial diseases (e.g. hypertension, cancer, atherosclerosis, diabetes) that may involve complex interactions of multiple genes (polygenic processes) and various environmental factors. The discovery of this explanatory category introduced advances in molecular medicine and new families of treatments. In criminological research the theoretical biosocial taxonomies of Lykken (1995), Mealey (1995) and Moffitt et al (2001) all include multi-factorial pathways in which biological factors are involved in complex interactions with environmental factors that unfold in several complex developmental pathways (Walsh 2002).
4. Autoimmune Diseases – This category includes several diseases that emerge when the person's immune system becomes overactive and attacks rather than defends the body (e.g. Lupus). While it may be a stretch, analogues of this category may include various psychological and neurotic conflicts leading to anti-social behavior. For example, Lykken (1995) describes a broad "genera" of neurotic/internally conflicted criminal types (paranoid personalities, limit-testing punishment seekers, and so on).

The above illustrates the broad links between theoretical pluralism and taxonomy and the more precise targeting of different intervention and treatment approaches based on improved understanding of the diverse causal categories within a domain. Medical interventions have clearly advanced in parallel with the clarification of the taxonomic diversity of disease categories and their underlying causes. We clearly do not claim an exact analogy between the criminological and medical domains and offer the above framework only as illustrative of the manner in which basic taxonomic research may facilitate new directions in determining the causes of crime, for designing more precise target populations and guiding more focused differentiated treatment and interventions in response to particular types of offenders and their crimes.

Theoretical pluralism also characterizes the emerging meta-discipline of dynamic or open systems theory that has recently entered developmental delinquency and child development studies (Richters 1997; LeBlanc 2005, 2006; Wachs 2000). Open-system concepts such as equifinality (multiple pathways to the same end) and multifinality (diverse end states emerging from the same initial state) imply a diversity of developmental pathways. Richters (1997) argues that equifinality as used in developmental psychopathology explicitly signifies that different structural/causal processes can underlie similar overt patterns of child problem behavior and that these processes jointly involve interactions between genetic influences, cognition, emotion, behavior and psychopathology (Cicchetti and Richters, 1993). Richters concludes that equifinality (or causal pluralism) is a ubiquitous characteristic of human functioning and development.

The Categorical vs. Dimensional controversy: A further pivotal empirical issue is the debate over general theory versus typological approaches. This focuses on the specific form of statistical distributions that underlie delinquent populations across theoretically relevant factors. This debate contrasts dimensional versus categorical representations of the underlying statistical data distributions of delinquency populations (Beutler and Malik 2002). Are such distributions relatively continuous and perhaps multivariate normal, or do they contain substantial density variations, high-density clusters and thus are clumpy or multimodal? Distributional concerns can be critical in multivariate situations with multiple explanatory or causal factors where latent high-density clusters may be suspected but are difficult to detect. If the underlying inter-point distribution of cases contains substantial density variation or multimodality then categorical and typological/categorical methods are arguably more appropriate and perhaps essential (e.g. latent class models, clustering methods, etc). Conversely, if the distribution is multivariate normal, or relatively continuous with minimal multimodality then dimensional methods (e.g. regression and path analysis, survival models, factor analysis, structural equation modeling, etc.) are more appropriate (Fielding 2007, Richters 1997, Meehl 1992).

This debate on dimensional versus categorical approaches pervades the behavioral and psychological sciences and is not fully resolved (Beutler and Malik 2002: Lykken 1991). In discussions of criminological theory and taxonomic models for delinquency Osgood (2005) acknowledged the critical relevance of this issue, and on balance, preferred the dimensional approach – which aligns well with the dominant general theory paradigm. However, he also acknowledged - and we agree - that the ultimate resolution of this controversy will emerge from careful empirical examinations of our data distributions in delinquency studies, across specific sets of factors, to assess the degree of multi-modality and the presence of reliable clustering structure. Several resolutions to this debate have been proposed in which these two general approaches are seen as complementary rather than mutually exclusive (Beutler and Malik 2002). For example, it is possible to conduct data analysis in a both/and approach that simply embeds categorical results within a broader dimensional framework. However, this debate is not yet resolved in the area of delinquency studies.

What Structural Features Signify the Presence of Types?

The above disagreements over the reality of delinquent "types" have often proceeded with little attention to what structural features can be taken to signify the strength or weakness of typological structure in data. Such structural features are generally not revealed, and remain larely invisible to standard correlational or variable-centered methods (Ragin 2000, Bergman 2000). These data structures include, for example: 1) the stability of cluster centers, 2) the boundary conditions of clusters and 3) the proportion of "unclassifiable" cases.

The stability of cluster centers: Stable cluster centers are a first indicator of the presence of type structures. The patterns identified by cluster centers (typically cluster centroids) are the basis of the narrative interpretations of each type. Cross-sample and cross method comparisons are conventionally used as tests of cluster stability. Such stability in turn hinges on the presence of sufficiently high-density regions within a multivariate distribution that can be reliably detected by pattern recognition procedures. Our later empirical taxonomic research pays particular attention to such multiple tests of stability as the basis for judging the reality of delinquent types.

Cluster Boundaries - Fuzzy/Probabilistic versus Crisp: A second issue concerns the common assumption that for type structures to be "real" the identified clusters must be "distinct" and have well-separated boundaries. However, this idea of well-separated clusters with distinct boundaries and empty regions between them, is a fairly extreme data structure that rarely appears in the behavioral and biological sciences. These sciences mostly exhibit clusters with considerable fuzziness at their boundaries and a straggling of outlier and hybrid cases in the spaces between major social or biological categories (Hey 2001; Lykken 1995). Lykken, in fact has noted that even an ideal taxonomy of antisocial offenders may include substantial outlier and hybrid cases. Additionally, several mathematically alternative "density-search" clustering procedures have been developed to detect varying kinds of cluster structures according to boundary conditions i.e. overlapping clusters, straggly cloud-like data clusters, compact spherical clusters, and so on. Specific algorithms also exist to detect cluster structures that vary in the strength of internal density: e.g. complete-link clusters, family-resemblance clusters, average-link clusters, single-link "natural" clusters, boundary based partitions, and so on.

In reviewing delinquency studies - where appropriate taxometric methods have been used - our conclusion is that type structures in delinquent populations do not offer distinct well-separated clusters. A degree of multi-modality or cluster structure does appear to exist in many relevant domains given the consistency with which central core dense regions of delinquent type patterns are repeatedly identified across different samples and clustering methods (Harris and Jones 1999; Frick 2004; Brennan, Breitenbach and Dieterich 2008). Such studies that incorporate cross validation tests that demonstrate stable recurrent data clusters suggest that a degree of typological structure cannot be rejected in this area.

However, we also acknowledge that cluster boundaries are often fuzzy and probabilistic in the domain of explanatory delinquency taxonomies and that any inappropriate or naïve use of clustering methods might easily fail to detect reliable clusters. Full details of the diverse forms of cluster-seeking methods and cluster structural forms, and appropriate validation tests, are given in several expository texts (Arabie, Hubert and deSoete 1996, Fielding 2007, Han and Kamber 2000).

What proportion of a sample is unclassifiable? Another sign of weaker typological structure is the percentage of cases that remain unclassified and outside the boundaries of any cluster. Such cases are not part of any clustering structure and larger percentage of such cases implies a weaker typological structure. Such outliers or hybrids are generally relegated to a "residue" non-classifiable class. In previous work we found that the number of outliers and hybrid cases in the residue class amounted to 15% - 47%, depending on clustering method, types of cluster definitions and sample. It also depends critically on whether irrelevant variables were included among the classification features. These will blur the boundaries between clusters since they have no discriminatory power and simply add noise to the data. Our prior results have shown that a majority of youth in most samples consistently enter the same clusters and thus support the conclusion that, a replicable multimodal structure containing a majority of delinquent youth is repeatedly found. This typological structure conforms closely to the "family resemblance" category structure described by Rosch (1978) that also appears to be widespread in nature (Hey 2001; Bryant 2000). Thus, on balance we concluded that a reliable and consistent categorical structure does exist in the explanatory domain of delinquency, but that it does not consist of highly distinct well-separated types. Thus, boundaries are fuzzy and a substantial percentage of youth will not belong to any type-profile.

SCOPE CONDITIONS AND THEORETICAL PLURALISM

Any shift in delinquency research from general nomothetic theories and general laws to theoretical pluralism and multiple contingent etiologies will heighten the need to establish scope conditions (SC) for each specific theory or etiological pathway. In most social and biological sciences, scope conditions are widely accepted as critical in various research designs (Goertz 2006; Richters 1997). They are used to select appropriate study samples and to restrict the range of generalizations and applicability of any theory e.g. to specific cultural contexts, specific population categories, disease categories, specific processes, stages in a developmental process, and so on. Cases falling under the SC of a theory are used to form homogeneous samples that can safely represent a particular causal category or mechanism (e.g. lupus, measles, Moffitt's LCP, neurotic offenders). The demarcated categories can then be tested, manipulated and measured to further refine and evaluate the proposed theory. Cases outside the SC may represent a totally different causal process, or may be used as explicit contrast categories. If such cases are included in any theory-testing sample or evaluation design, this may introduce unknown or latent heterogeneity to contaminate or distort research findings (Richters 1997; Meehl 1990; Lykken 1991).

The topic of SC is poorly developed in delinquency research since the dominant theoretical paradigm asserts, logically, that a "general" theory should apply to all youth and all forms delinquency. Thus, there is little need for any further specification of scope conditions. However, by ignoring scope conditions the resulting sample may unwittingly co-mingle a range of causally heterogeneous categories. Such "mixing" may change the sample wide correlations between predictors and outcomes and distort results depending on the mixing proportions of the underlying categories. This may preclude any valid substantive understandings stemming from any of the methods based on sample-wide correlation or covariance matrices e.g. path analysis, factor analysis, regression models, and so on (Richters 1997, Goertz 2006, Meehl 1992). In this regard Jack Block (2000) in examining the search for general theory in the context of child development research, wrote as follows:

> "Too often, it seems to me, psychologists assume unthinkingly a grand universality of the lawfulness of behavior. They do not inquire whether the covariance pattern of a set of variables within one group of individuals is reliably difference from the covariance pattern in another group of individuals. If there is such a reliable difference the possibility comes into play that we psychologists are dealing with importantly different kinds of individuals……If there indeed is, in the sample or population being studied, a mixture of two or more kinds of latent classes of individuals, it would advance conceptual understanding and predictability if we identify and keep analytically separate these commingled categories of persons" (Block 2000, p160).

Procedures to establish SC typically require guidance from a putative theory or some other means to define relatively homogeneous study samples. In disciplines with strong theory this is usually some conjunction of core factors of the theory. In disciplines like criminology with relatively weak theories, such conjunctions may be less useful and only an approximate atheoretical extensional definition may offer scope conditions to denote a relevant category e.g. a denotative definition may select one or several surface features as scope conditions, or may seek empirical clusters to give relatively homogeneous categories. A full discussion of SC methods is beyond the scope of this chapter and we refer readers to discussions of SC in typological and theoretical research (Goertz 2006, Richters 1997, George and Bennett 2005).

Current Status and Trends in Taxonomic Research in Delinquency

Turning away from general theoretical and philosophical issues we now examine the current status and several trends related to these as a prelude to our empirical research. The following appear relevant:

1. Emergence of Theoretical Pluralism and Typological Pathways in Delinquency

Given the above context across several behavioral, social and biological sciences, it seems paradoxical that many criminological theorists deny theoretical pluralism while most other biological and social sciences embrace pluralism [Beatty 1994, Richters 1997, Lykken 1991, Goertz 2006]. We grant, that from one perspective the multiple theory paradigm will violate the norm of scientific simplicity and parsimony.

We agree with Sampson and Laub (2005) that maximum simplicity and parsimony would be provided by a single unified theory encompassing all offenders and crimes. However, we are more inclined to agree with a statement (attributed to Einstein) that everything should be as simple as possible, but not simpler (cited in Thagard p. 34). For example, Thagard (1999) and others, argue that a uniform understanding does not only come from a general overarching theory but also from the availability of clearer and more coherent explanatory schemas.

However, several voices are now embracing an explicit theoretical pluralism as well as the taxonomic approach in criminology (Moffitt 1993, Huizinga, Esbenson and Weiher 1991, Lykken 1991, 1995; Brennan, Huizinga and Elliott 1978; Harris and Jones 1999, and others). Lykken (1991, 1995) has forcefully argued that the complexity of delinquency – with its multiple interactions between socialization factors, environmental factors, personality, genetic influences, gender, cultural and learning processes – is much more likely to produce structural heterogeneity and diverse types than a single global unified process.

To demonstrate this he delineated four broad explanatory categories of criminal offenders: normal offenders, sociopathic offenders, psychopathic offenders and neurotic or internally conflicted offenders. Each involved a distinct etiology and had several sub-categories. In proposing his theoretical taxonomy he rejected a single general theory and commented on the dominant approaches of delinquency theorists by commenting on:

> "The almost irresistible tendency for criminological theorists to oversimplify the causes of crime, to underestimate the variety of psychological peculiarities that can contribute to the underlying dispositions for criminal behavior" (1995, p 17).

McVie (2004, p 22), similarly, in the context of a large national longitudinal study of delinquency in Scotland comments on current theory development as follows:

> "The complex nature of the patterns in prevalence and frequency of offending for different offence types implies that a 'general' theory of offending is unwise, as it takes no account of offence classification or attempts to understand the differential groupings of offence or offender. Contra Sampson and Laub, it appears essential that a typology is developed, at least to understand juvenile offending which is diverse and multifarious in nature."

2. Recent Advances in Taxonomic Research in Delinquency

While the taxonomic approach to delinquency is still at an early stage of development the last decade has seen several advances that may lead to stronger and more cumulative findings. These are as follows:

Theoretical Advances indicating multiple types: First, advances in theoretical taxonomies from several related disciplines have offered compelling descriptions of diverse types of antisocial offenders (Lykken 1995; Mealey 1995; Moffitt 1993). Each of these taxonomies was offered as a theoretical integrative statement based on a broad range of psychological, social and biological evidence. The specific types proposed in these taxonomies show surprising overlap in the central causal mechanisms underlying the types – although Lykken's taxonomy addresses a broader range of sub-types. Moffitt's adolescent limited (AL) and life course persistent (LCP) taxonomy, in particular, have inspired a substantial number of empirical studies to clarify and validate her types (Moffitt 2003, Piquero and Moffitt 2005).

A further theoretical advance is the entry of the open systems and complexity paradigm into child developmental research and delinquency (LeBlanc 2005, 2006; Wachs 2000). This approach is friendly to taxonomic heterogeneity with its concepts of diverse "attractor" regions and bifurcations between states of youth adaptations within a multi-dimensional phase-space map with each state defined by a specific pattern of theory-relevant variables.

Methodological advances in taxonomy development: Paralleling these theoretical advances, the last decade has also seen continuing developments in methods of taxonomy development and validation (Fielding 2007, Lenzenweger 2004). Studies that use a single clustering method on a single sample are now obsolete and have largely disappeared from the literature. More sophisticated validation designs involving cross-method and cross-sample replication are now being routinely integrated into the development of taxonomies (e.g. McIntyre and Blashfield 1980; Milligan 1996). Multiple methods designs and two-stage clustering are also now routine (i.e. where a preliminary hierarchical clustering, e.g. Ward's minimum-variance, establish provisional classifications that are then refined by subsequent methods such as K-means partitioning). Advances have also been made in basic clustering methods e.g. mixture-models (Nagin and Paternoster 2000), semi-supervised clustering and bootstrapped aggregation methods (Brennan, Breitenbach and Dieterich 2008). New techniques from machine-learning (e.g. Support Vector Machines, Random Forests, etc) have given us efficient techniques to classify unidentified youth into pre-existing taxonomies and to address the need to establish theoretically homogeneous categories for theory testing studies and to establish scope conditions for diverse theories.

New empirical studies supporting heterogeneous delinquent types: An encouraging body of recent empirical taxonomic studies on diverse youth samples is steadily building support for the existence of causally heterogeneous delinquent types (Aalsma and Lapsley 2001; Harris and Jones 1999; Huizinga et al. 1991; Jefferson and Johnson 1991; Jones and Harris 1999; Mezzich et al. 1991; Potter and Jenson 2003; Skilling et al. 2001; Sorensen and Johnson 1996; Brennan, Breitenbach and Dieterich 2008, Brennan 2008). Additionally, the related field of child psychopathology has identified several developmental pathways leading to problem behaviors. Frick (2004) in reviewing this related discipline concluded there was sufficient evidence to indicate distinct developmental pathways leading to conduct disorder and that each pathway involves unique causal processes (see also Loeber 1996; Loeber et al. 1997).

3. Weaknesses in Prior Research on Explanatory Typologies on Delinquency

When Sampson and Laub (2005), and others, criticize the typological approach for unreliability we must agree that several methodological and design weaknesses have tended to undermine the impact, reliability and quality of taxonomic research. Thus, while the above advances are placing typological studies of delinquency on a more secure footing, we acknowledge several weaknesses that have hindered prior research – and which hopefully are now being avoided as this taxonomic effort moves forward. These weaknesses may explain why findings to date remain tentative and have lacked the cumulative development to support a more forceful challenge to the general theory paradigm.

1. *Small or inadequate samples:* Many prior studies of delinquent taxonomies used very small inadequate sample sizes – often under 200 cases. Small samples will produce very small clusters that often cannot be reliably identified. Taxonomic studies require much larger samples to ensure adequate reliability and stability of the various types (Milligan 1996).
2. *Inadequate coverage of explanatory factors:* An absence of key differentiating factors can undermine the ability to identify, differentiate or fully describe the structure of key type patterns. A comprehensive coverage of risk and need factors is needed when identifying or describing explanatory patterns (Lenzenweger 2004; Brennan 2008).
3. *Inadequate taxonomic methods and study designs*: Several prior studies of delinquency typologies used deficient taxonomic methods - e.g. clinical descriptions, inverse factor analysis, or a single cluster analysis applied to a single sample without cross-validation. However, recently more reliable research designs and appropriate validation techniques are now being incorporated into taxonomic studies (Harris and Jones 1999; Aalsma and Lapsley, 2001; Stefurak and Calhoun, 2006).
4. *Imposition of artificial cross-classifications that disguise the presence of latent classes*: Another hazard, particularly in tests of Moffitt's taxonomy, has been the use

of simple cross-classifications of age of onset against selected measures of criminal offending to identify types and operationalize her taxonomy. This approach has almost no chance of discovering natural patterns and may actually mask the natural diversity among offenders. Francis et al. (2004) discuss the hazards of this approach.

5. *Inadequate knowledge of key differentiating factors between offender types:* As noted elsewhere the initial selection of classification factors for a taxonomic study is often hazardous given our limited knowledge of latent types and weak guidance from extant delinquency theories. The basic problems at this stage are the inclusion of irrelevant factors or the exclusion of critical differentiating factors. Irrelevant variables introduce the danger of blurring the boundaries between clusters and thus lowering reliability. This selection of classification factors is of equal importance to any subsequent step (Milligan 1996; Lenzenweger 2004). It governs explanatory power, interpretative coherence, completeness of type description and the ability to discriminate between types and recognize latent types. A safe approach is to utilize a comprehensive coverage of theory-relevant factors. Recent integrated omnibus theories such as Farrington's (2003) are useful guides in the factor selection task by suggesting a broad coverage of key explanatory factors.
6. *Category contamination if latent undiscovered types exist*: In classification studies, where the number of types (K) is not sufficiently large, the presence of undiscovered latent types can introduce considerable distortion of the recovered clusters. Any unrecognized classes will be falsely merged into the recovered clusters to distort the type descriptions. This has been a particular danger, for example, in verification studies of Moffitt's categories (AL and LCP) where the researchers have not sufficiently identified other latent subtypes, thus producing contaminated descriptions of the two main categories.
7. *Absence of operational "matching" procedures*: Prior studies mostly fail to provide operational methods to identify "matches" to their types or rules for type recognition and matching. This omission has seriously crippled other researchers from conducting replication studies. Thus, matching could only proceed by "eyeballing" the specific feature matches of type profiles across studies. The recent introduction of powerful case matching procedures from the Machine Learning/Artificial Intelligence field largely resolves this weakness (Berk 2008, Brennan, Breitenbach and Dieterich 2008).

Given these weaknesses it is no surprise that many prior studies of delinquent taxonomies present their findings tentatively with pleas for replication (Harris and Jones 1999, Stefurak, Calhoun and Glaser 2004).

4. Integrating Recurring Types from the Prior Literature into Our Previous Taxonomy

To contextualize the present taxonomic study we briefly review the most likely matches between those delinquent types from the prior literature that appear fairly reliably across these prior studies with our taxonomic findings. In our prior study (Brennan, Dieterich and Breitenbach 2008) we developed a broad based explanatory taxonomy of seven delinquent types using two large samples of delinquent and problem youth (Development sample N = 1572; Replication sample N = 1453). We used multiple taxonomic methods and multiple cross-validation procedures to identify seven replicated delinquent types. The descriptions below link these seven types to the most likely matches from previously published delinquency taxonomies. For each of our seven types we found several likely or close replications. However, we note that these "matches" were based only on examining feature matches across types – and were not based on a quantitative pattern matching procedures such as Support Vector Machines (SVM) or K-Nearest Neighbor methods (for expositions of these methods see Han and Kamber 2000; Fielding 2007).

We concluded that these seven types may offer sufficient stability to begin the process of forming a consensus explanatory taxonomy of delinquent youth. The advances of this recent approach over prior delinquency typologies include: tested reliability across multiple methods and samples, internal coherence, external validity, precision of empirical profiles across a range of explanatory factors; and a broad matching to several recurring types from the past literature. These types, from our prior study, are as follows (Note: In the following description we use the numbering system from our previous study).

Type 1. Internalizing - A: Withdrawn, Abused and Rejected

Our cluster 1 had an extreme pattern of internalizing features - social withdrawal, hostility and suspicion – together with extremely violent parental abuse and neglect. The prior literature offered several similar internalizing abused neurotic types (Lykken 1995; Miller et al. 2004; Aalsma and Lapsley 2001; Harris and Jones 1999).

Type 2. Socially Deprived: Sub-culturally Socialized Delinquents

This appears to replicate the socially deprived ''lower class'' or sub-culturally ''socialized'' delinquent often mentioned in the sociological literature (Jesness 1988; Miller 1958; Van Voorhis 1994; Warren 1971). Its multiple features include: poverty and lower socio-economic class, criminal/drug-using parents, family disorganization, poor discipline, neglect and school failure. Lykken (1995) similarly described a ''common sociopath,'' as poorly socialized, often within an oppositional sub-culture, but also as psychologically ''normal''. Our cluster matched all the above features and also offered little evidence of low self control or serious internalizing psychological issues thus appearing psychologically normal and supporting Lykken's finding.

Type 3. Low-Control A: Versatile Offenders

Our taxonomy - contra Moffitt but consistent with Lykken - produced two highly impulsive low control/high delinquency clusters (3 and 6). These partly overlap Lykken's primary and secondary psychopaths. The present Cluster 3 largely matches the features of Lykken's (1995) primary psychopath in the following ways: impulsivity, low empathy, hostility, manipulative-dominance, low remorse, attention problems, disruptive school behaviors, criminal peers, high-risk lifestyle, drug abuse and serious criminal history. Other fairly close type replications with similar features are found in Moffitt's LCP, Alterman et al.'s (1998) ''Psychopathic'' and Vincent et al.'s (2003) ''Impulsive'' cluster.

Type 4. Normal ''Accidental/Situational'' Delinquents

Our type 4 category has very few risk factors, mostly minor delinquency and a relatively late age-at-first-adjudication. It partly matches Moffitt's AL type in its positive social resources, later onset and low delinquency. Lykken (1995) similarly describes a "normal" type with reasonably good socialization and competent parents. Other ''normal'' types - that are named as such - are found in Simourd et al. (1994), Aalsma and Lapsley (2001), Harris and Jones (1999) and Huizinga et al. (1991). Delinquency in this category is often explained by situational-accidental factors or peer influences (Warren 1971; Van Voorhis 1994).

Type 5. Internalizing Youth B: with Positive Parenting

Our Clusters 5 and 1 both exhibit an internalizing pattern of social withdrawal, isolation and mistrust. Both avoid delinquent peers, drugs and sex and have low adjudication rates. However, in stark contrast to the violent abusive parents of cluster 1, the parents of cluster 5 appear mostly non-abusive, competent and caring. Cluster 5 has several replicates e.g. Lykken's (1995) broad ''neurotic'' category contains a sub-type he describes as having positive parenting and normal socialization, but who are engulfed by some unconscious or emotional complexity (see also Harris and Jones's 1999 ''internally conflicted'' cluster).

Type 6. Low-Control B: Early Onset, Chronic Versatile Offenders with Multiple Risk Factors

Cluster 6 is very rare as well as unreliably identified. It is a more extreme version of Cluster 3 and perhaps simply forms a more extreme "variant" of a general low self-control category. It has multiple antisocial personality factors, high drug use, promiscuity, criminal peers, school attention problems and the highest parental crime and parental abuse. It had the earliest age-at-first-adjudication and the highest total adjudications. Similar descriptions in the literature and likely replications include: Lykken's secondary psychopath (1995), Mealey's (1995) primary sociopath, Moffitt's LCP category; as well as Sorenson and Johnson 1996; Blackburn's 1995 ''Secondary Psychopath;'' Aalsma and Lapsley's (2001) ''psychopath'' and Alterman et al.'s (1998) ''Psychopathic.'' However, this cluster was unstable in our cross-sample validation test – although we attribute this to sample differences since our second sample did not contain a sufficient number of the most serious delinquents.

Type 7. Normative Delinquency: Drugs, Sex and Peers

This cluster, like cluster 4, again reflects more ''normal'' youth with substantial school and family strengths. However, unlike Cluster 4, these youth exhibit a strong vulnerabilty to drugs, sex and peers. They show a later age-at-first-adjudication and had mostly non-violent offenses. Likely prior replicates include Moffitt's (1993) AL category; Lykken's (1995) ''dissocial sociopath'' that he describes as psychologically ''normal'' but engaged in a search for meaning and excitement that may involve drugs and sex; Harris and Jones' (1999) ''average normal'' and Alterman et al.'s (1998) ''drug-only clusters''.

We now shift to examine the degree to which this above taxonomy re-emerges on a new sample from a different locale. We use similar methods to identify, validate and cross-replicate the new taxonomic results.

METHODS

Sample

The current validation sample (n=3070) consists of adjudicated and non-adjudicated youth assessed in three statewide juvenile justice departments and two large juvenile justice county jurisdictions. This sample contains only males since the taxonomic structure of female delinquents is examined elsewhere (Brennan 2008a). The ethnic/racial breakdown of this validation sample is: 28% Caucasian, 57% African American, 0.4% Asian Americans, and 11% Hispanic. The ages range from 9 to18 with a mean of 15.58 years (Standard Deviation = 1.33). The ages at first adjudication range from 7 to17 with a mean of 13.38 (S.D. = 1.7). The number of total adjudications ranged from 0 to 19 with a mean of 3.06 (S.D. = 1.93). The number of felony adjudications ranged from 0 to 10 with a mean of 0.29 (S.D. = 0.77). These numbers reflect the fact that some non-adjudicated youth enter the sample by being referred to Juvenile Assessment Centers (JAC's) in their respective jurisdictions. Finally, this validation sample is independent of the original construction sample in our previous study (Brennan, Breitenbach and Dieterich 2008).

Other than gender this validation sample differs from the previous construction sample in two main ways. First, it has more African American youth (57%) than the original construction sample (27.4%). One of our main sampling sources was a statewide juvenile justice system from a southern state with a high proportion of African-American youth. Second, the new sample contains more minor delinquents than the original construction sample which had a mean = 1.2 and S.D. = 1.1 for felony adjudications. The range of agencies in the two samples was similar, except that the newer sample had more youth initially referred to JAC's many of whom were not adjudicated but had been referred for truancy, family problems, being incorrigible, and so on.

Measures

We designed this classification space to be comprehensive and theory-guided. Explanatory coherence is more likely in the presence of a set of theoretically relevant factors in the classification domain. We aimed at a broad coverage of features guided by the prior taxonomic literature and relevant theory. The conceptual platforms most closely guiding feature selection were Bronfenbrenner's (1979) ecological perspective and Farrington's (2003) Integrated Cognitive Antisocial Potential Theory. These identify well established theoretical domains of risk factors e.g. youth lifestyle and behaviors, youth attitudes and personality, school, leisure activities, peer relations, family, neighborhood characteristics and demographics. Each of these domains is included in the main instrument i.e. Youth COMPAS (Brennan and Dieterich 2003). This is a 171-item semi-structured assessment instrument with 32 scales. Each scale contains a set of ordinal level items with four or five response categories. For example, the response categories on the five-point items range from "definitely no" (1) at one pole to "definitely yes" (5) at the other. Example items from each of the scales are in Appendix A.

Table 1 (below) lists all of the Youth COMPAS scales, their respective numbers of items, mean scores, standard deviation and Cronbach's alpha in this sample. Most of these scales show alpha coefficients greater that 0.70 and thus fall into an acceptable range. These scores largely repeat those from our prior study. Full details of the Youth COMPAS scales, item content and measurement properties are available on request from the first author.

Table 1. Scale means and standard deviations and Alpha reliability coefficients

Input	Mean	SD	Min	Max	Alpha (Constr.)	Alpha (Validation)
Age at Assessment	15.62	1.31	9.2	18		
Felony Adjudications	0.29	0.81	0	14		
Total detentions	1.82	2.15	0	21		
Criminal Associates	1.97	0.76	1	4	0.82	0.86
Criminal Opportunity	2.16	0.62	1	4	0.82	0.77
Low Pro-social	3.12	0.64	1	4	0.66	0.78
Impulsivity	3.56	1.04	1	5	0.83	0.79
Low Empathy	2.48	1.13	1	5	0.79	0.60
No Remorse	2.34	1.00	1	5	0.78	0.76
Manipulative	3.10	0.99	1	5	0.82	0.73
Aggression	3.39	1.02	1	5	0.81	0.76
Violence Tolerance	2.79	1.18	1	5	0.88	0.84

Input	Mean	SD	Min	Max	Alpha (Constr.)	Alpha (Validation)
Social Isolation	2.14	1.03	1	5	0.87	0.84
Negative Cognition	2.75	1.08	1	5	0.83	0.77
Soft Drug Use	2.25	1.01	1	5	0.72	0.69
Hard Drug Use	1.10	0.28	1	4	0.63	0.70
Substance Trouble	2.15	1.27	1	5	0.89	0.89
Promiscuity	2.48	0.81	1	5	0.66	0.66
Academic Failure	3.00	1.07	1	5	0.39	0.66
Low Goals	1.88	1.07	1	5	0.77	0.83
Attention Problems	3.11	1.19	1	5	0.85	0.81
School Behavior	3.23	0.97	1	5	0.60	0.56
Fam. Discontinuity	3.12	1.17	1	5	0.69	0.62
Socioeconomic	2.70	1.27	1	5	0.88	0.88
Fam. Crime	2.31	0.92	1	5	0.85	0.82
Low Bonding	1.88	0.60	1	4	0.58	0.73
Inconsistent Discipline	2.27	1.09	1	5	0.89	0.91
Low Supervision	2.20	1.02	1	5	0.80	0.87
Neglect	2.10	1.02	1	5	0.86	0.80
Physical Abuse	1.87	1.06	1	5	0.81	0.83
Sexual Abuse	1.53	0.90	1	5	0.87	0.91
Parental Conflict	2.35	1.25	1	5	0.93	0.92
Neighborhood	2.46	1.28	1	5	0.88	0.89
Low Emotional Support	2.19	0.94	1	5	0.73	0.74
Youth Rebellion	2.70	1.03	1	5	0.79	0.76

Analytical Methods

1) Preliminary Data Transformations: We followed the generally accepted practice of initially transforming all raw scale scores into normalized Z-scores with zero mean and unit standard deviation (Milligan 1996).

2) Pattern Discovery: To identify type patterns in the new validation sample we used a bootstrapped aggregation (bagging) variant of K-Means clustering. The combination of bagging with K-Means was introduced by Dolnicar and Leisch (2000) to reduce problems related to initial starting points in K-Means clustering and the instability of clustering results due to outliers, hybrids, fuzzy boundaries and noisy data – all of which are typical in social science data. Bagging produces multiple classification models using each bootstrap sample of the data. These replication models are then integrated into a final aggregated classification model that typically is a more stable classification and is more robust to noise and outliers (Breiman 1996).

In the present analysis we used the bagging K-means implementation in R (R Development Core Team 2006) using all Y-COMPAS factors as input factors. We generated 1000 random samples (bags) from the validation sample with no outliers removed to create separate cluster solutions for each bag. In each replication we used two-thirds of the full training set to create each model, giving classification models that should be fairly independent so that the final aggregated model should be more robust to noise or outliers inherent in the training set. The 1000 cluster centers from these bags were then treated as data points and re-clustered with K-means. These stable cluster centers were then used as starting seed point centers for an overall K-means on the total sample to create a final taxonomic model.

3. Pattern Verification and Replication

(*a*) *Replications between Construction and Validation Sample:* To assess replication of the original typology from Brennan et al 2008 and the new typology from the present validation sample we use the McIntyre and Blashfield (1980) cross validation method.

This method can be applied to any two datasets A and B where similar clustering structure is expected. First, clustering methods are applied to A and B independently to give models M1 and M2. Second, a pattern-matching procedure, previously trained on the original clusters (Sample A), is then used to quantitatively match any cases in B that fit the original clusters of A to give model M3. This identifies and labels any cases in B that meet quantitative criteria to match M1. Third, (M3) is cross-tabulated against the independent clustering of B (M2) and an agreement coefficient is computed between the two partitions of B (e.g. Cohen's Kappa, Contingency Coefficient, etc).

We used a Support Vector Machine (SVM; Vapnik, 1998) for the pattern-matching step that was previously trained on the original typology from Brennan et al. (2008). SVM's have demonstrated impressive pattern matching performance for many practical applications (Caruana, 2006).

(b) *Replications of the overall typology in the Validation sample*: The Macintyre-Blashfield cross validation was also incorporated into the pattern discovery bagging analysis on the validation sample using a split-sample approach. Cohen's Kappa is again used to assess convergence of the two typological models arising from this method.

(c) *Replications of specific clusters from original and validation samples:* To assess replication of matching cluster centers from the original and validation samples we computed

Pearson's correlation coefficient (r) between the relevant pairs of cluster center vectors i.e. from the SVM defined 7 clusters from Brennan et al 2008 (M3) and the 7 clusters from the independent clustering of the validation sample (M2). In a second approach we demonstrate the matching of cluster pairs from the two independent solutions by clustering the joint set of 14 centroids using Ward's method and computed the resulting dendrogram. The fusion of cluster pairs at the base of the dendrogram directly illustrates the close matching between the seven pairs of cluster centers. Thirdly, we provide a graphical representation of this matching by mapping the M2 and M3 cluster centers into a 2D-Scatter Plot computed using Principal Component Analysis (PCA).

RESULTS

Generalizability and Internal Validation

Do the original seven clusters appear in the validation samples: The SVM when applied to the validation sample found that almost all cases in the validation sample could be matched to one of the seven clusters from the original study. Only 1% of the cases in the validation sample were not matched to one of the original seven clusters by the SVM procedure. Specifically, it found the following percentages of cases matching the original seven clusters (using the original numerical labels): cluster 1 (7.4%), cluster 2 (18.5%), cluster 3 (14%), cluster 4 (20%), cluster 5 (23.4%), cluster 6 (5%), cluster 7 (11%). The distributions of clusters were also similar, with the most infrequent cluster in the validation sample again being the extremely low self control/high delinquency cluster 6 with 5% while the more frequent clusters again included the socially deprived lower class youth (cluster 2), the normal situational (cluster 4) and the internalizing positive parent (cluster 5). While these percentages are not exactly the same as in the previous study, the general similarity is shown in the identification of the largest and smallest clusters. However, the more important point is that all of the original types re-emerged using the SVM in the validation sample.

Overall partition agreement between original and cross-validation typologies: The Macintyre-Blashfield (1980) method to examine the stability of clustering between the original and validation studies also found a strong matching between the original model (M3) and independent validation cluster model (M2). Cohen's Kappa was 0.64 for the overall match, with a contingency coefficient of 0.84 ($p < .000$), both indicating strong but not identical partition agreement. When the small original cluster 6 and its analogue in the validation sample were removed, kappa rose to 0.69 for the remaining six clusters, with the contingency coefficient remaining at 0.84. In the validation cluster model we found that 20% of the cases fell in the unclassifiable category. Thus, a large majority of youth in the independent sample (about 80%) was assigned to the new independent typology model (M2).

Replication of Specific Cluster Types

(a) *Cross classification analysis*: To examine the matching of specific cluster pairs we first examined the full contingency table of original clusters (M3) cross-classified against validation clusters (M2). This confirmed that 6 of the 7 original clusters re-emerged with strong overlapping memberships across the two classifications. However, the small unstable and highly delinquent original cluster 6 failed to replicate in the M2 partition and an alternative cluster 6 was formed (in M2). Our original paper speculated that the small unstable original cluster 6 was perhaps a fragment of the larger highly delinquent low self-control cluster 3. This was confirmed by the contingency table showing that a segment of original cluster 3 cases were re-assigned to the new cluster 6 in M2.

(b) *Pair-wise Correlations between original and validated clusters*: To more precisely examine the specific stability of profile pairs between original and validation partitions we computed Pearson's r between the vectors for the matched cluster pairs from both typologies (M3 and M2). The correlations between these matching pairs indicated very high profile similarities. These correlations in Table (2) range from 0.87 to .99 for the six matched pairs. This confirms the extreme stability and replication of these cluster prototypes from the original and validation analyses. The exception obviously was cluster 6:

Thus, the Cluster 6* profile in the M2 validation model clearly differs from the original model as indicated by it's very low correlation (0.01) with the earlier cluster 6. In all other cases the pair-wise correlations ranging from .87 to .99 indicate that essentially similar stable centroids emerge across the two typologies from original and replication samples.

Table 2. Correlations between original and validation cluster centers*

M3 Original Cluster Centers	1	2	3	4	5	6	7
M2 Validation Cluster Centers	2	1	3	7	5	6*	4
Pearson R for matched pairs	0.90	0.87	0.96	0.99	0.97	0.01	0.93

* Note: the numerical labels assigned to the clusters differ between the original study model (M3) and validation study model (M2). These numerical labels were purely arbitrary. The matching pairs are seen in each column of the above table.

Another approach to illustrate the close replications of the matched clusters from original and validation studies is shown in the dendrogram below. The Ward clustering of these 14 centroid vectors shows the six matched pairs almost immediately are grouped together at very high similarity levels at the base (left side) of the dendrogram. The six pairs can be seen being amalgamated into six small clusters at the earliest fusion steps of this Ward analysis, beginning with the pair (4, M7). The M designation in this figure refers to the validation sample clusters. The six paired matches (4-M7, 5-M5, etc) all occur close to the base of the dendrogram showing that their mutual similarity is very high. The one mismatched case (M6) in the dendrogram joins the other high delinquency, low self-control clusters (3, 6, and M3) but at a lower level of similarity. As expected these three vectors form a category of highly delinquent low-control clusters (see cluster descriptions below).

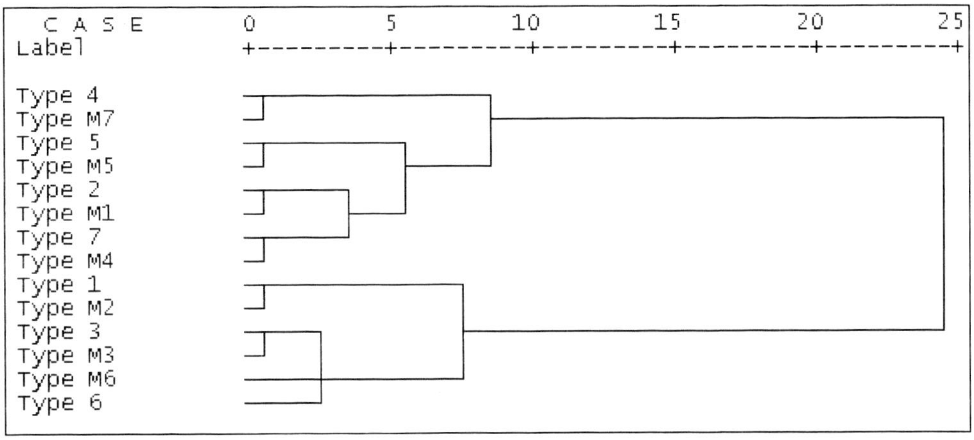

Figure 1. Dendrogram showing fusions of matched cluster pairs from original and validation sample (M).

In our third approach to illustrate the similarity of matching cluster profiles between original and validation clusters we a used Principal Component Analysis (PCA) to project the centers for fourteen clusters into a 2D space of the first two principal components. In the scatter plot the (+) markers indicate the seven cluster centers found in our replication data set (M2). The centers of the original construction sample are marked only with their number. This scatter plot shows that with the exception of cluster 6 the respective centers from the validation and original sample form six tight pairs indicating their high mutual similarity.

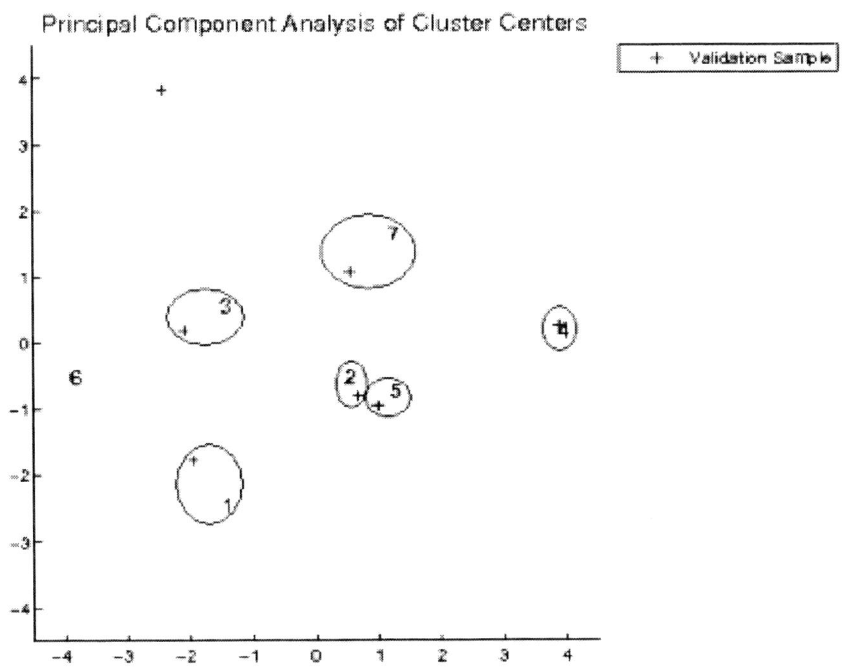

Figure 2. PCA scatter plot from the cluster centers of the original and validation sample (M).

External Validation

To examine external validation series of one-way ANOVAS with a Scheffe post-test procedure were applied to examine the associations between the new typology (M2) and five external delinquency history and demographic criterion variables that were not used in cluster development. Significant differences in such variables across types are conventionally viewed as supporting the external validation of a typology. Please note that the cluster number labels in these analyses now refer to the validation cluster model (M2). The results include many significant differences as follows:

1. *Age of each cluster*: Age differed significantly across the seven types ($F = 39.1$, $p<.000$). The Scheffe test indicated that clusters 2 and 5 were significantly younger at 15.1 and 15.3 respectively than other types, while clusters 4 (16.1) and 6 (16.2) fell into a significantly higher subset than other clusters.
2. *Age at first adjudication*: This age significantly differed between types ($F = 21.7$, $p <.000$). Clusters 2 (12.9) and 5 (12.8) were significantly younger at first adjudication than most clusters. Clusters 4 (13.8) and 6 (14.1) were significantly older.
3. *Total adjudications*: This differed significantly between types ($F = 6.7$, $p<.000$). The Scheffe test indicated that types 3 (3.4) and 4 (3.2) had significantly higher adjudications than other types, while type 7(2.8) had significantly fewer.
4. *Total Felony adjudications*: The types differed significantly on this variable ($F = 8.1$, $p<.000$). The small cluster 6 had a significantly higher average (.58) than other clusters, while clusters 1 and 2 fell in a significantly lower subset on the Scheffe test.
5. *Total detentions:* This differed significantly between types ($F = 6.8$, $p<.000$). The post hoc test indicated that type 7(1.4) fell in a subset significantly lower than other clusters, while types 2 and 3 were in a significantly highest subset.

These differences are largely consistent with the prior study. For example, the large "normal situational" type 7 again falls below the others in seriousness, extent of adjudications and detentions and is older at first adjudication. Similarly, the low self-control cluster 3 again has more adjudications and detentions than most other clusters. These differences are also consistent with the theoretical expectations for these types. The internalizing types (2 and 5) again have an early age of first adjudication that had previously characterized these two types in the original study.

Cluster Descriptions

In these descriptions we use the z-scores (Table 3) to build the narrative of each cluster. We use z scores of +/- 0.30 as indicators of relevant type characteristics following Costa et al (2002). These are highlighted in the table and are given in parenthesis in the narratives. We occasionally deviate from this rule if z scores are close to .30 and also form a coherent pattern with other key features of the profile. Please note that in the following descriptions we do not discuss matches to the prior literature – and also the number labels are now those that came with the validation analysis. The links to the prior literature are given in the final discussion section.

Table 3. Z scores for the eight male types (validation sample)

Input	1 (n=428)	2 (n=328)	3 (n=456)	4 (n=525)	5 (n=607)	6 (n=79)	7 (n=647)
Age at Assessment	−0.16	−0.26	0.12	0.38	−0.38	0.46	0.03
Felony Adjudications	−0.10	−0.11	0.00	0.04	−0.07	0.35	0.06
Total Number of Detentions	0.02	0.12	0.16	0.09	−0.01	−0.17	−0.18
Criminal Associates	−0.36	−0.06	1.02	0.51	−0.52	0.80	−0.66
Criminal Opportunity	−0.27	−0.16	0.73	0.43	−0.54	0.75	−0.36
Low Pro-social	0.30	0.12	0.55	−0.01	−0.18	0.21	−0.46
Impulsivity	−0.50	0.29	0.56	−0.01	0.44	0.47	−0.84
Low empathy	−0.20	0.08	0.96	−0.10	0.30	−0.07	−0.37
No remorse	0.09	0.24	0.80	−0.20	−0.14	−0.08	−0.54
Manipulative	−0.40	0.21	0.69	0.00	0.31	0.42	−0.78
Aggression	−0.47	0.42	0.57	−0.07	0.46	0.15	−0.87
Violence Tolerance	−0.54	0.40	0.68	−0.04	0.51	0.30	−0.79
Soc. Isolation	−0.25	0.70	−0.10	−0.38	0.38	−0.05	−0.53
Neg. Cognition	−0.37	0.59	−0.00	−0.30	0.41	−0.07	−0.75

Input	1 (n=428)	2 (n=328)	3 (n=456)	4 (n=525)	5 (n=607)	6 (n=79)	7 (n=647)
Soft drugs	−0.39	−0.10	0.48	0.65	−0.66	1.12	−0.56
Hard drugs	−0.28	−0.19	−0.15	−0.09	−0.32	3.51	−0.28
Substance Trouble	−0.38	−0.06	0.70	0.55	−0.56	1.25	−0.60
Promiscuity	−0.20	−0.13	0.45	0.43	−0.42	0.59	−0.50
Academic Failure	0.25	0.08	0.56	0.24	−0.18	0.20	−0.37
Low Goals	0.16	0.01	0.87	−0.01	−0.25	0.19	−0.35
School attendance	−0.10	0.44	0.45	0.06	0.21	0.34	−0.73
School behavior	−0.14	0.26	0.80	0.38	0.05	0.39	−0.81
Fam. discontinuity	0.22	0.81	0.02	−0.28	−0.10	−0.18	−0.57
Low Socioeconomic	0.30	0.71	0.42	−0.26	−0.11	−0.13	−0.59
Fam. Criminality	0.08	0.79	0.12	−0.18	−0.33	0.24	−0.51
Low bonds	0.26	0.55	0.45	−0.39	−0.32	0.01	−0.59
Discipline	0.49	0.81	0.56	−0.45	−0.43	0.15	−0.66
Low supervision	0.38	0.62	0.79	−0.33	−0.42	0.31	−0.61
Neglect	0.33	1.03	0.19	−0.40	−0.35	0.16	−0.64
Phys. abuse	−0.22	1.05	−0.11	−0.44	0.02	−0.06	−0.58
Sexual abuse	−0.34	0.34	−0.20	−0.39	0.01	−0.19	−0.45
Parental Conflict	0.11	0.82	0.09	−0.21	−0.44	0.42	−0.60
Bad Neighborhood	−0.16	0.35	0.55	0.11	0.36	0.03	−0.47
Low emotional support	0.21	1.00	0.23	−0.33	−0.36	0.29	−0.74
Youth rebellion	−0.41	0.57	0.41	−0.25	0.04	0.63	−0.90

Type 1 (N =428, 11%). Lower Socioeconomic Youth with Poor Family Socialization

The correlation between the original and present cluster is r = .90. This cluster - like its original counterpart – exhibits social deprivation and inadequate socialization. The youth are from lower socio-economic families (.30) with above average family disorganization (.22), inadequate discipline (.49), poor supervision (.38), neglect (.33), poor emotional support (.21) and weak family bonds (.26). School performance is relatively poor (.25) and the youth have few pro-social activities after school (.30). As in the original study, this type has little evidence of sexual (-.22) or physical abuse (-.34) and is not in rebellion against the parents (-.41). They do not show social withdrawal (-.25) or hostile negative social attributions (-.35) or aggression to others (-.47) and display no marked low-control personality features. They have lower than average involvement in drugs or promiscuity.

This cluster is a little younger than average (15.4). Its juvenile criminal history scores are about average. However, its age at first adjudication (13.2) is significantly younger than clusters 3, 4, 6 and 7.

Type 2 (N= 328, 8.5%) Internalizing Youth A: Withdrawn, Abused and Rejected

This pattern correlates at r = .87 with it original counterpart. This cluster has the same pattern of extreme abuse/neglect and an internalizing personality e.g. extreme physical abuse (1.1), sexual abuse (.34), emotional rejection (1.00), neglect (1.03), weak discipline (.81) and poor supervision (.62). This is accompanied by serious social isolation/withdrawal (.70), negative social cognitions/mistrust (.59), a hostile attitude to others (.42), above average tolerance of violence (.40) and some impulsivity (.29). The lifestyle features (drugs, promiscuity, peer associates and pro-social leisure activities) of this cluster all tend towards average – and thus are not quite as low as in the original matched cluster. These youth come from very poor (.71) and disorganized families (.81) with high rates of crime/drugs (.79) and reside in dangerous areas (.34).

External validation tests show that this cluster has significantly earlier mean age-at-first-adjudication (12.9) than several other clusters (4, 6, and 7).

Type 3 (N = 456, 11.8%) Low-Control A: Versatile Offenders

This cluster correlates very highly with its original counterpart at r = .96. It shares the same pattern of extremely low self-control, i.e., impulsivity (.56), low empathy (.96), manipulative-dominance (.69), aggression (.57), low remorse (.80) and a reckless high-risk lifestyle. Their lifestyle again involves criminal peers (1.02), high antisocial opportunity (.73), promiscuity (.45), common drugs (.48), getting into trouble as a result of drugs (.70) and few pro-social leisure activities (.55). These activities are conducted mostly in unsafe neighborhoods (.55). Their school experience is very negative: school failure (.56), attention problems (.45) and disruptive school behavior (.80). Family factors show low socio-economic status (.42) and residence in a higher crime neighborhood (.55). Parenting factors include very little supervision (.79), poor discipline (.56) and low bonding with the youth (.45). These youth, in turn, are highly rebellious against parents (.41).

This cluster's official criminal history coheres with the above extreme profile. It has the highest mean number for both adjudications (3.4) and detentions (2.2) compared the other clusters.

Type 4 (N =525, 13.6%) Normative Delinquents: Drugs, Sex and Peers

This is one of the larger clusters. It correlates at r = .99 with its original counterpart.

It has the same pattern of risks (drugs, sex, and peers) as in the original study. These youth are slightly older than average (.38) and have several family and personal strengths. Their families are not in the lowest socioeconomic strata (-.26), are not disorganized (-.28) and do not reside in dangerous areas. Sexual (-.39) and physical abuse (-.44) are far lower than average and there is no evidence of neglect (-.40), poor discipline (-.40) or weak supervision (-. 33). Family bonds are stronger than average (-.39). However, these youth exhibit a very risky lifestyle e.g. antisocial associates (.51), few pro-social leisure activities

(.43), promiscuity (.43), conventional drugs (.65), trouble from drug use (.55) but a relative avoidance of hard drugs (-.09). At school they show above average failure (.24) and negative behaviors (.38), but no loss of future goals. Personality shows no extreme low self-control factors and there are no signs of social isolation (-.38) or negative cognitive mistrust (-.30).

This type is significantly older (Ave. = 16.2) than clusters 1,2,3,5 and 7. The ANOVA analyses indicate a significantly later mean age-at-first adjudication than clusters 1, 2, 3, and 5. Otherwise, its official history scores are average.

Type 5 (N = 607, 15.7 %) Internalizing Youth B: With Positive Parenting

This cluster profile correlates very highly with its original counterpart at r = .97. It is again an internalizing type (like Cluster 2) with substantial negative social attributions (.41), hostile aggression (.46) and social withdrawal (.38). Their social isolation perhaps explains a relatively low-risk lifestyle (-.54) and an avoidance of delinquent peers (-.52) common drugs (-.66), hard drugs (-.32) and promiscuity (-.42). This cluster differs profoundly from Cluster 2 by the presence of caring, competent and non-abusive parents, who are not emotionally rejecting (-.32) or neglectful (-.35) and who do not shirk their supervision (-.42) and discipline (-.39) duties. These families give little evidence of serious disorganization (-.10) and have lower than average family crime/drugs (-.33) and low parental conflict (-.44).

This type is younger (Ave = 15.1) than average, with the post hoc test showing that it is significantly younger than clusters 3, 4, 6 and 7 (subset alpha = .05). It also has a significantly earlier mean age-at-first-adjudication than 4, 6 and 7; and significantly fewer felony adjudications than 6.

Type 6 (N = 79, 2%) Low Control B: High risk offenders

This small cluster does not have a high association with its original counterpart (r = .01). This cluster like cluster 3 has many serious criminogenic features. These youth follow a high risk lifestyle (.75), associate with anti-social peers (.80) and have the highest scores for soft drugs (1.12), hard drugs (3.51), drug related trouble (1.25) and promiscuity (.59). Their personality shows above average impulsivity (.47), manipulative-dominance (.42) and tolerance of violence (.30). At school they show disruptive behavior (.39 and attention problems (.34) but only slightly above average failure (.20). Surprisingly, their families are about average on most parenting and stability issues. However, these parents do not provide clear supervision (.31), are in serious conflict with each other (.42) while these youth show extreme rebellion against the parents (.63).

The profile of Cluster 6 has several similarities to the high risk cluster 3 but differs dramatically from 3 in it's greater drug involvement, especially hard drugs, in more positive parenting, family stability, less poverty and residence in safer neighborhoods.

Although the original counterpart was also highly delinquent, extremely rare, and had little self-control, these two type patterns, as note above, do not have a high association with each other. Thus, we again encounter the instability of this potential high risk, low self-control and rare cluster.

Type 7 (N = 647, 16.7 %) Normal "Accidental/Situational" Delinquents

This cluster correlates at r = 0.93 with its original counterpart. Relative to other clusters it has the lowest risk and need levels and appears virtually normal in comparison to all other clusters. These youth have higher socio-economic families (-.59), less family instability (-

.57), live in safer areas (-.47), have better supervision (-.61), more consistent discipline (-.66), less physical (-.58) and sexual (.45) abuse. Their families show less parental crime/drugs (-.51) and less parental conflict (-.60) than other clusters. These youth have less risky lifestyles (-.36), fewer high crime peers (-.66), less drugs (-.56) and less promiscuity (-.50). There are no obvious school problems. They are less socially isolated (-.70). Their personality pattern shows no clear tendency towards low self control. Bonding to parents shows less erosion (-.59) and the youth show less rebellion (-.90) than most of this sample.

The official criminal history of this cluster coheres with the above benign profile showing relatively low official delinquency. Their criminal record shows significantly lower mean adjudications compared with clusters 3 and 6.

Figure (3) below shows an alternative graphical representation of the z-scores of these seven clusters. All scales are scored with a directionality such that higher scores always represent more problems or higher risks. A bar extending to the left indicates a cluster has a lower mean score (less problems) than the grand mean. If the bar extends to the right the cluster has a higher mean score (more problems) than the grand mean. The scale inputs in the bar chart are sorted by domains that represent peers, substance abuse, attitudes, cognitions, school, neighborhood and family for easier comprehension.

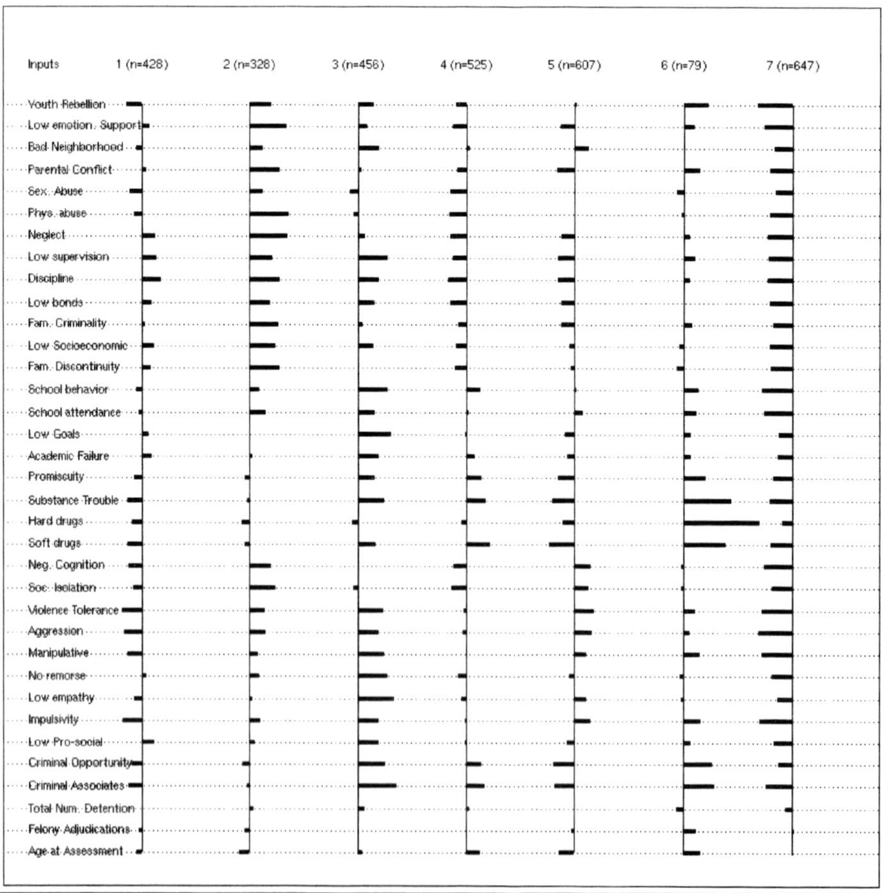

Figure 3. Z scores profiles for males only validation sample.

Discussion

In this discussion we first examine conclusions regarding the structural aspects of this taxonomy of delinquents. Second, we address the congruency, continuities and likely matches between our present taxonomy and the prior literature on explanatory delinquency typologies. This leads to some conclusions regarding the most reliable taxonomic structure and major explanatory types in this domain. We then comment on the relationship between taxonomic research and delinquency theory. This involves the transformation from raw empirical clusters towards progressively more scientific analytical categories. Finally, we note some limitations of this study.

Structural Features of This Taxonomy

What do our results imply regarding the structural aspects of a taxonomy of delinquents in the social-psychological explanatory domain? Basically, we found that the structural features of this updated delinquent taxonomy largely replicates our previous model. As noted previously most prior studies rarely discuss the structure of their taxonomies – leading to confusion over the data structures that constitute the taxonomic organization of delinquency samples. The following structural issues are critical:

Does the youth taxonomy generalize across regions? The present data shows that our original taxonomy is strongly replicated in the validation study and thus across a different locale and sample. The SVM procedure demonstrated that all seven of the original types re-emerged in the validation sample – including the small unstable cluster 6. The overall partition agreement between original and validation taxonomies was highly significant (Cohen's Kappa = 0.64; Contingency coefficient = 0.84 , $p < .000$). However, while showing strong overall agreement these coefficients also show that the two taxonomies are not identical and that the boundaries of clusters appeared unstable. This replicated our findings regarding boundaries in the first study.

Replication of specific types: In examining the replication of specific delinquent types we again found substantial stability. The data show that 6 out of the 7 original types had impressive replications in the validation sample with pair-wise correlations as follows: .90, .87, .96, .99, .97 and .93. These were the same six clusters that had high replication in the first study. Only the small low-control delinquent cluster 6 from the original study failed to replicate. However, we note that the two low-control clusters had several high delinquency features that overap and thus some similarity in their interpretations, despite the fact that they differ overall in their profile pattern.

Internal structure of clusters - Stable cores, graded membership and unstable boundaries: Our data suggest the following conclusions about the taxonomic structure.

1. Stable Central Prototypes: As shown above the replicated six cluster centers were very stable. Pairwise correlations in the range of 0.90 show the almost perfect stability of these six cluster centers across original and validation studies.
2. Unstable boundaries: We conclude that the type boundaries are somewhat unstable. This was shown by the kappa coefficients from the McIntyre-Blashfield split-half validation studies. Ranging from 0.64 to 0.69 these confirm strong but not perfect

agreement between the overall partitions. Since the cluster centers were clearly stable the disagreements likely relate to unstable boundary conditions. This underscores a point made by Brewer (1993) that natural classes are primarily defined not by boundaries but by their central cases; not by what is excluded, but by what they most strongly include.

3. Probabilistic membership levels within clusters: We also conclude that the internal structure of our delinquency types – denser stable cores, fuzzy boundaries and a gradation of membership - is consistent with a "family resemblance" definition of category structure (Rosch 1978; Bryant 2000). The membership probabilities of cases within each cluster also confirmed this gradation ranging from high probability central core members to boundary members with progressively lower probabilities.

Outliers and Unclassifiable cases: In the typology for the validation sample about 20% of cases fell in an Outlier/Hybrid class. This is lower than in the original study and is likely due to the fact that the present typology included only boys. Since this validation model is optimally adjusted to fit boys, this would reduce the proportion of non-classifiable cases. A separate study of a girls-only sample has provided profiles specifically orientated towards girls (Brennan 2008).

Hierarchical Structure: Seven or Five Clusters? We conclude that a hierarchical arrangement defines this taxonomy – with seven basic clusters nested within a broad 5-cluster solution. As in our original study, both 7 and 5-cluster taxonomies seemed viable each giving evidence of reliability, interpretative coherence and clear matches to the prior literature. The 5-cluster solution simply merges the two "internalizing socially withdrawn clusters" (2 and 5), and the two low self-control clusters (3 and 6) merge into one larger super-ordinate low self-control cluster. One represents the internalizing pattern, and the other, the low self-control pattern.

Conclusions regarding Multimodality: When multiple methods (K-Means, Bagged methods, Semi-supervised clustering) across multiple samples and separate studies converge on highly similar core clusters this suggest that some stable structure is present. Additionally, the apparent matching to clusters in the prior literature also supports the reliability of these findings. These multiple convergences suggest that the dense clusters and their core prototypes are stable reference points reflecting several dominant patterns among delinquent youth. Our results thus support a conclusion that these data distributions have sufficient multimodal structure that leads to the reliable identification of stable latent classes. This may address Osgood's (2005) and Sampson and Laub's (2005) challenge regarding the "existence" of differential types - although given fairly entrenched positions this may clearly require further replications. In this regard we note a recent comment by Skilling, Quinsey and Craig (2001)

> "If several taxometric methods indicated the presence of a taxon, and parameter estimates arrived at in different ways (derived within and across taxometric procedures) were numerically consistent, then there would be strong grounds for believing the taxon exists"

We note that such natural categories (taxons) would almost by definition create a high-density cluster in a measurement space of theory-relevant attributes.

Are These Taxonomic Findings Congruent with the Prior Theoretical and Taxonomic Literature?

We now examine the degree to which our present taxonomy identifies delinquent types that are potentially congruent with, and may represent replications of types from previous explanatory typologies in delinquency. The prior taxonomies of Lykken (1995) and Moffitt (1993) were theoretical statements. Lykken referred to his taxonomy as an "armchair" taxonomy, and Moffitt (2003) has indicated the need to clarify the number of types (K) in her taxonomy and add empirical precision to her theoretical prototypes. Additionally, the growing literature on explanatory delinquent typologies now offers several empirically defined taxonomies across a variety of social and psychological factors. Unfortunately, this literature is fragmented with diverse samples, diverse methods and mostly different measurement factors so that it is not easy to establish clear comparative or matching criteria. However, we attempted to examine continuities, corroborations and extensions to the most common prior theoretical and empirical taxonomies:

Type 1. Socially Deprived Delinquents – sub-culturally socialized: Our type 1 appears to replicate a socialized or sub-cultural delinquent type recurrently identified as emerging from social deprivation, poverty and sub-cultural socialization (Jesness 1988; Miller 1958; Van Voorhis 1994; Warren 1971). Our type 1 has the same conjunctive pattern of poverty, criminal/drug-using parents, low socio-economic status, family disorganization, poor discipline, neglect, and school failure; but little evidence of serious low social control or internalizing psychological issues. This also supports Lykken's (1995) contention that such ''common sociopaths'' (his term) although poorly socialized are, in fact, psychologically ''normal''. The theoretical process driving these "socialized delinquents" is that they have simply adapted to their sub-cultural environment (Miller 1985, Warren 1971).

Type 2. Internalizing and Abused: Isolated and Rejected: Several prior studies describe an internalizing delinquent type characterized by social withdrawal, hostility and neurotic behavior and a family background of serious violent abuse (Lykken 1995; Miller et al. 2004; Aalsma and Lapsley 2001; Harris and Jones 1999). Cluster 2 largely matches this type with its conjunction of internalizing features, social withdrawal, hostility, suspicion and extreme parental abuse, violence and neglect.

Type 3. Moffitt's LCP type and Low Self-Control Theory: Our cluster 3 appears to corroborate Moffitt's LCP as well as Lykken's (1995) "primary psychopath" concept. The key pattern of these types includes: impulsivity, low empathy, hostility, manipulative-dominance, low remorse, attention problems and disruptive school behaviors. Related behavioral features in our present cluster are: criminal peers, high-risk lifestyle, drug abuse and serious criminal history. Other potential replicates include Alterman et al.'s (1998) ''Psychopathic'' and Vincent et al.'s (2003) ''Impulsive'' cluster. Several theoretical models appear currently in contention to explain this type: Moffitt (1993), Lykken (1995), Gottfredson and Hirschi (1990), Hare (1996) and others.

An unresolved question is whether there are sub-types within this low-self control category. Both of our studies produced two sub-types (3 and 6). However, the instability of cluster 6 in both studies casts doubt on this finding and we acknowledge that it may be reasonable to simply offer a single super-ordinate category by combining these two clusters. Further work in this issue is required.

A second theoretical point concerns the scope conditions of the low self-control theory. Clearly, Cluster 3 largely exemplifies Gottfredson and Hirschi's General Theory of Crime in virtually every respect e.g. poor parental discipline and supervision, low-self control personality, higher opportunity and serious chronic delinquency. However, this pattern occurs only in a small percentage of the sample and does not apply to several other types. This challenges the claim that this is a "general" theory that applies to all youth and all delinquency. Thus, it would seem that the G/H theory requires a more constrained set of scope conditions.

Type 4. Normative Delinquency: Drugs, Sex and Peers: This basic pattern consists of apparently ''normal'' youth with some school and family strengths who exhibit high vulnerability and presumably interest in drugs, promiscuity and antisocial peers. They also show a later age-at-first-adjudication and commit mainly non-violent offenses. This type represents potential matches to Moffitt's (1993) AL category; Lykken's (1995) ''dissocial sociopath'' type he describes as psychologically ''normal'' but who seek meaning and excitement; see also Harris and Jones' 1999; Alterman et al (1998). Such youth may be simply exhibiting the well known concept of "normative delinquency" that reflects common adolescent risk-taking and autonomy-seeking behavior.

Type 5. Internalizing Youth B – Not abused and have Positive Parenting: Clusters 5 and 2 share a similar internalizing pattern of social withdrawal and isolation, mistrust and avoidance of delinquent peers, drugs and sex. However, in contrast to cluster 2, the parents of cluster 5 appear non-abusive, competent and caring. Matches to Cluster 5 in the prior literature include Harris and Jones's 1999 ''internally conflicted'' cluster; and a sub-type in Lykken's (1995) broad ''neurotic'' category he describes as having positive parenting and normal socialization, but who are engulfed by some unconscious or emotional complexity. The recurrence of two internalizing clusters in both of our taxonomic studies raises the possibility that at least two different causal processes may underlie this broad internalizing pattern.

Type 6. Low-Control B: Early Onset, Chronic Versatile Offenders with Multiple Risk Factors: This second, and quite rare, low self-control cluster remains tentative due to unstable boundaries and weak replication. However, in both studies it fell in the high delinquency low self control region, implying a variant of cluster 3. In fact, it has a similar profile to cluster 3 with extreme antisocial personality, high-risk lifestyle, drug use, promiscuity and criminal peers, as well as school attention problems, high parental crime and abuse. We will not attempt to link this cluster to matches in the literature due to this instability. More "discovery" work is required before any confidence could be placed on such matches.

Type 7. Normal ''Accidental/Situational'' Delinquents: Cluster 7 identifies a commonly recurring category with apparently few risk or need factors and a relatively late age-at-first-adjudication. Similar "normal" clusters are described in Simourd et al. 1994; Aalsma and Lapsley 2001; Lykken 1995; Harris and Jones 1999; Huizinga et al. 1991 and others. Theories for the delinquency of this type are often attributed to external situational-accidental factors or peer influences (Warren 1971; Van Voorhis 1994). This cluster partially matches Moffitt's AL type, although it does not have the strong affiliation to delinquent peers expected in Moffitt's type.

Traversing the Path From Empirical Clusters to Scientific/Theoretical Categories

We suggest that the clusters of delinquent types emerging from this study - although surviving various validation and reliability tests – cannot yet be viewed as theoretical or analytical categories. Some may never reach that status and may be replaced by more coherent and refined categories. In their present status they provide only an ostensive or denotative definition of a category – based on an overall empirical similarity across the classification factors. At this stage these clusters successfully reflect relatively homogeneous empirical categories of delinquent youth connected by a strong mutual similarity over a broad set of theory-relevant factors. Although we can reliably identify their membership using techniques such as SVM, these clusters are pre-theoretical in the sense that they do not yet clearly identify the underlying causal or theoretical "process" that may be producing each cluster.

These categories are not without some scientific progress as we attempt to develop them into an more precise set of analytical scientific categories. They have exhibited substantial internal homogeneity and stability. Each cluster has an explicit and fairly coherent central pattern around which most members coalesce and they appear to generalize across localities. We also have developed an explicit objective SVM-based procedure for reliable identification. These cluster patterns are also, to a degree, theory-guided, in the sense that they each reflect a specific pattern built on factors of known theoretical and predictive importance. Each pattern suggests it's own potential causal mechanism and may suggest how several current delinquency theories can be linked to a taxonomic analysis. This occurs to the degree that our taxonomic study used an input classification space was permeated by theory-relevant factors. Our input classification space specifically included over 30 factors drawn from several extant delinquency theories (opportunity, strain, social learning, low self-control, etc). Thus, a potential strength of this analysis is that the central "patterns" of each cluster may offer a starting point for the further delineation of the causal processes that may underlie each cluster (Brady 1994, Goertz 2006). Clearly, future challenges are to learn more about the causal processes that may underly these types. Additionally, the availability of quantitative identification procedures for each type may facilitate research on the developmental course of each type, specific risk prediction procedures for each; and more precision regarding differential treatment and interventions to address the specific needs of each type.

In summary, we view identifying raw empirical clusters as only a starting point in developing an acceptable taxonomy of delinquent youth. Much of our continuing analyses will aim to bolster this transformation from raw empirical clusters towards acceptable scientific categories. Daston (2000) has noted that the work of establishing scientific objects or categories is difficult and time-consuming and that these are often "elusive and hard-won" (p. 2). This is particularly the case for elusive latent classes or complex multidimensional categories (Quarks, genes, Moffitt's LCP, psychopaths, etc) and is particularly difficult in the high dimensional behavioral sciences. This shift from raw empirical clusters - based on surface similarities (phenotypes) – towards theoretically defined classes will ultimately shift the definition of these classes towards deeper theoretical criteria, and a transformation from poorly understood vague categories to more precisely measured analytical categories, with known defining features, ostensive definitions and ultimately connotative definitions based upon clearer theoretical processes. We view the present work as an early step on this journey towards a more powerful explanatory taxonomy of delinquent.

LIMITATIONS

A first limitation pertains to the often vague and diverse cluster descriptions given in the prior literature. Many prior studies fail to provide clear matching or identification rules for their types. Some prior types are described only theoretically. Thus, the matching process we used to identify the central features of prior types and match them to our seven types was sometimes difficult. Procedures such as SVM or K-Nearest Neighbor matching now offer useful tools for this challenge (Han and Kamber 2000). An important contribution of this study is that other researchers can have the ability to reliably identify our categories by following our outlined methodology using Youth COMPAS or similar instruments of their choice and the SVM tools. The study of new "scientific objects" or analytical categories will only cumulatively progress when we can ensure that across different studies or research teams we are talking about the same things (Daston 2000; Ragin 1992). However, unfortunately, the current status in delinquency typology is such that any integrative study of delinquent explanatory types will encounter this difficulty of poor identification and matching (Tremblay 2003).

The current overlapping nomenclature in delinquency and criminology is also problematic and disorganized and creates problems of matching. For example, Moffitt's LCP, Hare's psychopath, Lykken's Primary Psychopath, and Mealey's Primary Sociopath ALL have feature lists that substantially overlap. This compounds the difficulty of matching these theoretical categories and determining whether these different terms are referring to the same or different offender categories.

A second limitation is the lack of clear tests for the degree of multimodality or "clusterability" in any high dimensional multivariate data distribution. Thus, our conclusion of multimodality is based mainly on the consistent replication of highly similar clusters. Two factors cause us to be cautious regarding any final conclusion on multimodality: 1) the unreliability and fuzziness of boundaries, and 2) the relatively large number (20%) of outliers. Both of these features serve to weaken any taxonomic or multimodal data structure by blurring the boundaries between clusters, introducing unreliable cluster matches, and ruling out the possibility of "distinct" well-separated types. Another unresolved factor contributing to fuzzy boundaries is the difficulty of clearly identifying irrelevant variables. This has been a perennial challenge in pattern recognition work and no clear solution as yet has emerged (Han and Kamber 2000).

A third limitation is that the present study does not yet attempt to address the issue of "process". Our research so far has been primarily concerned to establish the robustness, stability and descriptive content of these delinquency type patterns. A shift from pattern to process explanation clearly will involve analysis of the sequencing, course and developmental processes within each of the delinquent types. Fortunately, the extreme multi-dimensionality and breadth of our data on each of these types, and the fact that many of our variables have "time markers" may support procedures such as "process-tracing" (George and Bennett 2005) that are designed to unravel the sequential processes that may underlie complex cases such as these complex holistic types. Current studies are underway to examine how different treatments affect the types we have identified.

APPENDIX A. YOUTH COMPAS

The following briefly describes the Youth COMPAS scales used in this study. Scale name abbreviations and factor loadings (in parenthesis) for selected key items in each scale are indicated. Full psychometric characteristics and theoretical justifications for each scale are available from the first author.

Antisocial Opportunity (CrimOpp): Hang around with friends (.66), parties w/o adults (.69).
Absence of prosocial engagement (LowProsoc): Church activities (.66), sports, music/hobbies (.66), school activities (.70).
Anti-social peers (CrimAssoc): Friends use drugs (.75), friends arrested (.70), friends dropped out (.65).
Social isolation (SocIsolate): Has trouble making friends (.77), no close friends (.62)
Common drugs (ComDrug): Alcohol use (.81), marijuana use (.78).
Hard drugs (HardDrug): Used cocaine (.72), used heroin (.62), has injected (.48).
Substance abuse trouble (SubTrbl): Poor judgment when high (.87), violent feelings when high (.83)
Sexual promiscuity (Promiscty): Frequency of intercourse (.78), number of partners (.68).
Impulsivity (Impulsiv): Takes risks (.64), makes quick decisions (.76), seen as reckless (.73).
Manipulative-dominance (Manipulate): Good at talking one's way out of trouble (.67), easily lies and gets away with things (.73), can dominate/threaten others (.55).
Empathy (LowEmpath): Feels sad when seeing other people cry (.81), guilt feelings when breaking a promise (.84).
Aggression/anger (Agress): Quick temper (.79), History of fights (.66), stays calm in arguments (.53).
Tolerance of violence (ViolTol): How wrong it is to hit someone to win an argument (.50), hit someone to teach them a lesson (.76).
Lack of remorse (LowRemor): Blames others/situation (.72), doesn't express regret (.63).
Negative social cognitions (NegCognit): Kids put you down (.78), few kids can be trusted (.63).
Academic failure/success (AcadFail): Usual grades (.79), number of classes failed (.80), times grade repeated (.57).
Attention problems (AttProbs): Trouble paying attention (.85), easily bored (.71).
Educational aspirations (LowGoals): Intends to graduate (.72), education is important (.81).
School behavior (SchoolBeh): Suspended (.72), argues/fights with students (.67), conflict w. teachers (.74).
Family discontinuity (FamDisc): Multiple caretakers (.64), separated from natural parent (.61), out-of-home placements (.72).
Social class and poverty (LowSES): Family receives social assistance/subsidized housing (.68), parent has unstable/low wage employment (.81), difficulty paying bills (.87).

Family criminality (FamCrime): Mother arrested (.62), father jailed (.60), sibling drug use (.51).

High crime neighborhood (Nhood): Friends or family assaulted (.73), drug sales (.84), witnessed fights/gunfire (.87).

Parental conflict/domestic violence (ParentConf): Parents threaten each other (.84), parents yell/fight (.78), parents attack each other (.82).

Inconsistent discipline (InconDiscp): parents have clear rules (.72), perceived fairness (.72), clear reasons for punishments (.75).

Inadequate supervision (PoorSuper): Parents check when youth returns home (.84), parents check on youth's friends (.65), parents monitor youth's activities (.85).

Emotional bonding with parents (EmotBonds): Feels close to mother (.73), close to father (.51), feels close to sibling (.70).

Parental neglect (Neglect): Youth feels neglected (.80), parents show no interest (.71), parents rarely talk to youth (.79).

Physical abuse (PhysAbuse): Youth is scared of being hurt (.86), parents violent when high/drunk (.78), youth removed from home because of abuse (.73).

Emotional support (EmotSupp): Mother is hostile (.64), kicked out of the house (.50). *Sexual abuse* (SexAbuse): Sexually abused by family member (.81), removed from home because of sexual abuse (.74).

Youth rebellion (YouthRebel): Youth intimidates parent/caretakers (.65), youth openly defies parents/caretakers (.82).

REFERENCES

Aalsma, M.C., and Lapsley, D. (2001). A typology of adolescent delinquency: Sex differences and implications for treatment. *Criminal Vehavior and Mental Health 11*: 173-191.

Alterman, A.I., McDermott, P.A., Caccioloa, J.S., Rutherford, M.J., Boardman, C.R., (1988). A typology of antisociality in methadone patients. *J. Abnom. Psychol.* 107 (3):412-422.

Arabie, P., Hubert, L.J., and DeSoete, G. (1996). *Clustering and Classification.* World Scientific, River Edge, NJ.

Beatty, J., (1994). Theoretical Pluralism in Biology and Systematics. Chapter in: *Interpreting the hierarchy of Nature – From Systematic Patterns to Evolutionary Process Theories.* Eds: Grande L and Rieppel O.

Bergman L. R., Cairns R.B. Nillson R-G and L. Nystedt. (2000) *Developmental Science and the Holistic Approach.* Lawrence Erlbaum Publishers, London.

Berk, R.A., (2008) *Statistical learning from a regression perspective.* Springer-Verlag.

Beutler, L.E., and Malik, M.L. (2002). Rethinking the DSM: a psychological perspective. *American Psychological Association,* Washington, DC.

Brady R.H. (1994) Pattern description, Process Explanation and the History of Morphological Sciences. Chapter in: Grange L. and O. Rieppel.(Eds) *Interpreting the Hierarchy of Nature: From systematic patterns to evolutionary process theories.* Academic Press, New York.

Breiman, L. (1996). *Bagging predictors.* Mach Learn 24:123-140.

Brennan T. (2008) Explanatory diversity among female delinquents: Examining taxonomic heterogeneity. Chapter in: Ruth Zaplin (Editor) *Female Crime and Delinquency: Critical perspectives and effective interventions* Jones and Bartlett Publishers

Brennan, T., Elliott, D., and Huizinga, D. (1978). The social psychology of runaways. Lexington, MA: Lexington Books.

Brennan, T., and Dieterich, W. (2003). *Youth COMPAS psychometrics: reliability and validity*. Northpointe Institute for Public Management, Traverse City, MI.

Brennan, T., Breitenbach M and W. Dieterich (2008) Towards an Explanatory Taxonomy of Adolescent Delinquents: Identifying Several Social-Psychological Profiles. *Journal of Quantitative Criminology*. Vol 24, No 2 179-203

Bronfenbrenner, U. (1979). The Ecology of human development: experiments by nature and design. Harvard University Press, Cambridge Mass.

Bryant, R. (2000). Discovery and decision: exploring the metaphysics and epistemology of scientific classification. Fairleigh Dickinson University Press, Madison, NJ.

Caruana, R. and A. Niculescu-Mizil (2006). An empirical comparison of supervised learning algorithms. In *ICML '06: Proceedings of the 23rd international conference on Machine learning*, New York, NY, USA, pp. 161–168. ACM.

Cicchetti, D., and Richters, J. E. (1993). Developmental psychopathology considerations in the study conduct disorder. Development and Psychopathology*, 5, 33 l- 344.*

Costa, P.T., Herbst, J., McCrae, R., Samuels, J., and Ozer, D.J. (2002). The replicablilty and utility of three personality types. *Eur. J. Pers* 16:73-87.

Dolnicar, S., and Leisch, F. (2000). Getting More Out of Binary Data: Segmenting Mardets by Bagged Clustering, Working Paper 71, SFB Adaptive Information Systems and Modeling in Economics and Management Science.

Elliot, D.S., Huizinga, D., and Ageton, S. (1985). *Explaining Delinquency and Drug Use*, Sage Publications, Beverly Hills, CA.

Farrington, D.P. (2003). Developmental and life course criminology: Key theoretical and empirical issues. *Criminology* 41:221-255.

Fielding, A.H. (2007). *Cluster and Classification Techniques for the Biosciences.* Cambridge University Press, Cambridge.

Francis B., Soothill K., and Fligelstone R. (2004). Identifying Patterns and Pathways of Offending Behavior. *European Journal of Criminology*, Vol 1 (1), 47-87.

Frick, P. (2004). Developmental pathways to conduct disorder: implications for serving youth who show aggressive and antisocial behavior. *Psychol. Schools* 41:823-834.

George, A. L., and Bennett, A. (2005). *Case Studies and Theory Development in the Social Sciences.* MIT Press, Cambridge, Mass.

Goertz, G. (2006). *Social Science Concepts: A User's Guide*. Princeton University Press, Princeton.

Han, J., and Kamber, M. (2000). *Data mining: concepts and techniques*. Morgan Kaufmann, New York.

Harris, P., and Jones, P.R. (1999). Differentiating delinquent youths for program planning and evaluation. *Criminal Justice and Behavior* 26(4): 403-434.

HeyJ. (2001) *Genes, Categories and Species*. Oxford University Press, Oxford.

Huizinga, D., Esbensen, F., Weiher, A.W. (1991). Are there multiple paths to delinquency? *J. Crim. Law Criminal* 82:83-118.

Jefferson T.W., and Johnson, J.H. (1991). Relationship of hyperactivity and sensation seeking to delinquent sub-types. *Crim. Justice Behav.* 18:195-201.

Jessness, C.F. (1988). The Jesness inventory classification system. *Crim. Justice Behav.* 15:78-91.

Jones, P.R., andHarris, P.W. (1999). Developing an empirically based typology of delinquent youths. *J. Quant Criminal* 15:251-276.

LaGrange, T.C., and Silverman R.A. (1999) Low self-control and opportunity: Testing the general theory of crime as an explanation for gender differences in delinquency. *Criminology* 37 (1): 41-72 Feb 1999.

LeBlanc, M. (2005) An Integrated Personal Control Theory of Deviant Behavior. Chapter in: Farrington D. (Ed). *Integrated Developmental and Life Course Theories of Offending.* Transaction Publishers, New Brunswick.

LeBlanc, M. (2006). Self control and social control of deviant behavior in context: development and interactions along the life course. Chapter in: Wikstrom P.H. and Sampson R.J. *The Explanation of Crime: Context, Mechanisms and Development.* Cambridge University Press: Cambridge.

Lenzenweger, M. (2004). Consideration of the challenges, complications, and pitfalls of taxometric analysis. *J. Abnorm. Psycol.* 113:10-23.

Loeber, R. (1996). Developmental coninuity, change, and pathways in male juvenile problem behaviors and delinquency. In: J.D. Hawkins (Ed.) *Delinquency and crime: current theories.* Cambridge University Press, New York, pp 1-28.

Loeber, R, Keenan, K., and Zang, Q. (1997). Boys' experimentation and persistence in developmental pathways toward serious delinquency. *J. CHild Fam. Stud.* 6:321-357.

Longshore, D., Eunice Chang, Shih-chao Hsieh and Nena Messina (2004). *Self-Control and Social Bonds: A Combined Control Perspective on Deviance. Crime and Delinquency,* Vol. 50 No. 4, 542-564

Longshore, D., and Turner, S. (1998). Self-control and criminal opportunity: Cross-sectional test of the general theory of crime. *Criminal Justice and Behavior*, 25(1), 81-98.

Lykken, D. T. (1991). What's wrong with psychology anyway? In D. Cicchetti and W. M. Grove (Eds.), *Thinking clearly about psychology* (Vol. 1, pp. 3-39). Minneapolis, MN: University of Minnesota Press.

Lykken, D. (1995). *The antisocial personalities.* Lawerence Erlbaum, Hillsdale NJ.

Mak, A.S. (1990).Testing a psychosocial control theory of delinquency. *Criminal Justice and Behavior*,17(2), 215-230.

McIntyre, R.M., and Blashfield, R.K. (1980). A nearest-centroid technique for evaluating the minimum-variance clustering procedure. *Multivariate Behav Res.* 15(2):225-238.

McVie, S. (2004). Patterns of deviance underlying the age-crime curve: The long term evidence. *Annual Conference.* British Society of Criminology.

Mealey, L. (1995). The sociobiology of sociopathy: an integrated evolutionary model. *Behav. Brain Sci.* 18:523-599.

Meehl, P. E. (1990). Appraising and amending theories: The strategy of Lakatosian defense and two principles that warrant it. *Psychological Inquiry. I,* 108-141.

Meehl, P.E. (1992). Factors and Taxa, Traits and Types, Differences of Degree and Differences in Kind. *Journal of Personality* 60, 117-74.

Mezzich, A.C., Coffman, G., and Mezzich, J.E. (1991). A typology of violent delinquent adolescents. *J. Psychiatry Law* 19:63-78.

Miller, M., Kaloupek, D.G., Dillon, A.L., and Keane, T.M. (2004). Externalizing and internalizing subtypes of combat-related PTSD: a replication and extension using the PSY-5 scales. *J. Abnorm Psychol.* 113:636-645.

Miller, W. (1958). Lower-class culture as a generating milieu of gang delinquency. *J. Soc. Issues* 14:5-19.

Milligan, G.W. (1996). Clustering validation: results and Implications for applied analyses. In P. Arabie, L. Hubert, and G. DeSoete (Eds.) *Lustering and classification.* World Scientific Press, River Edge, NJ, pp 345-379.

Moffitt, T.E. (1993). Adolescence-limited and life-course persistent antisocial behavior: a developmental taxonomy. *Psychol. Rev.* 100:674-701.

Moffitt, T.E. (2003). Life-course persistent and adolescent-limited antisocial behavior: a 10 year research review and a research agenda. In B.B. Lahey, T.E. Moffitt, and A. Caspi (Eds.) *Causes of conduct disorder and juvenile delinquency.* Guilford Press, Thousand Oaks, CA, pp 49-75.

Moffitt, T.E., Caspi, A., Rutter, M., and Silva, P.A. (2001). *Sex differences in antisocial behavior.* Cambridge University Press, Cambridge Mass.

Nagin, D. and Paternoster, R. (2000). Population heterogeneity and state dependence: state of the evidence and directions for future research. *J. Quant. Criminal* 16:117-144.

Osgood, D.W. (2005). Making sense of crime and the life-course. *Ann. Am. Acad. Polit. Soc. Sci.* 602:196-211.

Piquero, A. and Moffitt, T.E. (2005). Explaining the facts of crime: How the developmental taxonomy replies to Farrington's Invitation. In D. Farrington (Ed.) *Integrated developmental and life course theories of offending.* Transaction Publishers, London.

Potter, C.C., and Jenson, J.M. (2003). Cluster profiles of multiple problem youth: mental health problem symptoms, substance use, and delinquent conduct. *Crim. Justice Behav* 30:230-250.

Ragin C.C. (2000) *Fuzzy-set Social Science.* University of Chicago Press, Chicago.

Richters, J.E. (1997). The Hubble hypothesis and the Developmentalist's Dilemma. *Development and Psychopathology*, 9 (1997), 193-229.

Rosch, E. (1978). Principles of categorization. In E. Rosch and B.B. Lloyd (Eds.), *Cognition and Categorization.* Erlbaum, Hillsdale, NJ, pp27-48.

Rubenfeld S. (1976). Typological approaches and delinquency control: A status report. *Center for Studies in Crime and Delinquency*, NIMH, Washington D.C.

Salmon, W. C. (1984). *Scientific explanation and the causal structure of the world.* Princeton, NJ: Princeton University Press.

Sampson, R.J., and Laub, J.H. (2005). A life-course view of the development of crime. Ann *Am. Acad. Polit. Soc.* Sci 602:12-45.

Simourd, D.J., Hoge, R.D., Andrews, D.A., and Leschied, A.W. (1994). An empirically-based typology of male young offenders. *Can. J. Criminol* 36:447-461.

Skilling, T. A., Quinsey, V.L. and Wendy, M. Craig. (2001) Evidence of a Taxon Underlying Serious Antosical Behavior in Boys. *Criminal Justice and Behavior*, Vol. 28 No. 4, 450-470

Sorensen, E., and Johnson, E. (1996). Subtypes of incarcerated delinquents constructed via cluster analysis. *J. Child Psychol. Psychiatry* 37:293-303.

Stefurak, T., Calhoun G.B., and Glaser B.A. (2004). Personality typologies of male juvenile offenders using a cluster analysis of the Millon adolescent clinical inventory introduciton. *Int. J. Offender Ther Comp Criminal* 48:96-110.

Stefurak, T., James, R., Georgia, B. (2006). Subtypes of Female Juvenile Offenders: A Cluster Analysis of the Millon Adolescent Clinical Inventory, *International Journal of Law and Adolescence.*

Thagard, P. (1992). *Conceptual revolutions.* Princeton University Press, Princeton, N.J.

Van Voorhis, P. (1994). *Psychological classification of the adult male prison Inmate.* State University of New York Press, Albany, NY.

Vapnik, V.: *The Nature of Statistical Learning Theory.* Wiley, NY (1998).

Vincent, G.M., Vitacco M. J., Grisso T, and Raymond R. Corrado. (2003). Subtypes of Adolescent Offenders: Affective Traits and Antisocial Behavior Patterns. *Behavioral Sciences and the Law*, 21: 695–712 .

Wachs T.D. (2000). *Necessary but not sufficient: The respective roles of single and multiple influences on individual development.* American Psychological Association, Washingon D C.

Walsh, A. (2002). *Biosocial criminology.* Anderson Press, Cincinnati.

Warren, M.Q. (1971). Classification of offenders as an aid to efficient management and effective treatment. *J. Crim. Law Criminal Police* Sci 62:239-258.

In: Delinquency: Causes, Reduction and Prevention
Editor: Ozan Sahin and Joseph Maier
ISBN 978-1-60741-558-9

Chapter 2

JUVENILE DELINQUENCY AND FAMILY ENVIRONMENT INFLUENCES

Jean-Pascal Assailly*
INRETS
(French National Institute of Traffic Safety Research)

INTRODUCTION

There are nearly as many supposed causes of juvenile delinquency as authors writing on the subject! While a consistent sociological literature has been produced on the sociological mechanisms of the etiology of juvenile delinquency, and while an equally consistent psychosociological literature has also been produced about peer group influence on the same topic, much less has been published on the influence of family environment. Though, not all poor children become delinquent! We present here a review about what we have learnt from developmental psychopathology works concerning this question.

One of the reasons to study the family environment comes from longitudinal works on chronic aggressiveness and violence (Tremblay, 2003, 2008), or on antisocial (Moffitt, 2003) or delinquent behavior (Broidy, 2003; Lahey and al, 2003); these clearly indicate a continuity and a predictability of problems from childhood to adolescence, and the first environment to influence a person is the family. For example, 70% of antisocial problems at 11 years of age can be predicted by the judgment of the mother or of an educator before 3; the persistency is stronger when the initial manifestations are physical aggressions. This continuity is observed for boys but not for girls. So, delinquent behaviors of girls are more difficult to predict, and we still have to understand what orientates the trajectories of girls into delinquency.

Another lack in the knowledge is that we know even less about the symmetrical phenomenon of prosociality: which mechanisms explain the fact that a child does not become delinquent? In fact, respect of rules and respect of others could be as fascinating objects to study than transgression and antisociality for a psychologist, but society pays researchers to work only on what goes wrong (delinquency, traffic accidents, illnesses, etc), on late trains,

* E-mail: assailly@inrets.fr

not on what goes well, on trains on time! It is possible also that prosociality and antisociality have their own dynamics, with different underlying psychological mechanisms.

We present here the theoretical model we have built from our literature review, which is based on the interaction between social control of violence by the parents, and social learning of deviant behavior from the parents (Assailly, 2007). Usually, theorists in this field stress either social control (cf. Hirschi, 1969) or social learning (cf. Bandura, 1977), but we think these mechanisms are not exclusive and may be combined.

This interaction expresses itself through five main dimensions of what is a family environment; control is operated mainly through the second and third dimensions, learning through the two last ones.

1. The biological heritage: genetic and prenatal factors; behavior genetics works have shown the heritability of delinquent behaviors, more so in the case of an early onset (before 14 years of age); they have also shown non-genetic factors such as the selective mating of delinquent fathers and delinquent mothers!
2. The affective link of the mother-child dyad attachment, and the long-term consequences of emotional unsafety (and of course of the extreme negative parental behavior, abuse and neglect): defensive exclusion of affects, alexithymia, self-escape, low self-esteem, all of these are mediating psychological factors of antisociality.
3. The family structure and its evolution through time (divorce, recompositions, siblings, deaths, etc): the conflicts parent/parent and parent/child, notably parent-in-law/child, have been associated with the genesis of antisocial behavior. The issue of the importance of the biological father and its authority is questioned at the moment.
4. The behaviors of the parents themselves, the imitation and the intergenerational transmission of various social behaviors: social modeling, and indirect consequences of parental delinquency (on their educational supervision, for instance).
5. The parenting style, the type of control parents maintain on their children's behaviors during adolescence: coercitive, authoritarian styles have shown to have deletere effects, as well as permissive styles or psychological control.

Of course, interactions exist between these five dimensions and are more influent than the dimensions themselves.

For example, we know more precisely today that the parent/child relation is bidirectional: parents influence children but children influence parents too! So, we can distinguish three types of family influences: genetic factors, shared environment factors, unshared environment factors. Among the latter, interactions between the biological heritage and the affective link of the mother/child dyad attachment illustrate well this bidirectionality: genetic factors have produced a difficult temper of the child, in turn the mother reacts negatively to this temper and experiences more difficulties to create a secure attachment, insecure attachment will lead the child to perceive the world as hostile and to react with aggressiveness.

Another example is interaction between the biological heritage and the parenting style: genetic factors have produced a difficult temper of the child, in turn parents experience more difficulties to develop an « authoritative » parenting style, and will develop a much too permissive style, low supervision during the teenage years will promote contacts with delinquent peers.

Etc, etc…

Developmental psychopathology is a recent approach, created in the scientific space lying between psychology and epidemiology; their main interests are the developmental pathways, from birth to the end of life, that lead to inadaptation. This approach has generated various concepts like continuity, resiliency, transactions between genetic and environmental factors, critical periods, cumulative amount of stress, mediating and moderating factors, etc, in order to understand, for example, the road to delinquency.

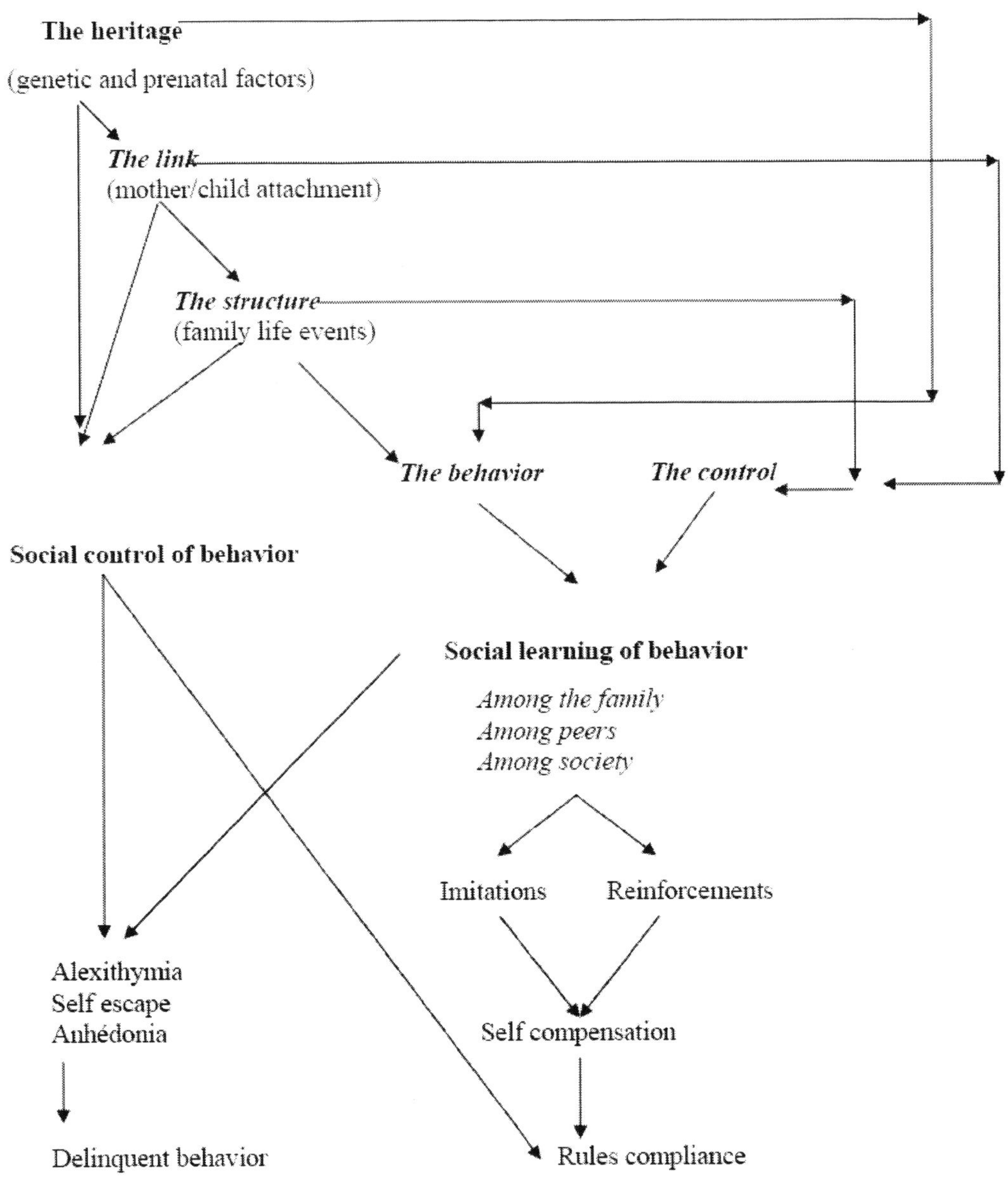

A social sequential model of the family etiology of delinquency.

1. Biological Heritage: Genetic Factors

1a) Heritability of Delinquent Behaviors

Generally speaking, behavior genetics works conclude to a stronger heritability of adult delinquency than of juvenile delinquency; this is probably due to the fact that juvenile delinquency may be transitory, that many adolescents display antisocial behaviors but do not persist to do it at adult age; adult delinquency may reveal more stable and more genetic traits than juvenile delinquency, which could be more influenced by peer pressure.

Concerning juvenile delinquency, the twins' study of Cloninger and Gottesman (1987) concluded to a weak heritability: 87% of concordance for monozygotic twins, compared to 73% for dizygotic twins. A study of siblings by Rowe and Rogers (1989) notes to the existence of genetic factors, but also to an imitation phenomenon: sins may display delinquent behaviors together. In three adoption studies, Cadoret and al. (1983) conclude to the existence of genetic factors; nevertheless, the « genetic risk » (delinquency of biological parents) acts only in interaction with « environnemental risk » (psychiatric problems and divorce in the adoptive family). Crime rate is important only among teenagers exposed to both types of risk.

Concerning adult delinquency, works are suggesting more important influences of genetic factors: Danish twins study (Christiansen, 1970), Danish adopted children study (Mednick and al., 1984), and Swedish adopted children study (Cloninger et al., 1982) all conclude to a strong heritability:

- in the Danish twins study, correlation for theft was .70 among monozygotic twins, compared to .36 for dizygotic twins; this produces a heritability of 66%. Crime prevalence was 14% among monozygotic twins, compared to 9% for dizygotic twins; nevertheless, an imitation effect was existing, and more strongly between monozygotic twins.
- in the Swedish adopted children study, 60% of variance was attributed to genetic factors, and 14% to a genotype/environment interaction (males in foster care in working class families or with unstable care were more at risk).

More recently, Rowe and al. (1997) have produced a reanalysis of the Cambridge longitudinal study (see detailed presentation in the chapter above about behaviors), trying do disentangle genetic and environmental factors.

Ironically, behavior genetics works end by revealing something that is not only genetic but also environmental, a strong correlation of .55 between the delinquent behaviors of the father and the mother! In fact, the father and the mother do not share common genes!

Two phenomenons can be distinguished here:

- social homogamy or mating: the father and the mother share the same ecological niche and so are subject to the same influences;
- phenotypical mating or selection: men and women choose their partners according to their characteristics (risk taking, addictions, antisociality, etc); this could be more under the influence of genetic factors than social mating.

In their analysis of the Cambridge data about the intergenerational transmission of delinquent behaviors, Rowe and al. (1997) have concluded to a strong heritability: genetic factors of delinquent personality are more influent than environmental factors (delinquent parents create a sort of family environment, low supervision for example, that may have an influence on their children's delinquent behavior). Nevertheless, one environmental factor was acknowledged in their study: the presence of a delinquent brother was increasing the probability of delinquent behavior of the subject; the presence of a non-delinquent brother was decreasing it.

Physical Aggressiveness

Works comparing mono-and dizygotic twins (see for example Brendgen et al., 2005) conclude to an important heritability of physical aggressiveness: nearly 50% of variance is attributed to genetic factors, the other 50% to non-shared environment factors.

Social Aggressiveness

Heritability of social aggressiveness is weaker: nearly 20% of variance is attributed to genetic factors, 60% to non-shared environment factors and 20% to shared environment factors.

So, social and physical aggressiveness may share the same genes but would be related to different environmental factors; the often-observed correlation between both types would result from a direct causal effect of physical aggressiveness on social aggressiveness.

1b) Genetic Factors and Age at Onset of Delinquency

One well-known result of delinquency research is the predictive value of age at first delinquent behavior: when delinquent behavior starts at adolescence, it may be very transitory (80% of teenagers display some kind or the other of antisocial behaviors during adolescence), but when it starts during childhood, the risk of an adult delinquency career is much stronger. Twins' studies have shown that early onset of delinquency is much more under the influence of genetic factors than later onset.

1c) Heritability of Associations between Delinquency and Other Problem Behaviors

The association between delinquency and precocious sexual activity may be under the influence of genetic factors (those ruling hormonal functioning, notably testosterone, see Rowe, 1994).

1d) Selective Mating of Delinquent Fathers and Delinquent Mothers

Selective mating of delinquent fathers and delinquent mothers is of course an important risk factor for the development of the child antisociality. Similarities concerning antisociality between the father and the mother have frequently been observed. When you consider selective mating about addiction and selective mating about antisociality together, it has been noted that selective mating about addiction can lead to selective mating about antisociality, but the reverse is not true (Vanyukov and al., 1996).

1e) Interactions between Genetic and Environmental Factors in the Etiology of Delinquency

Interactions between childhood maltreatment, the MAOA gene, and antisocial behavior have been observed in the Dunedin Longitudinal Study (Caspi, 2002, 2004): among sexually abused children, those presenting a variation of the MAOMA gene (low-functioning version) are twice more susceptible to develop aggressive behavior and three times more susceptible to be condemned for violent behaviors than sexually abused children not presenting this variation of the MAOMA gene; on the contrary, the presence of this gene is not associated to problems among children having not been abused, which also clearly shows the importance of environmental factors.

Of course, we are still in the prehistoric time of the understanding about the influences of genes related to neurotransmitters on offending behaviors! We know that serotonin plays an inhibitory role and dopamine a facilitating role on aggression, and therefore are related to the involvement in antisocial behavior. The fluctuations in biochemical levels and more generally modern neurobiology using cerebral imagery will help us to understand interindividual differences, as well as intra-individual evolutions like the decrease of risk taking after adolescence (Steinberg, 2008) or the age-crime curve (Collins, 2004).

2. The Link: Mother/Child Attachment Type

Attachment theory started with the publication of John Bowlby's seminal book on the child/mother attachment (1969). Attachment derives from the innate need of protection, this need activates attachment behaviors, which are all behaviors aiming to maintain a certain proximity with the maternal organism or its substitutes.

From these initial affective experiences, the human baby develops « internal working models » about the type of love and security he feels he can receive from others. Ethological observations (Ainsworth and al, 1978) have led to distinguish two types of attachment, secure and anxious, and three subtypes of anxious attachments: avoidant, resistant and disorganized. Two main factors influence the constitution of attachment type: the sensitivity of the mother to her baby's needs, her affective and emotional availability.

Longitudinal studies have shown that attachment behaviors in childhood turn into « states of mind » at the beginning of adolescence (Main and al, 1985): secure children turn into « autonomous » adolescents and adults, avoidant anxious attachments into « detached » states of mind, resistant anxious attachments into « preoccupied » states of mind, disorganized anxious attachments into « unresolved » states of mind. Detached and preoccupied states of mind may be considered as risk factors for aggressiveness and antisociality, as these subjects progressively learn to perceive the others as hostile, to develop negative expectancies, and to react aggressively to these perceived threats.

So, does attachment influence the etiology of delinquency? Bowlby already suggested it in a 40's paper entitled like a fable, " 44 young thieves ": the frequency of mother/child separation was noted, comparing with a control group. 40% of these young thieves had experienced long separations with their mother, and 70% had a « detached » state of mind, deprived of tenderness. These separations have produced the "defensive exclusion of affects "which is also present in the etiology of addictions, and this affective structure may persist even after the end of the separation.

The protective factor of a secure attachment relates well to the social control theory of Hirschi (1969): it is the social link that inhibits the development of delinquent behavior; young people engaging in delinquent behavior do so because they have nothing to loose in this domain.

Since Bowlby's seminal paper, many works have stressed the importance of affective problems between parents and their children in the etiology of juvenile delinquency. Numerous studies have noted the relationship between insecure attachment and child's aggressiveness (Cole and al, 1998, for example). Reciprocally, the quality of the mother/child attachment has been related to prosocial orientations of the child or the teenager (Radke-Yarrow and al., 1983), and this, among different cultural backgrounds (Ma, 2000, in Hong Kong for example).

In a longitudinal study of a national representative sample of teenagers about risk and protective factors of delinquency (Resnick and al., 1997), the protective factors against delinquent involvement were: intimacy with the parent, degree of parental attention perceived by the teenager, degree of satisfaction with the parent/child relationship, feeling of being loved by the parent.

Works on bullying show that family conflicts and affective relationships problems are associated to bullying (see Blaser and al., 2002, for example), and it is interesting to note that this is true whether young people are the victims or the perpetrators ...

Interactions between biological and psychological factors and between genetic and environmental factors have also been observed: For example, on the follow-up since birth of a cohort of 4,269 Danish boys (Raine and al., 1997), birth with complications or with neurological trouble of the child is not related to involvement in delinquent behavior eighteen years later, but birth with complications followed by maternal rejection of the child (4.5% of subjects) is related to involvement in delinquent behavior eighteen years later (18% of crimes).

This risk factor is specifically linked to violent crimes and not to non-violent delinquency or to recidivism, which supports the idea of a specific link between affective links and violence. We see here the importance of an early involvement of social work after births with complications, in order that these do not turn out to be a deletere risk factor: interventions on at risk families with a focus on maternal attachment behavior reduce by half ulterior arrests caused by teenagers antisocial behaviors (see the meta-analysis of Bakermans-Kranenburg and al., 2003).

Child Maltreatment and Delinquency

Children having been maltreated are more at risk to become delinquent; results vary between 9% and 29% of them (Ryan and al, 2005). In other terms, early childhood victimization increases the risk of later criminality by about 50% (Widom, 1989), whatever the type of offence. However, when delinquency is decreasing in the general population, it decreases also among maltreated children, as influencing factors of the decrease are the same in both populations. This being said, it is difficult to disentangle the effects of maltreatment from the other effects of social adversities following this experience.

Among the group of children having been maltreated, it is mainly those who have been in institutional care and those with unstable foster care (moreover for boys) who become delinquent (Ryan and al, 2008), the risk being 2.5 higher for residential care services than for a stable foster care, two observations easily understandable in the context of attachment theory. Approximately 16% of children placed into substitute care will develop a delinquent behavior, compared to 7% of all maltreatment victims who are not removed from their family. The instability of care seems to play in interaction with gender, as much less effects on delinquent behavior was observed among girls.

Of course, there are confounding factors in the comparison institutional/foster care: it is mainly the more severe cases of family disfunctioning that lead to institutional care, so it may not be the institutional care in itself but what the child has undergone before that has an effect on the development of delinquent behavior. However, it seems clear that placement instability attenuates social capital, which further weakens the social bonds that children in care have with significant individuals and institutions. Individuals with a weakened sense of social commitment, attachment and obligation are less bound by moral restraints and more susceptible to opportunities to engage in delinquent behavior.

Early Victimization, Trauma, Psychopathy and Delinquency

Early traumatization is considered as a causal or mediating risk factor for aggressive and violent behavior (Jaffee and al, 2004): it has a negative influence on the development of the ability to regulate anger. The syndrome of psychopathy is defined by such affective deficit, interpersonal deceptiveness, impulsive as well as antisocial tendencies (Forth and al, 1998) and is highly predictive of aggressive and violent behaviors in adulthood.

It has been shown that psychopathy mediates the association between early childhood victimization and violence (Krischer and al, 2008) on a population of incarcerated delinquent female and male juveniles; a sample of 185 detained adolescents has been compared to 98 adolescent students. Higher scores of traumatization have been observed in delinquent juveniles compared to school adolescents.

Early physical but also emotional traumatic experience was only associated to psychopathy in detained boys. In girls, other family-related variables such as nonparental living arrangements (number of foster homes), seemed to be more influential in developing the psychopathy syndrome than traumatization.

Maternal Incarceration and Child/Mother Attachment

With an estimate of one million US children whose mother has been in jail, these experiences may be a research field in themselves! When the father is incarcerated, more often the child stays with his/her mother, but when it is the mother, custody is more often with grandparents, and 10% of the children are in foster care.

The effects of this family life-event have been studied on a population of 54 Wisconsin children, aged 2 to 7 years (Poehlmann, 2005). 63% of these children expressed an insecure representation of attachment with their mother or with other persons, and typical loss behaviors, as described by Bowlby or Harlow.

Resiliency factors (children maintaining a long-term secure attachment) are: stable foster care, reactions of sadness rather than anger, age (less negative effects on older children: probably these are more able to " understand " this phase of separation than the younger children, the latter should therefore be subject to more careful attention when in this situation). Stability of foster care with a grandparent is even a stronger factor than the depression of the grandparent after the incarceration of the mother, which shows that this is clearly an attachment problem!

Furthermore, the way people talk to the child about the incarceration has an effect in itself, which is understandable in the context of resiliency theory (see Cyrulnik, 2008): positive effects when in a sincere, simple, direct manner; negative effects when things are hidden. So, this is an important, even if delicate, aspect for people in charge of the custody.

More surprisingly, visiting the mother in jail has negative effects: maybe the conditions of the visit reactivate attachment behavior but without any possible satisfaction of the need ...

Two Mediating Variables between Attachment and Delinquency: Alexithymia and Self Escape

Alexithymia, as introduced and conceptualized by Sifneos (1973) from observations of psychosomatic patients, relates to the difficulties or even inabilities of somebody to « read » and name his/her own emotions and feelings. As well, post-stress traumatic disorder is a good example of the manifestation of alexithymia. Alexithymia reveals a deficit in the cognitive processing and regulation of emotional states (Taylor and al., 1997).

Alexithymia has progressively been associated to a variety of other psychological problems: substance use and eating disorders (Taylor, 2000); risk taking in traffic and sports (Assailly, 2007). Concerning juvenile delinquency, this progressive « blindness » to one's own emotions has also been considered as a strong vulnerability factor in clinical works (Jeammet, 2001; Schreiber, 1992) or in empirical studies (Langevin and al., 2001; Moriarty and al, 2001; Zimmermann, 2006).

The frequency of alexithymia is much more important among populations of young delinquent people (47%) than among matched control groups (22%), and is similar to psychiatric clinical populations (in the Zimmermann study on 82 Swiss male adolescents, 36 offenders and 46 controls ranging in age from 14 to 18 years); the rate in the control group is in agreement with previous studies showing that approximately 23.5% of « normal adolescents » are alexithymic (Horton and al, 1992). With family dissociation, alexithymia is found as one of the most robust association of a psychological factor with juvenile delinquency.

These observations should have preventive implications in the field of young delinquents rehabilitation: they must be helped to « mentalize » and, for this, group therapies may be more appropriate than individual therapies with this target group, as subjects with high alexithymia respond by definition poorly to traditional psychotherapies. Group therapies can help these young people to become more emotionally aware and expressive, in order to facilitate certain maturational steps, converting motor behavior into verbal behavior.

Self escape is a concept originating from Carver and Scheier's self regulation theory (1981), which is another control theory approach to human behavior; this model relies on the difference between the real self and the ideal self; when what we are does not correspond to what we would like to be, self regulation has two attentional strategies: either self escape to shift attention from one's problems and frustrations to anything that can produce a diversion (alcohol, drugs, risk taking, etc), or self compensation to keep the attention on one's problems and frustrations in order to compensate and transform vulnerabilities into levers of adaptation.

We may also consider a " bridge » between the well-known criminological concept of « negative identity » of delinquent people and psychological concepts like alexithymia or self escape; in fact, numerous works have shown the relation between low self-esteem and delinquent behavior (cf. Lahey and al, 2003).

Two different developmental pathways may correspond to these associations, and both illustrate the etymological origin of the word « delinquency », which comes from *delinquere*, changing of place:

- Involvement in delinquent behavior may correspond to self-escape, the product of a difficult affective history, of insecure and anxious attachments that lead teenagers to alexithymia and acting out.
- Involvement in delinquent behavior may correspond to a « tentative trial » of self compensation (even without hope of success ...): a difficult affective history has produced an insecure attachment which in turn has produced a negative self image: to reinstall a good image of himself, the teenager may get involved in delinquent behaviors, in order to find a popularity, an aura, a prestige in his peers' eyes.

To conclude on the links, we'll say that the instability of family bonds creates the instability of social bonds, and hence of the social control of delinquent behavior, this mainly among boys.

3. The Structure: Influences of Life Events and Changes in the Family Structure (Parental Discord, Separations, Deaths, Moves, Siblings Births, etc)

For a long time, the instability of the family structure has been pointed to play a role in the development of delinquent behavior; separations would produce a deficit in the control of the socialization of young people. Moreover, those one-parent families being mainly the mother with her children, the single-mother would be confronted to two difficulties: financial resources generally weaker than those of the father, less effective authority on the children. Plus, this problem is more and more acute as separations and divorces follow an exponential growth in all industrialized countries.

Nevertheless, meta-analysis or reviews on the effects of divorce (Amato and al, 1991; Rodgers and al, 1998; Hetherington and al, 1982, 2002; Wallerstein and al, 1980) conclude that it was difficult to obtain a scientific consensus about the long-term effects of divorce in general, and on delinquent behavior of the children in particular, as this field of research is flawed by many confounding factors and methodological biases. In fact, divorce could be considered only as a risk marker: it would reveal negative factors that exist also in intact families (for example, family conflicts, as these are more influent than the separation itself).

This being said, two meta-analysis with an update ten years after (Amato and al, 1991; Amato, 2001) have concluded that there is a modest association between youth delinquency and parental divorce, and that the differences in delinquency between youth from intact families and those from divorced ones are currently increasing.

Several conceptualizations have been proposed about this problem: the social control model of Hirschi (1969) the social control/parental absence model (Demuth and al, 2004), the family crisis model (Biblarz and al, 1999), the economic strain model (Amato and al, 1991).

In his original social control model seminal paper, Hirschi (1969) only stressed the quality of the affective link between the child and the parent as a protective factor against the development of delinquent behavior; in this theoretical context, a child with a good relationship with his/her single mother should be less at risk than a child having difficult relationships with both parents! In fact, in the literature reviews, conflicts and links are often identified as confounding factors, and differences between types of family structures often disappear when affective conflicts are controlled.

In a more recent evolution of the model, the social control/parental absence model (see Gottfredson and al, 1990; Demuth and al, 2004), Hirschi recognized that the absence of one parent may have in itself deletere effects on the social development of the child, as the single parent would not be able anymore to provide a good affective relationship and a good supervision to the child. For example, on a nationally representative sample (7514 subjects having passed a medical check in the years 1966/1970 (certainly a bit old data!), Dornbusch and al. (1985) have shown that children living with single-mothers have too much autonomy in decisions and are more involved in deviant behavior and this, even after control of financial resources or educational level. The presence of another adult (which is not the child's biological father) in these monoparental structures increases parental control and decreases deviant behavior of young people, and this mainly among boys.

The family crisis model (Biblarz and al, 1999) put more emphasis on the emotional consequences of the separation and their effects on the child behavior. In this perspective, we understand that the results of studies stressing that death of one parent is less detrimental than divorce, as death creates less conflicts, and less resentment and less family crisis are possible. Several studies have confirmed this « hierarchy of disadvantage » two parents/death of one parent/separation or divorce (Amato and al, 1991; Glueck and al, 1950; Wadsworth, 1979; Wells and al, 1991).

The economic strain model (Amato and al, 1991) gives of course more importance to the lack of economic resources created by the separation. The social disadvantage (less money for cultural or sports activities, moves to more at risk neighborhoods, etc) experimented by the children would « push » them into delinquency. As said above, not all poor children become delinquent … so, it is not the family income per se but the loss of resources following the separation that is the risk factor, it is a comparative variable. In this context, rich single parent households should not have problems, as economic resources mediate the effect of family composition! Results of some studies (Mc Nulty and al, 2003, for example) support this model: divorce produces impoverishment in single-mother households, which in turn promotes deviant behaviors of the children.

So, it is difficult to decide which of the theoretical models fits better the data on family composition, family characteristics, family disruption and delinquency!

One of the difficulties is the definition of single-parent households: what means « the family "? Most of the time, the « family » resolves itself on a single-woman, with a series of « rotations » of other actors like brothers, sisters, grandparents, foster care children and mother's partners! So, to understand the genesis of antisocial behavior, you have to understand the influence of a single-mother and her social context and, for this, many methodological problems are still on the way when one wants to put in relation the family history and the said genesis:

- single-parent families cover a wide range of events: parental discord, separation, divorce, deaths, recomposition; these have very different effects on the children's social behavior, as meta analysis and reviews quoted above have shown;
- many studies are retrospective: so, how to know if the family problems are the cause or the consequence of the delinquent behavior of the young person?
- how is delinquency measured? The detected? The real one? The permanency of an antisocial behavior? What about the girls?
- very often, the same family factor considered as predicting delinquency is also predicting other phenomena like schizophrenia for example; so, it should be interesting to find and discriminate factors predicting only delinquency.
- confounding factors (social milieu, genetic factors, etc) play … as usual …

One work (Henry et al., 1993), originating from the well known Dunedin longitudinal study (924 New Zealand children born in 1973 and followed from birth up to 15 years of age) tried to avoid those methodological biases, comparing 50 children of 11 years-old with an antisocial behavior, 220 children without, and 37 children presenting other types of problems. This work shows that in a pool of 29 family variables, 9 are significantly associated to an antisocial outcome or other types of troubles (depression, anxiety). These nine variables explain 9% of the variance, once behavioral problems at age 5 had been controlled. Among these nine variables, the two more important are:

- the harmony between parents about discipline when the child was five years-old;
- the number of changes in the family structure during childhood.

The predictive value of these two factors is hence independent of the influence of the behavioral problems of the child. Moreover, these two factors will also predict « contacts with the police » when the child reaches 15 years of age, as well as the precociousness of these contacts; these two factors explain 15% of the variance for these contacts, once behavioral problems at age 5 had been controlled. One thing still to be discussed is the disharmony between parents about discipline: is it purely an environnemental factor, or is it also reflecting the influence of genetic factors (antisocial parents will have some difficulties to maintain harmony in their couple)? Let us remind that this work was not taking into account variables concerning the father, as these were not measured. A more important part of variance could have been explained if these would have been introduced.

One could think that single father families (indeed much more rare than single mother ones!) could be considered as « better » for the prevention of the development of antisocial behavior, on the two criteria of money and authority. On the contrary, fathers communicate less well with their children on the road to delinquency than mothers. Plus, the sex of the single parent plays in interaction with other variables: social class, ethnicity, etc. For example, the sex of the parent may be of importance among Caucasian, but not among afro-American or Hispanic families.

From a purely theoretical perspective, four hypotheses could be stressed about the influence of the parent:

1. the advantage of the same sex-parent; whether you consider psychoanalysis (the same sex-parent is essential in the construction of the Superego, this part of our subconscious dealing with rules and authority) or psychosociology (social learning by imitation and identification with the same sex-parent), the same sex-parent could be considered as a more important protective factor;
2. the advantage of the mother; attachment theory points the major importance of the affective link with the mother in the contention of the violence, and psychosociology points the better ability of mothers to create networks of social support;
3. the advantage of the father; in his absence, masculinity could be exaggerated, or the social control could be more difficult in the context of a deficiency in paternal authority;
4. the neutral hypothesis; when men and women find themselves in the situation of raising a child on their own, they adapt, and few differences would be observed between single-father and single-mother families.

Few studies have been done in this field, but the « advantage of the mother hypothesis » and hence attachment theory seems to fit more the data. Nevertheless, this factor plays in interaction with the social milieu: the advantage of single-mother households is observed only in Caucasian families, but not in afro-American and Hispanic ones, maybe the psychosocial differences between mothers and fathers are much less frequently observed in afro-American and Hispanic families.

For example, the study by Cao and al (2004) showed that being raised by a single mother does not have an influence on the young people delinquent behavior, once confounding factors are controlled, notably protective factors: the presence of other adults at home (« grannies » or « aunties » replacing the father?); the stability of presence at school (is it a social control by the school?). It also showed that social aid does not have an impact on these effects ... Contrary to the opinions of conservative politicians, social aid does not promote the emergence of delinquent behavior ... Finally, this study observes also the « usual » boys/girls difference: it is mainly the boys who become delinquent, particularly those raised by a single-mother; it is mainly on the boys that the absence of the father has an effect, one point for the same-sex parent hypothesis.

As well, another study by Eitle (2006) on several thousands of young people in Florida (2715 Blacks, 1257 Hispanics, and 5685 Caucasians) shows an effect of the parent's sex and rather concludes to the advantage of the mother hypothesis: girls are more susceptible to become delinquent when they are raised by a single father, controlling for other salient factors; but is it a cause or a consequence? When the girl becomes delinquent, maybe the mother puts her in custody with the father?

More recently, a study using data from the National Longitudinal Study of Adolescent Health (Add Health) was carried on 9,636 US teenagers (Mack and al, 2007); the results support the second hypothesis, attachment theory and Hirschi's original interpretation of social control theory: maternal attachment is a predictor of delinquency more important than family structure, a stronger explanation of delinquent behavior than other family processes such as maternal supervision, parental control or loss of economic resources.

To conclude on this question, all the results are not concordant for the moment, and even the neutral hypothesis keeps its possible validity! One can say that being raised by a single father (compared to a single mother) is a risk factor for the development of a delinquent behavior and that the reasons of this phenomenon have to be analyzed: attachment theory, and notably the light it puts on the contention of violence by an affective link, remains currently one of the best hypothesis. In the future, another research topic would be to analyze the differences in parenting styles or behavior between single mothers and fathers, and to determine how to help single fathers so that their children's risk of future delinquency and illicit substance use is reduced.

Concerning single mothers, another risk factor concerns the offspring of teenage mothers: living with a teenage mother increases the risk of developing antisocial and delinquent behaviors, (Conseur and al, 1997, for example). In fact, teenage factors covers a wide range of associated disadvantages and risks: parenting difficulties as the mother is not prepared to her role, frequent separations with the partner and hence lack of support, economic difficulties, etc.

Developmental behavioral genetics have also been applied to the correlation between parental divorce and offspring delinquency (Burt and al, 2008). In fact, this correlation is always thought to be of environmental origin, but the authors wanted to check if a passive gene/environment correlation was existing; this type of correlation means that behavior problems found in children of divorced parents could derive from a genetic factor which was also the cause of the parent's problems and, among these, of an increased risk of exposure to divorce. For this, an original design was built, incorporating adoption status and timing of parental divorce, on a sample of 610 adoptive and biological families: if there is a passive gene/environment correlation, nonadopted youth of divorced parents should manifest increased delinquency even if the divorce preceded their birth (as a genetic factor is involved); on the contrary, if there is only a shared environmental effect, adolescents should manifest increased delinquency only in response to divorce exposure, and this whatever the adoption status (as no genetic factor would be involved). Data fits the second hypothesis; it is a shared environmental factor and not common genes that drives the relationship between divorce and delinquency.

Another issue can also be related to this family structure/delinquency relationships problem: *how one gets out of delinquency?* In fact, the age/crime curve shows that offending peak at 19 years of age, and then declines progressively (Hirschi and al, 1983).

Precisely, works stress the notions of age-graded informal social control (Sampson et al, 1993) and of graduated reestablishment of social links, two notions originating from Hirschi's social bonding theory of delinquency (1969): it is the involvement in marriage and/or work that explain how the young person gets out of delinquency (Laub and al, 1998), ad this even after controlling for individual characteristics such as latent antisocial personality traits, for prior childhood and adolescent risk factors, and even after taking into account the possibility of selection effects. When a « good thing » happens to a « bad subject "!

It is not the marital status per se that causes the desistance process, but the stability of the marriage; this is why it is a progressive, graduated effect: in fact, the effect of marriage on desistance is mediated by changes in the time spent with delinquent peers (Warr, 1998, 2002).

Those stabilities, of marriage or work, could be considered as attachments; the difference is that if the events of childhood (mother/child attachment, poverty, low supervision, etc) are well predicting the entry into delinquency, these events are badly predicting the coming out or desistance of it. So, events and social links in late adolescence will be more influent on the desistance process.

This being said, not all married offenders desist from offending! Which factors explain the differences in adult outcomes and the moderation of social bonds effects?

Self-control may be one: in Dunedin Birth Cohort Study, the desistance-inducing effects of education, employment, family ties and partnerships were strongest among subjects with the lowest levels of self-control (Wright and al., 2001).

Genetic factors may also moderate the desistance effect of marriage: a recent behavior genetics study (Beaver and al, 2008), using data from the National Longitudinal Study of Adolescent Health (Add Health) showed that the dopaminergic polymorphisms (DAT1: Dopamine transporter gene; DRD2 and DRD4: Dopamine receptor genes) and MAOA gene had significant direct effects on desistance for males. For females, the serotonin transporter gene (5HTT) was associated with desistance. Significant interactions between marriage and DRD2, DRD4, and MAOA were observed in the prediction of desistance for males, a genotype/environment interaction: the possession of certain alleles conditions the effect that marriage has on desistance. This kind of work shows clearly the complementarity of biological and psychological approaches.

4. Behavior: Imitation and Social Learning from the Parents' Behaviors

In this section, we won't analyze what our parents do to us, but simply what they do themselves. Bandura's social learning model relies on this idea that the child can be a « video recorder » of his parents' behaviors. In fact, and as we will see in this part, among all the possible predictors of delinquency, the delinquent behavior of a parent is the strongest risk factor; this intergenerational reproduction has also been shown for traffic accidents and violations, or substance abuse (Assailly, 2007). Of course, the observation of an intergenerational similarity does not tell us why it is like this; for this, we have seen that genetic or affective factors may be the mechanisms in cause, and social learning, modeling or imitation could be one.

The observation of a familial aggregation of delinquency has been suggested as far as 1925 by Burt: he observed 53% of « lack of moral temper » among parents of delinquent children, compared to 17% among parents of non delinquent children, the choice of terminology may seem old fashioned today … and, as it is well known, the works of Burt have since been the object of suspicions among psychologists concerning the reliability of the data…

Nevertheless, several studies since that have confirm the hypothesis of a reproduction of delinquency in the family:

In 1950, Glueck and al. (1950) compared a group of 500 delinquent young people to a matched group of 500 non delinquent young people in Massachusetts: prevalence of criminal behavior was two to three times higher among parents (66% for the father, 45% for the mother) and among siblings (65%) of delinquent young people than among parents (32% for the father, 15% for the mother) and among siblings (26%) of non delinquent young people; so, this similarity is independent of quality of housing and school achievement. Most of delinquent subjects have been raised in numerous families (five and more children); of course, one wonders if the number of children is one factor that reinforces the family concentration of delinquency!

Later in the US, Mc Cord (1977) compared the condemnations of 115 fathers aged 47 in 1945 to the condemnations of their sons aged 47 in 1975, this study was aiming at the evaluation of family counseling as a delinquency prevention strategy … Intergenerational transmissions of delinquent behaviors are observed, according to the type of condemnation: 29% of sons whose fathers were condemned for violence are themselves condemned for violence, against 12% for sons whose fathers were not condemned for violence ; 40% of sons whose fathers were condemned for robbery are themselves condemned for violence, against 24% for sons whose fathers were not condemned for robbery ; 50% % of sons whose fathers were condemned for drunkenness are themselves condemned for violence, against 24% for sons whose fathers were not condemned for drunkenness. So, it seems that the transmission from the father to the son follows very specific paths! It is a pity that Mc Cord's work, a bit « old » now, has never been replicated, as it suggests that intergenerational transmission rates vary according to behavior, which is a very interesting topic.

More recently, British works (see Farrington and al., 1996, for example) showed the concentration with other data sources: 35% of British prisoners say that they have an incarcerated parent (and 44% of British prisoners under 21); in 70% of the cases, it was a sibling, in 30% a parent.

Those retrospective studies suggest hypotheses, but the definite experimental evidence is to be found in longitudinal studies, like the well-known Dunedin and Cambridge follow-ups.

In the Cambridge study (411 London boys from a working class area, born in 1953, and followed from 8 to 40 years of age, see the publications from West and Farrington in 1977 up until Farrington and Barnes in 1996) the most well known result is that 18% of children of non delinquent parents became delinquent, 42% of children whose one parent was delinquent became delinquent, and 62% when both parents were delinquent.

If the statistical distribution confirms the influence of the family environment, one result that is much more rarely commented is the very pessimistic observation that 18% of children of non-delinquent parents became delinquent! This shows also the limits of family influence!

The last data obtained in the follow-up of the cohort are:

	Median age	% of condemnations
Subject of the study	40	39%
Father	72	28%
Mother	68	14%
Parents	70	21%
Elder brother	46	50%
Younger brother	35	39%
Brothers	40	44%
Masculine children	40	42%
Elder sister	46	13%
Younger sister	34	12%
Sisters	40	12%
Siblings	40	31%
Family members	51	27%
Wife of the subject	39	10%

These percentages of condemnations seem incredibly high ... but one must remember that the cohort is from a very deprived area of London.

The fact that the rate for the fathers is lower than the rate for their sons is related to a cohort effect: when the fathers had the age of committing offences, justice was more lenient and condemning less often. This cohort effect is observed for men but not for women.

So, globally, 48% of children whose father was delinquent became delinquent, against 19% for those whose father was not delinquent. As well, 50% of children whose brother was delinquent became delinquent, against 19% for those whose brother was not delinquent; there is no difference whether it is an elder or a younger brother, which seems to indicate that transmission does not go necessarily from the older to the younger .

The concentration of delinquent behavior has been well shown by this study: 11% of the families were responsible of 50% of the condemnations, and as wondered above, number of children explains only very partially this phenomenon. Of course, concentration is not total, and in these longitudinal studies, non delinquent children of delinquent parents or delinquent children of non delinquent parents should be as much interesting to study than those illustrating the transmission process!

For example, there are father versus mother effects and siblings' effects:

- among boys of non delinquent fathers, 33% of those whose mother was delinquent became delinquent, against 18% of those whose mother was not delinquent;
- among boys of non delinquent mothers, 44% of those whose father was delinquent became delinquent, against 18% of those whose father was not delinquent;
- among boys of non delinquent fathers, 33% of those whose brother was delinquent became delinquent, against 11 % of those whose brother was not delinquent;
- among boys of non delinquent mothers and brothers, 33% of those whose father was delinquent became delinquent, against 15 % of those whose father was not delinquent;

One can notice that the paternal way of transmission of delinquency is the stronger, but that maternal and brotheral ways exist also.

For example, the delinquency of the mother predicts more strongly the delinquency of the daughter than the delinquency of the father. This delinquent behavior of the mother is associated to a dysfunctioning of parenting (too much harsch or erratic discipline, cruelty, neglect, parental discord), so we see that this topic is not very far from the affective link one…

The same-sex pattern of transmission seems to be very important: correlations of delinquent behaviors between fathers and sons are .45, correlations of delinquent behaviors between mothers and daughters are .50, as are correlations of delinquent behaviors between brothers or between sisters, but correlations between opposed sex pairs (mother/son, brother/sister) are two times weaker.

Among all the possible predictors of delinquency, the delinquent behavior of a parent or a sibling is the strongest, as shown above:

Odd Ratios found in the Cambridge study (Farrington, op cit):

Delinquent behavior of a parent:	3.4
Delinquent behavior of a brother:	3.2
Parenting deficit:	2.8
Low family income:	2.6
Low I.Q.:	2.3
Supervision deficit:	2.2

The Cambridge study results are probably the most valid about family transmission of delinquency, but many other works have found it, as shown by the meta-analysis from behavior genetics works of Walters (1992).

If Transmission Is Proved, What Are Its Mechanisms?

All the strong correlations or percentages or odd ratios above do not tell us why! As we have seen in the previous sections, it could be genetic, affective, life-events factors.

Various mechanisms are often suspected, but data do not always support the hypothesis:

Direct imitation: its influence seems weak as, in the Cambridge study, parents having committed their last offence before the birth of the subject have transmission rates as important as parents starting their delinquent career after the birth of the subject; moreover, delinquent acts committed together with the parent and his child are very infrequent. On the contrary, this mechanism may be more important among brothers, as delinquent acts committed together are much more frequent, especially if they are close in age.

Positive or negative reinforcement: its influence seems weak as well. Social workers reports indicate that delinquent parent do not approve the delinquent behaviors of their children (something close to « don't do what I do, do like I say "!) and do not encourage it. About other topics (risk taking, addiction), we showed (Assailly, 2007) that negative reinforcements coming from parents are only efficient when parents show also the « right example »; otherwise, the child is exposed to paradoxal communication and cognitive dissonance!

Birth order: it does not seem to play much, as the delinquent behavior of parents influence as much the elder and the younger siblings; so, it seems that a factor such as « time of exposure to the delinquent behavior of the father » does not exist.

Social labellisation: it does not seem so clear as well, as policemen do not generally know about the delinquent career of the father when they are arresting the son! This being said, some deprived areas may be more under social stigma and surveillance.

Finally, the most influencing mechanism seems to be the one we will analyze in the next section: the parental supervision, the type of control parents try to maintain on their children's behavior.

Siblings Influences and Delinquency

The similarity between siblings concerning delinquent behaviors has often been observed, correlations go from .35 to .50 according to proximity in age and sex; these correlations are, for example, well superior to those observed about personality traits .

Correlations are stronger among boys, which was highly predictable, for the children whose parents have been arrested (social learning), and for one-parent families (deficit of supervision).

The similarity is observed, even when controlling shared environment influences (mental health of the mother, matrimonial structure, family income). So, this similarity concerning delinquency between siblings cannot be explained by shared family environment experiences, but may be attributed to relationships between siblings and the social learning these relationships produce (see Fagan and al., 2003).

Intergenerational Transmission of Domestic Violence

It has been observed in South Africa (Abrahams and al., 2005) that men who have witnessed, during childhood, violent acts against their mother are more susceptible, when compared with a control group matched on alcohol use, to be arrested at an adult age for domestic violence, violence at work, or firearms possession.

In some ways, these subjects have concluded that violence could be « normative », and that conflicts could be solved by violence. So, interventions directed towards the reduction of domestic violence, as early as childhood, might have some effects in other aspects of social life.

Long Term Effects of Maternal Incarceration on Their Offspring's Delinquent Behavior

As seen in the section about the affective link, more than 1.5 million American children have an incarcerated parent in federal or state prison (2% of all minor children, 7% of African American children).. Various theoretical models may explain the effects of maternal incarceration upon their offspring's delinquent behavior: economical strain (when the mother is incarcerated, the child's caretakers may have more limited resources, some forms of assistance are lost, etc), social stigma (intergenerational transfer of deviant labeling or discrimination from the parent to the child), social control (incarceration hampers parental support and control).

Parental incarceration has been related to short term effects such as emotional problems (depression, anxiety, and low self-esteem) cfBraman, 2002), or problem behaviors such as school-related difficulties, running away, substance abuse, and aggressive/antisocial behavior (Bloom and al, 1993).

A question remaining is the long-term effects of maternal incarceration, and very few studies have been conducted about this.

One work (Huebner and al, 2007) tried to disentangle the effect of this factor from the other social confounding factors, using data from women and their children surveyed through the National Longitudinal Survey of Youth 1979: 1,697 American adult offspring aged 18 to 24 in 2000 and 1,258 mothers. 2.1% of mothers had been incarcerated at some point between 1979 and 2000, and 1.8% of children had mothers who had been incarcerated.

This study showed that offspring of incarcerated mothers was significantly more likely to be involved in the criminal justice system as adults; maternal absence appeared to be of great importance, but the effect of maternal absence was smaller than maternal incarceration. So, maternal incarceration has a direct effect on offspring outcomes, even after controlling for other risk factors.

Maternal incarceration did not appear to be a risk marker for poor home environments and other factors associated with risks of imprisonment: children of incarcerated mothers did report significantly lower levels of parental supervision, but maternal incarceration was not related to peer pressure and to parental efficacy, because a maternal heterogeneity was observed: some incarcerated mothers were providing poor home environments and supervision for their children, but some incarcerated mothers were efficient parents whose presence in the home was beneficial to their children. The findings also support the social stigmatization or labeling perspective: adult offspring of incarcerated parents may appear more threatening to the criminal justice system and could be more likely to be sanctioned formally when compared with offspring of parents with no prior contact with the system.

Some suggestions for policy related to the use of community sanctions may be drawn from this work: removing mothers from the home, because of incarceration, can increase the likelihood of negative outcomes for offspring, and keeping parents in the community may reduce the collateral consequences of incarceration for children. As women commit predominately drug and property crimes, community sanctions should be considered more frequently if we want to avoid the intergenerational transmission.

Intergenerational Transmission of Traffic Offences and Crashes

A growing traffic safety research literature (Carlson and al, 1970; Ferguson and al, 2001; Bianchi and al, 2004; Wilson and al, in press) points a rather unexpected observation in this field: traffic behavior and career of parents and their children are closely related! More detailed transmission data can be obtained from this literature, comparing same-sex parent and other-sex parent transmissions, comparing rates of transmission for alcohol, speed, highway code violations, etc. Anyway, it seems clear that, during 15 years, a young person cannot drive but that the back seat is the first seat of the « cinema », where all parental traffic behaviors are recorded!

The Associations between Delinquency and Addictions

The association between alcohol addiction and violence is well known, be it by clinical works on alcoholics in treatment, on violent people in treatment or by general population surveys. Nevertheless, everybody who drinks is not violent! When the association exists, it may have proximal causes, affective and cognitive impairments according to blood alcohol concentration for example; but it may also have distal causes, the family histories of violence and alcohol addiction for example.

Family histories influence the expectancies related to alcohol use, those learnt beliefs that are important in the type of alcohol use chosen by the subject. The expectancies are under the influence of the exposure to parental models of use, and are moderators of the alcohol/violence relationship.

So, when we talk of family histories of alcohol and violence, we are confronted to a « four inputs scheme » with all the possible combinations: father history of alcohol, mother history of alcohol, father history of violence, mother history of violence.

Interactions between father and mother histories exist: for example, for adult subjects whose father did not have alcohol problems, a mother history of violence has no effect on the severity of the violence when the subject is under the influence of alcohol, but, for adult subjects whose father did have alcohol problems, a mother history of violence has some effect on the severity of the violence when the subject is under the influence of alcohol (Chermack and al., 2006). These correlations are observed for boys but not for girls. This shows the necessity to use family disaggregated data!

Another type of interaction between alcohol and violence refers to the consequences of being a child of alcohol dependent parents: many consequences exist, the first one being to be more at risk to become dependent of alcohol when you grow up! Another consequence of the parental alcoholism is a deficit of social competencies of their children, and this has been observed on girls aged from 6 to 15 (Hussong and al., 2005). This effect varies according to the type of parental use, and one could think that when parental behavior improves in this domain, we should see later improvements in the social development of the child, but this is not always the case (see DeLucia and al., 2001): troubles persist among teenagers even after remission of the father alcoholism, as if there was a « critical period » after which resiliency was not possible anymore because problems associated with the father alcoholism (psychopathology, genetic vulnerability to alcohol addiction, parental supervision, etc) have already done harm. Maybe the initial severity of the alcohol addiction of the father is more important than its fluctuations, and once on a high-risk trajectory, the teenager's problems may become independent of the father's addiction problems.

5. Control: Parenting Styles

Family as a Citizenship Incubator…

Parenting styles have been classified by Baumrind (1985) in a three classes-categorization:

- *authoritarian:* the « Charybde » of coercition, where discipline is imposed with physical or psychological punishments;
- *permissive:* the « Scylla » of laxism, where there is no discipline at all … and where the child is left to him/herself for his/her decisions;
- *« authoritative » or democratic style*: the right median way, where persuasion is obtained through the dialogue parent/child, where rights, duties and decisions are negotiated.

A similar typology had been proposed by Maccoby and al (1983), which was based on two axis, discipline and warmth and added to a fourth style: disengagement (low discipline, low warmth).

Of course, this aspect of parenting is not only an educational choice, it reflects also the quality of the affective link: the more protective strategy, the « authoritative » style, is in fact only possible in the context of good enough affective relationships during adolescence, which will allow to maintain the dialogue. As well, « authoritative » style is not only a parental characteristics: it is also a reaction of the parental behavior to the child's temper, a child's difficult temper will not allow easily « authoritative » style! Plus, « authoritative » style is the most protective in terms of delinquency, safety, health, well-being, etc for the majority of children, but the children with a difficult temper may take more benefits from a more directive maternal style (Kochanska, 1997).

In fact, in the past, authoritanism was the norm, but « authoritative » style has become the « normative » parental behavior according to medias, psychology books, educational advices, etc, and most parents try to apply it … as long as they can!

Coercition theory (Patterson, 1982) suggests that the young person's antisocial behavior is a social learning, originating from a negative reinforcement: the child learns progressively that one's anger is efficient to control the behavior of somebody else … and the parents' control abilities are progressively lessened … As well, an association between parental authoritarian style and difficult relationships with peers or relationships with deviant peers have been observed: a coercitive parenting style creates coercitive relationships between the child and his/her peers, and constitutes an obstacle to prosocial skills learning.

As for affective links about which we observe a modeling, a transferability from the initial mother/child attachment type on the quality of other links, there is a transferability of authoritative parenting style: children of two years old who obey their mother, because of a warm control, will then better obey their father or other caregivers (Feldman and al, 2003); socialization starts indeed at home: mother's sensitivity and her parenting style predict the relationships that the child will have later with other educational actors.

Authoritative parenting can also be referred to behavioral control, which is one of the three main « molar » dimensions of parenting:

- attachment and affective support: these are linked to well being and social behavior as seen above;
- psychological control (intrusion): it is linked to psychopathology and antisociality;
- behavioral control: it is linked to compliance with rules and norms.

The differences in the effects of psychological versus behavioral control, and the importance of the latter for rules compliance have been observed in so many different cultures (USA, Germany, Bosnia, Columbia, Palestine, South Africa, India, China) that these may be considered as a universal dimension, which transcends cultural differences (see for example Barber and al., 2005).

Of course, despite this general trend, cultural differences may also be observed: for example, in some cultures, physical punishments may have less negative consequences, as these are more experienced as « normative "; for example, when comparing effects of maternal physical punishments on the child adaptation in China, India, Italy, Kenya, Philippines, and Thailand, it has been observed (Lansford and al., 2005) that the more maternal physical punishments are « normative », the less they have negative effects, but these still have negative effects on the anxiety and the aggressiveness of the child everywhere…

Similar observations have been made in the US: risks associated to physical punishment do not seem to apply within African-American samples (Deater-Deckard and al, 1996).

Many studies showed the impact of the parents' behavioral control type on their children's delinquent behavior..

For example, the impact of an authoritarian, coercitive parenting style on the development of the teenager's aggressive and violent behaviors has been observed in various longitudinal studies like the Cambridge follow-up (Rowe and al, 1997); the same associations have been observed about parental intrusion and psychological control. Coercitive style predicts physical aggressiveness of boys, intrusive style and psychological control predicts relational aggressiveness of girls. A genetic epidemiology work on 708 siblings (twins or not)showed that 60% of the variance of the teenager antisocial behavior may be attributed to a non shared environment effect (Reiss and al., 1995): an harsh, aggressive, impulsive or inconsistent specific parenting behavior.

At the other end of the spectrum, permissivity as well is a risk factor of delinquent development (Larzelere and al, 1990), and it mediates the effects of socioeconomic status on offspring's delinquency, as we said in the introduction, not all poor children become delinquent … In fact, the negative effect of permissivity operates through an absence of monitoring and an ignorance of what the child is really doing with rules, laws, psychoactive substances, cars, etc. This ignorance leads to an optimism bias and an illusion of control where parents try to convince themselves that their child is more respectful or more careful or more sober than the neighbor's children! So, it is only through the persistence of the dialogue parent/child in a trustful way that the « authoritative » or democratic style can be installed. Even when the peer group influences get more important with age, parenting style is still operating, for example in the supervision of peers selection.

In a longitudinal study of a national representative sample of teenagers about risk and protective factors of delinquency (Resnick and al., 1997), the protective factors against delinquent involvement were: physical presence of the parent before and after school, at dinner and in the evening, expectancies of the parent related to the school success of their children.

In the US, the probability of delinquent behavior among young Hispanics has been related to a weaker parental support to the studies continuation (Davalos and al., 2005). If the teenager gets progressively convinced that his/her parents show some interest for him/her only when there is a problem or when he/she commits a delinquent act, this could be considered as an incentive for delinquency!

As said above, affective relationship and parenting style interact: a bad quality of the affective relationship and the deficit of behavioral control are predicting together the teenager's involvement into delinquency; this has been observed in various sociocultural environments. Reciprocally, the warmth of the mother/child affective relationship moderates the effects on antisociality of a coercitive style based on physical punishments: it's only when bashing occurs in the context of a cold or hostile relationship between the child and the parent that it leads to delinquent behavior. Genetic behavior works have been conducted on this topic, comparing twins, adoptive and biological mothers (Deater-Deckard and al, 2006): what is observed is not a passive genotype/environment correlation, as adoptive mothers moderate in the same way the effects of physical coercition than biological mothers, whatever the age, sex or age at adoption of the child, but rather a shared environment effect; so, the general correlation of .27 between physical coercition and externalized problems of the child rises to .36/.40 with « cold » mothers and drops to .10/.19 with « warm » mothers ; nevertheless, an evocative genotype/environment correlation exists as well : mothers, whether biological or adoptive, treat in a different manner each child according to his/her temper ; these bidirectional effects aggravate progressively the parent/child conflicts at the beginning of the delinquent career, which promotes the delinquent evolution. We clearly see here how the interactions between characteristics of the family environment produce the most significant effects on the child's problems, more than the characteristics themselves.

CONCLUSION

From Cradle to Jail…

Our model, inspired by recent developmental psychopathology works, can be synthesized like this:

> Our relation to rules and laws is first built inside the family, which produces an informal social control operating well before formal social control coming from society. Family environment produces an internal control of transgression by the subject himself (interiorized values, norms, representations, attitudes, etc) as well as an external control of transgression by the family members, which depends of the evolutions of the family structure with time, of life events, and which is so more unstable. These social controls are both very dependent of attachment links and affective conflicts; the young person will not transgress rules, as this transgression would threaten the stability of the link. Family environment produces also a social learning, based on two mechanisms, imitation and reinforcement: being simply exposed to parental behaviors during a long time, like risk taking, substance abuse, car driving styles, etc, the child imitates many of these; being exposed to positive and negative reinforcements coming from his/her parents in reaction to his/her acts, the child learns progressively to

commit or refrain transgressions. As learning occurs also with peers after puberty, it is the balance between reinforcements coming from the parents and from the peers that will orientate the trajectory. To conclude, we'll say that this review of literature leads us to the concept of « spiralic » causality: one cause produces an effect, which becomes the cause of something else.

In this chapter, we have considered all types of juvenile delinquency as one dependent variable, as juvenile delinquency categorization was not our subject, but of course differential associations with family variables should be studied according to the type of juvenile delinquency.

For example, Leblanc (2006) suggested a three-classes typology from his works on French Canadian delinquent teenagers:

- « delinquency of opportunity » is the most frequent as it concerns an important proportion of youth; it covers minor offences, thefts and troubles. No precise family characteristics are related, as it concerns so many teenagers, except control. This delinquency has been related to low supervision (« children with the key »), which promotes contacts with deviant peers.
- « delinquency of transition » concerns much more serious offences (important thefts, violent acts), but it stops at the end of adolescence. Family dysfunction may be found for three of our family environment dimensions: structure, behavior and control
- « delinquency of condition » is the more severe form (start of delinquent behavior as early as 8 or 10 years of age, diverse forms of offences including violence, progressive severity of the offences, will continue in adult life). This delinquency can be related to the five family factors of our chapter.

Numerous interactions have been observed in the trajectories towards delinquency: for example, adopted children of delinquent biological father are more at risk to become delinquent, but this risk is three times higher when the adoptive family is dysfunctional. Even, the dissuasive effects of marriage on the delinquent career have been found under the influence of genetic factors! This clearly shows how biology and psychology of destiny are complementary and how one doesn't go without the other, like the various melodic lines in a Bach's contrapuntic theme!

Thinking about the intergenerational transmission of behaviors, each of us, as parent, should think about our own responsibility: when we behave in a wrong way in the presence of our children, we are guilty of producing delinquency, antisociality, traffic violations, substances abuse, etc, of the 22nd century, as their genesis begins there!

Of course, between 15 and 25 years of age, other actors influence teenagers delinquency, particularly peers and media, but we saw that exposure to media as well as supervision of peer selection are also under the parents' behavioral control.

We also saw that delinquency is much harder to predict for girls than for boys as noted in a previous publication on the genesis of risk taking and addiction (Assailly, 2007): the origin of boys' problem behaviors can be tracked back to infancy, the girls' problem behaviors in late childhood or adolescence. Of course, the fact that girls are much less delinquent than boys does not help the statistical signification of correlations!

To conclude, life can be described with the metaphor of mountain paths, some of these on the way to resiliency, some others to chronicity; the transactions between risk and protective factors play along the developmental paths, there is always a « window » for changes in the teenage years, as the same family environment characteristics produce very different effects according to the context or interactions with other variables.

BIBLIOGRAPHY

Abrahams, N., Jewkes, R. (2005). Effects of South African men's having witnessed abuse of their mothers during childhood on their levels of violence in adulthood, *American Journal of Public Health*, 95, 10, 1811-1816.

Ainsworth, M.D., Blehar, M.C. (1978). *Patterns of attachment: a psychological study of the strange situation*, Hillsdale, NJ, Erlbaum.

Amato, P.R., (2001). Children of divorce in the 1990's: an update of the Amato and Keith (1991) meta-analysis, *Journal of Family Psychology*, 15, 355-370.

Amato, P.R., Keith, B. (1991). Parental divorce and the well being of children: A meta–analysis, *Psychological Bulletin*, 110, 26–46.

Assailly, J.P. (2007). *Jeunes en danger. Les familles face aux conduites à risque (Young people at risk. Family environment and risk behavior)*, Paris, Imago.

Assailly, J.P. (1994). The psychogenetic approach to risk, in B. Munier and M.J. Machina (eds), *Models and experiments in risk and rationality*, 3-16, Kluwer Press, New York.

Bakermans-Kranenburg, M.J., Van IJzendoorn (2003). Less is more: meta-analyses of sensitivity and attachment interventions in early childhood, *Psychological Bulletin*, 129, 2, 195-215.

Bandura, A. (1977). *Social Learning Theory*, Prentice-Hall, New Jersey.

Barber, B.K., Stolz, H.E. (2005). Parental support, psychological control, and behavioral control: assessing relevance across time, culture and method, *Monographs of the society for research in child development*, 70, 4, 282.

Baumrind, D. (1985). Familial antecedents of adolescent drug use: A developmental perspective. In C. L. Jones and R. J. Battjes (eds.), *Etiology of Drug Abuse: Implications for Prevention*. NIDA Research Monograph 56, DHHS Publication No. ADM 85-1335. Washington, DC: U.S. Government Printing Office.

Beaver, K.M., Wright, J.P. (2008). Desistance from delinquency: The marriage effect revisited and extended, *Social Science Research*, 37, 736–752.

Bianchi, A., Summala, H. (2004). The « genetics » of driving behavior: parents' driving style predicts their children's driving style. *Accident Analysis and Prevention*, 36, 655-659.

Biblarz, T., Raftery, A. (1999). Family structure, educational attainment, and socioeconomic success: Rethinking the « pathology of matriarchy », *American Journal of Sociology*, 105, 321–365.

Blaser, R., Alsaker, F.D. (2002). Le harcèlement entre jeunes du même âge. L'arrière-plan familial des enfants et des adolescents impliqués (Bullying between same age peers. Family backgrounds), in Halfon, O., Ansermet, J., Laget, J., Pierrehumbert, B. (Eds.) *Sens et non sens de la violence*, Paris, PUF, 97-112.

Bloom, B., Steinhart, D. (1993). *Why punish children? A reappraisal of the children of incarcerated mothers in America.* San Francisco: National Council on Crime and Delinquency.

Bowlby, J. (1969). *Attachment and Loss*, New York, Basic Books.

Braman, D. (2002). Families and incarceration. In M. Mauer and M. Chesney-Lind (Eds.), *Invisible punishment: The collateral consequences of mass imprisonment* (pp. 120–135). New York: The New Press.

Brendgen, M., Dionne, G. (2005). Examining genetic and environnemental effects on social aggression: a study of 6-year-old twins, *Child Development*, 76, 4, 930-946.

Broidy, L.M., Nagin, D.S. (2003). Developmental trajectories of childhood disruptive behaviors and adolescent delinquency, a six sites cross national study, *Developmental Psychology*, 39, 222-245.

Burt, S.A., Barnes, A.R. (2008). Parental divorce and adolescent delinquency: ruling out the impact of common genes, *Developmental Psychology*, 44, 6, 1668-1677.

Cao, L., Cao, J. (2004). Family, welfare, and delinquency, *Journal of Criminal Justice*, 32, 565-576.

Carlson, W.L., Klein, D. (1970). Familiar vs. institutional socialization of the young traffic offender. *Journal of Safety Research* 2, 13–25.

Carver, C.S., Scheier, M.F. (1981). *Attention and self-regulation: a control theory approach to human behavior,* Springer-Verlag, New York.

Caspi, A. (2002). Role of genotype in the cycle of violence in maltreated children. *Science*, 297, 851–854.

Caspi, A., Moffitt, T.E. (2004). Maternal expressed emotion predicts children's antisocial bahavior problems : using monozygotic-twin differences to identify environmental effects on behavioral development, *Developmental Psychology*, 40, 2, 149-161.

Chermack, S.T., Wryobeck, J.M. (2006). Distal and proximal factors related to agression severity among patients in substance abuse treatment : family history, alcohol use and expectancies, *Addictive Behaviors,* 31, 845-858.

Cole, J.D., Dodge, K.A. (1998). Agression and antisocial behavior, In Damon, W. and Eisenberg, N. (Eds), *Handbook of child psychology. Social, emotional and personality development*, Vol 3, pp 779-862, Toronto, Wiley.

Collins, R.E. (2004). Onset and desistance in criminal careers: neurobiology and the age-crime relationship. *Journal of Offender Rehabilitation* , 39, 1–19.

Conseur, A., Rivara, F.P. (1997). Maternal and perinatal risk factors for later delinquency, *Pediatrics*, 99, 785-790.

Cyrulnik, B. (2008). *Autobiographie d'un épouvantail*, Paris, Odile Jacob.

Davalos, D.B., Chavez, E.L. (2005). Effects of perceived parental school support and family communication on delinquent behaviors in latinos and white non latinos, *Cultural Diversity and Ethnic Minority Psychology*, 11, 1, 57-68.

Deater-Deckard, K., Dodge, K.A. (1996). Physical discipline among African American and European American mothers : links to children's externalizing behaviors, *Developmental Psychology*, 32, 6, 1065-1072.

Deater-Deckard, K., Ivy, L. (2006). Maternal warmth moderates the link between physical punishment and child externalizing problems: a parent/offspring behavior genetic analysis, *Parenting : Science and Practice*, 6, 1, 59-78.

Demuth, S., Brown, S. (2004). Family structure, family processes, and adolescent delinquency : The significance of parental absence versus parental gender. *Journal of Research in Crime and Delinquency*, 41, 58–81.

De Lucia, C., Belz, A. (2001). Do adolescent symptomatology and family environment vary over time with fluctuations in paternal alcohol impairment ? *Developmental Psychology*, 37, 2, 207-216.

Dornbusch, S.M., Carlsmith, J.M. (1985). Single parents, extended households, and the control of adolescents, *Child Development*, 56, 326-342, 1985.

Eitle, D. (2006). Parental gender, single-parent families, and delinquency : exploring the moderating influence of race/ethnicity, *Social Science Research*.

Fagan, A.A., Najman, J.M. (2003). Sibling influences on adolescent delinquent behaviour : an australian longitudinal study, *Journal of Adolescence*, 26, 546-558.

Farrington, D.P. (1995). The 12th Jack Tizard Memorial Lecture : the development of offending and antisocial behaviour from childhood : key findings from the Cambridge Study in delinquent development, *J. Child Psychol. Pyschiat.*, 360, 6, 929-964.

Farrington, D.P., Barnes, G.C. (1996). The concentration of offending in families, *Legal and Criminological Psychology*, 1, 47-63.

Feldman, R., Klein, P.S. (2003). Toddler's self-regulated compliance to mothers, caregivers and fathers : implications for theories of socialization, *Developmental Psychology*, 39, 4, 680-692.

Ferguson, S.A. , Allan F. Williams (2001). Relationship of parent driving records to the driving records of their children, *Accident Analysis and Prevention* , 33, 2, 1, 229-234.

Forth, A. E., Burke, H. C. (1998). Psychopathy in adolescence: Assessment, violence and developmental precursors. In D. J. Cooke, A. E. Forth, and R. D. Hare (Eds.), *Psychopathy : Theory, research and implications for society* (pp. 205–229). Boston : Kluwer Academic.

Glueck, T., Sheldon, R. (1950). *Unraveling juvenile delinquency*, Cambridge, Mass., Harvard University Press.

Gottfredson, M., Hirschi, T. (1990). *A general theory of crime*, Stanford, CA: Stanford University Press.

Henry, B., Moffitt, T. (1993). Early family predictors of child and adolescent antisocial behaviour : who are the mothers of delinquents ? *Criminal Behaviour and Mental Health*, 3, 97-118.

Hetherington, E. M., Cox, M. (1982). Effect of divorce on parents and children. In M. E. Lamb (Ed.*), Nontraditional families : Parenting and child development* (pp. 233–288). Hillsdale, NJ: Lawrence Erlbaum Associates.

Hetherington, E. M., and Kelly, J. (2002). *For better or for worse : Divorce reconsidered.* New York: W.W. Norton.

Hirschi, T. (1969). *Causes of Delinquency*. University of California Press, Berkeley, CA.

Hirschi, T., Gottfredson, M.R. (1983). Age and the explanation of crime. *American Journal of Sociology* , 89, 552–584.

Horton, P. C., Gewirtz, H. (1992). Alexithymia—State and trait. P*sychotherapy and Psychosomatics*, 58, 91–96.

Huebner, B.M., Gustafson, R. (2007). The effect of maternal incarceration on adult offspring involvement in the criminal justice system, *Journal of Criminal Justice* , 35, 283–296.

Hussong, A.M., Zucker, R.A. (2005). Social competence in children of alcoholic parents over time, *Developmental Psychology*, 41, 5, 747-759.

Jaffee, S. R., Caspi, A. (2004). Physical maltreatment victim to antisocial child : Evidence of an environmentally mediated process. *Journal of Abnormal Psychology*, 113 (1), 44–55.

Jeammet, P. (2001). Approche psychodynamique de la violence chez les adolescents (Psychodynamic approach of adolescents violence), *Perspectives in Psychiatry,* 40 (3), 182–188.

Juby, H., Farrington, D. (2001). Disentangling the link between disrupted families and delinquency. *British Journal of Criminology*, 41, 22–40.

Kochanska, G. (1997). Mutually responsive orientation between mothers and their young : implications for early socialization, *Child Development*, 68, 94-112.

Krischer, M.K., Sevecke, K. (2008). Early traumatization and psychopathy in female and male juvenile offenders, *International Journal of Law and Psychiatry*, 31, 253–262.

Lahey, B.B. (2003). A developmental propensity model of the origins of conduct problems during childhood and adolescence, in Lahey, B.B., Moffitt, T.E., Caspi, A. (Eds), *Causes of conduct disorder and juvenile delinquency*, pp 76-117, New York, Guilford Press.

Langevin, R., Hare, R. D. (2001). Psychopathie et alexithymie chez un groupe de jeunes contrevenants (Psychopathy and alexithymia in a group of young offenders). *Revue de Psychoeducation et d'Orientation*, 30 (2), 227–236.

Lansford, J.E., Chang, L. (2005). Physical discipline and children's adjustment : cultural normativeness as a moderator, *Child Development*, 76, 6, 1234-1246.

Larzelere, R.E., Patterson, G.R. (1990). Parental management : mediator of the effect of the effect of socioeconomic status on early delinquency, *Criminology*, 28, 301-323.

Laub, J.H., Nagin, D.S. (1998). Trajectories of change in criminal offending : good marriages and the desistance process, *Amer. Soc. Rev.*, 63, 225-238.

Leblanc, M. (2006). Vers une criminologie appliquée de la conduite délinquante des adolescents (Towards an applied criminology of adolescent delinquent behavior), in Blatier, C. (Ed.), *Prévenir la délinquance dès la petite enfance*, pp 35-92, L'Harmattan, Paris.

Ma, H.K. (2000). Parental, peer, and teacher influences on the social behavior of Hong Kong Chinese adolescents, *Journal of Genetic Psychology*, 16, 1, 65-78.

Maccoby, E.E., Martin, J.A. (1983). Socialization in the context of the family : parent/child interaction, in Hetherington, E.M. (ed), *Handbook of child psychology : socialization, personality, and social development,* New York, Wiley.

Main, M., Kaplan, N. (1985). Security in infancy, childhood and adulthood : a move to the level of representation, in Bertherton, I. et al. (Eds.*), Growing points of attachment theory and research, Monographs for the society for research in child development*, 50, 1-2, 66-104.

Mack, K.Y., Leiber, M.J. (2007). Reassessing the family-delinquency association : Do family type, family processes, and economic factors make a difference ? *Journal of Criminal Justice*, 35, 51–67.

Mc Cord, J. (1977). A comparative study of two generations of native Americans, in Meier, R.F. (ed.), *Theory in Criminology*, 83-92, Beverly Hills, CA, Sage.

McNulty, T., Bellair, P. E. (2003). Explaining racial and ethnic differences in adolescent violence : Structural disadvantage, family well-being, and social capital. *Justice Quarterly*, 20, 1–31.

Mednick, S.A., Cudeck, R. (1984). The Danish high risk project : recent methods and findings, in Watt, N.F., Anthony, E.J., Wynne, L.C. and Rolf, J.E. (Eds.), *Chidren at risk for schizophrenia : a longitudinal perspective*, 21-42, New York, Cambridge University Press.

Moffitt, T.E. (2003). Life-course persistent and adolescent-limited antisocial behavior : a 10-year research review and a research agenda, in Lahey, B.B., Moffitt, T.E., Caspi, A. (Eds), *Causes of conduct disorder and juvenile delinquency*, pp 49-75, New York, Guilford Press.

Moriarty, N., Stough, C. (2001). Deficits in emotional intelligence underlying adolescent sex offending. *Journal of Adolescence*, 24, 743–751.

Patterson, G. (1982). *Coercive family process.* Eugene, OR: Castalia.

Poehlmann, J. (2005). Representations of attachment relationships in children of incarcerated mothers, *Child Development,* 76, 3, 679-696.

Radke-Yarrow, M., Zahn-Waxler, C. (1983). Children's prosocial dispositions and behavior, in Hetherington, E.M. and Mussen, P.H. (Eds.) *Handbook of child psychology*, Vol 4, 469-545, New York, Wiley.

Reiss, D., Hetherington, M. (1995). Genetic questions for environmental studies, *Arch. Gen. Psychiat.,* 52, 925-936.

Resnick, M.D., Bearman, R.W. (1997). Protecting adolescents from harm : findings from the National Longitudinal study on adolescent health, *JAMA*, 278, 10 September, 823-832.

Rodgers, B., Pryor, J. (1998). *Divorce and separation: The outcomes for children.* New York: Joseph Rowntree Foundation.

Rowe, D.C. (1994). *The limits of family influence. Genes, experience and behavior*, Guilford Press, New York.

Rowe, D.C., Farrington, D.P. (1997). The familial transmission of criminal convictions, *Criminology*, 35, 1, 177-201.

Ryan, J.P., Marshall, J.M. (2008). Juvenile delinquency in child welfare: Investigating group home effects, *Children and Youth Services Review* , 30,1088–1099.

Ryan, J.P., Testa, M.F. (2005). Child maltreatment and juvenile delinquency : investigating the role of placement and placement instability, *Children and Youth Services Review*, 27, 227-249.

Sampson, R.J., Laub, J.H. (1993). Crime and deviance over the life course : the salience of adult social bonds. *American Sociological Review* , 55, 609–627.

Schreiber, K. (1992). The adolescent crack dealer: A failure in the development of empathy. *Journal of the American Academy of Psychoanalysis*, 20 (2), 241–249.

Sifneos, P. E. (1973). The prevalence of « alexithymic » charcteristics in psychosomatic patients. *Psychotherapy and Psychosomatics*, 22, 255–262.

Steinberg, L. (2008). A social neuroscience perspective on adolescent risk-taking, *Developmental Review* , 28, 78–106.

Taylor, G. J. (2000). Recent developments in alexithymia. Theory and research. *Canadian journal of Psychiatry*, 45, 134–142.

Taylor, G. J., Bagby, R. M. (1997). *Disorders of affect regulation : Alexithymia in medical and psychiatric illness.* Cambridge, Cambridge University Press.

Tremblay, R.E. (2008). *Prévenir la violence dès la petite enfance (Preventing violence from infancy)*, Paris, Odile Jacob.

Tremblay, R.E. (2003). Why socialization fails : the case of chronic physical agression, in Lahey, B.J., Moffitt, T.E., Caspi, A. (Eds), *Causes of conduct disorder and juvenile delinquency*, pp 182-226, New York, Guilford Press.

Trzesniewski, K.H., Donnellan, B. (2006). Low self-esteem during adolescence predicts poor health, criminal behavior, and limited economic prospects during adulthood, *Developmental Psychology*, 42, 2, 381-390.

Vanyukov, M.M., Neale, M.C. (1996). Mating assortment and the liability to substance abuse, *Drug and Alcohol Dependence,* 42, 1-10.

Wadsworth, M. (1979). *Roots of delinquency : Infancy, adolescence and crime.* Lanham, MD: Rowman and Littlefield.

Wallerstein, J., Kelly, J. B. (1980). *Surviving the breakup : How children and parents cope with divorce.* New York: Basic Books.

Walters, G.D. (1992). A meta-analysis of the gene-crime relationship, *Criminology*, 30, 595-613.

Warr, M. (1998). Life-course transitions and desistance from crime. *Criminology* , 36, 183–216.

Warr, M. (2002). *Companions in Crime : The Social Aspects of Criminal Conduct.* Cambridge University Press, New York.

Wells, L. E., Rankin, J. H. (1991). Families and delinquency : A meta–analysis of the impact of broken homes. *Social Problems*, 38, 71−93.

West, D.J., Farrington, D.P. (1977). *The delinquent way of life,* London, Heinnemann.

Widom, C.S. (1989). The cycle of violence, *Science*, 244, 160-166.

Wilson, R.J., Meckle, W. (in press). Young Driver Risk in Relation to Parents' Retrospective Driving Record, *Journal of Safety Research.*

Wright, B.R.E., Caspi, A. (2001). The effects of social ties on crime vary by criminal propensity : a life-course model of interdependence, *Criminology* , 39, 321–352.

Zimmermann, G. (2006). Delinquency in male adolescents : the role of alexithymia and family structure, *Journal of Adolescence,* 29, 321–332

In: Delinquency: Causes, Reduction and Prevention
Editor: Ozan Sahin and Joseph Maier
ISBN 978-1-60741-558-9

Chapter 3

JUVENILE CRIMINALITY AND EXECUTIVE COGNITIVE FUNCTIONING IN AN ITALIAN SAMPLE OF LATE-ONSET ADOLESCENT DELINQUENTS

Maria Rosaria A. Muscatello, Antonio Bruno, Gianluca Pandolfo, Umberto Micò, Vincenzo M. Romeo, Paolo Micali Bellinghieri and Rocco Zoccali

Section of Psychiatry,
Department of Neurosciences,
Psychiatric and Anaesthesiological Sciences
University of Messina
Italy

ABSTRACT

Involvement in delinquent behavior is quite common during adolescence, and many authors consider it to be a transient phenomenon. However, the prevalence of mental disorders in juvenile delinquents appears to be relevant. It has been proposed that emotional disturbances are frequently associated with neuropsychological dysfunction as a result of a common biological, mainly genetic origin. Among cognitive dysfunctioning, impairment in executive cognitive functions (ECF) may be related especially to mental disorders, to failures in personality development, and to conduct and personality disorders. ECF include cognitive flexibility, hypothesis generation, abstract reasoning, problem solving, selective attention, inhibitory control and ability to organize and use information contained in working memory, all fundamental in social cognition and social behaviors. High prevalence rates (up to 80%) of ECF deficits have been reported in juvenile criminals. ECF and other neuropsychological and cognitive impairments, such as lower IQ and verbal deficits, have been associated with the pattern of antisocial and delinquent behavior starting in childhood (early-onset), but not with late-onset antisocial behavior. Based on this background, our purpose was to evaluate ECF in a sample of adolescents and young adults, with a pattern of late-onset delinquent behavior and no antecedents of conduct disorder, referred to the Social Services of the Department of Juvenile Justice of the city of Messina (Italy). The hypothesis tested with this design was that late-onset delinquent adolescents and young adults differ from nonantisocial controls matched for age and educational level on neuropsychological measures sensitive to ECF dysfunction (Stroop Color-Word task, or Stroop task; AB-AC; Raven's Standard Progressive Matrices (SPM); Verbal Fluency, both Phonemic and Semantic; and Winsconsin Card Sorting Test). Results showed significant differences between late-onset offenders and control groups on the following tasks: Stroop ($t = 3.570$; $p = < 0.0001$), SPM ($t = -7.174$; $p = < 0.0001$), and Phonemic Fluency ($t = -10.743$; $p = < 0.0001$). Chi-square analysis showed that a significantly greater number of late-onset offending participants scored in the clinical range on several ECF measures. Current findings add to the growing literature comparing juvenile offenders to other adolescent populations. These results imply that executive cognitive impairment, even subtle and subclinical, may be a contributing factor in the development and persistence of antisocial behaviors displayed by late-onset adolescent delinquents. The findings also suggest the need for additional research aimed to assess a broader range of cognitive abilities and specific vulnerability and risk factors for late-onset adolescent offenders.

INTRODUCTION

Delinquency and antisocial behavior by adolescents represent a major public health problem and "a constant source of fascination and concern for politicians, media commentators and academic analysts" (Muncie, 1999, p.2). According to the Office for Juvenile Justice and Delinquency Prevention [OJJDP] (2000), juvenile delinquent acts became more violent and serious during the late 1980s and the early 1990s, and juvenile arrests for violent crimes have increased 67% since 1986. Furthermore, a 30% increase in juvenile delinquency is estimated by the year 2010 (OJJDP, 2000). In a criminological frame, juvenile delinquency includes all public wrongs committed by youngsters between the ages of 12 and 20. In a broader sense, the concept of juvenile delinquency covers a multitude of different violations of legal and social norms, from minor offences to serious crimes, committed by juveniles (Vermeiren, 2003).

Involvement in delinquent behavior is quite common during adolescence (Carroll, 2006), and many authors share this opinion, viewing it as a transient phenomenon in adolescence (Teasdale and Powell, 1987), or a "normal feature of youth" (West, 1967, p. 42). As shown by the International Study of Self-Reported Delinquency (ISRD) (Junger-Tas, 1994) conducted in 13 Western nations, antisocial behavior by youths may be considered a "normative" phenomenon, as only between 3% and 34% of adolescents denied participating in all forms of antisocial behavior. Moreover, the United Nations Guidelines for the Prevention of Juvenile Delinquency (the Riyadh Guidelines, 1990) declare that "youthful behavior or conduct that does not conform to overall social norms and values is often part of the maturation and growth process and tends to disappear spontaneously in most individuals with the transition to adulthood". A distinction needs to be made between the term "delinquency", a legal phenomenon referring to officially registered unlawful behavior, and "antisocial behavior", which refers to acts that are considered inappropriate because they harm others or the society (Vermeiren, 2003). Adolescent delinquency is quite different from adult crime in many respects. According to the Surgeon General's Report (2001), 30% to 40% of males commit a serious violent offence by age 17; indeed, violence is a common phenomenon during adolescence. It must be further specified that most adolescent offenders, even violent offenders, do not continue offending into adulthood; offences peak at about age 17 years and then gradually decline over time during young adulthood (Blumstein et al., 1987). Temporary, situational antisocial behavior is quite common among adolescents, whereas it has been found that the most persistent 5–6% of all offenders account for about half of all crimes (Farrington et al., 1986). In these cases, antisocial behavior has been considered psychopathological because it is not normative, unusual, or the source of significant difficulties both for offenders and society (Raine, 1993). Another core feature of adolescent delinquency is its social pattern, since adolescents tend to offend in groups, whereas adult offenders tend to act alone, and this hallmark is thought to reflect the importance of peer relationships during development (Ash, 2006).

Developmental Issues in Juvenile Delinquency

Age of Onset and Behavioral Features

Several prospective cohort studies designed to identify predictors and correlates of delinquency have emphasized age of onset and the duration of delinquency as key features helpful to differentiate groups of delinquents on background factors and on the nature of their behavioral manifestations (Nagin et al., 1995). The dual taxonomy proposed by Moffitt (1993) regarding the relationship between age and antisocial behavior comprises two major patterns: a late-onset, adolescence-limited (AL), and an early-onset, life-course persistent (LCP) group. The first, larger group consists of adolescents demonstrating later onset of antisocial behavior, which is thought to represent an exaggerated pattern of rebellious behavior arisen as a result of the aid and comfort of the peer social context. The author considered adolescence-limited as a ubiquitous phenomenon due to its prevalence in the population; this pattern is restricted to adolescence, it is characterized by recovery by early adulthood, and it is largely contingent on environmental influences. Adolescence-limited delinquents, in contrast with the life-course-persistent type, may have sporadic crime-free periods and lack consistency in their antisocial behavior across situations, suggesting that their engagement in deviant lifestyles may reflect a sensitivity to reinforcement and punishment contingencies. Moffitt (1993) invoked the concept of "social mimicry", derived from ethology, to explain the beginning of adolescence-limited delinquency, that seems associated with a gap between expectations and achievements, and between biological and social maturity ("maturity gap"). In this acception, as the "mimic" species adopts the social behavior of the more successful species to approach to the desirable resources, adolescent delinquents may primarily imitate the behavior of their childhood-onset peers to achieve access to the mature status, with its features of independence and power. Moreover, adolescence-limited delinquency seems to be a by-product of modernization linked to the secular changes in health and work that modified the social and psychological status of the youngsters. In this context, a modeling role is exerted by the exposure to delinquent peer networks where life-course-persistent adolescents serve as core members of networks and role models or trainers for new members (Reiss, 1986). With the progression of chronological age, the assumption of more legitimate adult roles induce adolescence-limited delinquents to desist from criminal behavior; the antisocial conducts have been found to decline after adolescent teens leave high school, join the army, or get a full-time job (Sampson and Laub, 1990).

The second, smaller subgroup, named life-course persistent, includes youths with early-onset conduct problems whose antisocial behavior remains stable from preschool to adulthood and whose developmental trajectories are characterized by the influence of biological factors beyond disrupted social environments. Compared to the late-onset group, life-course persistent delinquents show greater levels of social problems and tendencies towards criminality. The main distinctive features of these offenders include cognitive, primarily verbal and attentional deficits, hyperactivity, impulsivity (Taylor et al., 1996), and early intense aggressiveness (Lochman and Wayland, 1994).

According to Moffitt (1993), prenatal and perinatal disruptions in neural development lead to neuropsychological deficits primarily in the domains of executive and verbal functioning. These individual variations in brain functions may engender differences between children in emotional reactivity, behavioral regulation, level of activity, self-control (especially impulse control), motor coordination, and cognitive abilities, such as attention, language, learning and reasoning. Furthermore, infants at risk for these deficits are also likely to be raised in environments that are poorly equipped, both financially and psychologically, to deal adaptively with a difficult child. Beyond biological factors, maladaptive parent-child interactions are central to this model; early behavioral difficulties in children evoke negative responses from parents, which in turn exacerbate the child's behavior problems. This reciprocal process results in an antisocial lifestyle maintained by a combination of pre-existing neuropsychological deficits, the negative consequences of ongoing antisocial behavior, and the absence of learned prosocial behavioral alternatives. As pointed out by Reid and Patterson (1989), temperamentally and cognitively disposed children are unlikely to develop antisocial behavior if they are raised in adaptive social environments. Moffitt's theory emphasizes the process of reciprocal interactions between personal features and environmental reactions to them; as claimed by the author, "Through that process, relatively subtle childhood variations in neuropsychological health can be transformed into an antisocial style that pervades all domains of adolescent and adult behavior. It is this infiltration of the antisocial disposition into the multiple domains of a life that diminishes the likelihood of change" (p.684). The distinction between LCP and AL patterns of offending suggests significant developmental insights into the nature of delinquent behavior and it has been supported by a number of studies. The Dunedin Multidisciplinary Health and Development Study (Moffitt et al., 1996) showed that boys with early-onset high conduct problem ratings from both parents and teachers during ages 5 through 11 years differed from those with later onset in that they had more impulsivity and attentional problems, lower IQ, worse neuropsychological performances, and greater family and peer difficulties. Late starters, on the other hand, began offending in middle-late adolescence probably as a result of social influences. Fergusson et al. (1996) found that life-course persistent adolescents were characterized by a number of risk factors such as social disadvantages, poor parenting, impulsivity and attention deficits, whereas adolescence-limited offenders were somewhere intermediate in social and individual characteristics between continuous offenders and consistent nonoffenders. Lahey et al. (1998), in a retrospective study aimed to differentiate childhood- and adolescent-onset Conduct Disorder (CD), found that the high levels of physical aggression were the main features of childhood-onset adolescents, who may have failed to learn to inhibit physical aggression during childhood. It has been proposed that childhood and adolescent-onset CD would not be the same disorder starting at different points during development, but different disorders starting at different developmental stages (Brame, 2001).

Beyond clinical and cohort studies, the dual taxonomy early- vs late-onset has received support from genetic studies showing that the earlier the onset of antisocial behavior, the more likely the influence of genetic factors on behavior problems, whereas the weight of environmental factors increases proportionally to age of onset (Taylor et al., 2000). The interaction between early vulnerabilities and a "criminogenic" environment has been confirmed by twin and adoption studies whose results account for significant variability in CD, antisocial personality disorder and aggression (Cadoret et al., 1995; Rutter et al., 1997). The effects of adverse genetic influences are moderated or reduced under favourable environmental conditions which may operate at the level of gene expression or interact with inherited psychological features (Reiss and Niederhiser, 2000). Overall evidences from genetic studies highlight the profound complexity of the nature of genetic influences on antisocial behavior. It seems likely that genetic factors directly influence temperamental and cognitive predisposition to antisocial behavior and that the magnitude of genetic influence is inversely related to the age of onset of behavior problems, even if heredity may continue to influence the onset of antisocial behavior in adolescence too (Lahey et al., 1999).

Beyond the age of onset, other approaches attempted to identify specific patterns of antisocial behavior. Gottfredson and Hirschi (1990) proposed that variations in criminal behavior can be explained by stable individual differences in antisocial propensity, whose hypothesized components include high activity level, physical strength, impulsivity, temperament (oppositionality, harm avoidance, and callousness), and low intelligence. Loeber et al. (1993) proposed three different pathways for antisocial behavior beginning in childhood: overt, covert, and authority conflict pathways. The overt path is characterized by aggression, bullying and proceeds to serious violence. The covert pathway includes aggressive acts that seem designed to avoid detection, lying and stealing, and vandalism; the assumption is that over time the individual progresses to damage to property, and to more extreme forms of substance abuse and health-risking sexual behaviors in adolescence. The third pathway, authority conflict, beginning with non-compliance to rules, is characterized by defiant and oppositional behaviors escalating to truancy and running away. Far from being a mean of classifying individuals, the over-mentioned pathways are intended as developmental trajectories of biological and psychological processes with their associated behaviors; as claimed by the authors, individuals whose behavior is limited to a single pathway are quite uncommon in clinical and community samples (Loeber and Coie, 2001).

Psychopathology in Juvenile Delinquents

From early studies (Glueck and Glueck, 1950), it was recognized that juvenile delinquency is associated with a number of psychopathological features. As shown by a number of studies of detained and incarcerated adolescents, the prevalence rates of psychiatric disorders in the delinquent population are 3 to 5 times higher than in general population (Doreleijers et al., 2000; Pliszka et al., 2000; Aarons et al., 2001). Moreover, comorbidity between psychiatric disorders is a major problem among detained youth; Abram et al. (2003) found that, on a sample of 1829 detained youth of both sexes, 17.3% of females and 20.4% of males exhibited only one disorder, whereas 56.5% of females and 45.9% of males met criteria for 2 or more of the following disorders: major depressive, dysthymic, manic, psychotic, panic, generalized anxiety, obsessive compulsive, and substance abuse. High rates of psychopathology among juvenile delinquents have attracted increasing attention, both as risk factors for the development of early and severe conduct problems (Lewis and Shanok, 1980; Neighbors et al., 1992; Ulzen and Hamilton, 1998) and as factors potentially related to long-term outcome (Vermeiren et al., 2002).

Childhood conduct problems, especially when they develop early, have significant implications for later mental disorders and criminal lifestyle, as resulted from both retrospective (Zoccolillo et al., 1992; Kratzer and Hodgins, 1997) and prospective studies (Babinski et al., 1999). As evidenced by the recent findings by McGue and Iacono (2005), adolescent problem behavior elevates the risk for a variety of adult disorders, mainly in the dimensions of substance abuse, antisocial personality disorder, and major depressive disorder. Similarly, Helgeland et al. (2005) demonstrated predictive relationships between adolescent emotional and disruptive disorders and adult personality disorders. Among the specific psychiatric disorders of childhood and adolescence, oppositional defiant disorder (ODD), conduct disorder, and attention-deficit hyperactivity disorder (ADHD) have been related with delinquency (Vermeiren, 2003). ODD consists of a recurrent pattern of manifestation of oppositional, hostile, negativistic and defiant behaviors, whereas the Diagnostic and Statistic Manual of mental disorders - DSM-IV (APA, 1994) definition of CD is "a repetitive and persistent pattern of behavior in which the basic rights of others or major age-appropriate societal norms or rules are violated." To be diagnosed as CD, DSM-IV requires that a young person manifests at least 3 out of 15 items; each of the 3 symptoms manifested must have occurred within the past 12 months and at least one of the symptoms must have been evident in the last 6 months. The symptoms are divided into four categories: Aggression (bullies, threatens, intimidates; starts physical fights; uses a weapon that can harm others; has been physically cruel to people or animals; has stolen while confronting a victim; has forced sex on someone); Destruction of Property (sets fires deliberately to cause serious damage; deliberately destroys property); Lying or Theft (breaks into other's property; often cons others, lies to get things or avoids responsibility; often steals valuables without confrontation); Serious Violation of Rules (often stays out late at night without permission, starting before age 13; has run away from home overnight at least twice; often plays hookey from school, starting before 13). Indeed, the DSM identifies two subtypes of CD based upon the age at onset, Childhood-Onset Type and Adolescent-Onset Type. The DSM recognizes that children with Childhood Onset CD "are more likely to have persistent Conduct Disorder and to develop adult Antisocial Personality Disorder than are those with Adolescent-Onset Type.", and this specification strictly resembles the predictive statement of life-course-persistent theory. Both ODD and CD are common diagnoses in child and adolescent psychiatry, with rates of CD ranging from 2% to 16% in boys and from 1% and 9.2% in girls (Loeber et al., 2000), and a certain degree of overlap between the two syndromes exist, since it has been estimated that upwards of 90% of clinic-referred children diagnosed with early onset CD also may meet criteria for ODD (Faraone et al., 1991; Walker et al., 1991). CD is an established childhood risk factor for late adolescent and early adult antisocial behavior, but it may continue to exert a long-term effect in later life, as it has been found that the number of symptoms of disruptive behavior has potent effects on antisocial behaviors and criminality, even into mid-adulthood (Simonoff et al., 2004).

Beyond ODD and CD, ADHD, which is characterized by two core dimensions, inattention and hyperactivity/impulsivity, is one of the most prevalent childhood psychopathological conditions, and it has been identified as a significant liability for social dysfunctioning (Nijmeijer et al., 2008) and later delinquency in males (Sourander et al., 2006). A recent prospective follow-up has found that children with ADHD are at significantly increased risk for criminal lifestyle, as measured by arrests, aggressive offenses and convictions; the risk is significantly higher in those subjects who develop substance use disorder and antisocial personality disorder in adolescence (Mannuzza et al., 2008). ADHD prevalence rates range from 14-19% in adjudicated adolescents (Vermeiren et al., 2000) to 8-72% in incarcerated adolescents (Vermeiren, 2003; Vreugdenhil et al., 2004). Regarding gender differences, a recent study showed that the prevalence rates of ADHD in adolescent and young adult female offenders is higher than in general female population and increases the risk for further psychiatric comorbidity (Rösler et al., 2008). Moreover, a significant proportion of children diagnosed with ADHD also warrant the diagnosis of CD; the comorbidity between the two conditions seems to be associated with a pattern of increased physical aggression and a greater variety of antisocial behaviors (Walker et al., 1987; Rey et al., 2005), higher anxiety and low self-esteem (Kuhne et al., 1997; Jarrett and Ollendik, 2008), more recidivism (Vermeiren et al., 2002), delinquency persistence (Pardini et al., 2006), neuropsychological deficits (Osterlaan et al., 2005), and learning disabilities (McNamara et al., 2008).

Cognitive and Executive Functions

A major theoretical framework for the understanding of developmental psychopathology and antisocial behavior was offered by Spreen (1989), who proposed that emotional disturbances are frequently associated with neuropsychological dysfunction as a result of a common biological, mainly genetic origin. The association between antisocial behavior and neuropsychological variables was found in a number of studies carried out with antisocial individuals, including juvenile delinquents who might also qualify as conduct-disordered (Buikhuisen, 1987; Gorenstein, 1990; Kandel and Freed, 1989). As in the adult literature, a substantial subset of youth who exhibit aggressive behavior suffer from neurological impairment (Teichner and Golden, 2000). As the appropriate functioning of the frontal lobes serves as a basis for appropriate social behavior as well as the basis for inhibition of inappropriate and irrelevant behavior (Grigsby and Stevens, 2000), it seems plausible that aggressive and antisocial children may lack sufficient frontal lobe functioning. Evidence for the hypothesis that neuropsychological dysfunctions in aggressive adolescents might be related to brain injury has been provided primarily by case studies of documented cerebral lesions, mainly frontal lobe injury in childhood which were associated on follow-up with persistent conduct problems (disinhibition of violent behavior, lying, and stealing) (Levine et al., 1985). Specific patterns of frontal lobe dysfunction, including impulsivity, poor insight, compromised planning ability and judgement, inflexible thinking, emotional deficits, and attentional difficulties, were found in CD youths (Lueger and Gill, 1990; Pennington and Bennetto, 1993) and in juvenile offenders (Wolff et al., 1982; Hawkins and Trobst, 2000; Séguin, 2004). Moffitt (1990) initially identified deficits in three specific areas: language abilities, executive function (EF), and cerebral dominance. Teichner and Golden (2000), in the conclusive remarks of their conceptual review, evidenced that a mixed pattern of neuropsychological deficits are displayed across studies, depending on the sampling method, methodological design, statistics employed, control groups, and assessment tools that were utilized. Whereas findings for visuospatial, sensory, and motor deficits have been relatively inconsistent, verbal deficits have been frequently displayed across the literature. Limited verbal abilities may reduce the capacity of problem solving, mediate verbal situations, and learn in academic environments, contributing over time to the unfavourable aspects of personality, poor self-regulation, and learning problems found in juvenile delinquents, especially if such dysfunction is present from an early age. Finally, Teichner and Golden (2000) noted that the association between executive dysfunction and antisocial behavior showed a marked variability across studies depending on the specific population, and the specific domain being evaluated, as executive function is a complex construct involving several dissociable abilities, such as cognitive flexibility, attention, planning abilities, concept formation (Robbins, 1996). However, a substantial amount of research has focused on the construct of executive cognitive functioning (ECF) (Moffitt et al., 1994; Paschall and Fishbein, 2002; Raine, 1993). ECF is a term that refers to the cognitive abilities implicated in goal-oriented processes such as the initiation and maintenance of efficient strategies (Lezak, 1985), and the programming and planning of motor behavior skills. They also include cognitive flexibility, hypothesis generation, temporal response sequencing, abstract reasoning, problem solving, selective attention, inhibitory control and ability to organize and adaptively use information contained in working memory (Giancola et al., 1998; Hawkins and Trobst, 2000; Morgan and Lilienfeld, 2000). ECF is considered necessary for socially appropriate adult conduct, as it is involved in the planning, initiation, and regulation of goal-directed behavior (Luria, 1980; Milner, 1995). Consequently, deficits in its function often contribute to poor behavioral self-regulation, social skills, judgement, and personality changes. Whereas a clinical impairment in ECF typically results from frontal lobes damage, oftentimes due to injury, subclinical impairment in ECF, which is observable or diagnosable mainly by neuropsychological assessments, may derive from a variety of biological and environmental factors in the context a biosocial model of vulnerability in which the interaction of perinatal complications, genetic influences and psychosocial factors play a substantial role (Hill, 2002). ECF are a complex construct including heterogeneous aspects which have been differently categorized according to various models. Pennington and Ozonoff (1996) include in ECF category abilities such as set-shifting, planning, working memory, contextual memory, inhibition, and fluency. Barkley (1997) included in ECF working memory, internalisation of speech, self-regulation of affect-motivation-arousal, and behavioral analysis-synthesis. A more empirical, problem-solving oriented framework, consider ECF as temporally ordered sub-phases such as (1) problem representation, (2) planning, (3) execution (including both intending and rule use), and (4) evaluation (including both error detection and error correction) (Zelazo et al., 1997). As ECF are associated to frontal lobe activity, functions involved in working memory has been associated with dorsolateral frontal lobe activity (Petrides et al., 1993).

Morgan and Lilienfeld (2000) performed a meta-analysis of executive dysfunction and antisocial behavior showing significant effect sizes (Cohen's *d*) of .40 for conduct disorder and .86 for juvenile delinquency. However, as suggested by the authors, performance on neuropsychological measures is multiply determined, and may reflect personality variables associated with Antisocial Behavior (ASB) (e.g., impulsivity, motivational deficits) rather than neuropsychological deficits. The magnitude of association between the constructs of ECF and antisocial behavior suggests that other factors, such as CD or ADHD, may account for this relationship. A key question has been whether the association between conduct problems and ECF deficits is attributable to ADHD, since there is a strong evidence linking ADHD to cognitive and executive deficits (Barkley, 2000; Oosterlaan et al., 2005). Neverthless, recent studies controlling for diagnostic comorbidity generally support the finding that, although ADHD clearly contributes to the executive function deficit in conduct problems, it cannot adequately explain all such deficits (Raine et al., 2005; Eme, 2007; Déry et al., 1999). Poorer ECF are related with increased antisocial behaviors in preschoolers (Hughes et al., 2000), and differentiate children with CD or aggressive children from normal controls (Séguin et al., 1999). As highlighted by Raine (2002), it seems likely that CD children with comorbid ADHD have the severest ECF deficits, whereas CD children without ADHD have a less strong, but significant ECF dysfunction. On the other hand, cognitive abilities, as expressed by higher scores on neuropsychological tasks, appeared to exhibit a protective effect against life-course-persistent forms of criminal activity (Moffitt, 1993; Piquero and White, 2003). Moreover, high academic achievement, which reflects good cognitive skills, was identified as a predictive factor of a low likelihood of serious antisocial behavior among other protective factors, such as older mother at age of birth of first child, good relations with peers, and high parental persistence of discipline (Lober et al., 2009)

Aim

Previous investigations have focused on executive dysfunctions in samples of juvenile delinquents. Some researchers in this field acknowledge that early-onset, life-persistent offenders demonstrate executive and verbal deficits (Loeber, 1990; Moffitt, 1990); moreover, strong associations among early neuropsychological deficits, low Verbal IQ, and persistent behavior problems throughout the childhood and adolescent years were found (Moffitt, 1993). Differences between the persistent and adolescent limited offence trajectories are thought to involve neuropsychological deficits that are linked to the kind of antisocial behavior that begins in childhood, whereas adolescence-limited subtype is viewed as a transient pattern influenced by social contingencies in absence of neurocognitive risk factors. It is widely accepted that the two patterns of onset (early- vs late-) have fairly different etiologies and developmental trajectories (Elkins et al., 1997), and that early-onset delinquents are characterized by higher psychopathology, social dysfunctioning, and cognitive impairments than late-onset subjects. However, in the most recent literature the evidence of marked differences between the early-onset persistent and late-onset adolescent limited offense trajectories is less consistent (Marmorstein and Iacono, 2005), since also adolescence-limited offenders showed enduring difficulties at follow-up. The presence of higher rates of mental health problems, substance dependence, financial problems and criminal behavior during adulthood (Moffitt et al., 2002) suggests that late-onset offending group displays a similar profile of problems in adulthood as the life-course persistent group, and therefore may warrant particular attention. Based on this background, the present chapter reports a study aimed to evaluate executive cognitive functioning in a sample of adolescents and young adults with late-onset delinquent behavior and no antecedents of CD, referred to the Social Services of the Department of Juvenile Justice of the city of Messina (Italy). The hypothesis tested with this design is that late-onset delinquent adolescents and young adults differ from nonantisocial controls matched for age and educational level on tasks of executive cognitive functions.

METHOD

Subjects

The study was conducted with a sample of male adolescents referred to the Department of Juvenile Justice, Messina (Italy). The initial data collection covered 11 months between 2007 and 2008. All male delinquents (103 youths) who were brought to the Department of Juvenile Justice for the first time during that period were contacted and asked to participate in the study. The potential subjects and their parents were given an outline of procedures, informed of their right of refusal, and were assured that refusal to participate would not influence their legal status. The study was introduced as a neuropsychological investigation on cognitive functions. Inclusions criteria were a pattern of late-onset antisocial behavior (after age fourteen) and the absence of mental disorders. Subjects were excluded if they had a history of disruptive childhood disorders (CD, ODD and ADHD), were currently affected by any major psychiatric disorder or were currently using psychotropic medications, had significant concurrent medical illnesses, reported a history of organic brain disorder including traumatic head injury (with loss of consciousness or cognitive sequelae) or central nervous system pathology, exhibited current substance and alcohol abuse, and had mental retardation. 21 subjects who incurred antisocial behaviors prior to age fourteen (early-onset) and/or reported symptoms of CD, ODD and ADHD were excluded from the study; 11 subjects were excluded for current substance or alcohol abuse. The final sample was formed by 71 Italian-speaking male subjects, aged 15–20 yrs. Control subjects were recruited from the general population via advertisements placed on notice boards at sport and leisure centres seeking adolescents interested in participating in research examining the neuropsychology of personality. The controls were 80 male subjects matched for age, educational level, socio-demographic features, and geographic residence. All were required to be medically healthy as a condition of study entry, with participants being excluded from the study if they had any past offending history.

Both clinical and control subjects provided written informed consent after a full explanation of the study design which had been approved by the local ethic committee. For minors, all parents of the boys referred to the Department of Juvenile Justice and of the controls received information on the study and signed an informed consent to allow their children to participate in the study.

Participants were interviewed in a private area, almost always within two days of intake. All subjects were screened for mental disorders by an psychiatrist with experience in interviewing high-risk youth using a non-structured psychiatric interview. All subjects were assessed using a neuropsychological battery. Both the psychiatric interview and the subsequent neuropsychological examination were conducted individually. Thus, the study was conducted anonymously, with rigorous procedures to ensure subject anonymity.

Instruments

A neuropsychological battery consisting of measures sensitive to executive cognitive dysfunction was administered to each subject both of late-onset offenders and control groups.

Stroop Color-Word Task

The Stroop Color-Word Task is considered a classic measure of frontal lobe function and it has been reported to distinguish patients with frontal damage from patients with lesion in other brain areas (Milner, 1964; MacLeod, 1991). In this task, the subject is instructed to name the color of the ink of an incongruent word-color stimulus (i.e., RED printed in green ink). As word reading is a more automatic cognitive process than color naming, subjects must resolve cognitive interference and inhibit the incorrect, response in order to properly respond. This cognitive interference commonly results in an increase in response time on incongruent trials. The cognitive processes underlying the Stroop task (i.e., response inhibition, interference resolution, and behavioral conflict resolution) are considered executive processes mediated by the frontal lobe. The Stroop task is a well validated instrument for studying typical and atypical development of executive processes (Dash and Dash, 1982); moreover, it has been used to assess neurocognitive function in antisocial personality disorder (Dinn and Harris, 2000). In the present study, a standard Stroop Color-Word Task (Golden, 1978) was administered to every subject. The Stroop test includes three time-limited (45-s) subtests. First, subjects are asked to read as quickly as possible a list of words printed in black ink that name colors (i.e., "red," "green," "blue"). During the second subtest, subjects are presented with a list of "XXXXX"s that differ in ink color. Subjects name the color of the ink for each "XXXXX." In the third subtest, subjects are then presented with a list of the words "red," "green," and "blue;" in this presentation, however, the ink color of the words is discordant with the presented word (i.e., the word "red" printed in blue ink). Again, subjects are asked to say the color of the ink and ignore the word's semantic meaning (conflict subtest). The third condition normally elicits what is called the 'Stroop' effect, a significant slowing of performance that is a normal finding in all subjects and patients, the essential diagnostic claim in neuropsychology is that this effect is greater in frontal lobe dysfunctions (Stuss et al., 2001).

Verbal Fluency Test

The ability to generate verbal material rapidly according to specified rules, as it is required in fluency tasks, is commonly impaired in patients with frontal lobe lesions, since the active search and retrieval of information necessary for adequate performance on fluency tasks are believed to be primarily mediated by the frontal lobes (Baldo and Shimamura, 1998). Magnetic resonance imaging (MRI) and positron emission tomography (PET) studies suggests that verbal fluency produces the activation of the frontal lobes, particularly the prefrontal cortex in the language dominant hemisphere (Phelps et al., 1997; Frith et al., 1991). Tests of verbal fluency are considered a valid and reliable measure of executive dysfunction, since rapid intrinsic response generation, with the initiation of elective retrieval strategies to organise thinking and the continual switching between retrieval strategies (Troyer et al., 1997), place relatively heavy demands on executive resources (Baddeley, 1996). The Verbal Fluency task consists of two subtests, phonemic and semantic fluency tests. The phonemic fluency test required participants to generate as many words as possible beginning with the letter F, then A, and finally S (excluding proper nouns and the same word repeated with different suffixes) in three 1-min trials (Borkowski et al., 1967). The phonemic fluency score was the total number of different correct words produced across the three trials. The semantic fluency test consisted of three 1-min trials in which participants first generated names of animals, then colours, and finally fruits. The semantic fluency score was the total number of correct unique responses given across the three trials.

Raven's Standard Progressive Matrices Test

Raven's Standard Progressive Matrices (SPM) is widely used as a test of general intellectual functioning, a measure of fluid intelligence (McGrew and Flanagan, 1998). Fluid intelligence is an important construct for assessing the ability to perform successfully across a wide range of situations, and it is thought to be the best predictor of performance in cognitively demanding occupations (Gottfredson, 1997). It has been suggested that the constructs of working memory capacity, abstraction, and executive function are important contributors to fluid intelligence (Garlick and Sejnowski, 2006). Indeed, apart from being a measure of intelligence, SPM may be consider an ECF test. The SPM is a multiple-choice paper and pencil test which is made of 60 visual pattern matching problems divided into five sets (A, B, C, and E), each progressively harder than the last. Section A involves simply filling in the missing part of an image. Later sections require more abstract reasoning. The participant is asked to complete series of drawings in which the last drawing is missing, selecting the appropriate one from a range of possible choices. The range of possible scores on the test are 0-60. The normative data are converted into percentile ranks for different age range for the interpretation of the individual scores (Raven et al., 1992).

AB-AC Test

AB-AC is a test of paired-associate learning used to measure proactive interference, defined as the degree to which prior learning affects later learning (Elvevåg et al., 2000). The test consists of 12 "moderately related" word pairs (e.g., lion–hunter), presented for three consecutive study-test learning trials. Then, an additional three learning trials is administered using the same cue words but paired with different response words (e.g., lion–circus). Cue words used in one list are repeated in a second list but are associated with different response. The first learned list of words produces proactive interference on the second list; indeed, subjects have to resolve memory interference and inhibit the incorrect response in order to properly manage retrieval of information from long-term memory. Frontal lobe dysfunction can result in a deficit in this process of learning associations and patients with frontal damage were found more susceptible to interference in tasks that require the inhibition of proactive interference during associative memory processes (Shimamura et al., 1995).

Wisconsin Card Sorting Test

The Wisconsin Card Sorting Test (WCST) (Heaton, 1981) is a widely used neuropsychological measure of executive functioning and is sensitive for assessing frontal lobe disorders (Robinson et al., 1980). The executive cognitive processes underlying the WCST task are strategic planning, organized searching, applying external feedback to shift mental sets, inhibiting impulsive responses, and directing behavior toward achieving a goal (Lezak, 1983). The WCST consists of four stimulus cards and 128 response cards that depict figures of varying forms (crosses, circles, triangles, or stars), colors (red, blue, yellow, or green) and numbers of figures (one, two, three, or four). Participants are asked to sort a deck of 64 cards according to the dimensions of color, form, and number of the stimulus cards. Following each card placement, the examiner informs participants whether their responses are correct or incorrect, but provides no additional information. After 10 consecutive correct matches, the sorting criterion is suddenly changed without the participant's knowledge, requiring the subject to use the examiner's feedback to develop a new sorting strategy. The WCST proceeds in this manner through five shifts in set, i.e., sorting principle among the three possible categories: Color, Form and Number. Of the indexes defined in the WCST manual (Heaton et al., 1993), number of categories achieved (CA), indicating the number of times a participant correctly sorted 10 consecutive cards, was analyzed for the purpose of the study.

Statistical Analyses

Data obtained from the study underwent check and quality control and, subsequently, descriptive and inferential statistical analysis. Continuous data were expressed as mean ± S.D. and significant differences between groups were assessed using the Student t test for two independent samples. Non continuous data were expressed as percentages and the comparison between the two groups was performed by using the chi-square test. Statistical significance was defined at $P < 0.01$. The statistical analysis was performed with Statistical Package for the Social Sciences (SPSS) 11.5 software (SPSS Inc, Chicago, IL, USA).

Results

The mean age of late-onset delinquent adolescents was 17.46 years (SD = 1.1), compared with a mean age of 17.11 (SD = 0.8) for the controls ($t = 0.169$, $p = 0.866$). Educational level (years) was 9.82 (SD = 3.38) for juvenile delinquents and 10.31 (SD = 3.15) for control subjects ($t = -0.873$, $p = 0.382$). Types of delinquency found in the sample of late-onset offenders were violent crimes including assault/physical injuries, rape, robbery (n = 19, 26.76%), property offences, such as extortion, vandalism, burglary, motor vehicle theft, arson (n = 40, 56.33%), and other miscellaneous offences (n = 12, 16.90%).

The means and the standard deviations for the neuropsychological measures are given in Table 1. The mean scores for Stroop task, AB-AC, SPM, Phonemic Fluency, Semantic Fluency, and WCST CA were all in the normal range.

Table 1. Comparisons between mean scores on neuropsychological tasks in late-onset offenders (n = 71) and controls (n = 80). Scores have been compared by Student's T Test for two independent samples.

	Late-onset offenders			Controls	
	Mean	S.D.		Mean	S.D.
Stroop *	41.9	29.8		27.6	18.9
Phonemic Fluency*	18.0	6.7		29.4	6.3
Semantic Fluency	32.8	9.2		35.7	9.5
SPM*	95.0	16.5		111.8	12.1
AB-AC	1.5	4.6		1.4	2.3
WCST CA	5.1	1.5		5.6	0.9

$^*p< 0.0001$.

To test the hypothesis of between-group differences on the measured variables, t tests were performed. Student t test for two independent samples (Table 1) evidenced significant differences between late-onset offenders and control groups on the following tasks: Stroop ($t = 3.570$; $p = < 0.0001$), SPM ($t = -7.174$; $p = < 0.0001$), and Phonemic Fluency ($t = -10.743$; $p = < 0.0001$). Late-onset offenders exhibited slower reaction times on the interference trial of the Stroop color-word set, although it should be noted that these differences were within the healthy functioning range. When required to inhibit a previous learned response pattern (conflict blocks), late-onset offenders displayed greater reaction time, though they were more likely to experience higher levels of interference than controls. On the Phonemic Fluency test, late-onset offenders produced fewer words (mean = 18, SD = 6.7) than control subjects (mean score = 29.4, SD = 6.3).

On measures of intellectual function there were significant differences between the groups in full scale IQ; relative to SPM, the average for late-onset offenders was 35 items correct, which in the Italian standardization correspond to the 51st percentile with an IQ equivalent of 95, whereas the average for controls was 46 items correct, corresponding to the 59th percentile and to an IQ equivalent of 111.8. Late-onset offenders did not demonstrate worse performance than controls on tasks measuring proactive interference in associative memory (AB-AC) ($t = .205$; $p = .838$), generation of category names (Semantic Fluency) ($t = -1.904$; $p = .059$), and executive functioning as evidenced by the index "categories achieved" (CA) of the WCST ($t = -2.321$; $p = .022$).

Relative to the frequencies (expressed in percentages) of subjects who reported scores in the clinical range within the two groups (see Figure 1), 9 subjects (12.7%) of the late-onset offender group exhibited performance deficits on Stroop task, vs none of the community control group, and 8 (11.3%) had lower IQ equivalent. The higher frequency of pathological subjects was found in the late-offender group on the Phonemic Fluency task: 59 subjects out of 71 (83.1% of the sample) vs only 11 controls (13.8%) showed an impairment of the rapid intrinsic response generation, where responses are minimally specified by external cues or triggers. Although group differences did not approach statistical significance, 21 (29.6%) late-onset offenders vs 27 (33.8%) controls exhibited an impaired performance on Semantic Fluency task, and 20 (28.2%) late-onset offenders vs 12 (15%) controls completed an insufficient number of categories on the WCST. Neither subjects nor controls exhibited performance deficits on AB-AC task.

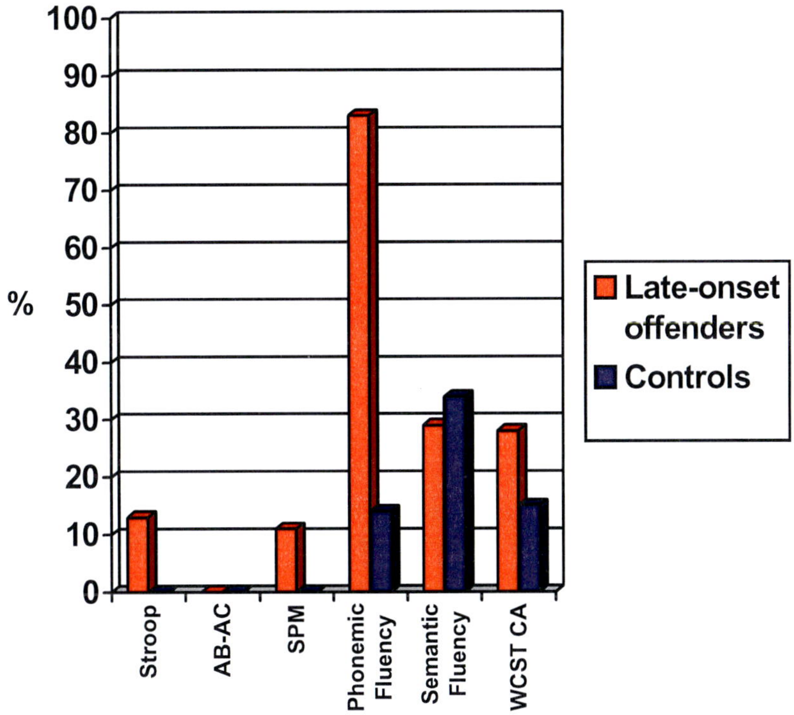

Figure 1. Frequencies of subjects who scored in the clinical range on neuropsychological tasks within the two groups.

CONCLUSION

The objective of this analysis was to examine the executive cognitive functioning in a sample of adolescents and young adults with late-onset delinquent behavior and no antecedents of CD, ODD and ADHD, referred to the Social Services of the Department of Juvenile Justice of the city of Messina (Italy). The leading hypothesis was that adolescents and young adults whose antisocial and delinquent behavior begins after age fourteen differ on tasks of executive cognitive functions from non-antisocial controls matched for age, social class, and geographic residence. For this purpose, the following measures considered sensitive to executive dysfunction (Morgan and Lilienfeld, 2000) were chosen: Stroop Color-Word Task; Verbal Fluency, both Phonemic and Semantic; Raven's Standard Progressive Matrices (SPM); AB-AC; and Wisconsin Card Sorting Test, "categories achieved" (WCST CA). Our results support the general hypothesis that late-onset offenders differ from community controls on several neuropsychological domains; although mean scores for both groups were within the normal range, there was a significant variability in scores within the two groups, as evidenced by high SD values. Further, chi-square analysis showed that a significantly greater number of late-onset offending participants scored in the clinical range on several ECF measures. The finding that late-onset offenders showed slower reaction times on the interference trial of the Stroop Color-Word Task indicates a general difficulty, even subclinical, to sustain high-level attention where interferent stimuli are presented and to maintain a consistent response intention in mind. As the Stroop test requires the inhibition of an overlearned response (word reading) in favor of a less automatic behavior (color naming), it has been considered an appropriate model for the examination of conflict resolution and the regulation of impulse control (Gruber et al., 2002). For the "conflict" condition, damage to the prefrontal lobes should disrupt performance most, since a main role of the frontal lobes is to control response options through organizing inhibitory processes, establishing response selection, or maintaining constant activation of the intended goal. Resistance to interference is a cognitive ability related to ECF, since maintaining goal-oriented processing might additionally involve gating task-irrelevant information (MacLeod and MacDonald, 2000). Our finding is generally consistent with the literature; mean scores in the impaired range on the Stroop Color-Word Task were found in a sample of 56 delinquent adolescents compared with normal subjects (Wolff et al., 1982).

On the Verbal Fluency task, our late-onset offending group was characterized by a significant difference in verbal output on the Phonemic Fluency Task when compared to controls. On a descriptive level, the process of word generation involves attention, an available word knowledge (i.e., semantic/lexical system) from which to select, retrieval from verbal declarative memory, and an executive ability to coordinate this process, including working memory to monitor performance and avoid breaking the rules (e.g., no proper nouns). Thus, when ECF are impaired, the flexibility necessary for the over mentioned strategies may be compromised as part of a difficulty in shifting between cognitive sets. Verbal deficits, often not previously diagnosed, were found in populations with antisocial behavior (Cohen, et al., 1998), and in incarcerated adolescent males vs controls (Davis et al., 1991). Moreover, the verbal skills deficits of delinquent adolescents are confirmed by the frequent incidence of selective learning disabilities and worse performance than controls on tests of reading, spelling, writing, expressive language, and receptive language functions (Teichner and Golden, 2000). As suggested by Brownlie et al. (2004), language impairment increases the risk of antisocial behavior, but these effects are not realized until late adolescence or early adulthood, except among individuals whose behavior problems are severe enough to meet criteria for a psychiatric diagnosis in earlier age. The cumulative effects of impaired communication skills may account for the increased levels of delinquency in language impaired boys, since they affect children's experiences in multiple social contexts. Behavior and antisocial problems of language impaired children may reflect their adaptations to situations in which the communication demands exceed their linguistic resources (Redmond and Rice, 2002). Within this frame, delinquent behavior may provide an alternate means of obtaining social status among peers for boys who have difficulty using social speech to endorse their social goals. Verbal deficits are also associated with a worse outcome; a follow-up study by Clegg et al. (2005) evidenced that language impaired boys still continued to experience problems in various domains in their mid-thirties, with substantial social adaptation difficulties and increased risk of mental disorders.

Regarding global intellectual functioning, our findings evidenced significant differences between the groups in IQ as documented by the mean score of 95 for late-onset offenders vs 111.8 for controls. It is widely accepted that better-developed cognitive skills protect against the development of antisocial behavior, and that lower intelligence is not only related to current delinquent activity, but it is predictive of adult antisocial behavior (Lynam et al., 1993; Moffitt and Silva, 1988; Stattin and Klackenberg-Larsson, 1993).

The relationship between intelligence and antisocial behavior has been widely investigated in previous studies which consistently reports a difference of 8 IQ points between antisocial adolescents and normal controls (Hirschi and Hindelang, 1977). More recently, Kratzer and Hodgins (1999) found that childhood problems and low global scores of intelligence distinguished early-onset offenders (i.e., life-course-persistent offenders) from all other offenders as well as nonoffenders. Starting from the observation that studies reporting low to moderate correlations between IQ and delinquency did not distinguish between early-onset, life-course persistent and late-onset, adolescence-limited delinquents, Moffitt (1990) separately analyzed data for the two groups, finding only a 1 point mean deficit for adolescent-onset delinquents but a 17-point mean deficit for childhood-onset offenders. These findings lead her to conclude that intelligence is unrelated to antisocial behavior for those individuals whose onset of delinquency occurs during adolescence. Contrarily to this, the 6-point difference found in our sample indicates that late-onset offenders were characterized by lower global intellectual functioning when compared with normal controls. This finding let us hypothesize that intelligence may be also involved in late-onset offending pattern among other features or risk factors.

The other neuropsychological measures of ECF, AB-AC task, Semantic Fluency, and WCST CA could not establish any statistically significant differences between the late-onset offenders group and controls. AB-AC, a task measuring verbal paired associate learning, have long been used for assessing learning ability in subjects with suspected or established neurological damage and memory impairment in both neurological and psychiatric samples (Landrø et al. 1993; Shimamura et al., 1995). To the best of our knowledge, AB-AC task has never been included among the neuropsychological tests used for the cognitive assessment of juvenile delinquents; however, a possible interpretation of our finding is that the process of proactive interference during associative memory tasks is unrelated to antisocial behavior.

Regarding semantic fluency, deficits on this task have been associated with impairment in the structure of the semantic knowledge system (Harvey et al., 1997; Paulsen et al., 1996). Differently from phonemic fluency impairment, which is associated with information processing problems and frontal lobe involvement (Kosmidis et al., 2005), semantic fluency deficits implicated temporal lobe involvement (Chen et al., 2000). Such deficits have been found in Alzheimer's patients, reflecting a breakdown in semantic structure which is consistent with the associated neuropathology of the neocortical temporal area (Fama et al., 2000). According to this evidence, it is almost intuitive to realize that late-onset offenders did not differ from community controls on semantic fluency task, since it does not reflect frontal lobe functioning and it appears to be compromised only in clinical samples of severe neurological illnesses.

Not surprisingly, our sample of juvenile delinquents was furtherly characterized by a performance on WCST within the normal range and no differences between them and controls were detected. This latter result is quite consistent with previous data; Appelloff and Augustine (1985) observed no group differences on WCST performances between 30 male delinquents and 30 nondelinquent controls. Similarly, WCST could not establish any statistically significant differences between the delinquents and controls in a study aimed to evaluate cognitive and neuropsychological abilities of 20 transnationally adopted delinquent adolescents in institutional care compared with 21 non-delinquent controls who were also transnationally adopted (Elmund et al., 2004). In contrast, Lueger and Gill (1990) assessed the neuropsychological functioning of 21 adolescent delinquents who were receiving rehabilitation for behavior and emotional problems compared with a group of volunteer normal and behavior-problemed youth at a community center. Perseverative errors on WCST, sustained attention errors, and poorer auditory verbal list recall were found in those subjects, both of delinquent and control groups, who were diagnosed as CD according DSM-III criteria (American Psychiatric Association, 1980). These results address the question that frontal lobe dysfunction is more directly related to CD than to delinquent behavior.

It has been suggested that WCST may not be an appropriate test for assessing subtle neuropsychological deficits in criminal samples; several prior researches found that WCST did not discriminate psychopaths from controls in terms of their ability to alternate between response sets (Hare, 1984), and it has been proposed that such samples are better characterized by distractibility (i.e., deficits of selective attention) than by perseverance, as assessed by the number of perseverative errors on WCST task (Pham et al., 2003).

Current findings add to the growing literature comparing juvenile offenders to other adolescent populations. These results implicate that executive cognitive impairment, even subtle and subclinical, may be a contributing factor in the development and persistence of antisocial behaviors displayed by late-onset adolescent delinquents. This possibility is both expected and likely, since existing research showed that juvenile delinquents demonstrate more cognitive difficulties than normal children (e.g., Yeudall et al., 1982). Abnormal neuropsychological profiles were found by Yeudall et al. (1982) in 84% of the delinquent adolescent group (n = 99) as compared to 11% of controls (n = 47 volunteers), with delinquents faring poorer on 74% of the neuropsychological variables as compared to controls. However, these findings need to be interpreted with caution, since controls were recruited among high school students, and a large percentage of the delinquent group reported a significant history of illicit drug use (alcohol, 93%; marijuana, 80.2%; hallucinogens, 67%; amphetamines, 62%; inhalants, 50%; opiates, 24%; miscellaneous drugs, 30%; tranquillizers, 17%; barbiturates, 16%). Our control sample was matched to juvenile delinquents for educational level; moreover, to rule out possible influences of psychoactive substances on neuropsychological assessment, subjects with a current history of substance abuse, illicit drug use, and psychotropic medications, have been excluded from the study. Previous investigations have focused on either language deficits or executive problems in antisocial adolescents: impulsive aggressive college students, compared with controls, were not impaired in language processing in general, but significant differences in performance appeared when the task demands required more executive modulation (planning, organization, and integration) (Villemarette-Pittman et al., 2002).

Indeed, the impairment of executive function can have a significant effect on the expression of other cognitive domains, mainly the verbal one. Poor language skills reduce the verbal mediation of behavior, and contribute to inefficiency in processing incoming stimuli and organizing purposive actions (Fuster, 1997).

The utility of differentiating between early- and late-onset delinquents has been emphasized by several authors (Moffitt, 1993; Patterson et al., 1989), and the main implication of this distinction is that the two patterns largely differ in many behavioral and developmental features. Early-onset offenders should be characterized be the severity and persistence of antisocial behavior, with high levels of physical aggression and an antisocial life-style that continues into adulthood, leading to repeated criminal convictions (Moffitt et al., 1996). Beyond family process variables (poor parental monitoring, disruptive family transitions, and inconsistent parental discipline) which are thought to play a prominent role in the development of early-onset persistent antisocial behavior (Patterson, 1982), the role of biological factors have been highlighted. According to Moffitt's theory (Moffitt, 1993), prenatal and perinatal disruptions in neural development lead to neuropsychological deficits, mainly in executive and verbal functioning. Indeed, neuropsychological deficits are associated with early-onset, life-course-persistent antisocial behavior, but not with the late-onset, adolescence limited form. Further studies have confirmed that the pattern of risk factors associated with an early age of onset of aggression is different from the pattern of risk factors associated with a later age of onset (Brennan et al., 2003). A prospective, longitudinal study of normal and abnormal development in a primarily low socioeconomic status, ethnically-diverse sample of 62 boys and 58 girls (Aguilar et al., 2000) reported that children with early-onset persistent behavior problems were characterized by more severe psychosocial adversity (life stress, composite risk scores, and life stress as experienced by mothers) within the first few years of life, whereas no significant differences were found on early measures of temperament or neuropsychological functioning. Differences on neuropsychological tasks emerged between the two groups on later tests of neuropsychological functioning only for early-onset adolescents, which suggested that their cognitive deficits were progressive rather than present at or near birth. Neverthless, more recent findings evidenced that late-onset antisocial behavior has many of the same negative correlates of persisting antisocial behavior (Marmorstein and Iacono, 2005). The follow-up of the New Zealand Study (Moffitt et al., 2002) reported the outcomes of 26-year-old males who had previously been assessed during ages 5 through 11 years and subdivided in two groups, early vs late, according to the age of onset (Moffitt et al., 1996). At the age of 26 years, the outcomes of both childhood-onset and late-onset groups were quite similar, with the early-onset subjects being the most elevated in psychopathic traits, mental disorders, substance abuse, and socio-relational dysfunctioning, and the late-onset subjects being less extreme but elevated in impulsivity, mental disorders, substance abuse, financial problems, and still perpetuating criminal activity (mainly property offenses).

As suggested by Elkins et al. (1997), onset of antisocial behavior in late adolescence or early adulthood may be associated with significantly more negative features than onset in early/mid-adolescence. Data from the Minnesota Twin Family Study – MTFS (Iacono et al., 1996) showed that fathers with onset of severe antisocial behavior after age 15 (late-onset) exhibited high levels of impulsivity, negative emotionality, substance abuse, and psychopatic personality traits.

Carroll et al. (2006) compared on a range of measures pertaining to impulsivity three groups of 43 early-onset offenders, 43 late-onset offenders, and 43 controls recruited from high school students, starting from the broad prediction that early-onset subjects would have performed worse than the other two groups on impulsivity tasks. Results evidenced that offenders significantly differed from non-offenders on several measures of impulsivity, whereas no significant differences were found within the offending population (early- vs late-onset). A community based study by Tweed et al. (1994) showed that approximately 50% of adults who demonstrated severe antisocial behavior in adulthood demonstrated no antisocial antecedents during childhood. Similarly, it has been furtherly estimated that 2.3% of men and 0.9% of women with adult antisocial behavior had no conduct problems in childhood or adolescence (Ridenour et al., 2002). Marmorstein (2006) found that, out of a population-based sample of 7612 subjects from the National Comorbidity Survey, approximately 2.3% of participants were characterized by late-onset antisocial behavior without history of CD or actual antisocial personality disorder (ASPD); in these subjects, the levels of comorbid diagnoses and disadvantage were similar to those of individuals with full ASPD diagnoses.

From these findings, it appears reasonable to assert that "late-onset delinquents are anything but normal; their problems are simply less severe" (Dishion and Patterson, 2006, p. 510).

Our findings extended research on late-onset adolescent delinquents and added new insight for the understanding of this developmental trajectory. However, the data were limited in their generalizability, as the sample was recruited from one city, Messina, and the extent to which the results would be replicated in other cities or even rural areas awaits continued research. Moreover, although frequently used measures of ECF were employed, other neuropsychological tasks may be further pursued for their discriminatory power. Among these tests, the Go/No-Go Task (Brown et al., 1989), a cognitive instrument specifically designed to measure ECF dimensions such as decision making, prevision abilities, reward/punishment sensitivity, and impulsivity may be included in further assessments. Despite limitations, the findings also suggest the need for additional research aimed to assess a broader range of cognitive abilities and specific vulnerability and risk factors for late-onset adolescent offenders, a "pathological yet overlooked group" (Marmorstein and Iacono, 2005). Juvenile offenders are a heterogeneous population in need of research and clinical attention. Research focusing upon the relationship between ECF deficits and antisocial behavior will have important theoretical and practical implications for understanding and preventing various forms of psychopathology and social dysfunctioning. Since ECF abilities may be influenced by environmental and psychosocial factors (Burt et al., 2007), the prevention of ECF impairment by broad public health strategies that target these aspects may be effective in minimizing exposure to these risk factors and preventing antisocial behavior. Interventions in pathways to antisocial behavior aimed to prevent its development should involve educational programs, violence prevention programs developed to improve cognitive and social skills among children, and cognitive remediation programs for the rehabilitation of executive function deficits (Strand, 2002). Subclinical ECF impairment with its related behavioral difficulties, mainly antisocial, can be effectively treated with both targeted and universal approaches (Paschall and Fishbein, 2002); moreover, the strategies mentioned above may be effective in inhibiting criminal activity (Redondo et al., 1999). Beyond the search for effective preventive and treatment programs, future epidemiological research on ECF impairment is needed to estimate prevalence and geographic concentrations, and to isolate contributory environmental conditions such as head injury, hostile or inconsistent parenting, poor socioeconomic condition, and exposure to toxins. Thus, effective interventions rely on understanding the relationships between frontal lobe dysfunction, neuropsychological deficits, impulse control, and antisocial propensity, considering that the construct of ECF impairment has remarkable empirical utility in explaining various dimensions of antisocial behavior and delinquent lifestyle.

References

Aarons, G.A., Brown, S.A., Hough, R.L., Garland, A.F., Wood, .P.A. (2001). Prevalence of adolescent substance use disorders across five sectors of care. *J. Am. Acad. Child Adolesc Psychiatry, 40*, 419-426.

Abram, K.M., Teplin, L.A., McClelland, G.M., Dulcan, M.K. (2003). Comorbid Psychiatric Disorders in Youth in Juvenile Detention. *Arch. Gen. Psychiatry, 60*, 1097-1108.

Aguilar, B., Sroufe, L.A., Egeland, B., Carlson, E. (2000). Distinguishing the early-onset/persistent and adolescence-onset antisocial behavior types: From birth to 16 years. *Development and Psychopathology, 12* , 109-132.

American Psychiatric Association. (1994). *Diagnostic and statistical manual of mental disorders.* (Fourth Edition). Washington, DC:Author.

Appellof, E.S., and Augustine, E.A. (1985). Prefrontal functions in juvenile delinquents. *Journal of Clinical and Experimental Neuropsychology, 7*, 79–109.

Ash, P. (2006). Adolescents in Adult Court: Does the Punishment Fit the Criminal? *J. Am. Acad. Psychiatry Law, 34*, 145-9.

Babinski, L. M., Hartsough, C. S., and Lambert, N. M. (1999). Childhood conduct problems, hyperactivity-impulsivity, and inattention as predictors of adult criminal activity. *Journal of Child Psychology and Psychiatry and Allied Disciplines, 40*, 347–355.

Baddeley, A.D. (1996). Exploring the central executive. *Quarterly Journal of Experimental Psychology, 49A*, 5-28.

Baldo, J. V., and Shimamura, A. P. (1998). Letter and category fluency in patients with frontal lobe lesions. *Neuropsychology, 12*, 259-267.

Barkley, R.A. (1997). Behavioral inhibition, sustained attention, and executive functions: Constructing a unifying theory of ADHD. *Psychological Bulletin, 121*, 65-94.

Barkley, R.A. (2000). Genetics of childhood disorders: XVII. ADHD, Part I: The executive functions and ADHD. *J. Am. Acad Child Adolesc. Psychiatry, 39(8)*, 1064-1068.

Blumstein, A., and Cohen, J. (1987). Characterizing criminal careers. *Science, 237*, 985-991.

Borkowski, J.G., Benton, A.L., and Spreen, O. (1967). Word fluency and brain damage. *Neuropsychologia, 5*, 135-140.

Brame, B. (2001). Developmental Trajectories of Physical Aggression from School Entry to Late Adolescence. *J. Child Psychol. Psychiat., 42(4)*, 503-512.

Brown, D., Fenwick, P., Howard, R. (1989). The contingent negative variation in a Go/No Go avoidance task: relationships with personality and subjective state. *International Journal of Psychophysiology, 7 (1)*, 35-45.

Brownlie, E.B., Beitchman, J.H., Escobar, M., Young, A., Atkinson, L., Johnson, C., Wilson, B., Douglas, L. (2004). Early Language Impairment and Young Adult Delinquent and Aggressive Behavior. *Journal of Abnormal Child Psychology, 32(4)*, 453-467.

Buikhuisen, W. (1987). Cerebral dysfunctions and persistent juvenile delinquency. In S.A. Mednick, T.E. Moffitt, and S.A. Stack (Eds.), *The causes of crime: New biological approaches.* (pp. 168-184). New York: Cambridge University Press.

Burt, S.A., McGue, M., Carter, L.A., Iacono, W.G. (2007). The different origins of stability and change in antisocial personality disorder symptoms. *Psychol. Med., 37(1)*, 27-38.

Cadoret, R. J., Yates, W. R., Troughton, E., Woodworth, G., and Stewart, M. A. (1995). Genetic–environmental interaction in the genesis of aggressivity and conduct disorders. *Archives of General Psychiatry, 52*, 916–924.

Carroll, A., Hemingway, F., Bower, J., Ashman, A., Houghton, S., Durkin, K. (2006). Impulsivity in Juvenile Delinquency: Differences Among Early-Onset, Late-Onset, and Non-Offenders. *Journal of Youth and Adolescence, 35(4),* 519–529.

Chen, R.Y.L., Chen, E.Y.H., Chan, K.Y., Lam, L.C.W., Lieh-Mak, F., 2000. Verbal fluency in schizophrenia: reduction in semantic store. *Australian and New Zealand Journal of Psychiatry 34*, 43-48.

Clegg, J., Hollis, C., Mawhood, L., Rutter, M. (2005). Developmental language disorders – a follow-up in later adult life. Cognitive, language and psychosocial outcomes. *Journal of Child Psychology and Psychiatry, 46(2)*, 128-149.

Cohen, N.J., Menna, R., Vallance, D.D., Barwick, M., Im, N., Horodezky, N.B. (1998). Language, social cognitive processing, and behavioral characteristics of psychiatrically disturbed children with previously identified and unsuspected language impairments. *Journal of Child Psychology and Psychiatry, 39*, 853-864.

Dash, J., and Dash, A.S. (1982). Cognitive developmental studies of the Stroop phenomena: Cross-sectional and longitudinal data. *Indian Psychol, 1(1)*, 24-33.

Davis, A.D., Sanger, D.D., Morris-Friehe, M. (1991). Language skills of delinquent and non-delinquent males. *Journal of Communication Disorders, 24(4)*, 251-266.

Déry, M., Toupin, J., Pauzé, R., Mercier, H., Fortin, L. (1999). Neuropsychological characteristics of adolescents with conduct disorder: association with attention-deficit-hyperactivity and aggression. *Journal of Abnormal Child Psychology, 27(3)*, 225-236.

Dinn, W.M., and Harris, C.L. (2000). Neurocognitive function in antisocial personality disorder. *Psychiatry Research, 97*, 173-190.

Dishion, T.J., and Patterson, G.R. (2006). The development and ecology of antisocial behavior. In D. Cicchetti and D. Cohen (Eds.), *Developmental psychopathology. Vol. 3: Risk, disorder, and adaptation.* (Revised ed., pp. 503-541). New York: Wiley and Sons.

Doreleijers, T., Moser, F., Thijs, P., van Engeland, H., and Beyaert, F. (2000). Forensic assessment of juvenile delinquents: prevalence of psychopathology and decision-making at court in the Netherlands. *Journal of Adolescence, 23*, 263-275.

Elkins, I.J., Iacono, W.G., Doyle, A.E., McGue, M. (1997). Characteristics associated with the persistence of antisocial behaviour: results from recent longitudinal research. *Aggression and Violent Behavior, 2(2)*, 101-124.

Elliott, F. (1978). Neurological aspects of antisocial behavior. In W. H. Reid (Ed.), *The psychopath: A comprehensive study of antisocial disorders and behaviors* (pp. 146–189). New York: Bruner/Mazel.

Elmund, A., Melin, L., von Knorring, A-L, Proos, L., Tuvemo, T. (2004). Cognitive and neuropsychological functioning in transnationally adopted juvenile delinquents. *Acta Paediatr, 93*, 1507-1513.

Elvevåg, B., Egan, M.F., Goldberg, T.E. (2000). Paired-associate learning and memory interference in schizophrenia. *Neuropsychologia, 38*, 1565-1575.

Eme, R.F.(2007). Sex differences in child-onset, life-course-persistent conduct disorder. A review of biological influences. *Clinical Psychology Review, 27*, 607-627.

Fama, R., Sullivan, E.D., Shear, P.K., Cahn-Weiner, D.A., Marsh, L., Lim, K.O., Yesavage, J.A., Tinklenberg, J.R., Pfefferbaum, A. (2000). Structural Brain Correlates of Verbal and Nonverbal Fluency Measures in Alzheimer's Disease. *Neuropsychology, 14(1)*, 29-40.

Faraone, S. V., Biederman, J., Keenan, K., Tsuang, M. T. (1991). Separation of DSM-III attention deficit disorder and conduct disorder: Evidence from a family genetic study of American child psychiatry patients. *Psychological Medicine, 21*, 109-121.

Farrington, D. P., Ohlin, L., and Wilson, J. Q. (1986). *Understanding and controlling crime.* New York: Springer Verlag.

Fergusson, D.M., Lynskey, M.T., Horwood, L.J. (1996). Factors associated with continuity and changes in disruptive behavior patterns between childhood and adolescence. *J. Abnor. Child Psychol., 24*, 533-553.

Frith, C. D., Friston, K. J., Liddle, P. P., and Frackowiak, R. S. J. (1991). A PET study of word finding. *Neuropsychologia, 29*, 1137-1148.

Fuster, J.M. (1997). *The prefrontal cortex*. Philadelphia, PA: Lippincott-Raven Publishers.

Garlick, D., and Sejnowski, T.J. (2006). There is more to fluid intelligence than working memory capacity and executive function. *Behavioral and Brain Sciences, 29(2)*, 134-135.

Giancola, P. R., Mezzich, A. C., and Tarter, R. E. (1998). Executive cognitive functioning, temperament, and antisocial behavior conduct-disordered adolescent females. *Journal of Abnormal Psychology, 107*, 629-641.

Glueck, S., and Glueck, E. (1950). *Unraveling juvenile delinquency*. Cambridge, MA: Harvard University Press.

Golden, C. J. (1978). *Stroop Colour and Word Test: A manual for clinical and experimental uses*. Stoelting Company, Illinois.

Gorenstein, E.E. (1990). Neuropsychology of juvenile delinquency. *Forensic Reports, 3*, 15-48.

Gottfredson, L. S. (1997) Why g matters: The complexity of everyday life. *Intelligence, 24*, 79-132.

Gottfredson, M., and Hirschi, T. (1990). *A general theory of crime*. Stanford University Press, Stanford, CA.

Grigsby, J., and Stevens, D. (2000). *The neurodynamics of personality*. New York: Guilford.

Gruber, S.A., Rogowska, J., Holcomb, P., Soraci, S., Yurgelun-Todd, D. (2002). Stroop Performance in Normal Control Subjects: An fMRI Study. *NeuroImage, 16*, 349-360.

Hare, R.D. (1984). Performance of psychopaths on cognitive tests related to frontal lobe function. *J Abnorm Psychol, 93*, 133-140.

Harvey, P.D., Lombardi, J., Leibman, M., Parella, M., White, L., Powchik, P., Mohs, R.C., Davidson, M. (1997). Verbal fluency deficits in geriatric and non geriatric chronic schizophrenic patients. *Journal of Neuropsychiatry and Clinical Neuroscience, 9*, 584-590.

Hawkins, K. A., and Trobst, K. K. (2000). Frontal lobe dysfunction and aggression: conceptual issues and research findings. *Aggression and Violent Behavior: A Review Journal, 5*, 147-157.

Heaton, R., 1981. The Wisconsin Card Sorting Test Manual. Psychological Assessment Resources, Odessa, FL.

Heaton, R.K., Chelune, G.I., Talley, J.L., Kay, G.G., Curtis, G. (1993). *Wisconsin Card Sorting Test Manual: Revised and Expanded.* Psychological Assessment Resources, Odessa, FL.

Helgeland, M.I., Kjelsberg, E., Torgersen, S. (2005). Continuities between emotional and disruptive behaviour disorders in adolescence and personality disorders in adulthood. *Am. J. Psychiatry, 162*, 1941-1947.

Hill, J. (2002). Biological, psychological and social processes in the conduct disorders. *Journal of Child Psychology and Psychiatry, 43(1)*, 133-164.

Hirschi, T., and Hindelang, M. (1977). Intelligence and delinquency: A revision and review. *American Sociological Review, 42*, 571-587.

Hughes, C., White, A., Sharpe, J, Dunn, J. (2000). Antisocial, angry, and unsympathetic: "hard-to-manage" preschoolers' peer problems and possible cognitive influences. *Journal of Child Psychology and Psychiatry and Allied Disciplines, 41(2)*, 169-179.

Iacono, W.G., Lykken, D.T., McGue, M. (1996). Psychophysiological prediction of substance abuse. In H. Gordon and M. Glantz (Eds.), *Biobehavioral etiology of drug abuse.* Rockville, MD: National Institute on Drug Abuse.

Jarrett, M.A., and Ollendik, T.H. (2008). A conceptual review of the comorbidity of attention-deficit/hyperactivity disorder and anxiety: Implications for future research and practice. *Clinical Psychology Review, 28*, 1266-1280.

Junger-Tas, J. (1994). *Delinquent behavior among young people in the Western World.* Amsterdam: Kugler Publications.

Kandel, E., and Freed, D. (1989). Frontal-lobe dysfunction and antisocial behavior: A review. *Journal of Clinical Psychology, 45*, 404- 413.

Kosmidis, M. H., Vassilis, T., Bozikas, P., Vlahou, C.H., Kiosseoglou, G., Giaglis, G., Karavatos, A. (2005). Verbal fluency in institutionalized patients with schizophrenia: Age-related performance decline. *Psychiatry Research, 134*, 233-240.

Kratzer, L. and Hodgins, S. (1999). A typology of offenders: A test of Moffitt's theory among males and females from childhood to age 30. *Criminal Behavior and Mental Health, 9*, 57-73

Kratzer, L., and Hodgins, S. (1997). Adult outcomes of child conduct problems: a cohort study. *Journal of Abnormal Child Psychology, 25*, 65-81.

Kuhne, M., Schachar, R., and Tannock, R. (1997). Impact of comorbid oppositional or conduct problems on attention-deficit hyperactivity disorder. *J Am Acad Child Adolesc Psychiatry, 36*, 1715-1725.

Lahey, B. B., Loeber, R., Quay, H. C., Applegate, B., Shaffer, D., Waldman, I., Hart, E. L., McBurnett, K., Frick, P. J., Jensen, P. S., Dulcan, M. K., Canino, G., and Bird, H. R. (1998). Validity of DSM-IV subtypes of conduct disorder based on age of onset. *J Am Acad Child Adolesc Psychiatry, 37*, 435-442.

Lahey, B.B., Waldman, I.D., McBurnett, K. (1999). Annotation: The Development of Antisocial Behavior: An Integrative Causal Model. *J. Child Psychol. Psychiat., 40(5),* 669-682.

Landrø, N.I., Ørbeck, A.L., Rund, B.R. (1993). Memory functioning in chronic and non-chronic schizophrenics, affectively disturbed patients and normal controls. *Schizophrenia Research, 10*, 85- 92.

Levine, M.D., Karniski, W.M., Palfrey, J.S., Meltzer, J., Fenton, T. (1985). A study of risk factor complexes in early adolescent delinquency. *American Journal of Development and Childhood, 139*, 50-56.

Lewis, D. O., and Shanok, S. S. (1980). The use of a correctional setting for follow-up care of psychiatrically disturbed adolescents. *American Journal of Psychiatry, 137*, 953-955.

Lezak, M. D. (1985). Neuropsychological assessment. In J. A. M. Frederiks (Ed.), *Handbook of clinical neurology, Vol. 1 (45): Clinical neuropsychology* (pp. 515-530). New York: Elsevier.

Lezak, M.D. (1983). *Neuropsychological Assessment, 2nd Edn.* Oxford University Press, New York.

Lochman, J.E., and Wayland, K.K. (1994). Aggression, social acceptance, and race as predictors of negative adolescent outcomes. *J. Am. Acad Child Adolesc. Psychiatry, 33*, 1026-1035.

Loeber, M., and Green, S. M. (1991). Anxiety, inhibition, and conduct disorder in children: Relations to social impairment. *J. Am. Acad Child Adolesc. Psychiatry, 30*, 187-191.

Loeber, R. (1990). Development and risk factors of juvenile antisocial behaviour and delinquency. *Clinical Psychology Review 10*, 1-41.

Loeber, R., and Coie, J. (2001). Continuities and discontinuities of development, with particular emphasis on emotional and cognitive components of disruptive behaviour. In J. Hill and B. Maughan (Eds.), *Conduct disorders in childhood and adolescence.* Cambridge: Cambridge University Press.

Loeber, R., Burke, J. D., Lahey, B. B., Winters, A., and Zera, M. (2000). Oppositional defiant and conduct disorder: a review of the past 10 years, Part I. *J. Am. Acad Child Adolesc. Psychiatry, 39*, 1468-1484.

Loeber, R., Burke, J.D., Pardini, D.A. (2009). Development and Etiology of Disruptive and Delinquent Behavior. *Annu Rev Clin Psychol. ANRV372-CP05-13* first posted online on January 20, 2009.

Loeber, R., Wung, P., Keenan, K., Giroux, B., Stouthamer-Loeber, M., Van Kammen, W.B., Maughan, B. (1993). Developmental pathways in disruptive child behavior. *Development and psychopathology, 5*, 101-132.

Lueger, R., and Gill, K. (1990). Frontal-lobe cognitive dysfunction in conduct disorder adolescents. *Journal of Clinical Psychology, 46*, 698-705.

Luria, A. (1980). *Higher cortical functions in man.* New York: Basic Books.

Lynam, D., Moffitt, T., and Stouthamer-Loeber, M. (1993). Explaining the relation between IQ and delinquency: Class, race, test motivation, school failure or self-control? *Journal of Abnormal Psychology, 102*, 187-196.

Lynn, R., Allik, J., Irwing, P. (2004). Sex differences on three factors identified in Raven's Standard Progressive Matrices. *Intelligence, 32*, 411-424.

MacLeod, C.M. (1991). Half a century of research on the Stroop effect: An integrative review. *Psychol. Bull., 109(2)*, 163-203.

MacLeod, C.M., and MacDonald, P.A. (2000). Interdimensional interference in the Stroop effect: uncovering the cognitive and neural anatomy of attention. *Trends in Cognitive Sciences, 4(1),* 383-391.

Mannuzza, S., Klein, R.G., Moulton III, J.L. (2008). Lifetime criminality among boys with attention deficit hyperactivity disorder: a prospective follow-up study into adulthood using official arrest records. *Psychiatry Research, 160*, 237-246.

Marmorstein, N.R. (2006). Adult Antisocial Behaviour Without Conduct Disorder:Demographic Characteristics and Risk for Cooccurring Psychopathology. *Can J Psychiatry, 51(4),* 226-233.

Marmorstein, N.R., Iacono, W.G. (2005). Longitudinal follow-up of adolescents with late-onset antisocial behavior: A pathological yet overlooked group. *J. Am. Acad Child Adolesc Psychiatry, 44(12),* 1284-1291.

McGrew, K.S., and Flanagan, D. (1998). *The intelligence test desk reference.* Boston: Allyn and Bacon.

McGue M., and Iacono, G.I. (2005). The association of early adolescent problem behavior with adult psychopathology. *Am. J. Psychiatry, 162*, 1118-1124.

McNamara, J., Vervaeke, S.L., Willoughby, T. (2008). Leraning disabilities and risk-taking behaviour in adolescents: a comparison of those with and without comorbid attention-deficit/hyperactivity disorder. *J. Learn. Disabil., 41(6),* 561-574.

Milner, B. (1964). Some effects of frontal lobectomy in man. In J. M. Warren and K. Akert (Eds.), *The frontal granular cortex and behavior* (pp. 313–334). New York: McGraw-Hill.

Milner, B. (1995). Aspects of human frontal lobe function. In H. Jasper, S. Riggio, and P. Goldman-Rakic (Eds.), *Epilepsy and the functional anatomy of the frontal lobe* (pp. 67–84). New York: Raven Press.

Moffitt, T. (1993). Adolescence-limited and life-course-persistent antisocial behavior: a developmental taxonomy. *Psychological Review, 100(4),* 674-701.

Moffitt, T. E., and Silva, P. A. (1988). IQ and delinquency: A direct test of the differential detection hypothesis. *Journal of Abnormal Psychology, 97*, 330-333.

Moffitt, T. E., Caspi, A., Dickson, N., Silva, P., and Stanton, W. (1996). Childhood-onset versus adolescent-onset antisocial conduct problems in males: Natural history from ages 3 to 18 years. *Development and Psychopathology, 8*, 399-424.

Moffitt, T. E., Lyman, D. R., and Sylva, P. A. (1994). Neuropsychological tests predicting persistent male delinquency. *Criminology, 2*, 277–300.

Moffitt, T.E. (1990). The neuro-psychology of delinquency: a critical review of theory and research. In: N. Morris, M. Tonry (Eds.). *Crime and justice: an annual review of research, vol. 12.* Chicago: University of Chicago Press, p. 99–169.

Moffitt, T.E., Caspi, A., Harrington, H.L. and Milne, B.J. (2002). Males on the life-course persistent and adolescence limited antisocial pathways: follow-up at 26 years. *Development and psychopathology, 14*, 179– 207.

Morgan, A.B., and Lilienfeld, S.0. (2000). A meta-analytic review of the relation between antisocial behavior and neuropsychological measures of executive function. *Clinical Psychology Review, 20*, 113-136.

Muncie, J. (1999) *Youth and Crime.* London: Sage.

Nagin, D.S., Farrington, D.P., Moffitt, T. (1995). Life-course trajectories of different types of offenders. *Criminology, 29*, 163-190.

Neighbors, B., Kempton, T., and Forehand, R. (1992). Co-occurrence of substance abuse with conduct, anxiety, and depression disorders in juvenile delinquents. *Addictive Behaviors, 17*, 379–386.

Nijmeijer,J.S., Minderaa, R.B., Buitelaar, J.K., Mulligan, A., Hartman, C.A., Hoekstra, P.J. (2008). Attention-deficit/hyperactivity disorder and social dysfunctioning. *Clinical Psychology Review, 28*, 692-708.

Office for Juvenile Justice and Delinquency Prevention. (2000). Juvenile arrest rates. Available online at: ojjdp.ncjrs.org

Oosterlaan, J., Scheres, A., Sergeant, J.A. (2005). Which executive functioning deficits are associated with AD/HD, ODD/CD and comorbid AD/HD+ODD/CD? *Journal of Abnormal Child Psychology, 33(1)*, 69-85.

Pardini, D., Obradović, J., Loeber, R. (2006). Interpersonal callousness, hyperactivity/ impulsivity, inattention, and conduct problems as precursors to delinquency persistence in boys: a comparison of three grade-based cohorts. *J. Clin. Child Adolesc Psychol, 35(1),* 46-59.

Paschall, M.J., Fishbein, D.H. (2002). Executive cognitive functioning and aggression: a public health perspective. *Aggression and Violent Behavior, 7*, 215-235.

Patterson, G.R. (1982). *A social learning approach: Vol. 3. Coercive family processes.* Eugene, OR: Castalia.

Patterson, G.R., DeBaryshe, B.D., Ramsey, E. (1989). A developmental perspective on antisocial behavior. *American Psychologist, 44*, 329-335.

Paulsen, J.S., Romero, R., Chan, A., Davis, A.V., Heaton, R.K., Jeste, D.V. (1996). Impairment of the semantic in schizophrenia. *Psychiatry Research 63*, 109-121.

Pennington, B. F., and Bennetto, L. (1993). Main effects or transactions in the neuropsychology of conduct disorder? Commentary on "The neuropsychology of conduct disorder." *Development and Psychopathology, 5*, 153-164.

Pennington, B. F., and Ozonoff, S. (1996). Executive functions and developmental psychopathology. *Journal of Child Psychology and Psychiatry, 37*, 51-87.

Petrides, M., Alivisatos, B., Evans, A.C., Meyer, E. (1993). Dissociation of human mid-dorsolateral from posterior dorsolateral frontal cortex in memory processing. *Proceedings of the National Academy of Sciences of the United States of America, 90*, 873-877.

Pham, T.H., Vanderstukken, O., Philippot, P., Vanderlinden, M. (2003). Selective Attention and Executive Functions Deficits Among Criminal Psychopaths. *Aggressive Behavior, 29*, 393-405.

Phelps, E. A., Hyder, P., Blamire, A. M., and Shulman, R. G. (1997). fMRl of the prefrontal cortex during overt verbal fluency. *NeuroReport, 8*, 561-565.

Piquero, A.R., White, N.A. (2003). On the relationship between cognitive abilities and lifecourse- persistent offending among a sample of African Americans: A longitudinal test of Moffitt's hypothesis. *Journal of Criminal Justice, 31*, 399-409.

Pliszka, S. R., Sherman, J. O., Barrow, M. V., and Irick, S. (2000). Affective disorder in juvenile offenders: a preliminary study. *American Journal of Psychiatry, 157*, 130-132.

Raine, A. (1993). The psychopathology of crime: criminal behavior as a clinical disorder. San Diego, CA: Academic Press.

Raine, A. (2002). Annotation: the role of prefrontal deficits, low autonomic arousal, and early health factors in the development of antisocial and aggressive behaviour in children. *Journal of Child Psychology and Psychiatry, 43(4)*, 417-434.

Raine, A., Moffitt, T., Caspi, A., Loeber, R., Stouthamer-Loeber, M., and Lynam, D. (2005). Neurocognitive impairment in boys on the life-course persistent antisocial path. *Journal of Abnormal Psychology, 114*, 38-49.

Raven, J.C., Court, J.H., Raven, J. (1992). *Standard Progressive Matrices. 1992 Edition.* Oxford: Oxford Psychologists Press.

Redmond, S.M., and Rice, M.L. (2002). Stability of behavioural ratings of children with SLI. *J Speech Lang Hear Res, 45(1)*, 190-201.

Redondo, S., Sanchez-Meca, J., Garrido, V. (1999). The influence of treatment programmes on the recidivism of juvenile and adult offenders: A European meta-analytic review. *Psychology, Crime and Law, 5*, 251-278.

Reid, J. B., and Patterson, G. R. (1989). The development of antisocial behavior patterns in childhood and adolescence. *European Journal of Personality, 3*, 107-119.

Reiss, A.J., Jr. (1986). Co-offender influences on criminal careers. In A. Blumstein, J. Cohen, J.A. Roth, and C. Visher (Eds.), *Criminal careers and career criminals* (pp. 121-160). Washington, DC: National Academic Press.

Reiss, D., and Neiderhiser, J.M. (2000). The interplay of genetic influences and social processes in developmental theory<. specific mechanisms are coming to view. *Development and Psychopathology, 12*, 357-374.

Rey, J.M., Sawyer, M.G., Prior, M.R. (2005). Similarities and differences between aggressive and delinquent children and adolescents in a national sample. *Australian and New Zealand Journal of Psychiatry, 39*, 366-372.

Ridenour, T.A., Cottler, L.B., Robins, L.N., Compton, W.M., Spitznagel, E.L., Cunningham-Williams, R.M. (2002). Test of the plausibility of adolescent substance use playing a causal role in developing adulthood antisocial behaviour. *J. Abnorm Psychol, 111*, 144-55.

Robbins, T.W. (1996). Dissociating executive functions of the prefrontal cortex. *Philosophical Transactions of the Royal Society of London, 351*, 1463-1470.

Robinson, A.L., Heaton, R.K., Lehman, R.A., Stilson, D.W. (1980). The utility of the Wisconsin Card Sorting Test in detecting and localizing frontal lobe lesions. *Journal of Consulting and Clinical Psychology, 48*, 605-614.

Rösler, M., Retz, W., Yaqoobi, K., Burg, E., Retz-Junginger, P. (2008). Attention deficit/hyperactivity disorder in female offenders: prevalence, psychiatric comorbidity and psychosocial implications. Eur *Arch. Psychiatry Clin. Neurosci, Sep 19*, DOI 10.1007/s00406-008-0841-8.

Ruff, R.M., Light, R.H., Parker, S.B., Levin, H.S. (1997). The Psychological Construct of Word Fluency. *Brain and Language 57*, 394-405.

Rutter, M., Dunn, J., Plomin, R., Simonoff, E., Pickles, A., Maughan, B., Ormel, J., Meyer, J., and Eaves, L. (1997). Integrating nature and nurture: Implications of person-environment correlations and interactions for developmental psychopathology. *Development and Psychopathology, 9*, 335-364.

Sampson, R.J, and Laub, J.H. (1990). Crime and deviance in the life-course. *Annal Review of Sociology, 18*, 63-84.

Séguin, J.R. (2004). Neurocognitive elements of antisocial behavior: Relevance of an orbitofrontal cortex account. *Brain and Cognition, 55*, 185-197.

Séguin, J.R., Boulerice, B., Harden, P.W., Tremblay, R.E., Phil, R. (1999). Executive functions and physical aggression after controlling for attention deficit hyperactivity disorder, general memory, and IQ. *J. Child Psychol. Psychiat., 40(8)*, 1197-1208.

Shimamura, A.P., Jurica, P.J., Mangels, J.A., Gershberg, F.B., Knight, R.T. (1995). Susceptibility to memory interference effects following frontal lobe damage: findings from tests of paired-associate learning. *Journal of Cognitive Neuroscience, 7*, 144-52.

Simonoff, E., Elander, J., Holmshaw, J., Pickles, SA., Murray, R., Rutter, M. (2004). Predictors of antisocial personality. Continuities from childhood to adult life. *British Journal of Psychiatry, 184*, 118-127.

Sourander, A., Elonheimo, H., Niemela, S., Nuutila, A.M., Helenius, H., Sillanmaki, L., Piha, J., Tamminen, T., Kumpulainen, K., Moilenen, I., Almqvist, F. (2006). Childhood predictors of male criminality: a prospective population-based follow-up study from age 8 to late adolescence. *J. Am. Acad Child Adolesc Psychiatry, 45(5)*, 578-586.

Spreen, O. (1989). The relationship between learning disability, emotional disorders, and neuropsychology: some results and observations. *Journal of Clinical and Experimental Neuropsychology, 11*, 117-140.

Stattin, H., and Klackenberg-Larsson, I. (1993). Early language and intelligence development and their relationship to future criminal behavior. *Journal of Abnormal Psychology, 102*, 369-378.

Stuss, D.T., Floden, D., Alexander, M.P., Levine, B., Katz, D. (2001). Stroop performance in focal lesion patients: dissociation of processes and frontal lobe lesion location. *Neuropsychologia, 39*, 771-786.

Taylor E, Chadwick O, Heptinstall E, Danckaerts M. (1996). Hyperactivity and conduct problems as risk factors for adolescent development. *J. Am. Acad Child Adolesc Psychiatry, 35*, 1213-1226.

Taylor, J., Iacono, W. G., and McGue, M. (2000). Evidence for a genetic etiology of early-onset delinquency. *Journal of Abnormal Psychology, 109*, 634-643.

Teasdale, J. and Powell, N. (1987). Youth Workers and Juvenile Justice. in Jeffs, T. and Smith, M. (Eds.) *Youth Work*. London: Macmillan.

Teichner, G., and Golden, C.J. (2000). The relationship of neuropsychological impairment to conduct disorder in adolescence: a conceptual review. *Aggression and Violent Behavior, 5(6),* 509-528.

The Riyadh Guidelines—United Nations Guidelines for the Prevention of Juvenile Delinquency, General Assembly resolution 45/112 of 14 December 1990, http://www.unhchr.ch/html/menu3/b/h_comp47.htm.

Troyer, A.K., Moscovitch, M., Winocur, G. (1997a). Clustering and switching as two components of verbal fluency: evidence from younger and older healthy adults. *Neuropsychology, 11*, 138-46.

Troyer, A.K., Moscovitch, M., Winocur, G., Alexander, M., Stuss, D. (1997b). Clustering and switching on verbal fluency: the effects of focal frontal and temporal-lobe lesions. *Neuropsychologia 36*, 499-504.

Tweed, J.L,, George, L.K., Blazer, D., Swartz, M., MacMillan, J. (1994). Adult onset of severe and pervasive antisocial behaviour: a distinct syndrome? *J Personal Disord, 8*, 192-202.

Ulzen, T. P., and Hamilton, H. (1998). The nature and characteristics of psychiatric comorbidity in incarcerated adolescents. *Canadian Journal of Psychiatry, 43*, 57-63.

U.S. Department of Health and Human Services. (2001). Youth Violence: A Report of the Surgeon General. Rockville, MD: DHHS.

Vermeiren, R. (2003). Psychopathology and delinquency in adolescents: a descriptive and developmental perspective. *Clinical Psychology Review, 23*, 277-318.

Vermeiren, R., De Clippele, A., and Deboutte, D. (2000). A descriptive survey of Flemish delinquent adolescents. *Journal of Adolescence, 23*, 277-285.

Vermeiren, R., Schwab-Stone, M., Ruchkin, V., De Clippele, A., and Deboutte, D. (2002). Predicting recidivism in delinquent adolescents from psychological and psychiatric assessment. *Comprehensive Psychiatry, 43(2)*, 142-149.

Villemarette-Pittman, N.R., Stanford, M.S., Greve, K.W. (2002). Language and executive function in self-reported impulsive aggression. *Personality and Individual Differences, 34*, 1533-1544.

Vreugdenhil, C., Doreleijers, T.A., Vermeiren, R., Wouters, L.F., van den Brink, W. (2004). Psychiatric disorders in a representative sample of incarcerated boys in the Netherlands. *J. Am. Acad Child Adolesc Psychiatry, 43(1)*, 97-104.

Walker, J. L., Lahey, B. B., Russo, M. F., Christ, M. A. G., McBurnett, K., Loeber, R., Stouthamer-Walker, J.L., Lahey, B.B., Hynd, G.W., Frame, C.L. (1987). Comparison of specific patterns of antisocial behavior in children with conduct disorder with or without coexisting hyperactivity. *Journal of Consulting and Clinical Psychology, 55*, 910-913.

West, D. J. (1967). *The Young Offender*. New York: International Universities Press.

Wolff, P. H., Waber, D., Bauermeister, C., Cohen, C., and Ferber, R. (1982). The neuropsychological status of adolescent delinquent boys. *Journal of Child Psychology and Psychiatry, 23*, 267-279.

Yeudall, L.T., Fromm-Auch, D., Davies, P. (1982). Neuropsychological impairment of persistent delinquency. *Journal of Nervous and Mental Disease, 170*, 257-265.

Zelazo, P.D., Carter, A., Reznick, J.S., Frye, D. (1997). Early development of executive function: A problem-solving framework. *Review of General Psychology, 1*, 198-226.

Zoccolillo, M., Pickles, A., Quinton, D., and Rutter, M. (1992). The outcome of childhood conduct disorder: implications for defining adult personality disorder and conduct disorder. *Psychological Medicine, 22*, 971-986.

In: Delinquency: Causes, Reduction and Prevention
Editor: Ozan Sahin and Joseph Maier
ISBN 978-1-60741-558-9

Chapter 4

Understanding the Delinquent Activities and Reputational Orientations of Adolescent Loners and Nonloners

Carol Tan[1], Stephen Houghton[2] and Annemaree Carroll[3]
[1]Nanyang Technological University
National Institute of Education, Singapore
[2]The University of Western Australia
Centre for Child and Adolescent Related Disorders
The Graduate School of Education, Australia
[3]The University of Queensland
School of Education, Australia

Abstract

Reputation enhancement theory is a dominant theory in the juvenile delinquency literature. It has clearly established that a delinquent identity requires public proof of a deviant disposition and that deviant acts are committed not alone, but in the company of others. Therefore, self-image is fostered by the visibility of actions to others, and perceptions and descriptions of oneself and others. If these are key elements on which the psychology of reputation is built, how then does this apply to adolescents who commit delinquent acts, but alone? Very little is known about the delinquent activities and reputational orientations of adolescent loners, yet recent research by the authors clearly shows the unique profiles of these individuals. In this chapter, we present the findings from a series of studies which we believe to be the only ones to date pertaining to the delinquent activities and reputational orientations of loners.

First, the instruments we have developed over time to measure these aspects of adolescents' behavior are briefly described along with their psychometric properties. Following this, we present empirical evidence from our research in which we employed various statistical analyses to compare the self-report delinquency and reputational orientations of adolescent loners and nonloners.

According to the U.S. Department of Justice (Snyder and Sickmund, 2006), 15% of all male arrests and 20% of all female arrests in 2003 involved a person younger than age 18 years. Moreover, when the offending behaviors were analyzed according to whether a juvenile was involved, this was true in 51% of arson arrests, 39% of vandalism arrests, 29% of motor vehicle theft and burglary arrests, 23% of weapons law violation arrests, 12% of drug abuse arrests, and 9% of murder arrests. Similar data are available from different countries. For example, in 2005 the most commonly reported offence categories among young people aged 10-25 in the United Kingdom were assault (committed by 16%), thefts (11%), criminal damage (4%), drug selling offences (4%), vehicle-related thefts (2%), burglary (1%), and robbery (1%). Of the young people who reported committing an offence, approximately 31% had done so in the past 12 months, while 28% had committed two or three offences and about 7% had committed six or more offences (Wilson, Sharp, and Patterson, 2006). In Australia, where the research reported in this chapter was conducted, juveniles most frequently engage in burglary and theft (50.9% of cases), driving offences (16.6%), order offences (9.6%), property damage (5.5%), offences against the person (8.9%), and drug offences (4.6%) (Fernandez and Loh, 2001). With reference to gender, males are much more likely to commit crimes than females, with the male to female ratio for serious juvenile violent crime being approximately four to one in the U.S. (Siegel, Welsh, and Senna, 2006). However, the number of female delinquents has been increasing faster than those for males; arrests of male delinquents having decreased by approximately 22% compared to females increasing by approximately 12%. Australia has also witnessed increases in the percentage of juvenile offenders who are female, from 21% in 1995-96 to 23% in 2003-04 while the rates of male juvenile offending have dropped by 27% since 1995, with a 19% drop in the past three years (Australian Institute of Criminology, 2006). Of particular note is that males are much more likely to commit particularly serious violent crimes than females (Siegel et al., 2006).

In our recent book (see Carroll, Houghton, Durkin, and Hattie, 2009), we present extensive research conducted over the past 15 years in detention centres, primary schools, and high schools in support of the empirical research literature (e.g., Haynie, 2001; Matsueda and Anderson, 1998; Thornberry, Lizotte, Krohn, Farnworth, and Jang, 1994; Warr, 2002) which has postulated that a person's involvement in delinquency is strongly correlated to his/her friends' involvement (see Kreager, 2004). However, not only do we build on this by showing how reputation enhancement theory (Emler, 1984; Emler and Reicher, 1995) has become a dominant theory explaining why young person's indulge (and continue to) in delinquent activities, but we also extend it by integrating goal setting theory to produce our reputation enhancing goals theory (see Carroll et al., 2009). Reputation enhancement theory on which our research is predicated will now be described, albeit briefly.

Reputation Enhancement Theory

Reputation enhancement theory (Emler, 1984) posits that a delinquent identity requires public proof of a deviant disposition; social visibility is therefore an important element which necessitates that deviant acts are not committed alone but in the company of others (Reicher and Emler, 1986). Visibility of actions to others, the audience to whom these actions are visible, and the perceptions and descriptions of ourselves and others which foster our self-image, are key elements on which the psychology of reputation has been built. According to Emler (1984), a peer audience is extremely important because companions, whether in crime or conformity, often generate and facilitate expressions of shared behavioral inclinations. For example, some young people pursue a law-abiding, conforming reputation (represented by attributes such as honesty, responsibility, and law-abidingness) because it is supported and approved by their peer audience. In contrast, others pursue a delinquent, nonconforming reputation, represented by toughness and aggressiveness, because it is supported by their peer audience (Emler, 1984).

Reputation is a complex social phenomenon arising from social processes within a community of individuals which link people to particular social identities. According to reputation enhancement theory (Emler, 1984), a reputation for bad behavior is a deliberate choice made by an individual, the reason for this being that delinquent action creates a tough reputation among outsiders, and also a means of proving one's credentials to the 'ingroup' to sustain one's self-identity (for a review, see Emler and Reicher, 1995). Furthermore, because positions in the group are consistently challenged by others and/or because reputations are jeopardized by incongruent behaviors, delinquents must constantly prove themselves to their delinquent peers by engaging in highly visible delinquent activities, in the presence of an audience (Reicher and Emler, 1986). According to Goodnight, Bates, Newman, Dodge, and Pettit (2006), deviant friend groups provide selective, positive reinforcement for deviant behavior.

In our recent interview-based research with juvenile detention centre personnel, primary and high school teachers and psychologists responsible for children with severe behavior problems, we found that contrary to reputation enhancement theory, some young offenders and mainstream school adolescents involved in delinquent activities appear to achieve a delinquent identity and enhance their reputations among peers by committing delinquent acts but without the presence of an immediate audience. Of the very limited research conducted, these young persons have been referred to as 'loners' (Demuth, 2004) or 'social isolates' (Adler and Adler, 1996). As will become evident in the following section, the nature of delinquent activities among loners is not clear, and there is also a lack of explanation regarding the link between delinquency and reputation in loners.

Adolescent Loners

In a comprehensive review examining the clinical significance of loneliness, Heinrich and Gullone (2006) make no specific mention of *loners*. Rather, the focus is on loneliness *per se*, which is defined as the aversive state experienced when a discrepancy exists between the interpersonal relationships one wishes to have, and those that one perceives they currently have (Peplau and Perlman, 1982). This state of loneliness is not only most prevalent during adolescence, but it also peaks at this time (see Perlman and Landolt, 1999), thus making adolescence a period of high risk for loneliness (Heinrich and Gullone, 2006). According to McWhirter, Besett-Alesch, Horibita, and Gat (2002), for many adolescents, loneliness can lead to even more serious problems, including delinquency.

There is no doubt that some adolescents experience loneliness and become loners. In early research, Parlee (1979) reported 79% of under 18 year olds felt lonely 'sometimes' or 'often'. Similar high figures were found by Culp, Clyman, and Culp (1995) when they asked high school students if they considered loneliness had been a problem during the past 12 months - 66% responded affirmatively. Taken to a more extreme level, Meloy et al. (2004) used the term "loner" in the context of a study of 34 adolescent mass murderers (Mean age = 17 years, range 11 to 19 years) and 30 adult mass murderers (Mean age = 38.3 years, range 19 to 59 years). Of the adolescent sample, 70% were described as "loners", while of the adults 94% were. In this context, there was "a marked tendency not to interact with others and to spend most time alone" (p. 296).

It is during this time of vulnerability (i.e., adolescence) that personal identities also become salient (Erikson, 1968) and are formulated on the basis of physical and psychological characteristics (e.g., beliefs and values) and with respect to social relationships (see Parkhurst and Hopmeyer, 1999). Weiss (1973) referred to "social loneliness" as something that results from the lack of a network of social relationships in which the person is part of a group of friends who share common interests and activities. According to Demuth (2004), loners report significantly greater feelings of isolation from friends, rejection by others, and marginalization within peer networks. It is not surprising therefore that adolescents who are loners perceive themselves in a negative and self-depreciating manner and form the opinions that they are inferior, worthless and unattractive (see Heinrich and Gullone, 2006). Since the research presented here is predicated on an examination of the applicability of reputation enhancement theory to loners, it is particularly worth noting that loners hold greater discrepancies about their actual selves and their ideal selves (i.e., who they would ideally wish to be) than do nonloners (Kuperschmidt, Sigda, Sedikides, and Voegler, 1999). However to date, this has not been investigated with regard to socially conforming and delinquent activities. Similarly, research suggests that loneliness has been linked to diminished levels of self-disclosure. Given that communication about oneself to an audience of delinquent peers is a central tenet on which reputation enhancement theory is built, this may also be an important point for investigation.

With reference to adolescent loners, the nature of their involvement in delinquent activities is unclear. In an investigation of high school adolescents aged 13-17 years, Demuth (2004) found that the 6.5% who were loners were significantly *less* likely to engage in serious public disorder and status offences than nonloners. This was supported by Kreager (2004) who also found that isolates were not necessarily more likely to engage in delinquent activities. Conversely, data from the National Longitudinal Study of Adolescent Health (see Kreager, 2004) revealed isolates who reported having significant trouble with others ('peer troubled isolates') were *more* likely to become involved in delinquent activities and to form delinquent peer associations than isolates who reported having little trouble with others ('invisible isolates').Thus, it appears that the nature of adolescent loners involvement in delinquent activities remains unclear. Furthermore, whether these individuals commit delinquent acts to establish and maintain a desired reputation is also unknown. Anecdotal evidence (Cordin, 2008; Houghton, Cordin, and Hopkins, 2008) suggests that some young offenders and mainstream adolescents do indeed achieve a delinquent identity and enhance their reputations among peers by committing delinquent acts, but without the presence of an audience. The delinquent activities committed by loners (compared to nonloners) remain unknown. Furthermore there is no evidence pertaining to reputation enhancement in loners.

Thus, the applicability of reputation enhancement theory has yet to be established with this population, particularly in terms of how their delinquent activities and reputational orientations differ to those of nonloners. We now describe a series of four sequentially linked studies to investigate these issues.

METHOD

Given the sequential nature of our series of inter-related studies, it is necessary to present each separately. The general procedure for each of the studies was however similar, as was the instrumentation administered. Therefore these two aspects of the research will be described first.

General Procedure

Prior to any of the studies being conducted, permission was obtained from the Human Research and Ethics Committees of the administering institutions. Once approval had been granted, the principals of randomly selected high schools were approached to ascertain their interest in the research and to obtain their permission to undertake the research. In almost all of the schools contacted, the principals agreed and an information sheet explaining the purpose and nature of the research, along with a consent form were sent to the homes of approximately 30 randomly selected students in each class, in each of the schools. In each of the studies reported here, a response rate of between 50% and 75% was obtained.

The various scales, which are described below, were administered to participants in groups of approximately 20 during regular class home room time. Prior to the dissemination of the scales, students were informed about the nature of the study and assured of confidentiality and anonymity. The scales were completed under examination like conditions, without peer discussion. Students who were identified by school personnel as experiencing literacy difficulties were administered the scales in smaller groups of four or five. In these cases, the researcher read the scales aloud verbatim.

In some of our research, data were obtained from young people resident in detention centers. Once approval to conduct the research had been obtained from the Directors of the centers involved, a similar procedure to that undertaken in mainstream schools was followed. That is, the instruments were administered to individuals in small groups of four to six. Where literacy difficulties were clearly evident, the questions were read to the participants. We decided to collect the data in small groups because of the problems frequently encountered in juvenile delinquent populations (e.g., low levels of literacy, emotional disturbances, and other symptoms). Previous research conducted by the authors has demonstrated that when working with detained youth and at-risk adolescents, small groups of between four and six students are most appropriate.

All instrumentation was administered by one of the researchers and a regular class teacher to the mainstream school participants in their regular classrooms. In the juvenile detention centers, however, the education officers undertook this task since they have established trusting relationships with their clients. Prior to the administrations, the institutional staff received verbal instructions in instrument administration and this was followed up with standardized written instructions on each testing session. The classrooms in each of the schools and the institutions were similar in terms of furniture layout. The administration of the instruments was also consistent across administrations. Participants were informed that should they encounter any problems with the questionnaires, they were to raise a hand to obtain support from the person(s) administering the questionnaires. In all of our research studies, the measures took approximately 30 to 60 minutes to complete and were completed under examination like conditions.

Instrumentation

The various instruments were included in one booklet, and administered to participants as follows: the *Adapted Self-report Delinquency Scale* (ASDS; Carroll, Durkin, Houghton, and Hattie, 1996), the *Reputation Enhancement Scale* (RES; Carroll, Houghton, Hattie, and Durkin, 1999), and the *Adolescent Loner Scale* (ALS; Tan and Houghton, 2008). Although these instruments along with their development and psychometric properties will now be described, albeit briefly, it is important to point out that while the ALS is relatively new, the ASDS and RES have undergone a stringent development over three separate, yet inter-related phases. In Phase, I, information pertaining to young persons' delinquent acts and reputational orientations was obtained from the research literature, previously established tests, and from interviews with high school adolescents, incarcerated youths, high school teachers, school psychologists, university researchers, and detention centre personnel to generate items. Duplicate items were subsequently removed from each of the scales and draft versions of the new scales were developed.

In Phase II, these versions were administered to 230 (114 males and 116 females) high school students randomly selected from four metropolitan senior high schools in the large Western Australian capital city of Perth. Of the 230 participants, 46 were aged 12-13 years (22 males and 24 females), 67 were 13-14 years old (36 males and 31 females), 50 were 14-15 years old (23 males and 27 females), and 67 were 15-16 years old (33 males and 34 females). All of the schools (student enrolments ranged from 788 to 1375) were in low to middle socioeconomic status metropolitan regions characterised by high percentages of blue collar workers with low household incomes. Data from the Phase II sample were analysed by maximum-likelihood exploratory factor analysis.

In Phase III, the scales were administered to 260 adolescent males. These were 80 incarcerated delinquents (Mean age = 16.1 years, range 11.6 to 18.1 years), 90 at-risk (Mean age = 14.4 years, range 12.2 to 17.2 years), and 90 not at-risk (Mean age = 14.4 years, range 12.2 to 17.6 years) males. The aim was to assess the extent to which the scales differentiated between delinquents and nondelinquents. At this stage, the findings of the previous Phase II analysis were cross-validated with the item responses of the Phase III participants using MICFA, a first-order, maximum-likelihood confirmatory factor analysis program (Krakowski and Hattie, 1993). To confirm the second-order factor structure, a structural equation modelling approach was used (Jöreskog and Sörbom, 1989). To determine whether our scales could differentiate delinquent, at-risk, and not at-risk adolescents, multivariate analyses of variance (MANOVAs) were then conducted. The estimates of reliability (Cronbach's alpha) were obtained for all subscales. (A full review of the development of these instruments, along with the data from exploratory and confirmatory factor analyses are presented in detail in Carroll et al., 2009.)

The Adapted Self-report Delinquency Scale (ASDS; Carroll et al., 1996) is a self-report scale which originally contained 52 items covering a wide spectrum of frequently occurring delinquent activities (from minor infractions to more serious offences) in Australia, with wording consistent with adolescent usage. Over time six items have been removed (e.g., items asking about police warnings and court appearances) because of the difficulties in verifying them. We have also removed five other items as they did not load on any of the factors (see Carroll et al., 2009). Consequently, a total of 41 items was utilised in much of the research reported here. A higher score on each of the delinquency dimensions (see below) is indicative of a young person engaging in more of those delinquent behaviors.

The most recent factor analysis (Carroll, Houghton, Wood, Perkins, and Bower, 2007) revealed similar consistency of the subscales to that of previous research (Carroll, Green, Houghton, and Wood, 2003; Houghton and Carroll, 2002) along with the following reliability coefficients: abuse of property (seven items), α = .91, hard drug-related offences (five items), α = .89, physical aggression (three items), α = .88, stealing offences (five items), α = 90, school misdemeanours (seven items), α = .86, soft drug use offences (five items), α = .88, and vehicle-related offences (nine items), α = .94.

The Reputation Enhancement Scale (RES; Carroll et al., 1999) is a 150-item self-report scale with five major scales measuring sociability, social desirability, social identity, self-identity, and communication of events. The five scales are: the *Sociability Scale*, which consists of eight items (α = .83) that determine the value participants place on friendship and group membership, and is measured using a six-point scale ranging from 'Strongly agree' to 'Strongly disagree'; the *Social Desirability Scale*, which is made up of 32 items examining admiration of law-abiding and law-breaking activities, the underlying value of reputation, and conformity or deviance to social attitudes; the scale uses a 6-point response format ('Not at all', 'Very little', 'Somewhat', 'Quite a bit', 'Very much', and 'Completely') and consists of four subscales with the following reliability coefficients: Self-perceived social deviance norms, α = .90, self-perceived social conformity norms, α = .81, evaluative reactions to others' social deviance, α =.91, and evaluative reactions to others' social conformity, α = .76; the *Social Identity* Scale, which comprises 30 items measuring participants' self-perception and how they would ideally like others to view them; the scale uses a 6-point scale response format ('Never', 'Hardly ever', 'Occasionally', 'Sometimes', 'Often', and 'Always'), and has four subscales with the following reliability coefficients: nonconforming self-perception, α =.91, conforming self-perception, α = .75, nonconforming ideal public self, α = 91, and conforming ideal public self, α = .82; the *Self Identity Scale*, which is made up of two sets of 12 semantic differentials measuring how participants describe themselves and how they would ideally like to be described in terms of power (e.g., strong-weak, tough-soft) and activity (e.g., mean-kind, nasty-friendly) attributes, and participants rate themselves using a 6-point scale, with semantic differential anchor points ranging from one extreme of a relevant variable (e.g., 'I think I am a leader') to the other extreme (e.g., 'I think I am a follower); the scale has four subscales with the following reliability coefficients: activity self-description, α = .75, power/evaluation self-description, α = .72, activity ideal private self, α =.82, and power/evaluation ideal private self, α = .73; the *Communication of Events Scale*, which consists of 56 items measuring patterns of disclosure of events to adults and/or peers using a 4-point response format of 'Friends', 'Parents', 'Other adults', and 'I would not want anybody to know'; the scale has four subscales with the following reliability coefficients: brag, α =.90, status, α = .91, face, α =.87, and rebel, α = .83.

For the present research, we carried out some modifications to the Social Desirability Scale. The original Social Desirability Scale comprised 32 items measuring admiration of law-abiding and law-breaking activities which reflected the underlying value of reputation, and conformity or nonconformity to social attitudes. Prior to this present research, male participants were only asked about the law-abiding and law-breaking activities of boys (i.e., social desirability items, for example, "If a boy steals, I would admire him" and "If a boy steals, most boys my age would admire him". Conversely, female participants were asked about their admiration for girls who were involved in law-abiding and law-breaking activities, such as, "If a girl obeys her parents, I would admire her" and "If a girl obeys her parents, most girls my age would admire her". In the research reported here, we sought to determine the admiration of members of the same and the opposite gender for the aforementioned activities. That is, all participants were requested to state their admiration for the law-abiding and law-breaking activities of both genders.

The *Adolescent Loner Scale* (ALS; Tan and Houghton, 2008) was originally a 10-item self-report scale developed to measure whether individuals are loners by choice or circumstances. The items on the ALS are based on the conceptual framework of loneliness in youth but were further extended to determine if an individual is a loner by personal choice or as a result of specific consequences such as peer rejection. Participants respond to items on the ALS using a 4-point Likert scale anchored with the descriptors 'Definitely not true' (score 0) to 'Definitely true' (3).

Tan and Houghton (2008) subjected the 10 items of the ALS to maximum likelihood factor analysis with (orthogonal) varimax rotation using SPSS Version 14.0 (SPSS Inc., 2005). Bartlett's test reached statistical significance, $\chi^2 = 438.45$, $df = 45$, $p < .001$, supporting the factorability of the correlation matrix. The Kaiser-Meyer-Olkin's (Kaiser, 1970, 1974) measure of sampling adequacy was also obtained and with a value of .75, exceeded the recommended value of .6, thereby suggesting sufficient common variance among the observed variables for factor analysis. In summary, two subscales comprising a 4-item loner by choice subscale and a 5-item loner by circumstances subscale were formed. The two factor solution explained a total of 51.1% of the variance, with Factor 1 (loner by choice) contributing 28.0% and Factor 2 (loner by circumstances) contributing 12.8%. The scores for the ALS instrument were then calculated for each of the factors, loner by choice and loner by circumstances. Factor scores for the two subscales were also calculated by summing the variables comprising each subscale. The alpha coefficients of the two subscales revealed a high degree of internal consistency for loner by choice (α = .79) and loner by circumstances (α = .74). A moderate positive correlation was also found between the two subscales, $r = .40$, $n = 149$, $p < .001$.

All instrumentation which requires less than four years of schooling to successfully read the instructions and items, was administered by the researchers to the school participants and by detention center education officers to the institutionalized participants in their regular classrooms. The classrooms in each of the schools and detention centers were similar in terms of furniture layout. The administration of the instruments was also consistent across administrations. Participants were informed that should they encounter any problems with the questionnaires, they were to raise a hand to obtain support from the researcher administering the questionnaires. In all research studies, the instruments completed were done so under examination like conditions.

STUDY ONE: SELF-REPORT DELINQUENCY AND REPUTATIONAL ORIENTATIONS OF ADOLESCENT LONERS AND NONLONERS

As this first study has been published elsewhere (Houghton, Carroll, Tan, and Hopkins, 2008), we will present the main findings pertaining to loners and nonloners, and only summarise the main findings regarding gender and age differences.

Participants

A total of 1460 (722 males, 738 females) 13 to 17 year olds were recruited from state government high schools in the capital cities of Brisbane, Queensland, and Perth, Western Australia. Of these young persons, 1328 were high school students and 132 were institutionalized youth. The high school youth came from schools in low to high socio-economic status regions, as determined by indexes defined at the postcode level from the socio-economic indexes for areas within Australia (Australia Bureau of Statistics, 1998). With regards to the institutionalized individuals, these came from the main juvenile detention centers in both of the capital cities. With the population of Queensland being the third largest and Western Australia the fifth largest in Australia, the capital cities of these two states provide a representation of the social and contextual milieus of Australian cities.

To identify any participants as loners we used the Sociability scale of the Reputation Enhancement Scale (Carroll et al., 1999). Individuals were identified as loners if their mean score on the Sociability Scale was 3 or less. To be assigned as a nonloner, an individual's mean score was required to be between 4 and 6. One hundred and thirteen participants (75 males, 38 females) were subsequently classified as loners (Mean age = 15.1 years, $SD = 1.39$) and 1343 (643 males, 700 females) were classified as nonloners (Mean age = 15.0 years, $SD = 1.45$).

Results

Two separate MANOVAs were conducted because scores on the variables of the ASDS are not totally independent of scores on the RES. First, we examined the delinquency variables according to Loner Status (loner, nonloner), Gender (male, female), and Age (13, 14, 15, 16, 17 years). Following this, we explored the effect of loner and nonloner status, gender, and age on the 16 variables of the RES (excluding the Sociability scale). Wilks' criterion was used to evaluate multivariate significance, and univariate F tests were conducted when significant multivariate results were obtained. To control for Type I errors, univariate F values were determined to be significant using Bonferroni-adjusted levels of .007 and .003 for the ASDS and RES variables, respectively. Effect sizes and power estimates were also calculated and Scheffé posthoc comparisons were conducted to explore mean differences.

Self-Report Delinquency

The 2 x 2 x 5 (Loner Status x Gender x Age) between-subjects MANOVA revealed no interaction effects and no main effect for Loner Status, but there were multivariate main effects for Gender [F (7, 1420) = 9.73, $p < .001$, partial $\eta^2 = .05$] and Age [F (28, 5121.31) = 2.99, $p < .001$, partial $\eta^2 = .02$]. Using the Bonferroni adjusted level, all seven types of delinquent activity reached statistical significance. What this showed was that males scored significantly higher than females on all delinquent activities.

With reference to Age, a significant difference was found for only soft drug use offences [F (4, 1426) = 4.48, $p < .002$, partial $\eta^2 = .01$] using a Bonferroni adjusted alpha level of .007. For soft drug use offences, Scheffé post-hoc results demonstrated that, with the exception of 14 year olds, 13 year old students reported significantly lower usage (M = 1.63, SD = 1.10) compared to their 15 (M = 2.22, SD = 1.46), 16 (M = 2.52, SD = 1.44), and 17 (M = 2.81, SD = 1.52) year old counterparts. There was generally an increase in soft drug use with age.

Reputation Enhancement

The 2 x 2 x 5 (Loner Status x Gender x Age) between-subjects MANOVA revealed no significant interaction effects but multivariate main effects for Loner Status [F (16, 1337) = 9.63, $p < .001$, partial $\eta^2 = .10$], Gender [F (16, 1337) = 10.35, $p < .001$, partial $\eta^2 = .11$], and Age [F (64, 5236.40) = 1.40, $p < .03$, partial $\eta^2 = .02$]. For Loner Status, using a Bonferroni adjusted alpha level of .003, the results of the univariate F tests (presented in Table 1) revealed significant differences on 11 of the 16 reputation enhancement variables. Nonloners scored significantly higher than loners on self-perceived social conformity norms, evaluative reactions to others social deviance, evaluative reactions to others social conformity, conforming self-perception, conforming ideal public self, activity self-description, power/evaluation self-description, activity ideal private self, power/evaluation ideal private self, and brag. Conversely, loners scored significantly higher than nonloners only on the face variable.

The univariate F tests and observed means for the main effect of Gender, demonstrated 11 of the 16 reputation enhancement variables differed at the .003 alpha level. Males reported significantly higher scores compared to females on five of the reputation enhancement variables, namely, self-perceived social deviance norms, nonconforming self-perception, nonconforming ideal public self, power/evaluation self-description, and face. Females, on the other hand, obtained significantly higher scores than males on six of the reputation enhancement variables of self-perceived social conformity norms, evaluative reactions to others social conformity, conforming self-perception, conforming ideal public self, activity self-description, and activity ideal private self. In general, females strived for a more socially acceptable reputation compared to their male peers.

The univariate F tests for the main effect of Age at a Bonferroni adjusted alpha level of .003 was significant for only one of the 16 reputation enhancement variables, the face variable [F (4, 1352) = 4.45, $p < .002$, partial $\eta^2 = .01$]. Scheffé post-hoc comparisons indicated no significant differences but the mean score for 14 year olds was highest compared to the other age groups.

Table 1. Univariate *F* Statistics, Observed Means, and Standard Deviations for the Reputation Enhancement Variables (df =1, 1352) with Loner Status (Loner vs. Nonloner) as the Independent Variable

						Loner		Nonloner	
Dependent variable	Mean square	*F*	*p*	Partial η^2	Power estimate	*M*	*SD*	*M*	*SD*
Self-perceived social deviance norms	.85	.96	.327	.001	.17	1.90	1.15	1.91	.94
Self-perceived social conformity norms	32.51	33.43	<.001	.024	1.00	2.76_a	1.05	3.53_b	1.02
Evaluative reactions to others social deviance	10.76	8.45	<.005	.006	.83	2.61_a	1.18	2.90_b	1.14
Evaluative reactions to others social conformity	10.63	13.32	<.001	.010	.95	2.91_a	1.04	3.43_b	.93
Nonconforming self-perception	.43	1.63	.515	.001	.25	2.53	1.45	2.18	1.07
Conforming self-perception	56.13	92.61	<.001	.064	1.00	3.55_a	1.11	4.45_b	.76
Nonconforming ideal public self	1.80	.42	.202	.000	.10	2.20	1.39	1.98	1.01
Conforming ideal public self	57.59	78.42	<.001	.055	1.00	3.85_a	1.38	4.82_b	.82
Activity self-description	16.37	24.88	<.001	.018	1.00	4.00_a	1.14	4.55_b	.80
Power/evaluation self-description	11.13	18.00	<.001	.013	.99	3.50_a	.81	3.83_b	.80
Activity ideal private self	13.09	20.62	<.001	.015	1.00	4.72_a	1.12	5.27_b	.79
Power/evaluation ideal private self	14.16	23.39	<.001	.017	1.00	4.48_a	1.00	4.90_b	.77
Brag	.86	10.36	<.002	.008	.90	$.24_a$	.29	$.35_b$	.29
Status	.31	2.93	.087	.002	.40	.35	.30	.40	.33
Face	.92	27.12	<.001	.020	1.00	$.24_a$	.30	$.12_b$	.18
Rebel	.12	5.19	.023	.004	.62	.14	.21	.09	.15

Note. Means within rows having no common subscripts differ at $p < .003$.

In summary, this initial research revealed significant differences in the reputational orientations of adolescent loners compared to nonloners. No significant differences were evident, however, in the delinquent activities of these two groups of adolescents. Nonetheless, because the trends for delinquent activities clearly indicated that loners reported higher levels of involvement, we suspected that the relatively small number of loners (n = 113) compared to the large numbers of nonloners (n = 1343) may have unduly affected the results. Therefore, to address this, we conducted a more stringent examination using a matched sample of 98 pairs of loners and nonloners. This is now reported.

Study Two: Establishing Differences In The Delinquent Activities And Reputational Orientations Of Adolescent Loners And Nonloners Using A Matched Sample

Method

Participants

Using the Sociability Scale of the RES, the subset of 113 participants who were identified as loners (75 male and 38 female, 13 to 17 years) in Study One were matched with nonloners whose chronological age was within five months. Due to missing data on the ASDS and the RES, however, 15 of the 113 could not be matched. The matching procedure thus resulted in a sample of 98 pairs (62 boys and 36 girls in each of the groups) whose mean ages were as follows: loners Mean = 15.1 years, SD = 1.40 and nonloners Mean = 15.1 years, SD = 1.41.

The settings, measures, and procedures for this matched sample study were identical to that of the first study because the sample was drawn from this larger dataset.

Results

As in the first study, the independent variables for the MANOVAs were Loner Status (loner, matched nonloner), Gender (male, female), and Age (13, 14, 15, 16, 17). The Wilks' criterion was used to evaluate the multivariate results and univariate F tests were examined when there were significant multivariate effects. Univariate F values were determined to be significant at Bonferroni adjusted alpha levels of .007 and .003 for the self-report delinquency and reputation enhancement variables, respectively. Effect sizes and power estimates are reported.

Self-Report Delinquency

A between-subjects MANOVA 2 × 2 × 5 (Loner Status × Gender × Age) revealed no interaction effects. There were, however, multivariate main effects for Loner Status [F (7, 170) = 2.08, $p < .05$, partial $\eta^2 = .08$], Gender [F (7, 170) = 2.66, $p < .02$, partial $\eta^2 = .09$], and Age [F (28, 614.37) = 1.56, $p < .05$, partial $\eta^2 = .06$]. For the main effect of Loner Status, the follow-up univariate *F* tests revealed significant differences for physical aggression [F (1, 176) = 8.11, $p < .004$, partial $\eta^2 = .04$], stealing offences [F (7, 176) = 7.56, $p < .006$, partial $\eta^2 = .04$], and vehicle-related offences [F (7, 176) = 7.83, $p < .005$, partial $\eta^2 = .04$]. Mean scores revealed that loners (physical aggression M = 1.81, SD = 1.29; stealing offences M = 1.84, SD = 1.29; and vehicle-related offences M = 1.67, SD = 1.24) reported higher involvement than their matched nonloners (M = 1.33, SD = .71; M = 1.33, SD = .74; and M = 1.21, SD = .60) respectively, on these (See Table 2).

For Gender, univariate *F* tests and observed means revealed that males reported significantly higher involvement than females for hard drug-related offences, physical aggression, stealing offences, school misdemeanours, soft drug use, and vehicle-related offences. There was no significant difference for abuse of property. While there was a significant multivariate main effect for Age, the follow-up univariate *F* tests indicated no significant differences among the five age groups for any of the seven self-report delinquency variables.

Reputation Enhancement

A 2 x 2 x 5 (Loner Status x Gender x Age) MANOVA revealed significant main effects for Loner Status [F (16, 161) = 3.60, $p < .001$, partial $\eta^2 = .26$] and Gender [F (16, 161) = 4.22, $p < .001$, partial $\eta^2 = .30$]. No significant interaction effects and no main effect were evident for Age.

As shown in Table 3, for the main effect of Loner Status the follow-up univariate *F* tests revealed indicated significant effects for four of the 16 reputation variables: self-perceived social conformity norms [F (1, 176) = 23.62, $p < .001$, partial $\eta^2 = .12$]; evaluative reactions to others social conformity [F (1, 176) = 10.20, $p < .003$, partial $\eta^2 = .06$]; conforming self-perception [F (1, 176) = 31.96, $p < .001$, partial $\eta^2 = .15$]; and conforming ideal public self [F (1, 176) = 26.06, $p < .001$, partial $\eta^2 = .13$]. Loners scored lower on self-perceived social conformity norms (M = 2.75, SD = 1.04), evaluative reactions to others social conformity (M = 2.90, SD = 1.05), conforming self-perception (M = 3.54, SD = 1.12), and conforming ideal public self (M = 3.88, SD = 1.36) than nonloners (M = 3.53, SD = 1.09; M = 3.37, SD = 1.01; M = 4.43, SD = .79; and M = 4.83, SD = .77) respectively, on these four reputation enhancement variables.

For the main effect of Gender, univariate *F* tests demonstrated significant differences for four of the 16 reputation enhancement variables: self-perceived social conformity norms [F (1, 176) = 24.58, $p < .001$, partial $\eta^2 = .12$]; evaluative reactions to others social conformity [F (1, 176) = 32.91, $p < .001$, partial $\eta^2 = .06$]; nonconforming self-perception [F (1, 176) = 17.57, $p < .001$, partial $\eta^2 = .09$]; and conforming ideal public self [F (1, 176) = 10.76, $p < .002$, partial $\eta^2 = .06$]. Mean scores indicated that males reported higher levels of nonconforming self-perception than females (M = 2.56, SD = 1.30 vs. M = 1.80, SD = .73). Conversely, females reported higher levels than males for self-perceived social conformity norms (M = 3.63, SD = .99 vs. M = 2.85, SD = 1.11), evaluative reactions to others social conformity (M = 3.68, SD = .89 vs. M = 2.82, SD = 1.02), and conforming ideal public self (M = 4.72, SD = .80 vs. M = 4.15, SD = 1.34).

Table 2. Univariate *F* Statistics, Observed Means, and Standard Deviations for the Self-Report Delinquency Variables (df =1, 176) with Loner Status (Loner vs. Matched Nonloner) as the Independent Variable

						Loner		Matched Nonloner	
Dependent variable	Mean square	F	p	Partial η^2	Power estimate	M	SD	M	SD
Abuse of property	5.87	5.97	.02	.033	.68	1.73	1.24	1.31	.73
Hard drug-related offences	2.22	2.26	.13	.013	.32	1.51	1.17	1.22	.79
Physical aggression	8.11	8.11	<.004	.044	.81	1.81_a	1.29	1.33_b	.71
Stealing offences	8.19	7.56	<.006	.041	.78	1.84_a	1.29	1.33_b	.74
School misdemeanours	.12	.07	.79	.000	.06	3.28	1.50	3.19	1.21
Soft drug use offences	6.48	3.67	.06	.020	.48	2.41	1.50	1.93	1.24
Vehicle-related offences	7.18	7.83	<.005	.043	.80	1.67_a	1.24	1.21_b	.60

Note. Means within rows having no common subscripts differ at $p < .007$.

Table 3. Univariate *F* statistics, observed means, and standard deviations for the reputation enhancement variables (df =1, 176) with Loner Status (Loner vs. Matched Nonloner) as the Independent Variable

						Loner		Matched Nonloner	
Dependent variable	Mean square	F	p	Partial η^2	Power estimate	M	SD	M	SD
Self-perceived social deviance norms	.02	.02	.882	.000	.05	1.88	1.08	1.88	.83
Self-perceived social conformity norms	24.17	23.62	<.001	.118	1.00	2.75_a	1.04	3.53_b	1.09
Evaluative reactions to others social deviance	11.08	8.70	.005	.047	.84	2.59	1.15	3.02	1.10
Evaluative reactions to others social conformity	9.57	10.20	<.003	.055	.89	2.90_a	1.05	3.37_b	1.01
Nonconforming self-perception	3.28	2.61	.108	.015	.36	2.46	1.43	2.10	.83
Conforming self-perception	30.01	31.96	<.001	.154	1.00	3.54_a	1.12	4.43_b	.79
Nonconforming ideal public self	1.16	.93	.337	.005	.16	2.17	1.36	1.91	.87
Conforming ideal public self	29.71	26.06	<.001	.129	1.00	3.88_a	1.36	4.83_b	.77
Activity self-description	6.66	6.81	.020	.037	.74	4.05	1.11	4.50	.86
Power/evaluation self-description	1.88	2.62	.107	.015	.36	3.55	.88	3.76	.81
Activity ideal private self	7.67	9.25	.004	.050	.86	4.78	1.08	5.29	.79
Power/evaluation ideal private self	7.15	8.98	.004	.049	.85	4.46	.99	4.89	.76
Brag	.26	3.15	.078	.018	.42	.25	.29	.35	.28
Status	.03	.33	.568	.002	.09	.37	.31	.40	.32
Face	.28	5.17	.030	.029	.62	.22	.28	.12	.19
Rebel	.20	5.93	.020	.033	.68	.15	.21	.09	.14

Note. Means within rows having no common subscripts differ at $p < .003$.

In summary, this more stringent examination revealed that adolescent loners reported significantly higher levels of involvement in physical aggression, stealing offences, and vehicle-related offences than their matched nonloners. With reference to reputational orientations, adolescent loners scored significantly lower on self-perceived social conformity norms, evaluative reactions to others social conformity, conforming self-perception, and conforming ideal public self, than non loners. This suggests that loners have less admiration for others who indulge in socially conforming activities, believe peers of their age also express the same belief, and they believe that others do not view them as conforming and ideally wish to be seen in this way.

During this research, we noted that different categories of loners and nonloners appeared to exist. For example, there were young persons who committed delinquent activities alone (loner delinquents), those who did so but in the company of others (nonloner delinquents), and there were also young persons who had no friends and who committed no acts of delinquency (loner nondelinquents), and there were others who had friends and did not commit delinquent acts (nonloner nondelinquents). We deemed it important to investigate the differences in delinquent activities and reputational orientations that may exist between these groups. The findings from our investigation are now presented.

Study Three: Loner Delinquents, Nonloner Delinquents and Nonloner Nondelinquents

Method

In our first research studies, we investigated the delinquent activities and reputational orientations of loners and nonloners. This loner/nonloner dichotomy provided valuable information. However, we continue examining the delinquent activities and reputational orientations of loners and nonloners in this section, but we do so according to the following four categories: *loner delinquents*, *nonloner delinquents*, *loner nondelinquents*, and *nonloner nondelinquents*. To achieve this, we established cutoff scores for the ALS to differentiate individuals with elevated levels of loneliness. Initially, frequency distributions and the normal distribution curves were generated with the ALS subscales (loner by choice and loner by circumstances). A visual examination revealed positively skewed distributions for both subscales. Specifically, for each subscale, the mass of the distribution was concentrated on the left portion of the figure, with a longer tapering tail to the right. This form of distribution where fewer participants scored higher on the subscales was anticipated given that a small proportion of the sample was expected to be loners. Next, cut off scores were estimated using the descriptive statistics for the ALS subscales. In this instance, a criterion of one standard deviation above the mean score was utilised to estimate the cut off scores for the loner by choice ($M = 2.38$, $SD = 2.79$) and loner by circumstances ($M = 3.56$, $SD = 3.01$) subscales which corresponded to scores of 5.17 and 6.57, respectively. Based on these cut off scores, 12 (8.1%) participants were identified as loners by choice only and 13 (8.7%) participants as loners by circumstances only. Ten participants (6.7%) had elevated scores in both ALS subscales and these were identified as loners both by choice and circumstances. As the sample sizes of the two ALS subscales were relatively small and inadequate for subsequent statistical analyses, they were merged with loners both by choice and circumstances ($n = 10$) to form a Loner group of $N = 35$. This represented 23.5% of our total sample of 149, which is described fully below.

Participants and Settings

We recruited 149 high school aged adolescents, some of whom had been suspended from school and/or had official records for antisocial behavior, from four separate high schools and one Restorative Education Project (REP; an in-school support unit providing specialised school intervention programmes for suspended students with severe behavioral difficulties) in the metropolitan area of the Western Australian capital city of Perth. The schools were spread across different socioeconomic status areas, with two being in low-status areas, one in a low to middle status area and one in a high status area, as indexed by their postal codes from the socio-economic indexes for areas within Western Australia (Australian Bureau of Statistics, 2003). Consequently our sample was represented by two groups, namely individuals presenting with antisocial behavior and individuals with no records of antisocial behavior or behavioral problems.

Antisocial Behavior Group

This group contained 73 participants (49% of the total sample), ranging in age from 11.8 to 18.5 years (Mean age = 14.6 years, $SD = 1.4$) of which 41 were males and 32 were females. All had school records documenting their involvement in antisocial behavior which ranged from repetitive school misdemeanors and general disruptiveness in classrooms and around the school through to physical and verbal assaults of teachers and/or peers. Using the cut off scores described earlier, 24 participants in this group were classified as *loner delinquents* and 49 as *nonloner delinquents*.

Community Comparison Group

This group comprised 77 adolescents (39 males and 38 females) ranging in age from 11.8 to 17.4 years (Mean age = 13.9 years, $SD = 1.5$) recruited from the same schools as the Antisocial Behavior Group. No participants in this group were recruited from the REP and none had official records showing suspension, antisocial behavior or behavioral problems during their time at school. Using the cut off scores described earlier 11 were classified as *loner nondelinquents* and 65 were *nonloner nondelinquents*. The loner/nonloner, delinquent/nondelinquent status data are shown in Figure 1.

Results

Two separate one way between-groups MANOVAs were conducted using SPSS version 14.0 (SPSS Inc., 2005) to determine whether there were significant group differences in terms of delinquent activities and reputational orientations. Of the four levels within the independent variable, Loner-Delinquent Group, only three levels (loner delinquents, nonloner delinquents, and nonloner nondelinquents) were utilised in this phase. The fourth level, loner nondelinquents, was excluded from the MANOVA due to small cell size ($n = 11$) which was inadequate for inclusion in the MANOVA.

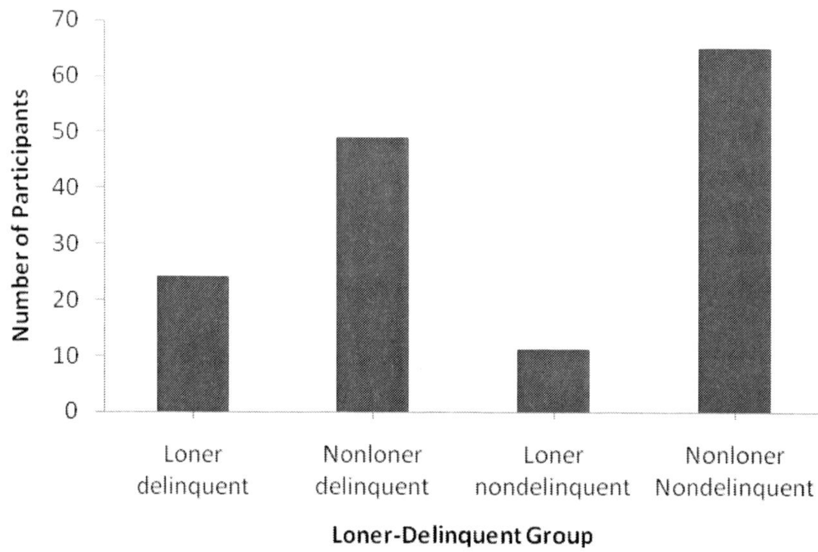

Figure 1. Frequency distribution for Loner-Delinquent Group.

The Pillai's Trace criterion was used to evaluate multivariate significance with an alpha level of .05 and below given its robustness when sample sizes are unequal and the assumption of homogeneity of variance-covariance matrices is violated, as reflected in the two MANOVAs (Tabachnick and Fidell, 2007). Follow-up univariate F tests were conducted where multivariate results were significant. Univariate F values were considered as significant utilising more stringent Bonferroni-adjusted alpha levels of .007 and .003 for the ASDS and RES variables respectively to control for inflated Type 1 errors due to multiple testing (Tabachnick and Fidell, 2007). In addition, effect sizes and power estimates are reported. Pairwise Scheffé post hoc comparisons were also conducted to examine mean differences.

Group Differences in Delinquent Activities

When we investigated the Loner-Delinquent Group differences, there was a multivariate main effect, F (8, 258) = 2.40, $p < .02$; Pillai's Trace = .14; partial $\eta^2 = .07$. As can be seen in Table 4, follow-up univariate F tests indicated that all seven delinquent activities were statistically significant, using a Bonferroni adjusted alpha level of .007: abuse of property, F (2, 131) = 9.70, $p < .001$, partial $\eta^2 = .13$; hard drug-related offences, F (2, 131) = 10.13, $p < .001$, partial $\eta^2 = .13$; physical aggression, F (2, 131) = 8.71, $p < .001$, partial $\eta^2 = .12$; stealing offences, F (2, 131) = 12.09, $p < .001$, partial $\eta^2 = .16$; school misdemeanours, F (2, 131) = 9.08, $p < .001$, partial $\eta^2 = .12$; soft drug use offences F (2, 131) = 11.65, $p < .001$, partial $\eta^2 = .15$; and vehicle-related offences, F (2, 131) = 6.94, $p < .002$, partial $\eta^2 = .10$.

Table 4. Univariate *F* Statistics, Observed Means, and Standard Deviations for the Adapted Self-Report Delinquency Variables (df=2, 131) with Group (Loner delinquent, Nonloner delinquent, Nonloner nondelinquent) as the Independent Variable

						Loner Delinquent		Nonloner Delinquent		Nonloner Nondelinquent	
Dependent variable	Mean square	F	p	Partial η^2	Power estimate	M	SD	M	SD	M	SD
Abuse of property	4.21	9.70	$< .001$	.129	.98	1.93_{ab}	1.02	1.62_{abc}	.72	1.26_{bc}	.39
Hard drug-related offences	1.97	10.13	$< .001$	.134	.98	1.51_{a}	.96	1.13_{bc}	.30	1.03_{bc}	.13
Physical aggression	6.61	8.71	$< .001$	.117	.97	2.10_{ab}	1.34	1.69_{abc}	.94	1.26_{bc}	.55
Stealing offences	4.74	12.09	$< .001$	.156	.99	2.00_{ab}	1.04	1.51_{abc}	.66	1.25_{bc}	.34
School misdemeanours	15.76	9.08	$< .001$	.122	.97	3.70_{ab}	1.55	3.37_{ab}	1.45	2.53_{c}	1.11
Soft drug use offences	10.82	11.65	$< .001$	.151	.99	2.30_{ab}	1.21	2.11_{ab}	1.08	1.38_{c}	.75
Vehicle-related offences	1.86	6.94	$< .002$	.096	.92	1.58_{ab}	.93	1.29_{abc}	.51	1.11_{bc}	.26

Note. Means within rows having no common subscripts differ at $p < .007$.

Scheffé post hoc comparisons indicated that the mean scores of loner delinquents were higher than the mean scores of nonloner nondelinquents on all seven delinquent activities: abuse of property (M = 1.93, SD = 1.02 vs. M = 1.26, SD = .39); hard drug-related offences (M = 1.51, SD = .96 vs. M = 1.03, SD = .13); physical aggression (M = 2.10, SD = 1.34 vs. M = 1.26, SD = .55); stealing offences (M = 2.00, SD = 1.04 vs. M = 1.25, SD = .34); school misdemeanours (M = 3.70, SD = 1.55 vs. M = 2.53, SD = 1.11); soft drug use offences (M = 2.30, SD = 1.21 vs. M = 1.38, SD = .75); and vehicle-related offences (M = 1.58, SD = .93 vs. M = 1.11, SD = .26).

In addition, nonloner delinquents reported significantly higher levels than nonloner nondelinquents on two of the seven delinquent activities, namely, school misdemeanours (M = 3.37, SD = 1.45 vs. M = 2.53, SD = 1.11) and soft drug use offences (M = 2.11, SD = 1.08 vs. M = 1.38, SD = .75). Of particular note was that loner delinquents reported significantly higher levels of hard drug-related offences (M = 1.51, SD = .96) than nonloner delinquents (M = 1.13, SD = .30).

Group Differences in Reputational Orientations

A one way MANOVA established a significant multivariate main effect of Loner-Delinquent Group, F (40, 192) = 2.39, $p < .001$; Pillai's Trace = .67; partial $\eta^2 = .33$ on the reputation enhancement variables.

As shown in Table 5, follow-up univariate F tests utilising a Bonferroni adjusted alpha level of .003 revealed nine reputation enhancement variables reached statistical significance: boy's self-perceived social deviance norms, F (2, 114) = 8.63, $p < .001$, partial $\eta^2 = .13$; boy's evaluative reactions to others social deviance, F (2, 114) = 10.29, $p < .001$, partial $\eta^2 = .15$; girl's evaluative reactions to others social deviance, F (2, 114) = 16.42, $p < .001$, partial $\eta^2 =$ .24; conforming self-perception, F (2, 114) = 6.10, $p = .003$, partial $\eta^2 = .10$; nonconforming self-perception, F (2, 114) = 10.84, $p < .001$, partial $\eta^2 = .16$; nonconforming ideal public self, F (2, 114) = 10.31, $p < .001$, partial $\eta^2 = .15$; activity self-description, F (2, 114) = 11.69, $p <$ .001, partial $\eta^2 = .17$; activity ideal private self, F (2, 114) = 9.46, $p < .001$, partial $\eta^2 = .14$; and face, F (2, 114) = 5.99, $p = .003$, partial $\eta^2 = .10$.

Scheffé post hoc comparisons indicated loner delinquents scored significantly higher than nonloner nondelinquents on five reputation enhancement variables, namely, boy's evaluative reactions to others social deviance (M = 3.19, SD = 1.27 vs. M = 2.17, SD = .99), girl's evaluative reactions to others social deviance (M = 3.11, SD = 1.33 vs. M = 1.86, SD = .72), nonconforming self-perception (M = 2.92, SD = 1.33 vs. M = 1.93, SD = .76), nonconforming ideal public self (M = 2.74, SD = 1.24 vs. M = 1.93, SD = .76) and face (M = .29, SD = .35 vs. M = .09, SD = .13). Loner delinquents, however, scored significantly lower than nonloner nondelinquents on conforming self-perception (M = 3.81, SD = 1.28 vs. M = 4.59, SD = .60), activity self-description (M = 3.55, SD = 1.13 vs. M = 4.66, SD = .80) and activity ideal private self (M = 4.33, SD = 1.21 vs. M = 5.37, SD = .74).

Table 5. Univariate F Statistics, Observed Means, and Standard Deviations for the Reputation Enhancement Variables (df =2, 114) with Group (Loner delinquent, Nonloner delinquent, Nonloner nondelinquent) as the Independent Variable

						Loner Delinquent		Nonloner Delinquent		Nonloner Nondelinquent	
Dependent variable	Mean square	F	p	Partial η^2	Power estimate	M	SD	M	SD	M	SD
Boy's self-perceived social deviance norms	5.84	8.63	<.001	.131	.96	1.98_{abc}	.99	2.22_{ab}	1.06	1.53_{ac}	.51
Boy's self-perceived social conformity norms	2.03	1.54	.22	.026	.32	3.55	1.27	3.68	1.25	3.28	1.03
Boy's evaluative reactions to others social deviance	12.50	10.29	<.001	.153	.99	3.19_{ab}	1.27	3.05_{ab}	1.17	2.17_{c}	.99
Boy's evaluative reactions to others social conformity	3.14	2.96	.06	.049	.57	3.57	1.17	3.27	1.06	2.95	.96
Girl's self-perceived social deviance norms	2.94	5.67	.004	.090	.85	1.91	.91	1.99	.86	1.52	.52
Girl's self-perceived social conformity norms	2.47	2.02	.14	.034	.41	3.56	1.04	3.80	1.23	3.35	1.04
Girl's evaluative reactions to others social deviance	15.32	16.42	<.001	.224	1.00	3.11_{ab}	1.33	2.74_{ab}	1.08	1.86_{c}	.72
Girl's evaluative reactions to others social conformity	3.08	2.77	.07	.046	.54	3.68	1.01	3.59	1.05	3.16	1.07
Conforming self-perception	4.27	6.10	<.004	.097	.88	3.81_{ab}	1.28	4.48_{abc}	.89	4.59_{bc}	.60
Nonconforming self-perception	10.23	10.84	<.001	.160	.99	2.92_{ab}	1.33	2.68_{ab}	1.06	1.93_{c}	.76
Conforming ideal public self	4.26	5.12	.01	.082	.81	4.10	1.37	4.72	.97	4.88	.66
Nonconforming ideal public self	7.98	10.31	<.001	.153	.99	2.74_{ab}	1.24	2.35_{abc}	.99	1.77_{bc}	.64
Activity self-description	9.04	11.69	<.001	.170	.99	3.55_{ab}	1.13	4.19_{abc}	.87	4.66_{bc}	.80
Activity ideal private self	7.40	9.46	<.001	.142	.98	4.33_{ab}	1.21	5.18_{abc}	.91	5.37_{bc}	.74
Power/evaluation self-description	1.27	2.04	.13	.035	.41	3.60	.65	4.05	.85	3.87	.78
Power/evaluation ideal private self	2.03	2.94	.06	.049	.56	4.44	1.03	5.00	.81	4.85	.78
Brag	.38	4.10	.02	.067	.72	.25	.31	.45	.32	.48	.29
Status	.04	.42	.66	.007	.12	.38	.32	.46	.30	.41	.32
Face	.26	5.99	<.004	.095	.87	$.29_{ab}$	.35	$.14_{abc}$	.23	$.09_{bc}$	.13
Rebel	.03	.60	.55	.010	.15	.17	.25	.16	.26	.12	.18

Note. Means within rows having no common subscripts differ at $p < .003$.

In comparison, nonloner delinquents obtained significantly higher mean scores on boy's self-perceived social deviance norms, M = 2.22, SD = 1.06; boy's evaluative reactions to others social deviance, M = 3.05, SD = 1.17; girl's evaluative reactions to others social deviance$M$ = 2.74, SD = 1.08; and nonconforming self-perception, M = 2.68, SD = 1.06 than nonloner nondelinquents (M = 1.53, SD = .51; M = 2.17, SD = .99; M = 1.86, SD = .72; and M = 1.93, SD = .76, respectively). Although it did not reach statistical significance, nonloner delinquents (M = 5.18, SD = .91) reported a higher mean score than loner delinquents (M = 4.33, SD = 1.21) for activity ideal private self (p = .004).

Summary

As expected loner delinquents committed more of all delinquent acts than their nonloner nondelinquent counterparts. In addition, nonloner delinquents were more involved in school misdemeanours and soft drug use offences than nonloner nondelinquents. What separated the loner delinquents from the nonloner delinquents was their greater involvement in hard drug-related offences. With reference to reputation, loner delinquents (compared to nonloner nondelinquents) perceived peers of their age admired boys involved in socially deviant activities, but conversely believed these same peers also admired girls involved in socially *conforming* acts. These loner delinquents believe that others do not view them as conforming, ideally wish to be seen in this way, and they do not communicate positive things to anyone. They also describe themselves as delinquent and ideally wish to be seen by others in this way.

In comparison to nonloner nondelinquents, nonloner delinquents expressed greater levels of admiration towards (and believed peers of their age to have the same opinion) boys who committed socially deviant acts. They also perceived that their peers admired girls involved in socially *conforming* activities. Finally, they were of the opinion that others saw them as nonconforming individuals.

Given these encouraging findings, we decided to add the fourth group to our research, namely loner nondelinquents, so that a greater level of comparison could be undertaken. This is now reported.

Study Four: Loner Delinquents, Nonloner Delinquents, Loner nondelinquent, and Nonloner Nondelinquents

Method

In an attempt to further understand the delinquent activities and reputations of loners compared to nonloners, we generated the fourth level of the Loner-Delinquent Group, that is, loner nondelinquent (LND; n = 11). This subset of LND (four males and seven females, 12.5 to 15.0 years) was then closely matched to participants in the loner delinquents (LD), nonloner delinquents (NLD), and nonloner nondelinquents (NLND) groups on gender and chronological age (within 10 months). This matching procedure yielded quadruple sets of 11 participants for each group with mean ages for the LD, LND, NLD, and NLND groups of 13.9 years (SD =.72), 13.7 years (SD =.89), 13.9 years (SD =.75) and 13.7 years (SD = .83), respectively. This permitted us to carry out some preliminary analyses to test if the LND group was different from the other three levels of the Loner-Delinquent Group (LD, NLD, NLND).

According to Hair, Black, Babin, Anderson, and Tatham (2006), the *t*-test assesses the statistically significant difference between two independent sample means for a single dependent variable, and works with small group sizes. Given that there were four levels of the independent variable, Loner-Delinquent Group, there were a total of six different combinations of independent sample means for comparison: LD vs. LND, LD vs.NLD, LD vs.NLND, LND vs.NLD, LND vs.NLND, and NLD vs.NLND. In addition, there were a total of 27 dependent variables (seven ASDS variables and 20 RES variables). In this instance, for each of the six combinations of independent sample means, independent-sample *t*-tests (two tailed) were conducted, utilising an alpha level of $< .05$, to determine whether there were significant differences in group means on each of the 27 dependent variables.

Results

Loner delinquents vs. Loner nondelinquents

There were statistically significant differences on seven variables. LD scored higher than LND on delinquent activities as follows: school misdemeanours ($M = 3.97$, $SD = 1.87$ vs. $M = 2.55$, $SD = .92$; $t\,(14.55) = 2.28$, $p < .04$), abuse of property ($M = 1.91$, $SD = .92$ vs. $M = 1.12$, $SD = .14$; $t\,(10.46) = 2.82$, $p < .02$), physical aggression ($M = 1.91$, $SD = 1.03$ vs. $M = 1.09$, $SD = .16$; $t\,(10.45) = 2.60$, $p < .03$), and for reputational orientations on nonconforming self-perception ($M = 2.98$, $SD = 1.51$ vs. $M = 1.73$, $SD = .55$; $t\,(12.58) = 2.58$, $p < .03$). Conversely, LD scored lower than LND on the reputation variables of activity self-description ($M = 3.55$, $SD = 1.37$ vs. $M = 4.68$, $SD = .73$; $t\,(20) = -2.43$, $p < .03$), activity ideal private self ($M = 4.33$, $SD = 1.33$ vs. $M = 5.55$, $SD = .39$; $t\,(20) = -2.91$, $p < .01$), and brag ($M = .23$, $SD = .33$ vs. $M = .69$, $SD = .31$; $t\,(19) = -3.26$, $p < .005$). These differences are represented pictorially in Figure 2.

Loner delinquents vs. Nonloner delinquents

No significant group differences were evident between LD and NLD on any of the delinquency and reputation enhancement variables.

Loner delinquents vs. Nonloner nondelinquents

As can be seen in Figure 3, LD had significantly higher mean scores than NLND on five variables. For delinquency these were: school misdemeanours ($M = 3.97$, $SD = 1.87$ vs. $M = 2.22$, $SD = .78$; $t\,(13.37) = 2.87$, $p < .02$), soft drug use offences ($M = 2.16$, $SD = 1.20$ vs. $M = 1.27$, $SD = .33$; $t\,(11.48) = 2.38$, $p < .04$), abuse of property ($M = 1.91$, $SD = .92$ vs. $M = 1.26$, $SD = .30$; $t\,(12.08) = 2.23$, $p < .05$), and physical aggression ($M = 1.91$, $SD = 1.03$ vs. $M = 1.18$, $SD = .27$; $t\,(11.39) = 2.26$, $p < .05$). In addition, LD scored significantly lower than NLND on one reputation variable, namely activity ideal private self ($M = 4.33$, $SD = 1.33$ vs. $M = 5.47$, $SD = .96$; $t\,(20) = -2.30$, $p < .03$).

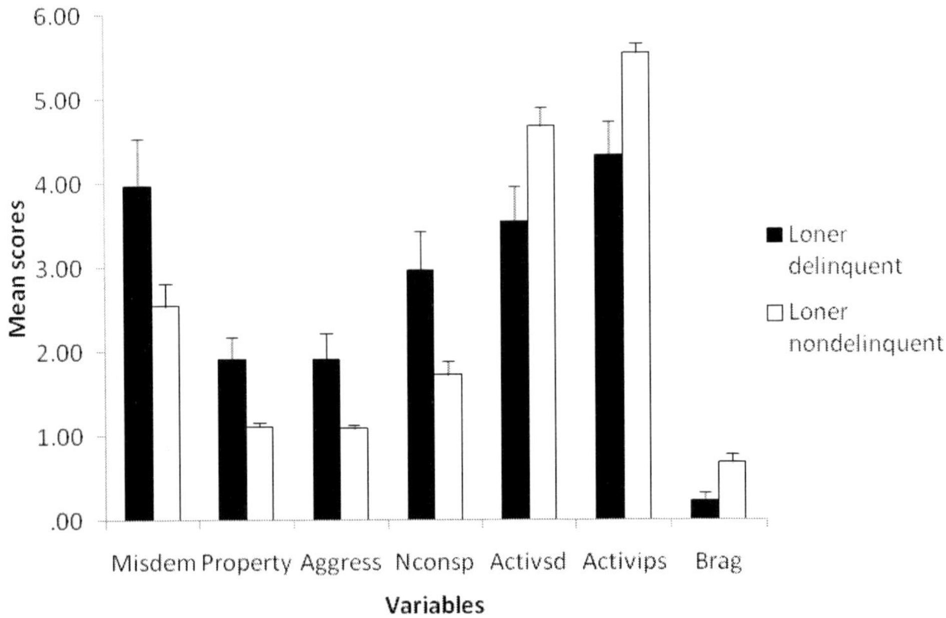

Figure 2. The mean scores of loner delinquent and loner nondelinquent groups as a function of ASDS and RES variables with standard errors of the means.

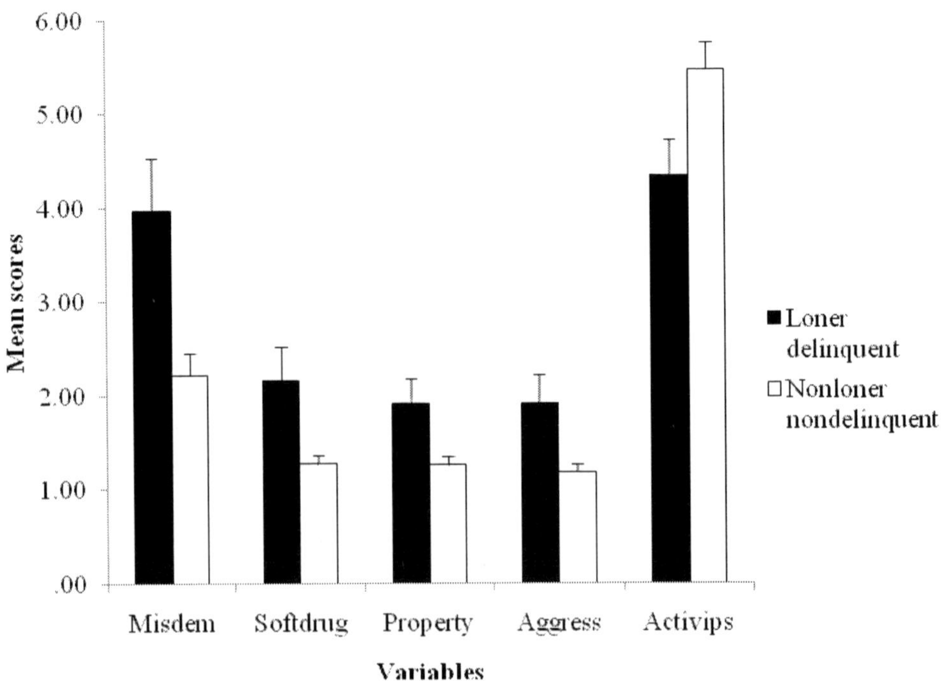

Figure 3. The mean scores of Loner delinquent and Nonloner nondelinquent groups as a function of ASDS and RES variables with standard errors of the means.

Loner nondelinquents vs. Nonloner delinquents

The fourth series of independent-samples *t*-tests indicated that LND had significantly lower mean scores than NLD on abuse of property (M = 1.12, SD = .14 vs. M = 1.97, SD =.91; t (10.48) = -3.10, p < .01) and physical aggression (M = 1.09, SD = .16 vs. M = 1.94, SD = .98; t (10.51) = -2.85, p < .02).

For the reputation enhancement variables, LND also scored significantly lower than NLD on nonconforming self-perception (M = 1.73, SD = .55 vs. M = 2.99, SD = 1.17; t (14.21) = -3.25, p < .007), nonconforming ideal public self (M = 1.76, SD =.84 vs. M = 2.73, SD = 1.13; t (20) = -2.27, p < .04), power/evaluation self-description (M = 3.50, SD = .56 vs. M = 4.15, SD =.85; t (20) = -2.12, p < .04), and status (M = .21, SD = .19 vs. M = .52, SD = .24; t (19) = -3.24, p < .005). LND, however, reported significantly higher mean score than NLD on brag (M = .69, SD = .31 vs. M = .33, SD =.27; t (19) = 2.84, p < .02). These differences are represented pictorially in Figure 4.

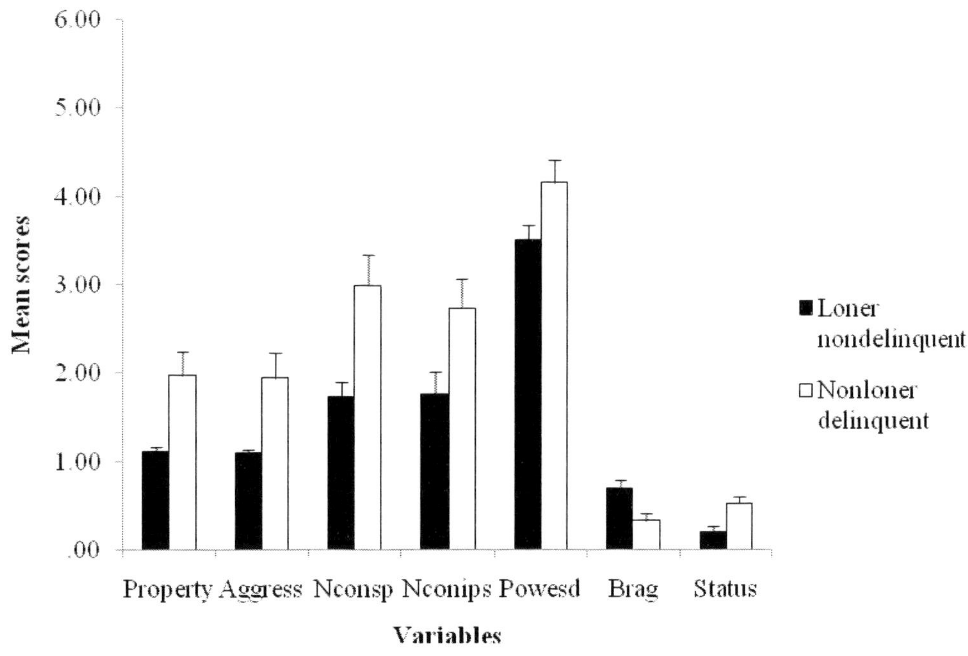

Figure 4. The mean scores of loner nondelinquent and nonloner delinquent groups as a function of ASDS and RES variables with standard errors of the means.

Loner nondelinquents vs. Nonloner nondelinquents

The fifth set of independent-samples *t*-tests focused on LND and NLND. The differences in the mean scores of these groups were statistically significant for only two variables, power/evaluation self-description and brag. LND (M = 3.50, SD = .56) scored significantly lower for power/evaluation self-description as compared to NLND (M = 4.09, SD = .68), t (20) = -2.22, p < .04. Conversely, LND (M = .69, SD = .31) scored significantly higher than

NLND (M = .41, SD = .19) for the brag variable, t (19) = 2.50, p <.03. These differences are represented pictorially in Figure 5.

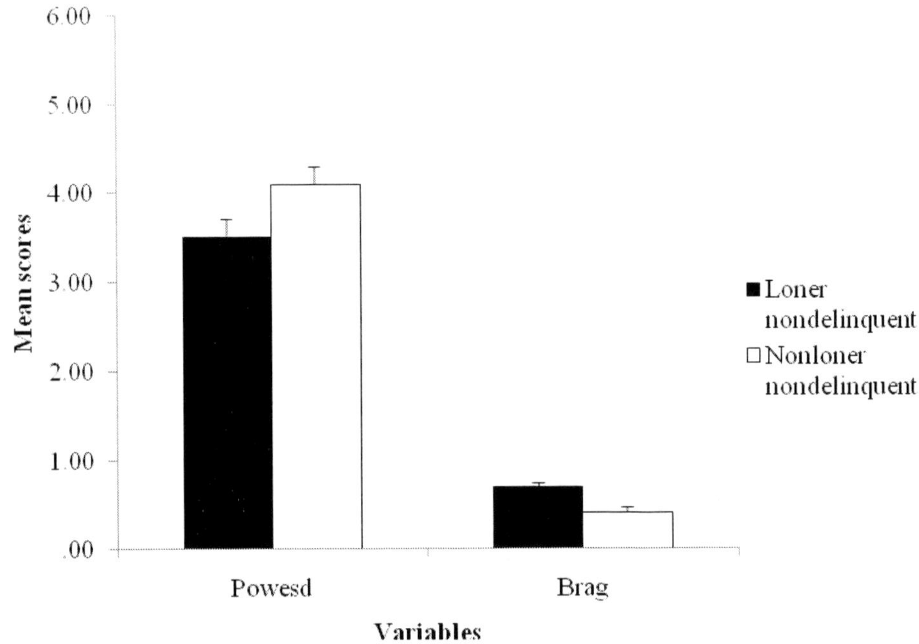

Figure 5. The mean scores of loner nondelinquent and nonloner nondelinquent groups as a function of ASDS and RES variables with standard errors of the means.

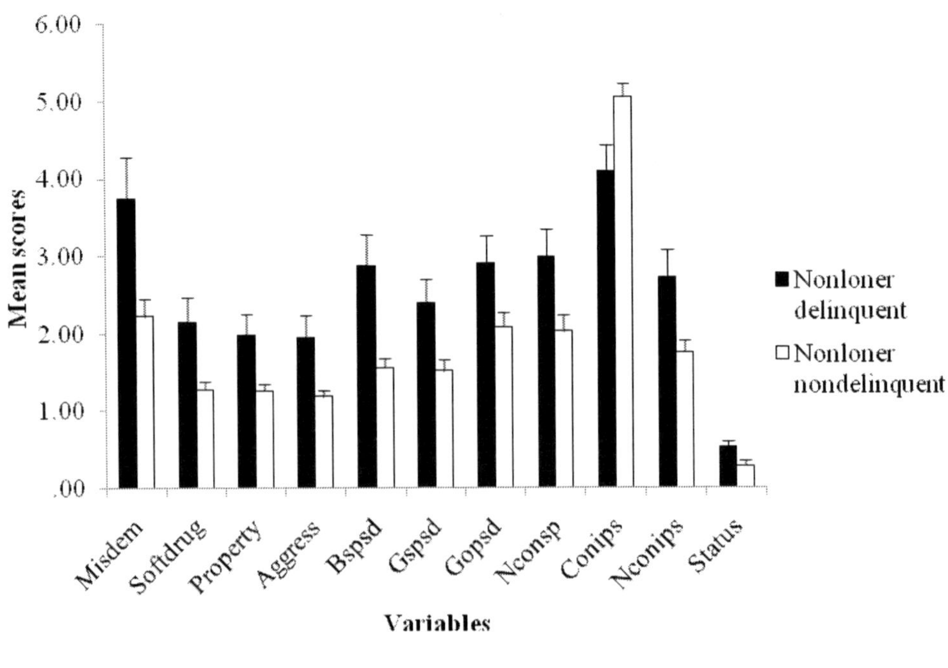

Figure 6. The mean scores of nonloner delinquent and nonloner nondelinquent groups as a function of ASDS and RES variables with standard errors of the means.

Nonloner delinquents vs. Nonloner nondelinquents

The final cluster of independent-samples *t*-tests for NLD and NLND yielded significant differences in the mean scores for 11 of the dependent variables.

For delinquency, NLD reported significantly higher mean scores than NLND on school misdemeanours ($M = 3.74$, $SD = 1.80$ vs. $M = 2.22$, $SD = .78$; $t\ (13.60) = 2.57$, $p < .03$), soft drug use offences ($M = 2.15$, $SD = 1.06$ vs. $M = 1.27$, $SD = .33$; $t\ (11.86) = 2.60$, $p < .03$), abuse of property ($M = 1.97$, $SD = .91$ vs. $M = 1.26$, $SD = .30$; $t\ (12.14) = 2.48$, $p < .03$), and physical aggression ($M = 1.94$, $SD = .98$ vs. $M = 1.18$, $SD = .27$; $t\ (11.56) = 2.48$, $p < .04$), Similarly, for reputational orientations NLD reported significantly higher mean scores than NLND on boy's self-perceived social deviance norms ($M = 2.87$, $SD = 1.35$ vs. $M = 1.56$, $SD = .40$; $t\ (11.79) = 3.10$, $p < .01$), girl's self-perceived social deviance norms ($M = 2.39$, $SD = 1.02$ vs. $M = 1.52$, $SD =.47$; $t\ (14.13) = 2.60$, $p < .03$), girl's evaluative reactions to others social deviance ($M = 2.91$, $SD = 1.14$ vs. $M = 2.08$, $SD =.63$; $t\ (20) = 2.10$, $p < .05$), nonconforming self-perception ($M = 2.99$, $SD = 1.17$ vs. $M = 2.02$, $SD =.72$; $t\ (20) = 2.34$, $p < .04$), nonconforming ideal public self ($M = 2.73$, $SD = 1.13$ vs. $M = 1.75$, $SD =.52$; $t\ (14.07) = 2.60$, $p < .03$), and status ($M = .52$, $SD =.24$ vs. $M =.29$, $SD =.25$; $t\ (20) = 2.25$, $p < .04$). Conversely, NLD ($M = 4.09$, $SD = 1.15$) scored lower mean scores than NLND ($M = 5.05$, $SD = .57$) on conforming ideal public self, $t\ (20) = -2.49$, $p < .03$. These differences are represented pictorially in Figure 6.

CONCLUSION

The research findings presented in this chapter appear to be the first that have linked the delinquent activities of adolescent loners with reputational orientations. Moreover, the findings from the series of studies reported highlight some important differences between loners and nonloners irrespective of their delinquent/nondelinquent status. These differences have important implications for reputation enhancement theory and its applicability to young person's involved in delinquent activities. To conclude this chapter, we highlight these differences.

First, with reference to loner delinquents, these individuals commit significantly more property offences, stealing offences, vehicle-related offences, physically aggressive acts, and school misdemeanours, and indulge (to a greater extent) in both soft and hard drug-related offences than nonloner nondelinquents. These findings provide support for the National Longitudinal Study of Adolescent Health (see Kreager, 2004) that found that isolates who reported having significant trouble with others ('peer troubled isolates') were *more* likely to become involved in delinquent activities. Conversely, our findings are the opposite of those by Demuth (2004) and Kreager (2004) that isolates are not necessarily more likely to engage in delinquent activities.

In terms of reputational orientations, an interesting picture emerges. While loner delinquents believe that peers of the same age more openly admire boys who indulge in socially deviant activities, they also believe that these same peers admire girls who are involved in socially conforming activities. Loner delinquents see themselves as delinquent and nonconforming, believe that others view them in this way, actually desire others to view them as such, and ideally wish to be seen in this nonconforming light. Finally, they do not communicate positive things to their parents or anyone else. The data from the comparisons of the four small, but distinctive, samples presented in the final study of our research also reveal some interesting findings which not only support the larger scale analyses but also suggests that there are different activities and reputations associated with loner delinquents, loner nondelinquents, nonloner delinquents, and nonloner nondelinquents. While many of these aspects of reputation enhancement are in line with our previous extensive research findings with detained and mainstream primary and high school delinquents (see Carroll et al., 2009), subtle differences are evident particularly in relation to how members of the opposite sex are viewed. However, we suspect that there may be more marked differences between loner and nonloner delinquents in reputational orientations, but because our loner scale is in its infancy, these differences are not detected.

The major question remains with regards to reputation - How do loners fit with the theory? Social visibility and the committing of delinquent acts in the company of others (i.e., an audience; Reicher and Emler, 1986) are NOT key elements on which loners build their reputations. Furthermore, loners do not have to prove their credentials to an 'in group' to sustain a self-identity (Emler and Reicher, 1995). Nevertheless, they do appear to be in pursuit of a particular reputation. We suspect that for loners, an "immediate" audience is not important. That is, others who witness the delinquent acts as they are committed. Nevertheless, our research suggests that a wider audience still becomes aware of the loners actions over time. Thus an audience is still important but the question remains as to how the delinquent acts committed alone become known to others? This is clearly an area for further investigation.

Our findings also resonate with Kuperschmidt et al. (1999) who reported that adolescents who are loners hold greater discrepancies about their actual selves and their ideal selves (i.e., who they would ideally wish to be) than do nonloners. Indeed, reputation is a complex social phenomenon arising from social processes within a community of individuals which link people to particular social identities. In the case of loners, it may be even more complicated, yet this complexity may offer opportunities for positive peer interaction based intervention strategies prior to the most vulnerable period, namely adolescence.

In conclusion, understanding the nature of delinquency of adolescent loners along with their motivations for involvement in such acts has important implications. Determining the applicability of reputation enhancement theory to this under researched population of vulnerable individuals will advance theoretical understanding. From this, intervention strategies might be developed which facilitate the everyday functioning of loners and hence reduce their involvement in delinquent activities.

REFERENCES

Adler, P.A., and Adler, P. (1996). Preadolescent clique stratification and the hierarchy of identity. *Sociological Inquiry, 66*, 111-142.

Australian Bureau of Statistics (1998). *1996 Census of population and housing: Socio-economic indexes for areas* (ABS Cat. No. 2039.0). Canberra: Author.

Australian Bureau of Statistics (2003). *Census of population and housing: Socio-economic indexes for areas (SEIFA), Australia, 2001* (ABS Cat. No. 2033.0.30.001). Canberra: Author.

Australian Institute of Criminology (2006). *Australian crime: Facts and figures 2005*. Canberra: Author.

Carroll, A., Durkin, K., Houghton, S., and Hattie, J. (1996). An adaptation of Mak's Self-Reported Delinquency Scale for Western Australian adolescents. *Australian Journal of Psychology, 48*, 1-7.

Carroll, A., Green, S., Houghton, S., and Wood, R. (2003). Reputation enhancementand involvement in delinquency among high school students. *International Journal of Disability, Development and Education, 50*, 253-273.

Carroll, A., Houghton, S., Durkin, K., and Hattie, J. (2009). *Adolescent Reputations and Risk: Developmental Trajectories to Delinquency*. New York: Springer.

Carroll, A., Houghton, S., Hattie, J., and Durkin, K. (1999). Adolescent reputationen hancement: Differentiating delinquent, nondelinquent, and at-risk youth. *Journal of Child Psychologyand Psychiatry and Allied Disciplines, 40*, 593-606.

Carroll, A., Houghton, S., Wood, R., Perkins, C., and Bower, J. (2007). Multidimensional self-concept: Age and gender differences in Australian high school students involved in delinquent activities. *School Psychology International, 28*, 237-256.

Cordin, R. (2008). *Psychopathic-like-traits and aggression in suspended mainstream school children and adolescents*. Unpublished doctoral dissertation, The University of Western Australia, Perth.

Culp, A. M., Clyman, M. M., and Culp, R. E. (1995). Adolescent depress mood, report of suicide attempts and asking for help. *Adolescence, 30,* 827-837.

Demuth, S. (2004). Understanding the delinquency and social relationships of loners. *Youth and Society, 35*, 366–392.

Emler, N. (1984). Differential involvement in delinquency: Towards an interpretationin terms of reputation management. In B. A. Mahler and W. B. Maher (Eds.), *Progress in experimental personality research* (Vol. 13, pp. 173–237). New York: Academic Press.

Emler, N., and Reicher, S. (1995). *Adolescence and delinquency: The collective management of reputation*. Cambridge, MA: Blackwell.

Ennett, S. T., and Bauman, K. E. (1993). Peer group structure and adolescent cigarette smoking: A social network analysis. *Journal of Health and Social Behavior, 34*, 226–236.

Erikson, E. H. (1968). *Identity youth and crisis*. New York: Norton.

Fernandez, J. A., and Loh, N. S. N. (2001). *Crime and justice statistics for Western Australia: 2001*. Perth: Crime Research Centre, The University of Western Australia.

Goodnight, J. A., Bates, J. E., Newman, J. P., Dodge, K. A., and Pettit, G. S. (2006).The interactive influences of friend deviance and reward dominance on thedevelopment of externalizing behavior during middle adolescence. *Journal of Abnormal Child Psychology, 34*, 573–583.

Hair, J. F., Black, W. C., Babin, B. J., Anderson, R. E., and Tatham, R. L. (2006). *Multivariate data analysis* (6th ed.). New Jersey: Pearson Prentice Hall.

Haynie, D. L. (2001). Delinquent peers revisited: Does network structure matter? *American Journal of Sociology, 106*, 1013–1057.

Heinrich, L. M. and Gullone, E. (2006). The clinical significance of loneliness: A literature review. *Clinical Psychology Review, 26,* 695-718.

Houghton, S., and Carroll, A. (2002). Longitudinal rates of self-reported delinquencyof at-risk and not at-risk high school students. *Australian and New ZealandJournal of Criminology, 35,* 99–113.

Houghton, S., Cordin, R., and Hopkins, S. (2008). *Psychopathic-like-traits and aggression in children and adolescents.* Manuscript submitted for publication.

Houghton, S., Carroll, A., Tan., C., and Hopkins, S. (2008). Self-reported delinquency and reputational orientations of high school and incarcerated adolescent loners and nonloners, *Journal of Forensic Psychiatry and Psychology, 19,* 205-227.

Jöreskog, K. G., and Sörbom, D. (1989). *LISREL 7: User's reference guide.* Mooresville, IN: Scientific Software.

Kaiser, H. F. (1970). A second generation Little Jiffy. *Psychometrika, 35,* 401-415.

Kaiser, H. F. (1974). An index of factorial simplicity. *Psychometrika, 39,* 31-36.

Krakowski, K. A., and Hattie, J. (1993). *MICFA: A first-order confirmatory structural analysis program.* Graduate School of Education, The University of Western Australia, Perth.

Kreager, D. A. (2004). Strangers in the halls: Isolation and delinquency in school networks. *Social Forces, 83,* 351–390.

Kuperschmidt, J. B., Sigda, K. B., Sedikides, C., and Voegler, M. E. (1999). Social self-discrepancy theory and loneliness during childhood and adolescence. In K. J. Rotenberg and S. Hymel (Eds.), *Loneliness in childhood and adolescence* (pp. 263-279). Cambridge, England: Cambridge University Press.

Matsueda, R. L., and Anderson, K. (1998). The dynamics of delinquent peers anddelinquent behavior. *Criminology, 36,* 269–306.

McWhirter, B. T., Besett-Alesch, T. M., Horibita, J., and Gat, I. (2002). Loneliness in high risk adolescent: The role of coping, self-esteem and empathy. *Journal of Youth Studies, 5,* 69-84.

Meloy, J. R., Hempel, A.G., Gray, B. T., Mohandie, K., Shiva, A., and Richards, T. C. (2004). A comparative analysis of North American adolescent and adult mass murderers. *Behavioral Sciences and the Law, 22,* 291–309.

Parkhurst, J. T. and Hopmeyer, A. (1999). Developmental change in the souces of loneliness in childhood and adolescence: Constructing a theoretical model. In In K. J. Rotenberg and S. Hymel (Eds.), *Loneliness in Childhood and Adolescence* (pp. 56 - 79). Cambridge, England: Cambridge University Press.

Parlee, M. B. (1979). The friendship bond. *Psychology Today, 13,* 43-54.

Peplau, L. and Perlman, D. (1982). Perspectives on loneliness. In L.A. Peplau and D. Perlman (eds.), *Loneliness: A Sourcebook of current theory, research and therapy* (pp. 1-18). New York: Wiley.

Perlman, D. and Landolt, M. A. (1999). Examination of loneliness in children-adolescent and in adults: Two solitudes or a unified enterprise. In K. J. Rotenberg and S. Hymel (Eds.), *Loneliness in childhood and adolescence* (pp. 325 – 347). Cambridge, England: Cambridge University Press.

Reicher, S., and Emler, N. (1986). Managing reputations in adolescents: The pursuitof delinquent and nondelinquent identities. In H. Beloff (Ed.), *Getting into life* (pp. 13–42). London: Methuen.

Siegel, L. J., Welsh, B. C., and Senna, J. J. (2006). *Juvenile delinquency: Theory, practice and law* (9th ed.). Belmont, CA: Thomson/Wadsworth.

Snyder, H. N., & Sickmund, M. J. (2006). *Juvenile offenders and victims: 2006 national report.* Washington, DC: U.S. Department of Justice, Office of Justice Programs, Office of Juvenile Justice and Delinquency Prevention.

SPSS Inc. (2005). *Statistical package for the social sciences* (Version 14.0) [Computer software]. Chicago, IL: SPSS Inc.

Tan, C. and Houghton, S. (2008). The *Adolescent Loner Scale.* Unpublished.

Tabachnick, B. G., and Fidell, L. S. (2007). *Using multivariate statistics* (5th ed.). Boston: Allyn and Bacon.

Thornberry, T. P., Lizotte, A. J., Krohn, M.D., Farnworth, M., and Jang, S. J. (1994). Delinquent peers, beliefs, and delinquent behavior: A longitudinal test ofinteractional theory. *Criminology, 32*, 47–84.

Warr, M. (2002). *Companions in crime: The social aspects of criminal conduct.* Cambridge, UK: Cambridge University Press.

Weiss, R. S. (1973). *Loneliness: The experience of emotional and social isolation.* Cambridge, MA: MIT Press.

Wilson, D., Sharp, C., and Patterson, A. (2006). *Young people and crime: Findings from the 2005 offending, crime and justice survey* (Home Office Statistical Bulletin 17/06). London: Home Office.

In: Delinquency: Causes, Reduction and Prevention
Editor: Ozan Sahin and Joseph Maier
ISBN 978-1-60741-558-9

Chapter 5

DELINQUENCY AND ANTISOCIAL BEHAVIOUR AMONG HIGH RISK YOUNG PEOPLE IN ADOLESCENCE

Patrick McCrystal* and Kareena McAloney
Institute of Child Care Research
School of Sociology Social Policy and Social Work

INTRODUCTION

This chapter presents an investigation of the patterns of offending and antisocial behaviour amongst young people from the age of 11-16 years who are categoried as high risk or vulnerable to delinquency and antisocial behaviour. The chapter will draw upon findings from the first five datasweeps of the Belfast Youth Development Study (BYDS), a longitudinal study of the onset and development of adolescent problem behaviour. Through a detailed exploration of the onset and development of delinquency and antisocial behaviour from the age of 11-16 years it will provide insights for targeting and development of appropriate interventions for school aged high risk young people who do not attend mainstream school in adolescence. The findings will form the empirical base for a discussion of the key issues around appropriate interventions and the development of conclusions in relation to young people who have received comparatively less attention in the delinquency literature but who are considered more likely to offend during adolescence.

WHAT IS ADOLESCENCE?

An important and primary issue for this chapter is identifying the period of adolescence. Defining adolescence is itself a contested issue in the youth development literature. For many it corresponds to the teenage years up to the age of eighteen years and the commencement of

* Corresponding Author: Dr. Patrick McCrystal, Institute of Child Care Research, School of Sociology, Social policy and Social Work, Queens University Belfast 6 College Park Belfast BT7 1LP. Phone: 00442890975991; Fax: 00442890975900; Email: P.McCrystal@qub.ac.uk

legal adulthood. However, recently researchers are increasingly taking the period from the end of primary education at the age of the eleven years up to the end of teenage years which includes the period traditionally known as youth transition (16-18 years) and the beginning of emerging adulthood (Arnett, 2000) as one that includes a number of drug transition stages. This chapter will cover the period the period 11-16 years which in the UK marks the period of compulsory secondary education to the end of statutory education. However as the chapter shows a number of young people will stop attending mainstream school before the age of 16 years and for this reason are of particular importance for policy makers but comparatively less is known about their experience during adolescence, particularly in the UK. The reasons for this are elaborated upon later in this chapter.

Adolescence has been defined as a transitional stage between childhood and adulthood that may have inescapable implications and consequences for later life (Nicholson and Ayers, 2004). Adolescence is conceived of as a period lasting up to ten years which is divided into three stages; early (10-13- years old), middle (14-16 years old) and late adolescence (17 + years old) according to Petersen and Leffert (1995). This exploration of young people is interested particularly in middle adolescence which is a period marked by greater interest in experimentation and may signal the initiation into risk-taking behaviours (Rutter et al 1998).

This experimentation can lead to an increase in delinquency, sexual experimentation, challenges to parental authority and conflict surrounding beliefs and values (Fishbien and Ajzen, 1975). Evidence also exists to suggest that during these years more serious substance using behaviours develop (Goulden and Sondhi, 2001). Research has highlighted that many psychological disorders, such as major depression (Angold et al, 1998) certain anxiety disorders and eating disorders (Steinhaus et al, 1993) emerge during the early to middle stages of adolescence. It is also argued that the middle adolescent period is the peak period for offending and risk-taking in boys with the average criminal career beginning at around fifteen years old (Farrington et al, 1998).

The information above presents a rationale for focusing on middle adolescence in particular as research indicates that experimentation with a variety of risk-taking activities is central to this particular phase of development. For the majority there is a marked fall in criminal behaviour during early adult life, though a minority continue to persist in their offending 'careers'. In many ways it has been the management of this 'problem population;' until the point at which they 'grow up' which has been seen as the key task in controlling crime. In some respects, however, this appears to be becoming increasingly difficult.

Delinquency and Antisocial Behaviour in Adolescence

Delinquency is an expression of conformity to (sub cultural) norms that runs counter to the values of the wider society (Western et al, 2003). Cloward and Ohlin (1960) describe three types of criminal sub-cultures: criminal, violent and retreatist and identify the neighbourhood structure as a key influence on the formation of each subculture. The criminal-subculture occurs in lower socio-economic status, but socially organised neighbourhoods, and is typically directed towards property crime. The violent subculture is typically directed towards violent or gang affiliated baheviour and is characterised by socially disorganised neighbourhoods. The final subculture, retreatist, encompasses those individuals who do not 'flourish' in either the criminal or violent subculture, and is characteristic of drug related offending.

It is only one element of a much larger syndrome of antisocial behaviour that tends to persist over time (Farrington, 1984). However, this time generally corresponds to the teenage years with delinquent behaviours noted during the teenage years and into early twenties. Whilst the relationship between the age of delinquent behaviour has been the subject of considerable debate there is no generally agreed consensus on a single age for delinquent behaviour other than the teenage years are the peak period for delinquency. This appears to have lead to the generally accepted view that a significant proportion of young people will just mature

out of crime. Others suggest that the key issue here is not that the level of delinquency becomes less prevalent into early adulthood but the nature and frequency of delinquency and antisocial behaviour changes as more serious and violent offences become more prevalent during the later teenage years and into early adulthood.

Graham and Bowling (1995) suggest the peak age of offending is 15 years for property, expressive, and serious offences; 16 years for violent offences crime; 20 years for drug offences. Expressive and violent offences were most prevalence among 14-17 year olds; and theft and motor offences among 22-25 year olds. The Cambridge Study of Delinquent Behaviour (Great Britain) 1961-81 noted that the peak age of offending was 17/18 years (Farrington, 1984). Whilst it is generally accepted that young people are most often associated with delinquent behaviour, it is usually young males who are seen as the main offenders here. In 1995, for example, the ratio of males to females convicted for all indictable offences by young offenders was 3.3:1 (Criminal Statistics England and Wales, 1995).

Hawkins et al (1992) in a seminal paper *Risk and Protective Factors for Alcohol and Other Drug Problems in Adolescence and early Adulthood: Implications for Substance Abuse Prevention* presented a list of behaviours associated with antisocial behaviour problems in adolescence. These factors, the authors claim, show much consistency in effects across cultures, races and in particular genders in the USA Europe and Australia and are to be found in communities, families, schools, peer groups and individuals. A further principle of the work of Hawkins et al (1992) is a general positive relationship between the number of risk factors present at one time and the likelihood of negative behaviour in adolescence, although the quality of the association would appear to be a stronger indication of the role of each factor.

In relation specifically to delinquency there is a range of risk factors that increase the likelihood of a young person committing an offence. Loeber and Dishon (1983) suggest the most important predictors for male offending are poor parent child-management techniques; offending by parents and sibling; low intelligence and low educational attainment; and separation from parents. Loeber and Stouthamer (1987) note however that low socio-economic status was a rather weak predictor of delinquency. The results obtained from British longitudinal surveys of delinquency (Farrington, 1984) report similar outcomes as those obtained in comparable surveys in North America, the Scandinavian countries (Wikstom 1987), and New Zealand (Fergusson et al, 1993) and, indeed, with results obtained in British cross-sectional surveys (Graham and Bowling 1996).

However, the causal status of known risk factors to delinquency remains to be clarified and no single risk factor can explain delinquency and antisocial behaviour in adolescence, but the greater the number of risk factors, the greater the likelihood of early onset offending

(Hawkins et al, 2002). In relation to substance abuse a large literature base supports associations between alcohol use/abuse and crime (Rutter et al, 1998). One explanation for this is because they share the same set of risk factors (Jessor et al, 1991; Catalano and Hwakins, 1997). Fergusson and Harwood (2000) from their analysis of the Christchurch Longitudinal Study showed that alcohol abuse in late adolescence increases involvement in crime (especially violent crime).

It is clear that many groups are working with offenders suffering from drug and alcohol addiction in an effort to reduce re-offending. Unsurprisingly, a recent government report also highlighted excessive drinking as the main underlying factor in the rise of teenage crime and anti-social behaviour, observing that young people '...who drank alcohol once a week or more committed a disproportional volume of crime, accounting for 37 per cent of all offences' (Pavis et al, 1997). These figures increased to 63% as young people became older and where binge drinking patterns could be identified (Home Office, 2004).

A number of theories have attempted to conceptualise the nature of offending, many of which have placed a strong emphasis on the social world of the offender and the role that social networks, norms and values have on behaviour. Examples of these theories include social control theory (Hirschi, 1969), sub-cultural theory (Wolfgang and Ferracuti, 1967), lifestyles-exposure theory (Hindelang, 1973) and routine activities theory (Cohen and Felson, 1979). Each of these theories proposes that offending behaviour is a product of the relationship between an individual and society. Social control theory asserts that it is the ties or bonds that individuals form with others and their acceptance and adherence to societal norms and values which influence participation in offending or anti-social behaviour. Similarly sub-cultural theory (Wolfgang and Ferracuti, 2003) premises that membership of certain groups can result in the development and acceptance of values, norms and behaviours which supports and encourages deviance and delinquency. The related theories of lifestyle-exposure and routine activities link involvement in crime to particular situation contexts which arise out of the social networks of the individual. Hindelang (1973) suggest that an individual's lifestyle – the locations in which they spend time, the activities they participate in and the people they associate with, determine involvement in criminal activity. Routine activities theory proposes that criminal events are a function of a favourable environment – determined by the presence of a suitable target or victim in a location accessible to the perpetrator and outside the sphere of protective guardianship.

Although distinct theories of delinquency have been developed, there is appears to be a consensus that the social environment and relationships of an individual are influential in criminal involvement. A significant body of research has lent weight to these theories, particularly in empirical investigations of adolescent delinquency. One particular area that is emerging in the literature is the relationship between victimisation and offending. Victims and offenders are traditionally viewed as two distinct categories of individuals, defined by their respective roles and experiences of a particular event. Yet a substantial body of research suggests that victims and perpetrators may be very similar, sharing similar environmental and social factors which facilitate exposure to violence and crime (e.g. Fagan, Piper and Cheng, 1987). As Fattah (1991:123) points out 'criminals are more frequently victimized than non-criminals and ... victims of violent crime themselves have considerable criminal involvements'.

High Risk Groups in Adolescence

Catalano et al (1998) defined high risk groups as those either exposed to multiple risk factors, or to an elevated level on one particular risk factor. They describe the term 'at risk' in relation to children and young people as referring to children and youth who are in danger of failing at school, in their social life, or in making a successful transition to work. Educational, social and vocational failure are predictable to some extent by a range of factors, including, ethnic status, family circumstances, language, type of school, geography and community. (Day et al, 1997).

The role of school and/or education in the lives of young people is key here. Existing research findings suggest that children and young people often survive exposure to a single risk factor, but that exposure to multiple risks significantly increases the risk of maladaptive outcomes (Rutter, 1979)

Lloyd (1998) takes this definition further when identifying specific high risk groups such as the homeless, those 'looked after' by local authorities or in foster care, truants, those excluded from school, young offenders, children from families with substance-abusing parents or siblings, and young people with conduct or depressive disorders. Many of these categories, i.e. the homeless, those 'looked after' and young offenders consist of relatively small numbers of young people particularly in early adolescence. The main challenges to researching young people considered to belong to high risk subsamples include the resources required to identify these hard to reach groups and then encouraging them to participate in research. These young people can be suspicious towards adults who are unfamiliar to them who arrive and begin asking questions about personal and sensitive issues. These challenges go some way to explaining the comparatively limited base on this subject.

The existing research on these young people consistently reports higher levels of delinquency and antisocial behavior compared with those who are categorised as not being vulnerable (e.g. Audit Commission 1996; Powis et al, 1998). Others have highlighted those attending Emotional Behavioural Difficulty Units (EBD) as at a high risk or vulnerable to delinquency and antisocial behavior during adolescence (Kress and Elias, 1993). These young people are rarely included in school based surveys, the main information source of offending behavior between the age of 11-16 years. As a result comparatively little is known about the offending behaviours of these young people. One of the reasons they are considered to be at a high risk to delinquency and antisocial behaviour is because of exclusion from mainstream school, and identified behavioural problems and/or conduct disorders (Phil and Peterson 1991; Davis and Florian 2004).

The comparatively limited empirical base of delinquency and antisocial behaviour amongst high risk young people makes it difficult to produce clear conclusions about what is best for them when developing best practice. This task has become substantially more challenging when compared with those who continue to attend mainstream school. Even where targeted surveys were undertaken, these have generally been undertaken on a cross sectional basis involving one-off questionnaire/interview surveys with the high risk samples. Whilst these studies provide a 'snapshot' relevant to the time and location of research, the samples in such studies are generally comparatively small, making their generalisability to all young people difficult. Whilst the existing evidence from these studies remains limited, there is even less evidence on the experience of these young people being studied over a longer period of time which would greatly assist the development of appropriate targeted interventions at all stages throughout adolescence. As a result establishing the resources for researching delinquency and antisocial behaviour amongst high risk young people presents a major challenge for researchers before such studies can begin.

Unlike much of the empirical research on adolescent delinquency and antisocial behaviour, studies with vulnerable groups of young people tend to be undertaken outside mainstream school settings, and on a cross-sectional basis due to the difficulties of identifying and accessing appropriate samples (Powis et al, 1998). More generally, young people who are categorised as belonging to at least one high risk group are considered to have a higher propensity to offend and therefore may benefit from targeted intervention. There is comparatively limited level of research upon which to base such interventions for young people who constitute high risk groups compared to their peers who continue to attend school. Longitudinal data on the prevalence and nature of offending among these groups represents a particular gap in the literature (Lloyd, 1998; Manski et al, 2001). The High Risk Booster Sample of the Belfast Youth Development Study has attempted to address the general information gap on at risk young people on a longitudinal basis.

The Belfast Youth Development Study

The empirical evidence presented in this chapter is drawn from the Belfast Youth Development Study being undertaken at the Institute of Child Care Research, located with the School of Sociology Social Policy and Social Work at Queens University Belfast, Northern Ireland. This section describes the study which includes a High Risk Booster Sample, one of the innovative aspects of the study.

The Belfast Youth Development Study (BYDS) is a longitudinal study of adolescent problem behaviour. It began in 2001 when the study cohort of approximately 4500 young people entered postprimnary school at the age of eleven years. Its aim is to study the onset and development of adolescent problem behaviour during adolescence. This involved an annual survey of the study cohort in order to build a picture of the issues associated with the onset, progression and desistance from problem behaviours from the age of 11-16 years. This was achieved through a traditional longitudinal research design within participating schools across three towns in Northern Ireland. All schools in each town were invited to participate, three quarters agreed. Three quarters of the sample cohort lived in Belfast, the main urban centre in Northern Ireland. The other two towns were about thirty miles north of Belfast and twenty-five miles south of the city respectively. These two towns were selected because they were considered to have emerging problems around illicit drug use and would provide important insights into the experience of young people growing up in these areas in relation to the behaviours associated with delinquency and antisocial behaviour. The main data collection involved an annual data collection sweep in each of the 43 mainstream schools that agreed to participate in the research. This represented 19 per cent of all postprimary schools in Northern Ireland.

In addition, an annual data collection sweep amongst young people living in each town who did not attend mainstream school was undertaken as part of the BYDS. This included those attending alternative education provision for school excludees, young people attending Emotional and Behavioral Difficulty Units, and those living in state care at the time of the research. These subsamples are young people who have been traditionally considered vulnerable to or at a high risk to marginalisation in society duirng adolescence and beyond. They are young people who are usually excluded from surveys of school aged young people due to the resource implications of undertaking such research on those who are traditionally hard to access and include in research which is a time consuming process.

The high risk booster sample of the BYDS utilized a repeated cross-sectional approach to data collection which involved surveying all those who met the inclusion criteria at each annual data sweep (Menard, 1991). This approach was adopted to overcome the challenges of using a traditional longitudinal approach with a sample that is very difficult to track over a long period of time. Full details of the research and data collection procedures for each high risk sample are available elsewhere (McCrystal et al, 2007a). The findings from such surveys are also less generalisable beyond the participating sample making them less attractive to funders and therefore more challenging for researchers to undertake such studies. As a result the experience of these young people has received less attention in the research literature and from policy makers.

The BYDS has addressed this gap in the UK literature to some extent through its High Risk Booster Sample. The delinquency and antisocial behaviour of these young people was studied from the age of 11-16 years. As a prospective longitudinal study the BYDS also provides important insights more generally to the onset and development of delinquency and antisocial behaviours during adolescent. This approach is the most informative method for studying developmental changes over time to reveal developmental pathways leading to positive and negative outcomes. Other advantages of using a prospective longitudinal study are for the development of temporal problems that will assist in the inference of causality, to identify the specific timing of the onset of problem behaviour (Farrington, 1991), in particular delinquency.

The BYDS used a self report measure of delinquency and antisocial behaviour. This consisted of a scale that included fourteen items of delinquency and antisocial behaviour. The items in the scale were asked in a question format. In the first year the participants were asked have you ever committed any of the following items? From years 2-5 this was asked as *In the past 12 months, have you....*

- Not paid the correct fare on a bus or train
- Taken something from a shop or store without paying for it?
- Behaved badly in a public place so that people complained or you got into trouble?
- Stolen or ridden in a stolen care or a van or on a stolen motorbike?
- Taken money or something else that did not belong to you from school?
- Carried a knife or weapon with you for protection or in case it was needed in a fight?
- Deliberately damaged or destroyed property that did not belong to you (for example, windows, cars or streetlights)
- Broken into a house or building to steal something?
- Written things or sprayed paint on property that did not belong to you (for example a phone box, care building, or bus shelter)?
- Used force, threats or a weapon to get money or something else from somebody?
- Taken money or something else that did not belong to you from your home without permission?

- Deliberately set fire or tried to set fire to someone's property or a building (for example, a school)?
- Hit, kicked or punched someone on purpose to hurt or injure them?
- Broken into a car or van to steal something out of it?

Those who answered *yes* each year were then asked to indicate the frequency of each item for the period of each datasweep. Frequency measures were 1-2 times; 3 to 5 times; 6 to 9 times; and 10 or more times.

Whilst questions are raised about the validity of self-report data on illegal activity, such data can on the other hand contain more comprehensive information than official statistics on delinquent behaviour of young people as they record behaviours not reported, or otherwise known, to authorities (Loeber and Farrington, 1994). Others claim that young people are willing to report accurate information on minor and serious delinquent acts (Farrington et al, 1996).

To a considerable extent the limited level of empirical evidence of delinquent and antisocial behaviour with high risk young people reflects methodological difficulties in studying this group. As a result much of the research on these young people involved small samples with few population-based perspectives and very few studies have tracked these individuals over time. Existing research in this area is generally cross-sectional with the limitations associated with such studies including their relevance beyond the time and location of the study. Within the Belfast Youth Development Study these challenges were overcome when investigating delinquency and antisocial behaviours of high risk young people from the age of 11-16 years through use of a repeated cross-sectional research design that identified all those living within three towns of the BYDS who were the same age as the mainstream school sample but were not attending school at the time of each data collection sweep.

Other factors contributing to the poor knowledge base results from firstly, these young people are frequently excluded from studies examining offending behaviour, because they are seen to be 'atypical' and thus not representative of the population under study. Secondly, the administration of self-report surveys can be problematic for these young people, because of limitations in skills central to the completion of a questionnaire (e.g. comparatively poor literacy and reading comprehension). Some commentators (e.g. Kessler and Klein, 1995) have suggested that the lack of usable data reflects methodological difficulties in obtaining empirical evidence of relevant data from these young people. The limited data base has implications for the development of appropriate resources, both classroom-based education, and for defining the approaches to intervention, once delinquent behaviour has been identified.

The High Risk Booster Sample of the Belfast Youth Development

The less structured lifestyles of some young people including those who are not attending mainstream school makes them a more difficult group to research (Nilson, 1999). This also makes studying their lifestyles over a long period of time particularly challenging, which goes some way to explaining the cross sectional nature of much of the research undertaken with these young people. The BYDS is addressing this gap in the literature through inclusion of an annual survey of its High Risk Booster Sample. As the description of this subsample clearly implies, this component of the BYDS includes young people considered to be high risk to delinquency and antisocial behaviour in adolescence and included school excludees, young people attending Emotional and Behavioral Difficulty Units, and those living in state care at the time of the research. The delinquency and antisocial behaviours of these young people are the main interest of this chapter. The comparatively limited research on their delinquency and antisocial behaviour may raise questions about the extent to which current education and prevention initiatives have been developed to meet their specific needs. Within the BYDS delinquency and antisocial patterns of a number of these vulnerable groups were studied from the age of 11-16 years.

Many school based studies do not include booster samples of the type included in the BYDS. One of the reasons for this is the difficulty involved with identifying and accessing such young people. Such findings suggest that school based surveys may be underestimating the true level of delinquency and antisocial behaviour amongst school aged young people generally. Other studies have highlighted the diverse and at time heterogeneous nature of such young people particularly when compared with those attending mainstream school. For example, boys are more likely to be excluded from school, and young people with emotional and behavioural difficulties are over represented in exclusion rates by over six times their proportion in the school population (Hayden, 1997).

For many years it has been argued that effective intervention needs to be targeted for particular recipients especially high risk and/or vulnerable young people as their needs may vary. Targeting specific needs and experiences of such recipients has become a key principle for effective intervention initiatives including age and appropriateness (White and Pitts, 1998) with a focus on vulnerable groups (HAS, 2001) which is also a cost effective approach. Furthermore the earlier prevention strategies are implemented, the more likely they are to be effective. To succeed, targeting preventive interventions relies on the accurate identification of the needs of these groups. Despite the extensive range of information on risk and protective factors to delinquency and antisocial behaviour, there is relatively little known about what works to prevent these behaviours amongst vulnerable groups. One exception was reported by Smyth and Saulnier (1996) who found that interventions with high-risk young people could be effective when programmes were culturally relevant, included outreach and incentives, and involved peers or families. However, efficient identification of high risk groups remains a particular challenge for researchers practitioners and policy makers.

Patterns of Delinquency and Antisocial Behaviour in the BYDS

In this section the patterns of delinquency and antisocial behaviour from age 11-16 years will be explored through an analysis of responses to the delinquency scale used in each datasweep of the BYDS. The section will begin with an analysis of the delinquency and antisocial behaviour trends for the mainstream school cohort of young people participating in the BYDS. This will provide contemporary and comparative insights into this behaviour amongst school aged young people who continued attending school until the age of 16 years. An analysis of the trends for each of the high risk groups of the BYDS will then be presented in order to highlight the emerging trends of delinquency and antisocial behaviour amongst these young people from age 11-16 years.

Table 1. Percentage of young people participating in the BYDS school survey committing at least one delinquent behaviour each year by age

Age of Respondents	At least 1 delinquency item in past 12 months (%)	Males (%)	Females (%)
11/12 years	64	77	49
12/13 years	75	84	67
13/14 years	77	84	71
14/15 years	70	76	65
15/16 years	68	76	60

The first point to make here is the high proportion of all young people who had reported at least one delinquent item or behaviour (see Table 1). In the first year of the study when the young people were aged 11/12 years nearly two thirds (64%) reported at least one delinquent offence. This increased to approximately three quarters in year 2 (75%) when aged 12/13 years and year 3 (77%) when aged 13/14 years. The prevalence then fell slightly in year 4 when the young people were aged 14/15 years to 70% and 68% in the fifth year of the study when aged 15/16 years. At each stage of the research more males than females reported at least one delinquent behaviour. The gender gap was widest in year one when 77% of males reported at least one delinquent item compared with less than half (49%) of all females. During the third year of the study the highest proportion of males (84%) and females (67%) reported at least one delinquent item, this fell to 76% of males and 60% of females in year 5.

The level of delinquency and antisocial behaviour increased steadily during the first three years of the study and was highest by the age of 14 based on the mean number of delinquent offences committed (see table 4). In year 1 this was a mean of 2.1 items rising to 2.8 in year 2 and 3.0 in year 3. It then fell to 2.5 in year 4 and 2.4 in year 5. The most frequent type of delinquency was rowdy behaviour followed by graffiti, theft from home and vandalism, avoidance of payment on public transport and shoplifting. This pattern was consistent across the five years of the study with the highest prevalence reported in the third year of the study (see table 5). Males were more likely to commit each of these offences at each stage of the study but the gender gap narrowed as the study progressed and the young people aged through adolescence.

In relation to more serious delinquency, the prevalence rates of this activity remained comparatively low throughout the five years of the study. The more serious offences were 'joyriding' (car theft), arson, burglary, robbery with a weapon, and theft from a car. The most frequent level of serious delinquency was 'joyriding' which peaked at 9 percent in the third year of the study with arson peaking at 6 percent in the third year also. Burglary (5%) robbery with a weapon (3%) and theft form a car (4%) also peaked in the third year of the study amongst the full school cohort. A substantially higher proportion of males committed each of these offences with the gap only narrowing for joy riding (car theft). This analysis provides a baseline of delinquency and antisocial behaviour for school aged young people in Northern Ireland. It provides a useful benchmark upon which to compare young people who are categorised as belonging to high risk groups and who also participated in the BYDS.

Tables 2 and 3 present the numbers of young people who were identified within the high risk categories of the BYDS. It includes the proportion of males in each sample including the proportion of males in the mainstream school survey (approximately 4000 young people each year).

Table 2. Numbers of young people excluded from school identified for inclusion in the study

Survey Year	Participants	Refusals	Absentees	Total
Year 8 (11/12 years)	12 (92%)	3	10	25
Year 9 (12/13 years)	29 (90%)	6	4	39
Year 10 (13/14 years)	48 (88%)	3	15	66
Year 11 (14/15 years)	51 (69%)	4	21	76
Year 12 (15/16 years)	75 (65%)	4	34	113

NB: Proportion of males in brackets.

Table 3. Number of young people attending EBD Units and participating in the BYDS

Survey Year	EBD Participants (%)	Proportion of Males in Mainstream School Survey (%)
Year 8 (11/12 years)	10 (90%)	55
Year 9 (12/13 years)	12 (83%)	48
Year 10 (13/14 years)	16 (94%)	48
Year 11 (14/15 years)	10 (90%)	47
Year 12 (15/16 years)	4 (75%)	47

NB: Proportion of males in brackets.

Data on those young people living in state care was only available for years 3-5 of the BYDS. In year three 31 young people lived in state care with 74 per cent males, in year 4 there were 31 young people living in state care (62% males) and 19 in year 5 (58% males).

The first point to make about the High Risk Booster Sample of the BYDS is the smaller numbers of young people who met the criteria for participation in the research. This will go some way to explaining the comparatively small research resource that has been allocated to studying the experiences of these young people in adolescence generally and in the area of delinquency and antisocial behaviour in particular.

The other important point to make here is the high proportion of males who meet the criteria for inclusion in this part of the BYDS, particularly during the first three years of the study. This is particularly significant as the BYDS contained a majority of female participants during the second to fifth years of the mainstream school survey. For this reason an analysis of the gender patterns of delinquency amongst these groups was not undertaken.

The first point to make about the patterns of delinquency for these young people is the higher number of delinquent acts committed by young people making up the High Risk Booster Sample of the BYDS at each stage of the research regardless of their age. For all young people regardless of their 'risk' status the mean number of delinquent acts peaked in year 3 of the study when the young people were aged 13/14 years, with a fall in the mean numbers of delinquent acts in the two subsequent years (see Table 4).

Table 4. Frequency of Delinquency

No. of Delinquent items	Year 1 School*	Year 1 Excludees **	Year 1 EBD	Year 2 School*	Year 2 Excludees**	Year 2 EBD	Year 3 School*	Year 3 Excludees **	Year 3 EBD	Year 3 In care
0	36	17	0	25	3	8	23	8	6	16
1-3	41	25	50	42	38	50	41	33	31	29
4-6	15	33	10	21	31	33	23	17	19	16
6-9	5	17	20	7	19	0	10	23	19	23
10+	2	8	10	3	7	0	3	19	25	16
Mean	2.1	2	4.2	2.8	4.7	3.5	3	5.3	5.6	5.0

No. of Delinquent items	Year 4 School*	Year 4 Excludees**	Year 4 EBD	Year 4 In care	Year 5 School	Year 5 Excludees	Year 5 EBD	Year 5 In care
0	30	14	20	24			0	11
1-3	41	35	30	41			75	47
4-6	19	33	20	12			0	26
6-9	8	10	20	21			25	11
10+	3	8	10	3			0	5
Mean	2.5	4.1	4.6	3.4		4.1	2.8	3.0

* School Sample; ** School exclude.

Table 5. Frequency of each delinquent behaviour by type of subsample

Delinquent items	Year 1 School*	Year 1 Excludees**	Year 1 EBD	Year 2 School*	Year 2 Excludees**	Year 2 EBD	Year 3 School*	Year 3 Excludees **	Year 3 EBD
Fare	18	45	50	23	14	8	26	27	31
Shoplift	19	42	50	19	59	42	21	58	50
Rowdy	29	50	40	40	62	42	42	71	63
Joyride	4	17	20	7	21	25	9	38	31
Sch theft	6	8	10	13	14	8	15	8	13
Weapon	15	58	50	18	28	25	17	38	44
Vandal	19	42	30	23	55	33	28	56	63
Burglary	3	8	10	4	17	17	5	27	31
Graffiti	26	42	40	37	62	50	41	65	56
Rob	2	0	0	3	17	0	3	8	19
Hm theft	26	50	30	37	38	33	37	40	25
Arson	4	8	10	6	17	0	7	17	25
Fight	4	50	50	47	55	50	48	65	88
Car theft	3	25	50	3	14	17	48	17	25
Delinquent items	Year 3 In care	Year 4 School*	Year 4 Excludees**	Year 4 EBD	Year 4 In care	Year 5 School	Year 5 Excludees	Year 5 EBD	Year 5 In care
Fare	39	21	14	10	18	28	31	0	53
Shoplift	39	17	31	30	29	15	27	25	21
Rowdy	61	37	61	60	47	34	54	50	37
Joyride	23	9	22	20	18	9	31	0	5
Sch theft	23	10	10	10	15	12	15	0	32
Weapon	32	16	33	50	27	14	31	25	21
Vandal	55	23	47	50	29	22	41	25	26
Burglary	23	4	18	30	6	4	17	0	11
Graffiti	52	38	63	60	44	32	51	75	32
Rob	10	3	12	20	9	3	11	25	11
Hm theft	42	27	20	20	18	25	25	0	26
Arson	29	6	18	30	24	6	16	25	11
Fight	55	4	53	60	50	37	51	25	42
Car theft	19	3	6	10	9	3	14	0	11

* School Sample; ** School excludes.

For more serious delinquency e.g. joyriding (care theft), arson, robbery with a weapon, the annual prevalence rates for these behaviours was lower than other types of delinquency (i.e. antisocial behaviour and acquisitive crime). The patterns of behaviour across each category of young people showed consistently higher prevalence rates across each year of the study for the high risk groups of the BYDS compared with the full school cohort (see Table 5). Figures 1-3 provide examples of this pattern of behaviour for these including comparisons with the mainstream cohort.

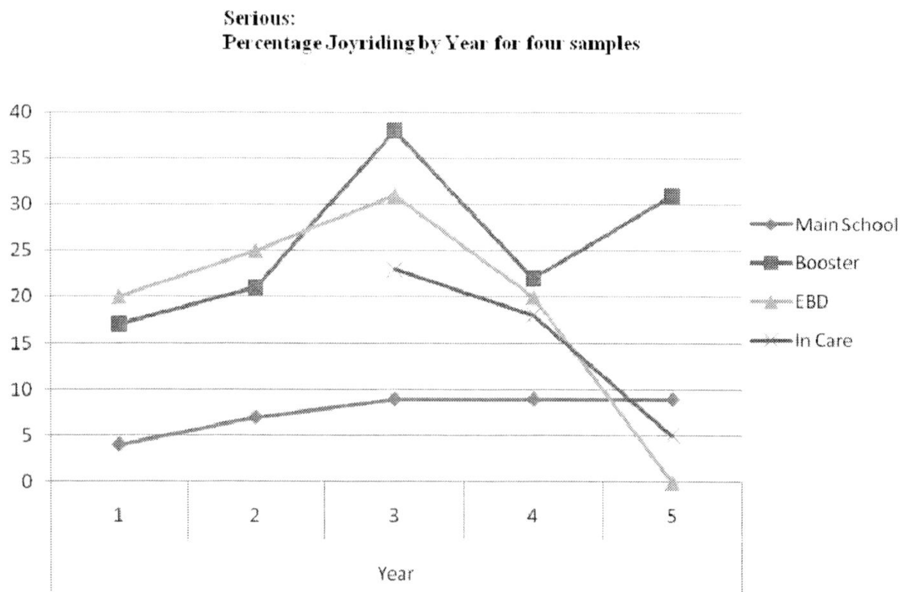

Figure 1. Percentage of joyriding (car theft) by categories of participants in the BYDS.

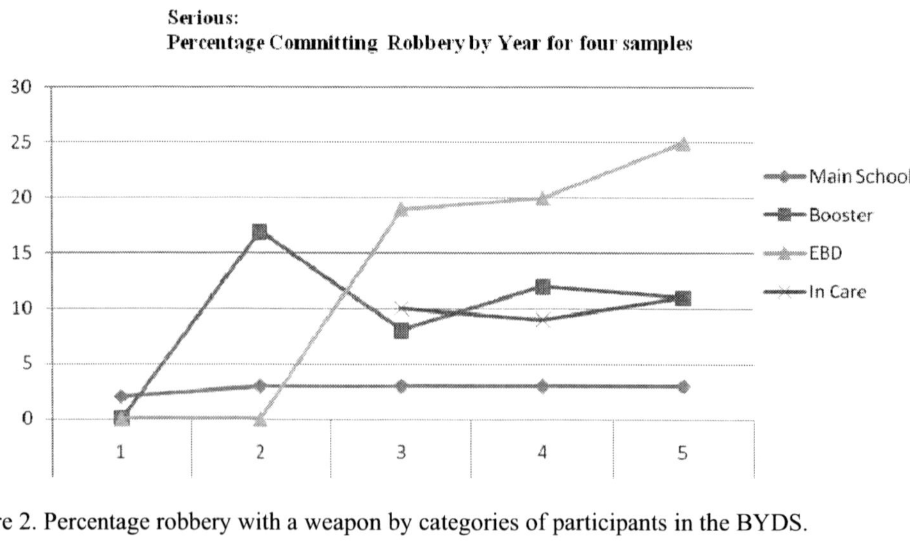

Figure 2. Percentage robbery with a weapon by categories of participants in the BYDS.

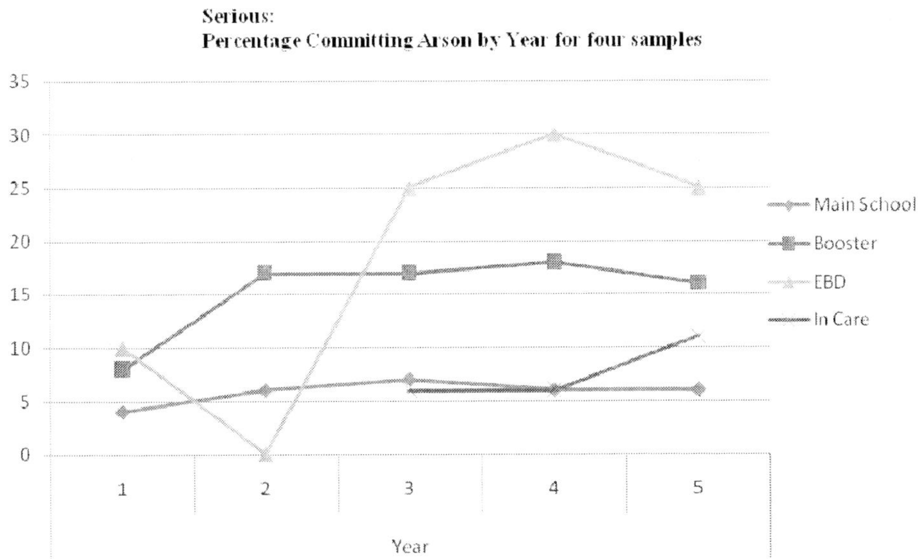

Figure 3. Percentage of arson by categories of participants in the BYDS.

The frequency of each delinquent behaviour followed a similar pattern to lifetime use as the high risk groups regardless of the subsample of young people. The EBD sample reported more frequent delinquency and antisocial behaviour followed by the school excludees and then the young people living in state care. The frequency of delinquency and antisocial behaviour was higher for each category of high risk cohort than for those attending mainstream school, reaching a high during the fourth year of the study when all the young people participating in the BYDS were 14/15 years of age. A lower level frequency of each delinquent activity was noted during the fifth year of study when all young people were aged 15/16 years. Figures 4-6 provides examples of these types of behaviour.

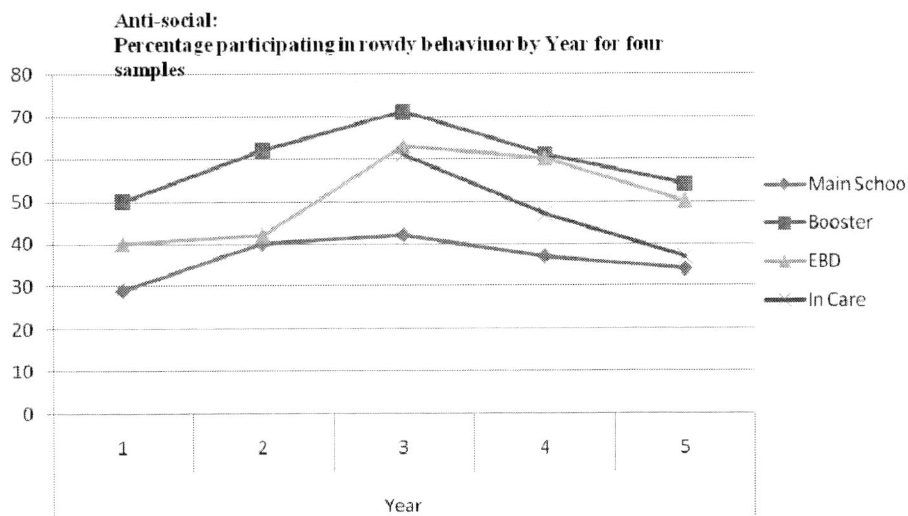

Figure 4. Percentage of rowdy behaviour by categories of participants in the BYDS.

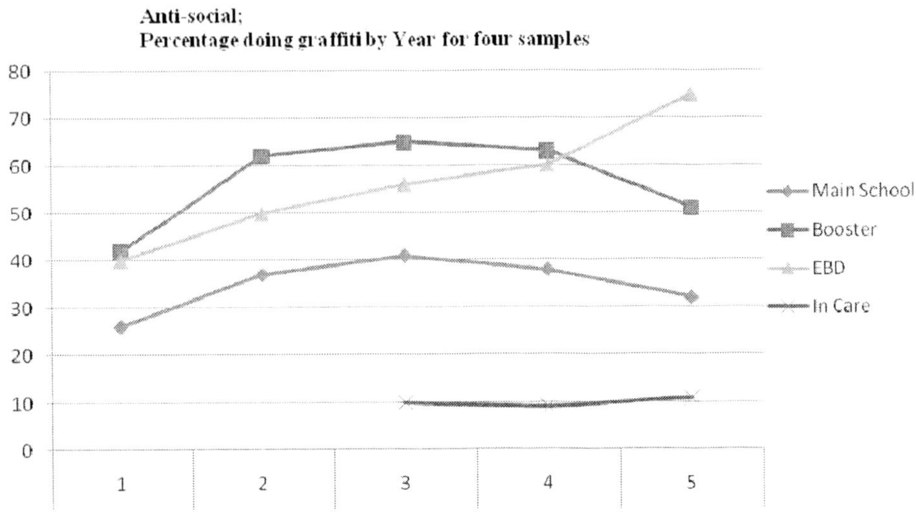

Figure 5. Percentage of graffiti by categories of participants in the BYDS.

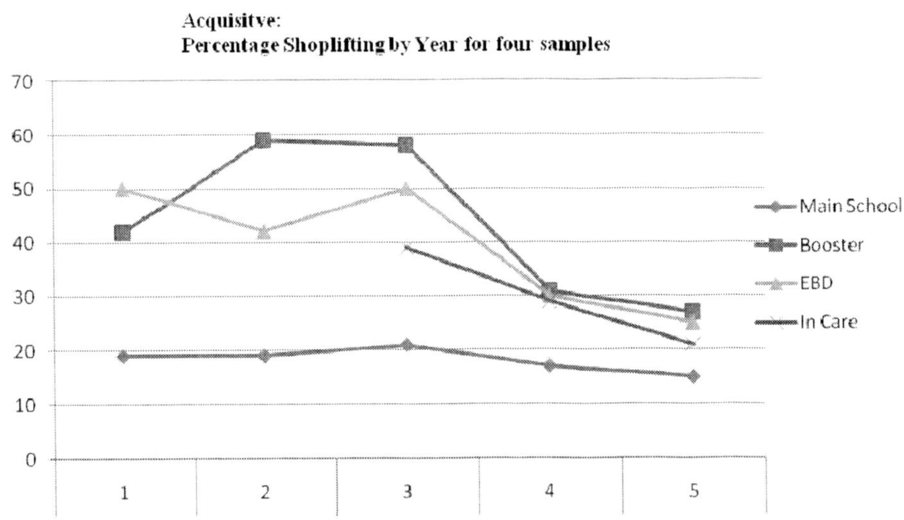

Figure 6. Percentage of shoplifting by categories of participants in the BYDS.

Explaining delinquency in the High Risk Booster Sample of the Belfast Youth Development Study

In contrast to those who were not attending school at the time of the research (school excludees; EBD sample), substantially higher levels of delinquency and antisocial behaviour was reported at all stages of the research. This reached a high of approximately eight out of ten participants during the third year of the research and remained at this level for the rest of the study. Amongst the school sample, delinquency was comparatively lower at the beginning of the research rising gradually each year until the fourth stage of the study when the young people were aged 14/15 years. At this stage more than four out of ten of the full mainstream school sample reported delinquency year of the research.

These findings are important for several reasons. Firstly, they appear to support the categorization of each subsample of the BYDS as a vulnerable or high risk group to delinquency and antisocial behaviour. Although without a full analysis of all contributing variables it is not possible to call this a causal relationship. Secondly, they highlight the key stage at which the level of lifetime delinquency appears to reach a high noticeably during the fourth year of the study when the young people were aged 14/15 years. These insights are useful for both the timing and individual targeting of intervention initiatives to all school aged young people, regardless of their educational status or the type of education they are receiving.

The general patterns of delinquency and antisocial behaviour appear similar in relation to the age of onset and the development of these behaviours on a more regular basis. For example the levels of more frequent delinquency and antisocial behaviour showed noticeable increases until the around the age of 14 years when it appeared to stabilize as the majority of vulnerable groups reported the highest mean number of delinquent behaviours. However all the traditional high risk samples produced substantially higher levels of delinquency compared with the mainstream sample regardless of whether they were a school based (i.e. 'in care') or non-school sample (i.e. school excludes; EBD sample).

The delinquency and antisocial behaviour trends reported by the high risk subsamples of the BYDS have shown that non school attending young people, and other members of traditional school based vulnerable groups (i.e. those 'in care') were much more likely to engage in delinquent and antisocial behaviour. Other similar patterns were noted amongst each sample of vulnerable young people regardless of their school status. For example the high risk samples were more likely to be male, live in a disrupted family, report indicators of social deprivation and attend non grammar schools. In Northern Ireland academic ability remains the main selection criteria for grammar schools at the end of primary educational when aged 11 years (McCrystal et al, 2006; 2007 a, b).

Developing a Framework for Evidence Based Interventions for High Risk Young People in Adolescence

In this section the implications of the findings presented in this chapter will be discussed in order to provide insights into the structure and timing of prevention initiatives for the reduction of delinquency and its causes amongst high risk young people during adolescence. The timing and placement of interventions within appropriate educational settings is key to their success but this is not always straightforward. The use of instruction approaches that rely heavily on the production and processing of verbal discourse may particularly disadvantage young people who are not attending mainstream school as classroom groups may be unsuitable for teaching them about delinquency and antisocial behaviour. Factors such as reduced information-processing and limited communication abilities make it difficult for these young people to engage in discussion topics and integrate new ideas and information. The notion of evidence-based practice has proved enormously challenging in mainstream school-based drug education, for example, Wallace and Staiger (1998) and offers increased challenges to the delivery of such initiatives to young people who have stopped attending formal school based education settings.

The area of high risk young people has not been graced with the same level of concern or debate with respect to preparing its young people to deal with these issues in society compared with young people in mainstream education. Given that mainstream settings consist of a heterogeneous group of young people with highly varying levels of academic and psychosocial risk, gaining a better understanding of how to prevent delinquent and antisocial behaviour by high risk young people will help us to reduce some of the variance with respect to the levels of risk experienced by these young people, as well as offering insights to inform practice in both mainstream and special education settings. Perhaps it would be insightful to consider where every young person sits on the continuum of risk versus protective factors. In this way, interventions designed to address delinquency and antisocial behaviour, like other aspects of educational curriculum, can be tailored more specifically to individual learning requirements, and can be measured against meaningful and identifiable outcomes. This approach could be supported by further research to evaluate the effectiveness of health promotion for high risk young people in order to clarify the most appropriate approaches to the development and delivery of delinquency and antisocial behaviour prevention initiatives to deal with such problems.

These approaches could consist of easily understood material on delinquent behaviour by high risk young people which could provide accurate information on which to develop informed decision-making strategies for making a decision about such behaviour. The delivery of such programmes should include skills based interventions; culturally relevant elements that are delivered alongside initiatives to address other social and health problems faced by these young people. Furthermore, to be effective these programmes should be delivered by appropriately qualified individuals and include issues relevant to their peer group, family and general lifestyle environment in which they life. They should be regularly updated standardized and monitored to assess their value to what can be a changing social environment. In addition individual sessions of short duration can have a negative impact on young people and their attitude towards delinquency and antisocial behaviour, as can threatening messages and wrong information (EMCDDA, 2002). The methods used in teaching need to be age appropriate and may be either interactive or non interactive or both. An important message for the development of effective interventions for high risk young people should be to highlight the methods that are inappropriate as well as those that will work when producing such initiatives.

Young delinquents, particularly in the pre-teenage years, are a group not usually recognised as needing services to prevent them from becoming future serious, violent offenders (Loeber and Dishon, 1983). These young people present potentially serious problems for society generally as they grow up if their delinquency and antisocial behaviour tendencies remain and even become established as may be evident from the increased prevalence of these behaviours noted in the findings from the BYDS. Despite this, they are a group about who comparatively little is known, especially amongst those who are considered particularly vulnerable or at risk to these behaviours in adolescence. The earlier targeted interventions are delivered the more likely they are to be effective, particularly as these young people can become an expensive burden on society, now and in the future (Farrington et al, 2001) making the timing of such interventions an important issue.

The findings from the BYDS show that to be effective interventions need to be considered before young people leave primary education at age 11 years as many had already reported delinquency and antisocial behaviour by this age, in some cases at quite high levels. This is particularly important when the behaviours associated with delinquency and antisocial behaviour are highlighted particularly the levels of substance abuse associated with this behaviour (McCrystal et al, 2006).

Another significant factor was the dramatic increase in the number of young females reporting delinquency and antisocial behaviour from year 1 to year 2 amongst the mainstream cohort, when the gender balance became much more even and remained so from this point onwards. This may imply that there is increasing evidence for the development and implication of gender specific intervention strategies. However the implications for the gendered nature of interventions was difficult to assess amongst the high risk cohorts of young people due to the predominantly male nature of these groups particularly during the first three years of this study. Consideration should also be given to the development of a series of strategies that are also age specific to the developmental stage at which these young people had reached, as the levels of offending appeared to stabilise and even fall during the final year of the BYDS. The reasons for this were unclear and perhaps require a more qualitative research approach to fully unravel this finding.

To be effective interventions need to take a whole person approach rather than focus only on one particular behaviour like delinquency with particular attention given to the individual needs of the target group. Existing initiatives for adolescents are developed from existing evidence which is usually drawn from school based surveys which undermines their value to those attending EBD units or have been excluded from school. For interventions to be most effective they need to be targeted to the specific needs of recipients, especially when designed for young people vulnerable to drug misuse as their needs may vary with those in mainstream school settings. Targeting the specific needs through an understanding of the experiences of recipients has become a key principle for effective practice in the area of drug prevention that focuses on vulnerable groups (HAS, 2001) a principle that can also be applied to delinquency and antisocial behaviour among these young people. Despite the extensive range of information on risk and protective factors (e.g. Hawkins et al, 1992), there is relatively little known about what works amongst vulnerable or high risk groups (Roe and Becker, 2005). One exception was reported by Smith and Saulnier (1996) who found that interventions with high-risk young people could be effective when programmes were culturally relevant, included outreach and incentives, and involved peers or families.

It will not be sufficient, however, to amass only a quantitative data base. In this respect, a clearer understanding of the role played by delinquent behaviour, during the adolescent and early adult years of this population will provide an important foundation for future research. To this end, studies that employ in-depth interviews with the young people themselves, their parents, teachers, and community carers are needed. Whilst the BYDS has highlighted a number of relevant issues to delinquency and antisocial behaviours amongst high risk young people, its reliance on quantitative research methods makes it difficult to define all the key issues and their operationalisation.

CONCLUDING REMARKS

The majority of empirical evidence on delinquency and antisocial behaviour in adolescence has been gathered from school-based surveys. The existing literature has shown that some young people are at a higher level of risk to delinquency and antisocial behaviour. Despite this, a limited information base exists on delinquency and antisocial behaviour amongst these young people. The reasons for this include difficulties with obtaining relevant data on delinquency and antisocial behaviours, developing appropriate measuring instruments to meet their varying levels of literacy for both cross sectional and longitudinal research. In addition the relatively small numbers of high risk young people means the findings are often not generalizable to the majority of young people in mainstream school. Initiatives designed to keep all young people within mainstream education further ensures the numbers in this population remain small. In order to fully address their needs for targeted and appropriate intervention strategies, a valid empirical base is necessary as an initial step. Having identified the difficulties involved in obtaining such empirical based evidence the example of the high risk booster sample of the BYDS overcame these difficulties showing it is possible to develop an appropriate empirical base upon which delinquent prevention strategies can be developed for high risk young people.

The findings from high risk booster sample of the BYDS have highlighted a number of challenges for policy makers and practitioners with responsibility for addressing the delinquent behaviour among young people considered to be vulnerable to this behaviour. Firstly is the identification of the scale of the problem. The high risk booster sample of the BYDS has highlighted the scale of delinquency amongst its target population and in doing so the importance of researching the issue throughout the developmental period of adolescence. An understanding of the scale of this challenge is a necessary prerequisite for determining the scope and level of intervention required which also has resource implications and often an inhibitory effect on such research. The findings from the high risk booster sample of the BYDS have provided important insights into the scale of the problem as well as when interventions may have maximum impact during adolescence. The findings support early intervention at the beginning of postprimary education particularly before the age of 14 years with evidence suggesting interventions may be necessary at primary school level before young people reach the age of 11 years. However it is even more difficult to identify and target high risk young people at this stage.

The second key challenge is the design and development of targeted education and prevention initiatives to address the level of intervention required. All mainstream schools are required to deliver personal health and social education to their pupils but such programmes are not developed for the specific needs of those who stop attending mainstream school. The challenge here includes both the identification of these young people and delivering targeted interventions.

A further challenge is the delivery of targeted initiatives to those most in need as many of the high risk booster sample were not regular school attenders or in receipt of school based interventions. Monitoring the impact of such interventions through effective evaluations that assess their short and longterm impacts on the delinquency and antisocial behaviors of recipients are also required to ensure such interventions are ‘fit for purpose’. The high risk booster sample of the BYDS has demonstrated an ability to engage and track groups of vulnerable young people throughout adolescence. Perhaps the key challenge to the success of the issues raised here is making such assessments feasible through addressing the resource implications of delivering the suggestions made here. As the specific details of resource requirements are not yet known it is difficult to calculate this. However, it is clear that some additional requirements will be necessary for example the design and operationalisation of age related targeted interventions.

Interventions for addressing delinquency and antisocial behaviour should ideally be empirically based. The empirical base for delinquency among vulnerable young people at risk to delinquency is comparatively limited. This means that our knowledge base upon which the most appropriate interventions are based remains incomplete. The high risk booster sample of the BYDS has highlighted the potential value of undertaking research with young people who are considered vulnerable to delinquency and antisocial behaviour. In doing so it has highlighted potentially appropriate intervention approaches and in doing so increased this knowledge base for both practitioners and policy makers as well has indicating the timing when the delivery of such interventions may have their greatest impact.

ACKNOWLEDGMENTS

The Belfast Youth Development Study is funded by the Research and Development of Office of the Health and Personal Social Services of the Department of Health and Social Services for Northern Ireland.

REFERENCES

Advisory Council on the Misuse of Drugs. (2006). *Pathways of problems.* Hazardous use of tobacco, alcohol and other drugs by young people in the UK and its implications for policy. London: Avisory Council on the Misuse of Drugs.

Angold, A., Messer, S.C., Stangl, D., Farmer, E.M., Costello, E.J. and Burns, B.J. (1998) Perceived parental burden and service use for child and adolescent psychiatric disorders. *American Journal of Public Health*, 88 (1), 75-80.

Arnett, J.J. (2000) Emerging adulthood: A theory of development from late teens through twenties. *American Psychologist*, 55, 469-480.

Audit Commission (1996). *Misspent youth: Young people and crime.* London: Audit Commission.

Catalano, R.F. and Hawkins, J.D. (1997). The social development model: A theory of antisocial behaviour. In J.D. Hawkins (Ed.), *Delinquency and crime: Current theories* (pp.149-177). Cambridge: Cambridge University Press.

Catalano, R.F., Haggerty, K.P., Gainey, R.R., Hoppe, M.J., and Brewer, D.D. (1998). Effectiveness of prevention with youth at high risk of drug abuse. In W.J. Bukoski and R.I. Evans (Eds.), *Cost benefit/cost-effectiveness research of drug prevention: Implication for programming and policy*. Rockville: NIDA Research Monograph 176.

Criminal Statistics England and Wales (1995). London: Home Office.

Cohen, L.E. and Felson M. (1979). Social change and crime rate trends: A routine activity approach. *American Sociological review,* 44, 588-608.

Crome, I.B., and McArdle, P. (2004). Prevention programmes. In H. Crome, E. Ghodse, P. Gilvarry and P. McArdle (Eds.), *Young people and substance misuse.* London: Royal College of Physicians.

Davis, P. and Florian, L. (2004). Teaching strategies and approaches for pupils with special educational needs: A scoping study. Department for Education and Employment *Research Brief No. 516* (Nottingham, DfES Publications).

Day, C., van Veen, D., and Walraven, G. (1997). *Children and youth at risk and urban education, research, policy and practice.* Leuven: EERA and Garant.

European Monitoring Center for Drugs and Drug Addiction (2002). The state of the drugs problem in the acceding and candidate countries to the Europen Union. Annual report 2002. Luxembourg: Office of the Official Publications of the European Communities.

Espiritu, R.C., Huizinga, D., Crawford, A.,and Loeber, R. (2001). Epidemiology of selfreported delinquency. In *Child Delinquents:Development, Intervention, and ServiceNeeds,* edited by R. Loeber and D.P.Farrington. Thousand Oaks, CA: Sage Publications, Inc., pp. 47–66.

Fagan, J., Piper, E.S. and Cheng, Y-T. (1987). Contributions of Victimization to Delinquency in Innner Cities. *The Journal of Criminla Law and Criminology, 78, 3,* 586-596,

Farrington, D.P. (1984). Measuring the natural history of delinquency and crime. In R.A. Glow (ed). *Advances in the behavioural measurement of children*, 1, 217-63.

Farrington, D.P. (1991). Childhood aggression and adult violence: Early precursors and later life outcomes. In: D.J. Pepler and K.H. Rubin (eds) *The development and treatment of childhood aggression.* (pp 5-29). Hillsdale: NJ: Erbaum.

Farrington, D.,P., Barnes, G.C., and Lambert, S.(1996). The concentration of offending in families, *Legal and Criminological Psychology*, 1, 47-63.

Farrington, D.(2001). Multiple risk factors for multiple problem violent boys. In: R.R. Carrado, R. Roesch, S.D., Hart and J.K. Gierowski, (Eds). *Multiple problem violent behaviour.* Amsterdam: IOS Press.

Fattah, E.A. (1991). *Understanding Criminal Victimization: An Introduction to Theoretical Victimology.* Scarborough Ontario: Prentice-Hall

Fergusson, D.M., Harwood, L.J., and Lynskey, M.T. (1993). The effects of conduct disorder and attention in middle childhood on offending and scholastics ability at age 13. *Journal of Child Psychology and Psychiatry*, 32, 899-916.

Fishbein, M., and Ajzen, I. (1975). *Belief, Attitude, Intention, and Behavior: An Introduction to Theory and Research. Reading*, MA: Addison-Wesley

Graham J. and Bowling, B. (1995) *Crime prevention stratgeies in Europe and North America.* Monsey, NY: Criminal Justice Press..

Graham J. and Bowling, B. (1996). *Young people and crime.* London: Home Office Study 145. London: Home Office.

Goulden, C. and Sondhi, A. (2001). *At the margins: Drug use by vulnerable young people in the 1998/1999 youth lifestyles survey.* London: Home Office Research Study 228.

HAS. (2001). *The substance of young needs.* London: Drugs Prevention Advisory Service.

Hawkins, J.D., Catalano, R.F., and Miller, J.Y. (1992). Risk and protective factors for alcohol and other drug problems in adolescence and early adulthood: Implications for substance abuse prevention. *Psychological Bulletin*, 112, 64-105.

Hayden, C. (1997). Excluded from primary school: Debates, evidence responses. Buckingham: Open University Press.

Hindelang, M.J. (1973). *Causes of Delinquency*: A partial replication and extension, Social Problems, 20, 127-47.

Hirschi, T.(1969). *Causes of Delinquency*. Berkeley CA: University of California Press.

Home Office (2004).Underage Drinking Findings from the 2004 *Offending, Crime and Justice Review*. www.homeoffice.gov.uk/red/pdf506/r277.pdf

Kress, J.S. and Elias, M.J. (1993). Substance abuse prevention in special education populations: Review and recommendations. *Journal of Special Education*, 27(1), 35-51.

Lloyd, C. (1998). Risk factors for problem drug use: Identifying vulnerable groups. *Drugs: Education, Prevention and Policy*, 5 (3), 217-232.

Loeber, R. and Dishon, T.(1983). Early predictors of male delinquency: A review. *Psychological Review*, 94, 68-99.

Loeber, R. and Stouthamer-Loeber, M. (1987). Family Predictors as Correlates and Predictors of Juvenile Conduct Problems and Delinquency. In: M. Tonry and N. Morris (eds), *Crime and Justice: An Annual Review of Research*. Chicago: University of Chicago Press.

Loeber, R. and Farrington, D.P. (1994). Problems and Solutions in Longitudinal and Experimental Treatment Studies of Child Psychopathology and Delinquency. *Journal of Consulting and Clinical psychology*, 62, 887-900.

Manski, C.F., Pepper, J.V. and Petrie, C.V. (Eds.) (2001). Informing America's policy on illegal drugs: what we do not know keeps hurting us. Committee on data and research for Policy on Illegal Drugs. Committee on Law and Justice and Committee on National Statistics (Washington, National Research Council).

McCrystal, P., Higgins, K. and Percy, A. (2006) Brief Report: School Exclusion drug use and delinquency in adolescence. *Journal of Adolescence*, 29, 829-836.

McCrystal, P., Percy, A. and Higgins K. (2007a). The cost of drug use in adolescence: Young people, money and substance abuse. *Drugs: Education, Prevention and Policy*, 14(1), 19-28.

b). Drug use amongst young people attending emotional and behavioural difficulty units during adolescence: a longitudinal analysis. *Emotional and Behavioural Difficulties*, 12(1), p49-68.

Menard, S. (1991). *Longitudinal research*. London: Sage Publications.

Nicholson, D and Ayers, H. (2004). *Adolescent problems*. Fulton: David Publishers.

Nilson, M. (1999). Drug use among vulnerable groups of young people: comments. *Drugs: Education, Prevention and Policy*, 6 (12), 204-204.

Cloward, R.A. and Ohlin, L.E. (1960). Delinquency and Opportunity - A Theory of Delinquent Gangs. New Tork: Free Press.

Pavis, S., Cunningham-Burley, S. and Amos, A. (1997). Alcohol Consumption and Young People: Exploring Meaning and Social Context. *Health Education Research*, 1997, 12, 3, 311-322.

Peterson, A. and Leffert, N. (1995). What is special about adolescence? In *Psychosocial disturbances in young people*, edited by M. Rutter. Cambridge: Cambridge University Press pp.3-36.

Phil, R. and Peterson, J. (1991). Attention-deficit hyperactivity disorder, childhood conduct disorder, and alcoholism: Is there an association? *Alcohol Health and Research World*, 15 (1), 25-31.

Powis, B., Griffiths, P., Gossop, M., Lloyd, C., and Strang, J. (1998). Drug use and offending behaviour among young people excluded from school. *Drugs: Education, Prevention and Policy,* 5 (3), 245-256.

Roe, S. and Becker, J. (2005). Drug prevention with vulnerable young people: a review. *Drugs: Education, Prevention and Policy*, 12, 85-99.

Rutter , M. Giller, H, and Hagall, A. (1998). *Antisocial Behaviour by Young People.* Cambridge: University Press.

Snow, P.C., Wallace, S.D., and Munro, G.D. (2001). Drugs education with special needs populations: Identifying and understanding the challenges. *Drugs: Education, Prevention and Policy*, 8 (3), 261-273.

Steinhausen, H-C., Wilms, J., and Spohr, H-L (1993). Longterm psychopathological and cognitive outcome of children with fetal alcohol syndrome. *Journal of the American Academy of Child and Adolescent Psychiatry*, 32, 990-94.

Western, J.S., Lynch, M. and Ogilvie, E. (2003). Understanding Youth Crime. *An Australian Study*. London: Ashgate.

Wikstrom, P-O (1987). *Patterns of crime in a birth* cohort. Stockholm: University of Stockholm Department of Sociology.

Wolfgang, M.E. and Ferracuti, F. (2003). *The Subculture of Violence.* London: The International Behavioural and Social Scinces Library.

In: Delinquency: Causes, Reduction and Prevention
Editor: Ozan Sahin and Joseph Maier
ISBN 978-1-60741-558-9

Chapter 6

ADOLESCENT RELIGIOSITY AS A PROTECTIVE FACTOR FOR DELINQUENCY: REVIEW OF EVIDENCE AND A CONCEPTUAL FRAMEWORK FOR FUTURE RESEARCH

Robert D. Laird[1], Matthew D. Marrero[1] and Loren D. Marks[2]
[1]Department of Psychology, University of New Orleans
[2]School of Human Ecology, Louisiana State University

ABSTRACT

The first section of this chapter reviews evidence showing that although greater religiosity has been associated with less involvement in delinquent and analogous behaviors, the mechanisms and processes through which religiosity is linked to delinquent behavior are not well understood. In the second section of the chapter, a conceptual framework and theory for studying the religion-delinquency association will be presented. The framework adapts and builds on Gottfredson and Hirschi's (1990) General Theory of Crime. The third section of the chapter presents results of the initial study guided by the framework. Data are drawn from a longitudinal study of development during the transition from middle childhood to adolescence. Participants (n = 181) completed standard self-report assessments. Results provide initial evidence that the link between religiosity and delinquent behavior problems can be explained by the reduced opportunities and dispositions to engage in delinquent behavior more common among highly religious than less highly religious adolescents.

INTRODUCTION

Greater religiosity has been associated with less delinquency and risk-taking behavior (Wallace and Williams, 1997). However, the mechanisms and processes through which religiosity is linked to delinquency and risk-taking behavior (i.e., alcohol, tobacco and drug use; delinquency; risky sexual behavior; risky driving) are not well understood (Cotton, Zebracki, Rosenthal, Tsevat, and Drotar, 2006; Miller and Thoresen, 2003; Wallace and Williams, 1997). In the first section of this chapter we will review available evidence pertaining to whether greater adolescent religiosity is associated with lower levels of delinquent and risk-taking behavior. We will focus on delinquency and risk-taking behavior because research in this area is quite sparse and because delinquency and risk-taking behavior are correlated and assumed (by the primary theoretical perspective guiding our work) to be influenced by similar processes. In the second section of the chapter, a conceptual framework and theory for studying the religion-delinquency association will be presented. The framework adapts and builds on Gottfredson and Hirschi's (1990) General Theory of Crime (GTC) to propose that delinquency and risk-taking behavior in middle to late adolescence is the product of risk-taking dispositions and risk-taking opportunities. The third section of the chapter will present an initial test of the theorized processes and pathways. The final section of the chapter will discuss findings from the initial test and offer directions for future work.

Based on survey data, 95% of married couples and parents in the U.S. report a religious affiliation (Mahoney, Pargament, Tarakeshwar, and Swank, 2001), and about 60% say religion is "important" or "very important" to them (McCullough, Hoyt, Larson, Koenig, and Thoresen, 2000). For "a substantial minority," religion is reportedly "the single most important influence in [life]" (Miller and Thoresen, 2003, p. 25). Conversely, only 2% of Americans say they do not believe in God (Sherkat and Ellison, 1999). Even given the tendency of U.S. survey respondents to over-report their religious participation, religious beliefs and activities continue to be reported as salient (Christiano, 2000; Dollahite, Marks, and Goodman, 2004). If the cumulative research on religion is taken at face value, religion does not directly influence about 10% of the population, matters little to another 20-30%, is important to another 40%, and is "most important" to 10-20%. These data, however, are drawn from adult samples. *The Handbook of Religion and Health* (Koenig, McCullough, and Larson, 2001) examines more than 1,200 studies and 400 reviews, but only about 5% of the accumulated work specifically addresses adolescents. A recent interest in the interface between religion/spirituality and adolescent development is manifested by two multi-authored handbooks (Roelhkepartain, King, Wagener, and Benson, 2005; Yust, Johnson, Sasso, and Roehlkepartain, 2006). However, neither volume presents primary research—the editors' and authors' aims are conceptual, thereby seeking to lay a foundation for future research in this nascent area.

Perhaps the landmark research in the domain of adolescent religiosity is Smith's (2005) book-length, mixed-method study with a sample of more than 3,000 U.S. youth. Smith reports that 8% of American youth are *devoted* (attend services weekly or more), 27% are *regulars* (2-3 services a month), 17% are *sporadic* (a few times a year), 12% are *disengaged* (not religious), and 37% of the sample were categorized as "other/mixed" (p. 220). In addition to providing a useful typology, Smith (2005) offers two overarching conclusions that are directly relevant to this chapter: (a) "highly religious teenagers appear to be doing much better in life than less religious teenagers" (p. 263); and (b) "a modest amount of religion...does not appear to make a consistent difference in the lives of U.S teenagers...only the more serious religious teens" seem to benefit (p. 233).

Wallace and Williams (1997) propose that religiosity is a neglected and understudied influence on adolescent delinquency and risk-taking behavior. They note that: (a) there is little communication between scholars who study religion and scholars who study adolescents; (b) research on adolescent religiosity rarely addresses risk-taking behaviors; (c) research on adolescent risk-taking has largely ignored evidence of a relation between religion and health; and (d) when studies of adolescent risk-taking have included religion, religion or religiosity is typically viewed as a control or nuisance variable. Following this preamble, Wallace and Williams (1997) proceed to review a handful of studies documenting evidence that religion (operationalized in numerous ways) is associated with reduced risk-taking behavior in two broad areas: (a) alcohol, tobacco, and other drug use; and (b) sexual behavior. There is a "moderate but significant" negative relationship between religiosity and substance use. With respect to sexual behavior, Wallace and Williams (1997) conclude that the literature suggests that "highly religious adolescents initiate sex later, have fewer sexual partners, and have sex less often that their less religious peers" (p. 452). A meta analysis of 19 studies (and 79 effects) testing the effect of religion on crime in adult samples (Baier and Wright, 2001) reached a similar conclusion that religious beliefs and behaviors have a moderate deterrent effect on criminal behavior with a mean effect size of $r = -.12$. Similar conclusions have been reached in reviews of literature linking religiosity and adult mental health and adjustment (Donelson, 1999; Levin and Chatters, 1998).

In the eleven years since Wallace and Williams' review, evidence of a potential protective effect of religiosity on a wide range of adolescent risk taking behaviors has continued to accumulate. Consider the following examples. In a large-scale, national study (Sinha, Cnaan, and Gelles, 2007), greater religiosity among 11 to 18 year olds was associated with less smoking, alcohol use, truancy, sexual activity, marijuana use, and depression. Analyses of the National Longitudinal Survey of Youth (Hardy and Raffaelli, 2003), show that religiosity among 15-18 year olds was associated with a lower likelihood of first sexual intercourse over a two year period but that the initiation of sexual intercourse was not related to change in religiosity. In another study, religiosity was associated with less substance use and also buffered the negative impact of life stress on increased substance use from grades 7 to 10 (Wills, Yaeger, and Sandy, 2003). Religious beliefs and behaviors also were associated with less alcohol use and abuse in a sample of inner city African American adolescents (Goggin, Murray, Malcarne, Brown, and Wallston, 2007), and greater religiosity among 14-19 year olds was linked to less alcohol use and problem drinking (Brown, Parks, Zimmerman, and Phillips, 2001).

Despite the continued accumulation of evidence that greater adolescent religiosity is associated with less negative risk-taking behavior, little progress has been made toward understanding why and how religiosity is linked to less risk-taking behavior. In the sections that follow we present a heuristic model of why and how religiosity may inhibit adolescent involvement in delinquency and risk-taking behavior. In developing the model we draw from and seek to integrate research from the sociology of religion, adolescent development, and criminality/deviance literatures.

Conceptual Model

In their GTC, Gottfredson and Hirschi (1990) theorize that crime will take place if people are given the opportunity to commit a crime when they are prone to take advantage of the opportunity. Gottfredson and Hirschi (1990) proposed that their GTC was applicable to criminal behavior and analogous acts. Risk-taking behavior is consistent with the range of analogous acts discussed by Gottfredson and Hirschi. Thus, we extend the GTC framework to risk-taking behavior in adolescence and propose that adolescents will engage in delinquent and risk-taking behavior when they have opportunities to take risks combined with a disposition to engage in risk-taking behavior. Furthermore, we elaborate on the GTC to incorporate religiosity as an external influence on the propensity-opportunity-risk-taking process (and in doing so elaborate on Gottfredson and Hirshi's hypothesis that the link between religion and crime is spurious due to shared associations with low self-control). The conceptual model is shown in Figure 1. Delinquent and risk-taking behavior is hypothesized to be predicted by dispositions (path A), opportunities (path B), and the interaction between dispositions and opportunities (path C). Adolescent religiosity is hypothesized to be associated with dispositions (path D) and opportunities (path E) and to moderate associations between dispositions and risk-taking behavior (path F) and between opportunities and risk-taking behavior (path G). The sections that follow present each of the four key concepts (risk-taking behavior, religiosity, dispositions, and opportunities) and discuss potential indicators of each concept. We also review research documenting associations consistent with the proposed model.

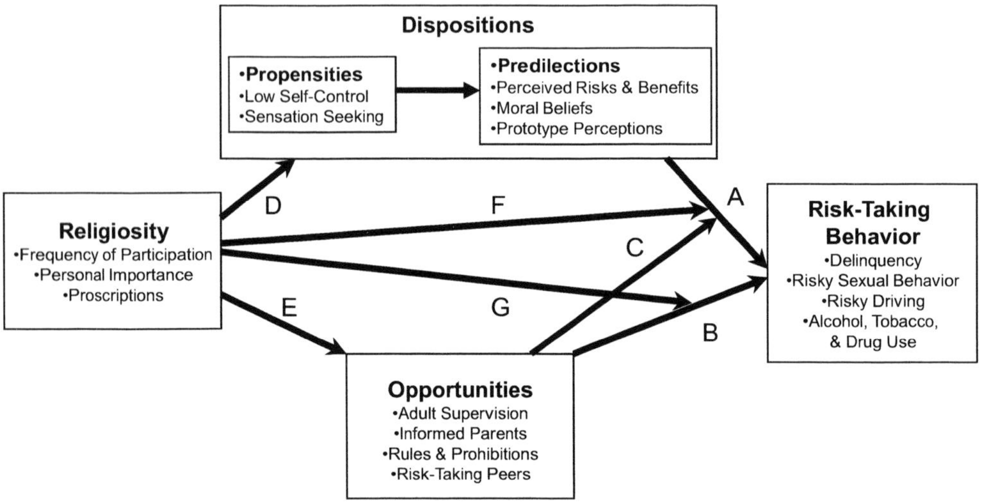

Figure 1. Adapting the General Theory of Crime to Study Religiosity.

Risk-Taking Behavior in Adolescence

In elaborating on the model, we will focus on four types of risk-taking behavior: substance use (alcohol, tobacco, and drugs), delinquency, risky sexual behavior, and risky driving behavior. These behaviors were selected because they are relatively common during middle to late adolescence, yet they qualify as risk-taking behaviors because involvement in these behaviors contribute to the leading causes of death in the middle to late adolescence age group (Biglan, Brennan, Foster, and Holder, 2005). Adolescent involvement in many of these risk-taking behaviors is formally discouraged by society broadly and by parents and religious organizations in particular, although not all of the behaviors are discouraged to the same extent. These risk-taking behaviors are consistent with the "analogous behaviors" presumed to be explained by the GTC.The pattern of associations is expected to be generally consistent across the range of behaviors, in part because risk-taking behaviors are expected to be intercorrelated, and may, according to GTC, share a common cause (Biglan et al., 2005; Feldstein and Miller, 2006; Gottfredson and Hirschi, 1990).

Conceptualizing Religiosity

Many pre-1985 sociological studies measured religiosity with minimal breadth and depth and included only one or two indicators to conceptualize and represent religion or religiosity. Indeed, religion was frequently little more than a token variable, raising questions regarding the construct validity of religion as presented in many studies (Marks, 2005). In psychology, Miller and Thoresen (2003) similarly indicate that "measurement of spiritual/religious constructs...has usually been poor in quality" (p. 26). On one hand, these points lead a scholar to read social science research on religion with a healthy skepticism. On the other hand, it is noteworthy that the construct of religion has—in spite of frequently limited and simplistic measurement—been a statistically significant factor in a myriad of studies; a point that seems to indicate a salient connection between religion and individual outcomes, even if researchers often fail to satisfactorily measure, much less explain, the processes at work (Dollahite et al., 2004).

Many of the problems related to the inadequate measurement of religiosity stem from the inadequate conceptualization of religion. In this chapter we employ Marks' (2005, 2006) three dimensional conceptualization of religion as being comprised of: (a) beliefs (personal, internal beliefs, framings, meanings, and perspectives; often including a sense of relationship with God); (b) practices (outward, observable expressions of faith such as prayer, scripture study, rituals, traditions, or less overtly sacred practice or abstinence that is religiously grounded); and (c) faith community (support, involvement, and relationships grounded in one's congregation or religious group). An adequate measure of religiosity should address each of these three dimensions at some level. Accordingly, in our framework we emphasize three components of religiosity: (a) frequency of religious participation (an indicator of the faith community dimension of religion); (b) personal importance of religion (a self report measure that reflects the beliefs dimension); and (c) religion proscriptions (an indicator based in the practices dimension, which includes abstinences that are faith-based; including the avoidance of alcohol, drugs, crime, and extramarital sex).

A final point regarding the conceptualization of religiosity in our study is that "most studies of religion and spirituality are cross-sectional and most measures assess religion and spirituality as stable, enduring constructs" (Hill and Pargament, 2003, p. 71). The implicit bias in this conceptualization is that religiosity is static—a bias that likely stems from the fact that most extant data are from relatively stable adult samples. Religiosity should be conceptualized in a more fluid way that allows for developmental changes and shifts through adolescence. We need to consider the possibility that religiosity can measurably increase or decrease over time and that any protective function of religion may increase or decrease over the course of adolescence.

Dispositions

Our conceptualization of dispositions includes both propensities and predilections to engage in risk-taking behavior. As such, our disposition conceptualization embraces research on both temperament/personality traits and belief/cognitive evaluations within the risk-taking literature. In our model, for example, a disposition to engage in risky behavior may have its origins in low self-control or in a belief that potential harm from engaging in risky behavior is minimal. In contrast to Gottfredson and Hirschi (1990), but consistent with the conclusions reached in Pratt and Cullen's (2000) meta-analysis and those in Piquero and Tibbetts' (1996) analyses, we propose that propensities and predilections are additive contributors to one's disposition to engage in a particular behavior, particularly risk-taking behaviors that are relatively normative in the late adolescent population (see also Walker, Ainette, Wills, and Mendoza, 2007). However, we also anticipate that strong propensities are likely to be positively associated with predilections, such that individuals with low self-control or high sensation-seeking tendencies are more likely than those with a high self-control or low sensation-seeking tendencies to hold favorable opinions regarding risk-taking behavior (Piquero and Tibbetts, 1996).

In the psychological literature, temperament and personality traits are the most commonly studied propensities for risk-taking with impulsivity and sensation-seeking demonstrating reliable and consistent associations with a range of risk-taking behaviors. Zuckerman (1994) noted that sensation seeking is "a trait defined by the need for varied, novel, and complex sensations and experiences and willingness to take physical and social risks for the sake of such experiences" (Zuckerman, 1979, p. 10). Greater sensation-seeking has been linked to higher of levels of legal and illegal drug use (Crawford, Pentz, Chou, Li, and Dwyer, 2003; Zuckerman, 1983), delinquency (Newcomb and McGee, 1991; White, LaBouvie, and Bates, 1985), engagement in risky sexual behaviors (Arnett, 1990; Zuckerman, Tushup, and Finner, 1976), and dangerous driving (Arnett, 1991; Zuckerman and Neeb, 1980).

In the sociological and criminology literatures, studies have focused on low self-control. Gottfredson and Hirschi (1990) propose that low self-control is the primary propensity for crime and that self-control is primarily influenced by parental socialization efforts in the first decade of life. Self-control is broadly conceptualized in GTC as comprised of six characteristics: risk seeking, preference for physical activities, non-verbal communication, shortsightedness, volatile temper, and impulsivity. Numerous studies have shown that this conceptualization of self-control is related to engaging in criminal acts (Pratt and Cullen, 2000), illicit and licit substance use (e.g., Arneklev, Grasmick, Tittle, and Bursik, 1993; Vaszonyi, Pickering, Junger, and Hessing, 2001; Wood, Pfefferbaum, and Arneklev, 1993), risky sexual behavior (Jones and Quisenberry, 2004), and risky driving (Jones and Quisenberry, 2004; Hartos, Eitel, Haynie, and Simons-Morton, 2000). A meta-analysis indicated that the effect size for the association between self-control and criminal behavior among adults is about $r = .25$ whereas the effect size for the association between self-control and analogous risk-taking behaviors is about $r = .35$ (Pratt and Cullen, 2000). Although the GTC conceptualization of self-control incorporates risk-seeking, some have proposed that self-control and sensation-seeking tendencies are two different pathways to problem behavior (Wills, Sandy, and Yaeger, 2000), or that sensation-seeking is the most predictive characteristic of self control (Arneklev et al., 1993). Therefore, we have included both self-control and sensation-seeking in our propensity conceptualization.

Consistent with our conceptualization of predilections, the rational choice framework (Cornish and Clarke, 1986; Nagin and Paternoster, 1993) emphasizes situational inducements and impediments to criminal behavior, most notably the perceived cost or harm of engaging in specific acts. The rational choice framework also emphasizes adolescent's personal moral beliefs regarding whether involvement in a particular behavior is wrong under the assumption that such beliefs impede criminal behavior. Although Gottfredson and Hirschi (1990) are critical of the rational choice perspective, Piquero and Tibbetts (1996) present a model that integrates the GTC and rational choice perspectives. In their test of the integrated model, rational choice variables (i.e., perceived sanctions, pleasure, and situational shame) mediated much of the association between self-control and intentions (measured using hypothetical vignettes) to shoplift and drive drunk. In a similar study, Schoepfer and Piquero (2006) found that moral beliefs regarding how wrong the potential action was moderated the link between self-control and intentions to steal and fight such that low-self control was associated with greater intentions to steal and fight when moral beliefs were low, but self-control was not associated with intentions to steal and fight when moral beliefs were high. Furthermore, Evans, Cullen, Burton, Dunaway, and Benson (1997) found that moral beliefs and self-control were additive predictors of deviant behavior. Likewise, Arnett (1990) found that propensities (i.e., sensation seeking) and predilections (i.e., perceived risk) were additively related to having sex without contraception in a sample of 145 adolescent females.

Another perspective on predilections comes from social perception theory, which focuses on the perceptions or prototypes that people hold of individuals who engage in certain behaviors (Gibbons and Gerrard, 1995). Having a favorable prototype of individuals who engage in risk-taking behavior is considered a risk factor for engaging in the behavior yourself. Research on drug use and sexual behavior has linked favorable prototypes to risk taking behavior (Blanton, VandenEijnden, Buunk, Gibbons, Gerard, and Bakker, 2001; Gibbons and Gerard, 1995; Gibbons, Gerard, Boney-McCoy, 1995). More positive prototype perceptions have been found to predict increased substance use and sexual behavior among adolescents even when controlling for self-control (Wills, Gibbons, Gerrard, Murry, and Brody, 2003; see also Pratt and Cullen, 2000). Perceived benefits, risks, moral beliefs, and prototype perceptions are included in the model as risk taking predilections. In general, greater religiosity is expected to be negatively associated with dispositions and predilections, but sub-components of religiosity are expected to be linked to specific measures of dispositions and predilections (e.g., more frequent attendance is expected to be linked to self-control whereas proscriptions are expected to be more strongly linked to perceived costs and prototype perceptions). Previous research has demonstrated that dispositions and predilections can mediate between contextual experiences (e.g., parenting) and problem behavior (Curry and Youngblade, 2006; Simons, Simons, Chen, Brody, and Lin, 2007).

Opportunities

Although Gottfredson and Hirschi (1990) propose that criminal acts are most likely to occur when an individual with low self-control is presented with an opportunity to commit a crime, they argue that opportunities for crime are everywhere but devote little attention to opportunities in their theorizing. Moreover, researchers testing GTC have devoted much more attention to studying the link between self-control and criminality than to studying opportunities (Pratt and Cullen, 2000), and tests of GTC using naturally occurring variation in opportunities are limited (e.g., Jones and Quisenberry, 2004). However, the adolescent development literature has identified several individual-level variables that can be conceptualized as expanding or limiting risk-taking opportunities for adolescents (LaGrange and Silverman, 1999). Therefore, we have relied heavily on the adolescent development literature to identify potential variables to index risk-taking opportunity.

Unlike adults, adolescents are expected to be supervised and disciplined by their parents or other adults (e.g., teachers). In addition, it is our assumption that most adolescent risk-taking behavior, particularly negative risk-taking behavior, takes place outside of adult supervision, and often, in the presence of peers. Lack of adult supervision has often been found to be associated with child and adolescent misbehavior (e.g., Cohen, Farley, Taylor, Martin, and Schuster, 2002). Therefore, the amount of time adolescents spend outside of adult supervision could serve as an index of opportunity, with adolescents spending more time unsupervised having more opportunity to engage in risk-taking behavior.

Along similar lines, parental monitoring and rule-setting have been identified as forms of distal supervision (Laird, Criss, Pettit, Bates, and Dodge, in press) and are consistent predictors of adolescent risk-taking behavior (see Dishion and McMahon, 1998; Crouter and Head, 2002). Monitoring is conceptualized as a dyadic process through which parents can track the behavior of adolescents when they are not being directly supervised by adults. Recent data provide strong evidence that adolescents play a large role in determining the amount and accuracy of the information that parents obtain regarding the adolescent's whereabouts and activities (Stattin and Kerr, 2000; Laird, Criss, Pettit, Bates, and Dodge, 2008). A lack of parental knowledge predicts increases in risk-taking behavior (Laird, Pettit, Bates, and Dodge, 2003a; 2003b) and high levels of knowledge moderate peer relationship and personal risk factors, including genetic risks (Dick, Viken, Purcell, Kaprio, Pulkinen, and Rose, 2007; Laird et al., 2008). Adolescents are expected to engage in less risk taking behavior when they have informed parents. Informed parents may more effectively limit risk-taking opportunities than less informed parents. Additionally, adolescents who opt to keep their parents informed may be less likely to engage in risk-taking behavior.

Parental rules and prohibitions are thought to provide adolescents with behavioral guidance in their parents' absence. Clear rules and prohibitions, when followed by adolescents, also can function to limit risk-taking opportunities (Beck, Hartos, and Simons-Morton, 2006; Guilamo-Ramos, Jaccard, Dittus, and Bouris, 2006; Wight, Williamson, and Henderson, 2006). Thus, three family-level variables (i.e., unsupervised time, poorly informed parents, and limited rules and restrictions) are included in the model as indicators of greater risk-taking opportunities. LaGrange and Silverman's (1999) results support this conceptualization of opportunities. Specifically, variables consistent with our conceptualization of unsupervised time, poorly informed parents, and limited rules were found to interact with measures of self-control to predict general delinquency, property offenses, violent offenses, and drug offenses. Other studies also have found that the association between self-control and antisocial behavior was attenuated by parenting (Jones, Cauffman, and Piquero, 2007; Wight, Caspi, Moffitt, and Silva, 2001). Conceptualizing parenting during adolescence as an influence on opportunities may help to explain why parenting continues to be associated with delinquent behavior when controlling for self-control (e.g., Burt, Simons, and Simons, 2006).

Gottfredson and Hirschi (1990) downplay the role of other individuals as influences on crime and criminality by arguing that: (a) most crimes are committed by a single individual; (b) individuals who commit crimes with others also commit crimes alone; and (c) the propensity to commit crimes and the propensity to affiliate with other like-minded individuals have a shared cause (i.e., low self-control). However, compared to adults, adolescents are more likely to engage in risk-taking behavior with or when surrounded by peers (Dishion, Andrews, and Crosby, 1995; Simpson, 1996; Udry, 1998; Warr, 1996; Zimring, 1998). Numerous studies have documented strong and consistent associations between adolescents' misbehavior and the misbehavior of their peers (Elliot and Menard, 1996; Pratt and Cullen, 2000; War, 2002). Moreover, Pratt and Cullen's (2000) meta-analysis indicated that deviant peer associations and low self-control are additive predictors of crime and analogous behaviors. While research indicates that much of the link between adolescent and peer behavior can be considered a selection effect, wherein risk-taking adolescents form friendships with risk-taking peers; affiliations and friendships with risk-taking peers are likely to provide more risk-taking opportunities than affiliations and friendships with risk-aversive peers (Evans et al., 1997; Thornberry, Lizotte, Kron, Farnworth, and Jang, 1994). Wight et al., (2001) found that antisocial peers interact with self-control so that low-self control is most strongly associated with criminal behavior among individuals with antisocial friends. Goodnight, Bates, Newman, Dodge, and Pettit (2006) also found that impulsivity interacted with antisocial friends to predict increases in externalizing behavior problems. Likewise, Slater (2003) found that peer pressure was more strongly associated with marijuana use among individuals high in sensation seeking than low in sensation seeking. Data from these three studies show a pattern consistent with our proposed model and suggest that risk-taking peers may interact with propensities to increase risk-taking behavior.

Religiosity and the Propensity-Opportunity Theory of Risk-Taking Behavior

Previous research on religiosity and risk-taking behavior conducted in the propensity-opportunity framework during adolescence is very limited. Only a few studies have tested specific hypotheses from our proposed model, and tests that have been conducted are largely limited to main effects using cross-sectional data. Walker, Ainette, Wills, and Mendoza (2007) found that religiosity was linked to substance use through both self-control and tolerance for deviance (which, in turn was linked to substance use through friends' substance use). Wills et al. (2003) found that low self-control predicted substance use and sexual behavior through social-cognitive constructs and peer relations. However, the impact of religion on substance use and sexual behavior was not mediated through self-control or peer relationships. No tests of moderation were included in their analyses. Yanovitsky (2005) found that low religiosity, high sensation-seeking, low parental monitoring, and deviant peer affiliations were additive predictors of the intention to use marijuana. Interactions among these factors were not tested. These three studies attest to the potential of the propensity-opportunity framework as an aid to understanding how and why greater religiosity protects adolescents from risk-taking behavior. However, the studies test a limited set of hypotheses and rely on cross-sectional data.

RESEARCH QUESTIONS AND ANALYSES GUIDED BY THE MODEL

The next section of this chapter will illustrate how our conceptual model can be used to frame and attempt to answer questions about how and why adolescent religiosity may be negatively associated with delinquent and risk-taking behavior. From the conceptual model we selected four hypotheses to test using data from an ongoing longitudinal study of parent-adolescent relationships. Specifically, we hypothesize that adolescent participants' reports of greater religiosity will be associated with fewer behavior problems and less delinquent behavior. Furthermore, greater religiosity is hypothesized to be associated with fewer opportunities to misbehave (i.e., less time unsupervised by adults and less antisocial behavior by friends) and a decreased propensity to misbehave (i.e., greater self control). In addition, we hypothesize that fewer opportunities to misbehave and a greater propensity to avoid misbehavior will mediate the association between religiosity and behavior problems and delinquent behavior.

Participants and Procedures

Data were drawn from a longitudinal study of development during the transition from middle childhood to adolescence. Participants (N=181) range in age from 12 to 15 years old. Fifty percent of participants are European American and 44% are African American. Approximately half of the participants are male and 75% live in a two parent home. Participants' parents reported a median yearly income between \$40,000 and \$60,000 with 12.6% earning less than \$20,000, and 36.8% earning greater than \$80,000.

Measures

Measures were derived from questionnaires verbally administered during a visit to the participants' homes. Our religiosity measure focused on the three dimensions of religiosity emphasized by our conceptual model; beliefs ("How important is religion to you in your daily life?), practices ("How often do you pray?"), and community ("How often do you attend religious services?"). Response options were presented as four or five point scales. A religiosity composite score was calculated as the mean response to the three items after standardizing responses to adjust for scaling differences ($\alpha = .74$).

Measures of unsupervised time and antisocial peer involvement served as indices of opportunities to engage in delinquent behavior. To assess unsupervised time, participants reported how often (from "never" to "everyday") they spend time in activities outside of adult supervision using items newly developed for this study. Participants responded to seven items (e.g., "How often do you stay at home when no adult is there? How often do you hang out around the neighborhood with no adult around?"). A composite unsupervised time score was computed as the mean of the seven items ($\alpha = .73$).

Antisocial peer involvement was assessed using items adapted from Dishion, Patterson, Stoolmiller, and Skinner (1991). Participants reported how often (from "never" to "all the time") their friends engaged in mildly antisocial behavior using 10 items (e.g., "Do your friends get into fights with other kids, do your friends use bad language, do your friends get into trouble at school?"). A composite antisocial peer involvement score was computed as the mean of the 10 items ($\alpha = .75$).

A measure of self-control served as an index of adolescents' propensity to avoid misbehavior. Self-control was assessed using the Low Self-Control Scale (LSC; Grasmick, Tittle, Bursik, and Arneklev, 1993). The Low Self-Control Scale is comprised of six sub-scales tapping the dimensions of self control that Gottfredson and Hirschi (1990) argued were most relevant to crime and delinquency. The six sub-scales are labeled impulsiveness (e.g., "I often act on the spur of the moment"), simple tasks (e.g., "I frequently try to avoid tasks that I know will be difficult"), risk-seeking (e.g., "Sometimes I feel I will take a risk just for the fun of it"), physical activities (e.g., "I almost always feel better when I am on the move than when I am sitting and thinking"), self-centeredness (e.g., "I try to look out for myself first, even if it makes things difficult for other people"), and control-temper (e.g., "Often, when I am angry at people, I feel more like hurting them than talking to them about why I am angry."). Participants indicated how much they agreed (from "strongly disagree" to "strongly agree") with each of the 24 items. A composite *self-control* score was computed as the mean of 24 items ($\alpha = .88$) after items were reverse coded so that higher scores indicate greater self control.

The Problem Behavior Frequency Scale (Farrell, Kung, White, and Valois, 2000) was used to assess behavior problems. The Problem Behavior Frequency Scale is a 32 item assessment comprised of five sub-scales labeled rule breaking (e.g., "broke a rule at home"), physical aggression (e.g., "hit or slap another kid"), non-physical aggression (e.g., "insult someone's family"), delinquency (e.g., "steal from someone"), and drug use (e.g., "smoke cigarettes"). Participants reported the frequency (from "0 times" to "7 or more times") of their involvement in each behavior over the past month. A composite *behavior problems* score was computed as the mean of the 26 non-delinquency items ($\alpha = .92$) and a separate *delinquency* score was computed as the mean of the six delinquency items ($\alpha = .82$).

Analyses and Results

The analyses that follow were conducted to test four hypotheses. Our first hypothesis was that greater religiosity will be associated with fewer behavior problems and less delinquent behavior. Bivariate correlations were computed to test the association between religiosity and behavior problems and between religiosity and delinquent behavior. Results support our first hypothesis. Adolescents reporting greater religiosity also report fewer behavior problems ($r = -.19, p = .01$) and less delinquent behavior ($r = -.16, p = .04$).

Our second hypothesis was that greater religiosity will be associated with fewer opportunities to misbehave. As a reminder, opportunities to misbehave were operationalized as unsupervised time and antisocial peer involvement. Bivariate correlations were computed to test the associations between religiosity and unsupervised time and between religiosity and antisocial peer involvement. Results support our second hypothesis. Adolescents reporting greater religiosity also report less unsupervised time ($r = -.16, p = .04$) and less antisocial peer involvement ($r = -.40, p < .001$).

Our third hypothesis was that greater religiosity will be associated with a stronger propensity to avoid misbehavior. A stronger propensity to avoid misbehavior was operationalized as greater self control. A bivariate correlation was computed to test the association between religiosity and self control. Results support our third hypothesis. Adolescents reporting greater religiosity also report greater self control ($r = .22, p = .005$).

Our fourth hypothesis was that the association between religiosity and behavior problems will be mediated through opportunities (unsupervised time and antisocial peer involvement) and propensity (self control). Data were analyzed using multiple regression to determine whether the four criteria for mediation proposed by Baron and Kenny (1986) were satisfied. Baron and Kenny's (1986) first criterion is that there must be a significant association between the independent variable and the dependent variable. The results from the first hypothesis test demonstrate that the data met this criterion. As noted above, greater religiosity is significantly associated with less behavior problems and less delinquent behavior. Baron and Kenny's (1986) second criterion is that there must be a significant association between the independent variable and the mediating variable. The results from the second and third hypothesis tests demonstrate that the data met the second criterion. As noted above, greater religiosity is significantly associated with less unsupervised time, less antisocial peer involvement, and more self-control. Baron and Kenny's (1986) third criterion is that there must be a significant association between the mediating variable and the dependent variable. Six multiple regression analyses were conducted to determine whether the data met the third criterion. Behavior problems and delinquent behavior were regressed on unsupervised time, antisocial peer involvement, and self control separately. Results from our analyses demonstrate that the data met the third criterion. Less unsupervised time is associated with fewer behavior problems ($\beta = .46, p < .001$) and less delinquent behavior ($\beta = .31, p < .001$). Additionally, less antisocial peer involvement is associated with fewer behavior problems ($\beta = .51, p < .001$) and less delinquent behavior ($\beta = .42, p < .001$). Finally, greater self control is associated with fewer behavior problems ($\beta = -.56, p < .001$) and less delinquent behavior ($\beta = -.39, p < .001$).

Baron and Kenny's (1986) fourth criteria for mediation is that the association between the independent variable and the dependent variable becomes non-significant after controlling for the mediating variable. In order to test the fourth criteria, behavior problems and delinquent behavior were regressed on religiosity and each of the potential mediators, separately. First, a series of multiple regressions were computed to test whether opportunity mediates the association between religiosity and behavior problems. Controlling for unsupervised time, religiosity is no longer significantly associated with behavior problems ($\beta = -.13, p = .08$) or delinquent behavior ($\beta = -.12, p = .72$). Controlling for antisocial peer involvement, religiosity is no longer significantly associated with behavior problems ($\beta = .03, p > .72$) or delinquent behavior ($\beta = .01, p = .99$). Results from the multiple regression analyses indicate that our measures of opportunity fully mediate the association between religiosity and behavior problems according to Baron and Kenny's (1986) criteria.

Next, a series of multiple regression analyses were computed to test whether our measure of propensity mediates the association between religiosity and behavior problems. Controlling for self control, religiosity is no longer significantly associated with behavior problems ($\beta = -.07, p = .30$) or delinquent behavior ($\beta = -.07, p = .31$). Results from the multiple regression analyses indicate that self control fully mediates the association between religiosity and behavior problems according to Baron and Kenny's (1986) criteria.

When using the method proposed by Baron and Kenny (1986), a weak association between an independent variable and a dependent variable can become non-significant when the indirect effects are small. Also, Baron and Kenny's (1986) method does not provide an index of the size or strength of the indirect effects. A stronger test for mediation is to test the significance of indirect effects. Path models were specified to test the indirect effects of the association between religiosity and behavior problems through opportunities and propensities. This approach allows us to use bootstrapping to estimate the size and significance of the indirect effects, as the standard errors for product terms may have unusual distributions (MacKinnon, Fairchild, and Fritz, 2007; McCartney, Burchinal, and Bub, 2006).

The results from the tests of indirect effects provide further evidence supporting our fourth hypothesis that opportunities and propensity mediate the association between religiosity and behavior problems. The standardized indirect effects and standard errors can be found in Table 1. The indirect effects from religiosity to behavior problems and delinquent behavior through unsupervised time, antisocial peer involvement, and self control are all significant.

Table 1. Indirect Effects of Religiosity on Behavior Problems and Delinquent Behavior

	Behavior Problems		Delinquent Behavior	
Mediator	Indirect Effect	Standard Error	Indirect Effect	Standard Error
Unsupervised Time	-.066*	.036	-.047*	.027
Antisocial Peer Involvement	-.217**	.050	-.165**	.046
Self Control	-.118**	.044	-.088**	.036

Significance of indirect effects computed using bias-corrected bootstrapped standard errors.
Standardized estimates, *$p < .05$, ** $p < .01$.

CONCLUSION

The study presented in this chapter aimed to replicate previous research establishing religiosity as a protective factor for adolescent delinquency and risk-taking and to demonstrate the utility of a new theoretical framework for understanding why and how religiosity may be protective. Results indicate that delinquent behavior and behavior problems more generally, were less frequent among adolescents reporting more personal religiosity as compared to adolescents reporting less religiosity. As anticipated, the link between religiosity and delinquent behavior was mediated by indicators of opportunity and dispositions providing general support of both Gottfredson and Hirschi's (1990) GTC and our adaptation and expansion of the GTC to study religiosity.

Drawing on our adaptation of Gottfredson and Hirschi's (1990) GTC, our model proposes that delinquent behavior in adolescence results from risk-taking opportunities combined with a risk-taking disposition. In the expansion of the general model, religion is specified as a protective factor that limits risk-taking opportunities and reinforces a propensity to avoid risk-taking. Two theorized pathways linking religiosity to delinquent behavior were tested and support was found for both pathways. In terms of risk-taking opportunities, adolescents reporting greater religiosity also report less unsupervised time and less antisocial peer involvement. Unsupervised time and antisocial peer involvement fully mediated the association between religiosity and delinquent behavior. Thus, results provide evidence that one pathway from religiosity to delinquent behavior is through adolescents' lack of risk-taking opportunities. In terms of risk-taking dispositions, adolescents reporting greater religiosity also report greater self-control and self-control fully mediated the association between religiosity and delinquent behavior. Thus, results provide evidence that a second pathway linking religiosity to behavior problems and delinquent behavior is through adolescents' greater propensity to avoid risk-taking behaviors. Self-control is the primary propensity discussed by Gottfredson and Hirschi (1990) and results from this study indicate that low self-control is linked to greater delinquency and with less religiosity as anticipated.

Strengths of the current study include a theory-based measure of religiosity and a conceptual model for testing the paths linking religiosity and delinquent behavior in adolescence. However, enthusiasm for conclusions reached in the current study should be restrained due to a number of study limitations. Religiosity was measured based on Marks' (2005, 2006) three dimensional theory of religiosity which captures an individual's religious beliefs, practices, and community. The set of three items tapping each of the dimensions was internally consistent and associated with opportunities, propensities, and delinquency as anticipated. However, while the three item scale is an improvement over previous operationalizations of religiosity, the concept remains weakly operationalized and a broader set of items assessing each dimension more comprehensively is necessary to significantly enhance our understanding of the link between religion and delinquency.

In the current study, unsupervised time and antisocial peer involvement served as indicators of opportunity restrictions. The conceptual model provided in this chapter specifies additional indicators of opportunity restrictions that may also link religiosity and risk-taking behavior. While this chapter provides preliminary support of this conceptualization and hypothesized pathway, future studies should consider additional indicators of opportunity restrictions. Likewise, self-control served as the indicator of dispositions for risk-taking. The conceptual model described in this chapter identifies additional factors that may serve as propensities and predilections for risk-taking that may also be influenced by religiosity. Future studies should consider these additional dispositions to determine whether findings from this study represent a general process or whether findings are unique to self-control.

As with many studies conducted in the GTC framework, the current study focused exclusively on main effects linking dispositions, opportunities, and delinquency. While explicit tests of mediation are an improvement over previous studies, key moderation hypotheses remain to be tested. Whereas the current study showed that greater religiosity is linked to weaker dispositions and fewer opportunities, it will be important to determine whether religiosity protects adolescents with stronger risk-taking dispositions and more opportunities from engaging in delinquent behavior. To the extent that the effects of religiosity are primarily mediated through dispositions or opportunities, associations between religion and delinquency may be primarily indirect or spurious (as hypothesized by Gottfredson and Hirschi, 1990), and any causal or protective role of religion remains in doubt. However, evidence that religiosity moderates associations between risk factors and delinquent behavior, would shift the emphasis toward religiosity serving as an important ameliorative factor for delinquent behavior and indicate that the link between religion and delinquency deserves more attention.

Finally, the current study is cross-sectional like most of the studies in this area. Longitudinal studies are needed to better understand the potentially complex interplay among religion, delinquency, dispositions, and opportunities. It may be that religion is a protective factor and that religion inoculates adolescents from developing predilections and propensities that would lead to greater risk-taking behavior. However, it is as equally conceivable that there are considerable selection effects whereby the individuals least predisposed to engage in risk-taking behavior remain or increase their religious involvement and commitment during adolescence whereas those more predisposed to take risks decrease their religious involvement. In other words, it is possible that the same characteristics that dispose one to take risks also discourage involvement in religious institutions that limit or prohibit risk-taking behavior. Longitudinal data are required to map the common developmental pathways and to determine whether religion is a prospective protective factor or whether selection effects account for a large portion of any apparent protective effects of religion.

In sum, this chapter makes the case that there is compelling evidence that justifies further study of religion as a protective and potential ameliorating factor for delinquent behavior and a range of analogous adolescent health risk-taking behaviors. Drawing on Gottfredson and Hirschi's (1990) GTC, a conceptual framework that provides guidance and a roadmap for future work in the area is presented. Cross-sectional data were presented to illustrate the utility of the framework and to demonstrate how key constructs can be operationalized and how hypothesized associations can be tested. Results provide general support for two pathways drawn from the broader conceptual framework. Conclusions identify a range of new directions and research questions that could be addressed using the conceptual framework to contribute to a richer understanding of the link between religion and delinquency.

Acknowledgments

We thank the teachers and principals from the East Baton Rouge Parish School System and the families who participated in this research. This research was supported by a grant from the National Science Foundation (BCS 0517980). Address correspondence to Robert Laird, Department of Psychology, University of New Orleans, New Orleans, LA 70148. rlaird@uno.edu.

References

Arneklev, B. J., Grasmick, H. G., Tittle, C. R., and Bursik, R. J. (1993). Low self-control and imprudent behavior. *Journal of Quantitative Criminology, 9*, 225-247.

Arnett, J. (1990). Contraceptive use, sensation seeking, and adolescent egocentrism. *Journal of Youth and Adolescence, 19*, 171-180.

Arnett, J. (1991). Still crazy after all these years: Reckless behavior among young adults aged 23-27. *Personality and Individual Differences, 12,* 1305-1313.

Baier, C. J., and Wright, B. R. E. (2001). 'If you love me, keep my commandments': A meta-analysis of the effect of religion on crime. *Journal of Research in Crime and Delinquency, 38*, 3-21.

Baron, R. M., and Kenny, D. A. (1986). The moderator mediator variable distinction in social psychological research: Conceptual, strategic, and statistical considerations. *Journal of Personality and Social Psychology, 51*, 1173-1182.

Beck, K. H., Hartos, J. L., and Simons-Morton, B. G. (2006). Relation of parent-teen agreement on restrictions to teen risky driving over 9 months. *American Journal of Health Behavior, 30*, 533-543.

Biglan, A., Brennan, P. A., Foster, S. L., and Holder, H. D. (2004). *Helping adolescents at risk: Prevention of multiple problem behaviors*. New York, NY, US: Guilford Press.

Blanton, H., VandenEijnden, R. J. J. M., Buunk, B. P., Gibbons, F. X., Gerrard, M., and Bakker, A. (2001). Accentuate the negative: Social images in the prediction and promotion of condom use. *Journal of Applied Social Psychology, 31*, 274-295.

Brown, T. L., Parks, G. S., Zimmerman, R. S., and Phillips, C. M. (2001). The role of religion in predicting adolescent alcohol use and problem drinking. *Journal of Studies on Alcohol, 62*, 696-705.

Burt, C. H., Simons, R. L., and Simons, L. G. (2006). A longitudinal test of the effects of parenting and the stability of self-control: Negative evidence for the general theory of crime. *Criminology: An Interdisciplinary Journal, 44*, 353-396.

Christiano, K. J. (2000). Religion and the family in modern American culture. In S. K. Houseknecht and J. G. Pankhurst (Eds.) *Family, religion, and social change in diverse societies (pp. 43-78)*. New York: Oxford University Press.

Cohen, D. A., Farley, T. A., Taylor, S. N., Martin, D. H., and Schuster, M. A. (2002). When and where do youths have sex? The potential role of adult supervision. *Pediatrics, 110*, e66.

Cornish, D., and Clarke, R. (1986). *The reasoning criminal: Rational choice perspectives in offending*. New York: Springer-Verlag.

Cotton, S., Zebracki, K., Rosenthal, S. L., Tsevat, J., and Drotar, D. (2006). Religion/spirituality and adolescent health outcomes: A review. *Journal of Adolescent Health, 38*, 472-480.

Crawford, A. M., Pentz, M. A., Chou, C.-P., Li, C., and Dwyer, J. H. (2003). Parallel developmental trajectories of sensation seeking and regular substance use in adolescents. *Psychology of Addictive Behaviors, 17*, 179-192.

Crouter, A. C., and Head, M. R. (2002). Parental monitoring and knowledge of children. In M. H. Bornstein (Ed.), *(2002). Handbook of parenting: Vol. 3: Being and becoming a parent (2nd ed.)* (pp. 461-483). Mahwah, NJ: Lawrence Erlbaum Associates, Publishers.

Curry, L. A., and Youngblade, L. M. (2006). Negative affect, risk perception, and adolescent risk behavior. *Journal of Applied Developmental Psychology, 27*, 468-485.

Dick, D. M., Viken, R., Purcell, S., Kaprio, J., Pulkkinen, L., and Rose, R. J. (2007). Parental monitoring moderates the importance of genetic and environmental influences on adolescent smoking. *Journal of Abnormal Psychology, 116*, 213-218.

Dishion, T. J., and McMahon, R. J. (1998). Parental monitoring and the prevention of child and adolescent problem behavior: A conceptual and empirical formulation. *Clinical Child and Family Psychology Review, 1*, 61-75.

Dishion, T. J., Patterson, G. R., Stoolmiller, M., and Skinner, M. L. (1991). Family, school, and behavioral antecedents to early adolescent involvement with antisocial peers. *Developmental Psychology, 27*, 172-180.

Dishion, T. J., Andrews, D. W., and Crosby, L. (1995). Antisocial boys and their friends in early adolescence: Relationship characteristics, quality, and interactional process. *Child Development, 66*, 139-151.

Dollahite, D. C., Marks, L. D., and Goodman, M. (2004). Religiosity and families: Relational and spiritual linkages in a diverse and dynamic cultural context. In M. J. Coleman and L. H. Ganong (Eds.), *The handbook of contemporary families* (pp. 411-431). Thousand Oaks, CA: Sage.

Donelson, E. (1999). Psychology of religion and adolescents in the United States: Past to present. *Journal of Adolescence, 22*, 187-204.

Elliott, D. S., and Menard, S. (1996). Delinquent friends and delinquent behavior: Temporal and developmental patterns. In J.D. Hawkins (Ed.), *Delinquent behavior and crime: Current theories* (pp. 28-67). New York: Cambridge University Press.

Evans, T. D., Cullen, F. T., Burton Jr, V. S., Dunaway, R. G., and Benson, M. L. (1997). The social consequences of self-control: Testing the general theory of crime. *Criminology, 35*, 475-504.

Farrell, A. D., Kung, E. M., White, K. S., and Valois, R. F. (2000). The structure of self-reported aggression, drug use, and delinquent behaviors during early adolescence. *Journal of Clinical Child Psychology, 29*, 282-292.

Feldstein, S. W., and Miller, W. R. (2006). Substance use and risk-taking among adolescents. *Journal of Mental Health, 15*, 633-643.

Gibbons, F. X., and Gerrard, M. (1995). Predicting young adults' health risk behavior. *Journal of Personality and Social Psychology, 69*, 505-517.

Gibbons, F. X., Gerard, M., and Boney-McCoy, S. (1995). Prototype perceptions predict pregnancy prevention. *Personality and Social Psychology Bulletin, 21*, 85-93.

Goodnight, J. A., Bates, J. E., Newman, J. P., Dodge, K. A., and Pettit, G. S. (2006). The interactive influences of friend deviance and reward dominance on the development of externalizing behavior during middle adolescence. *Journal of Abnormal Child Psychology, 34*, 573-583.

Goggin, K., Murray, T. S., Malcarne, V. L., Brown, S. A., and Wallston, K. A. (2007). Do religious and control cognitions predict risky behavior? I. Development and validation of the Alcohol-related God Locus of Control Scale for Adolescents (AGLOC-A). *Cognitive Therapy and Research, 31*, 111-122.

Gottfredson, M. R., and Hirschi, T. (1990). *A general theory of crime*. Stanford, CA, USA: Stanford University Press.

Grasmick, H. G., Tittle, C. R., Bursik, R. J., and Arneklev, B. J. (1993). Testing the core empirical implications of Gottfredson and Hirschi's general theory of crime. *Journal of Research in Crime and Delinquency, 30*, 5-29.

Guilamo-Ramos, V., Jaccard, J., Dittus, P., and Bouris, A. M. (2006). Parental expertise, trustworthiness, and accessibility: Parent-adolescent communication and adolescent risk behavior. *Journal of Marriage and Family, 68*(5), 1229-1246.

Hardy, S. A., and Raffaelli, M. (2003). Adolescent religiosity and sexuality: An investigation of reciprocal influences. *Journal of Adolescence, 26*, 731-739.

Hartos, J. L., Eitel, P., Haynie, D. L., and Simons-Morton, B. G. (2000). Can I take the car? Relations among parenting practices and adolescent problem-driving practices. *Journal of Adolescent Research, 3*, 352-267.

Hill, P. C., and Pargament, K. I. (2003). Advances in the conceptualization and measurement of religion and spirituality: Implications for physical and mental health research. *American Psychologist, 58*, 64-74.

Jones, S., and Quisenberry, N. (2004). The general theory of crime: How general is it? *Deviant Behavior, 25*, 401-426.

Jones, S., Cauffman, E., and Piquero, A. R. (2007). The influence of parental support among incarcerated adolescent offenders: The moderating effects of self-control. *Criminal Justice and Behavior, 34*, 229-245.

Koenig, H. G., McCullough, M. E., and Larson, D. B. (Eds.) (2001). *Handbook of religion and health.* New York: Oxford.

Lagrange, T. C., and Silverman, R. A. (1999). Low self-control and opportunity: Testing the general theory of crime as an explanation for gender differences in delinquency. *Criminology, 37*, 41-72.

Laird, R. D., Criss, M. M., Pettit, G. S., Bates, J. E., and Dodge, K. A. (2009). Developmental trajectories and antecedents of distal parental supervision. *Journal of Early Adolescence, 29,* 258-284.

Laird, R. D., Criss, M. M., Pettit, G. S., Bates, J. E., and Dodge, K. A. (2008). Parents' monitoring knowledge attenuates the link between antisocial friends and adolescent delinquent behavior. *Journal of Abnormal Child Psychology, 36,* 299-310.

Laird, R. D., Pettit, G. S., Bates, J. E., and Dodge, K. A. (2003a). Parents' monitoring-relevant knowledge and adolescents' delinquent behavior: Evidence of correlated developmental changes and reciprocal influences. *Child Development, 74*, 752.

Laird, R. D., Pettit, G. S., Dodge, K. A., and Bates, J. E. (2003b). Change in parents' monitoring knowledge: Links with parenting, relationship quality, adolescent beliefs, and antisocial behavior. *Social Development, 12,* 401-419.

Levin, J. S., and Chatters, L. M. (1998). Religion, health, and psychological well-being in older adults: Findings from three national surveys. *Journal of Aging and Health, 10*, 504-531.

MacKinnon, D. P., Fairchild, A. J., and Fritz, M. S. (2007). Mediation analysis. *Annual Review of Psychology, 58,* 593-614.

Mahoney, A., Pargament, K. I., Tarakeshwar, N., and Swank, A. B. (2001). Religion in the home in the 1980s and 1990s: A meta-analytic review and conceptual analysis of links between religion, marriage, and parenting. *Journal of Family Psychology, 15*, 559-596.

Marks, L. D. (2005). Religion and bio-psycho-social health: A review and conceptual model. *Journal of Religion and Health, 44,* 173-186.

Marks, L. D. (2006). Religion and family relational health: An overview and conceptual model. *Journal of Religion and Health, 45,* 603-618.

McCartney, K., Burchinal, M. R., and Bub, K. L. (2006). Best practices in quantitative methods for developmentalists. *Monographs of the Society for Research in Child Development, 71*(3, Serial No. 285).

McCullough, M. E., Hoyt, W. T., Larson, D. B., Koenig, H. G., and Thoresen, C. (2000). Religious involvement and mortality: A meta-analytic review. *Health Psychology, 19,* 211-222.

Miller, W. R., and Thoresen, C. E. (2003). Spirituality, religion, and health: An emerging research field. *American Psychologist, 58*, 24-35.

Nagin, D. S., and Paternoster, R. (1993). Enduring individual differences and rational choice theories of crime. *Law and Society Review, 27*, 467-496.

Newcomb, M. D., and McGee, L. (1991). Influence of sensation seeking on general deviance and specific problem behaviors from adolescence to young adulthood. *Journal of Personality and Social Psychology, 61*, 614-628.

Piquero, A., and Tibbetts, S. (1996). Specifying the direct and indirect effects of low self-control and situational factors in offenders' decision making: toward a more complete model of rationale offending. *Justice Quarterly, 13*, 481-510.

Pratt, T. C., and Cullen, F. T. (2000). The empirical status of Gottredson and Hirschi's general theory of crime: A meta-analysis. *Criminology, 38*, 931-964.

Rohelkepartain, E. C., King, P. E., Wagener, L. M., and Benson, P. L. (2005). *The handbook of spiritual development in childhood and adolescence.* Thousand Oaks, CA: Sage.

Schoepfer, A., and Piquero, A. R. (2006). Self-control, moral beliefs, and criminal activity. *Deviant Behavior, 27*, 51-71.

Sherkat, D. E., and Ellison, C. G. (1999). Recent developments and current controversies in the sociology of religion. *Annual Review of Sociology, 25*, 363-394.

Simon, R. L., Simons, L. G., Chen, Y.-F., Brody, G. H., and Lin, K.-H. (2007). Identifying the psychological factors that mediate the association between parenting practices and delinquency. *Criminology: An Interdisciplinary Journal, 45*, 481-517.

Simpson, H., (1996). *New to the road: Reducing the risks for young motorists.* Youth Enhancement Service, UCLA School of Medicine. Los Angeles.

Sinha, J. W., Cnaan, R. A., and Gelles, R. J. (2007). Adolescent risk behaviors and religion: Findings from a national study. *Journal of Adolescence, 30*, 231-249.

Slater, M. D. (2003). Sensation-seeking as a moderator of the effects of peer influences, consistency with personal aspirations, and perceived harm on marijuana and cigarette use among younger adolescents. *Substance Use and Misuse, 38,* 865-880.

Smith, C. (w/ Denton, M. L.) (2005). *Soul searching: The religious and spiritual lives of American teenagers*. New York: Oxford.

Stattin, H., and Kerr, M. (2000). Parental monitoring: A reinterpretation. *Child Development, 71*, 1072-1085.

Thornberry, T., Lizotte, A., Krohn, M., Farnworth, M., and Jang, S. (1994). Delinquent peers, beliefs, and delinquent behavior: A longitudinal test of Interaction Theory, *Criminology, 32,* 47-84.

Udry, J. (1998). The National Longitudinal Study of Adolescent Health (Add Health), Waves I and II, 1994-1996. Carolina Population Center, University of North Carolina. Chapel Hill, NC.

Vazsonyi, A. T., Pickering, L. E., Junger, M., and Hessing, D. (2001). An empirical test of a general theory of crime: A four-nation comparative study of self-control and the prediction of deviance. *Journal of Research in Crime and Delinquency, 38*, 91-131.

Walker, C., Ainette, M. G., Wills, T. A., and Mendoza, D. (2007). Religiosity and substance use: test of an indirect-effect model in early and middle adolescence. *Psychology of Addictive Behaviors, 21*, 84-96.

Wallace, J. M., Jr., and Williams, D. R. (1997). Religion and adolescent health-compromising behavior. In J. Schulenberg, J. L. Maggs and K. Hurrelmann (Eds.), *Health risks and developmental transitions during adolescence.* (pp. 444-468). New York, NY, US: Cambridge University Press.

Warr, M. (1996). Organization and instigation in delinquent groups. *Criminology*, 34, 11-37.

Warr, M. (2002). *Companions in crime: The social aspects of criminal conduct.* New York: Cambridge University Press.

White, H. R., LaBouvie, E. W., and Bates, M. E. (1985). The relationship between sensation seeking and delinquency: A longitudinal analysis. *Journal of Research in Crime and Delinquency, 22*, 197-211.

Wight, B. R., Caspi, A., Moffitt, T. E., and Silva, P. A. (2001). The effects of social ties on crime vary by criminal propensity: A life-course model of interdependence. *Criminology, 39*, 321-351.

Wight, D., Williamson, L., and Henderson, M. (2006). Parental influences on young people's sexual behaviour: A longitudinal analysis. *Journal of Adolescence, 29*, 473-494.

Wills, T. A., Gibbons, F. X., Gerrard, M., Murry, V. M., and Brody, G. H. (2003). Family communication and religiosity related to substance use and sexual behavior in early adolescence: A test for pathways through self-control and prototype perceptions. *Psychology of Addictive Behaviors, 17*, 312-323.

Wills, T. A., Sandy, J. M., Yaeger, A. (2000). Temperament and adolescent substance use: An epigenetic approach to risk and protection. *Journal of Personality, 68*, 1127-1151.

Wills, T. A., Yaeger, A. M., and Sandy, J. M. (2003). Buffering effect of religiosity for adolescent substance use. *Psychology of Addictive Behaviors, 17*, 24-31.

Wood, P. B., Pfefferbaum, B., Arneklev, B. (1993). Risk-taking and self-control: Social psychological correlates of delinquency. *Journal of Research in Crime and Delinquency,* 16, 111-30.

Yanovitzky, I. (2005). Sensation seeking and adolescent drug use: The mediating role of association with deviant peers and pro-drug discussions. *Health Communication, 17*, 67-89.

Yust, K., Johnson, A. N., S. E. Sasso, S. E. and Roehlkepartain, E. C. (Eds.) (2006). *Nurturing childhood and adolescent spirituality: Perspectives from the world's religious traditions.* Lanham, MD: Rowman and Littlefield.

Zimring, F. E. (1998). *American youth violence.* Oxford, England: Oxford University Press.

Zuckerman, M. (1979). *Sensation seeking: Beyond the optimal level of arousal.* Hillsdale, NJ: Earlbaum.

Zuckerman, M. (1983). A biological theory of sensation seeking. In Zuckerman, M. (Ed.), *Biological bases of sensation seeking impulsivity, and anxiety* (pp. 37-76). Hillsdale, NJ: Lawrence Erlbaum, Associates.

Zuckerman, M. (1994). *Behavioural expressions and biosocial bases of sensation seeking. New York*: Cambridge University Press.

Zuckerman, M. and Neeb, M. (1980). Demographic influences in sensation seeking and expressions of sensation in religion, smoking, and driving habits. *Personality and Individual Differences, 1,* 197-206.

Zuckerman, M., Tushup, R., and Finner, S. (1976). Sexual attitudes and experience: Attitude and personality correlates and changes produced by a course in sexuality. *Journal of Consulting and Clinical Psychology, 44*, 7-19.

In: Delinquency: Causes, Reduction and Prevention
Editor: Ozan Sahin and Joseph Maier
ISBN 978-1-60741-558-9

Chapter 7

PSYCHOPATHIC-LIKE-TRAITS AND AGGRESSION IN AUSTRALIAN CHILDREN AND ADOLESCENTS SUSPENDED FROM SCHOOLS

Stephen Houghton*, Robin Cordin and Sarah Hopkins
Centre for Child and Adolescent Related Disorders
The Graduate School of Education
The University of Western Australia

ABSTRACT

New instrumentation measuring psychopathic-like-traits and aggression in children and adolescents suspended from mainstream school were developed. One hundred and seventeen psychopathy related items and 63 aggression items were generated from reviews of current instrumentation and interviews with school personnel, psychologists, and detention centre officers.

These were subsequently reduced to 56 and 20, respectively. Data from one pilot study and the preliminary analysis of data from a larger scale study analyzed using item affectivity and discrimination resulted in 43 psychopathy items and 20 aggression items being retained. Maximum likelihood factor analyses of data from 137 suspended mainstream school students revealed four factors for psychopathy (Callous/Unemotional, Narcissism, Thrill- Seeking, and Moral Detachment of Self) and three for aggression (Physical Aggression, Reactive Verbal Aggression and Proactive Verbal Aggression). Cronbach's alpha revealed high internal consistency.

Psychopathy is a specific form of personality disorder that is characterized in the adult literature by at least three major symptom dimensions: On the *Interpersonal* level - an arrogant and deceitful interpersonal style involving manipulation, dishonesty, grandiosity, and glibness; On the *Affective* level - a defective emotional experience, involving shallow emotions and a pronounced lack of remorse, empathy, and lack of personal responsibility for one's own actions; associated with a *Socially deviant* (not necessarily criminal) lifestyle involving impulsivity, irresponsibility, and sensation seeking behavior (Cleckley, 1976; Cooke and Michie, 2001; Hare, 1991, 2006; McCord and McCord, 1964; Millon, 1981). According to Hare (2006) "Psychopathy has been described as the single most important clinical construct in the criminal justice system and as what may be the most important forensic concept of the early 21st century" (p.709).

It has been recognized that there exists a subgroup of children and adolescents who exhibit characteristics that are similar to adults with psychopathy (Frick, et al., 2000). According to Hare (1999), however, the very idea of psychopathy in childhood may be inconceivable for some people. Vaughn and Howard (2005) also acknowledged the likelihood that people would be uncomfortable applying this term to children and suggested it be used with extreme caution. For reasons such as the label having an unjustifiable negative influence on young persons' rehabilitation plans and sentence length, debate still surrounds the moral and ethical appropriateness of labeling juveniles with this construct (Chauhan, Reppucci, and Burnette, 2007; Edens, Guy, and Fernandez, 2003; Skeem and Petrila, 2004). Indeed, Johnstone and Cooke (2004, p. 105) asserted, "there is potential for devastating consequences as a result of the misuse of the construct", while Chauhan, Reppucci, and Burnette (2007) pointed out that the label may become permanent and associated with adverse consequences in adulthood. Conversely, Salekin and Lochman (2008) suggested that claims about the potential harming effects of the disorder have likely been overstated and are not based on science. With this in mind, a pressing need remains to better understand the construct of juvenile psychopathy, even though since the mid 1990s interest and debate in the construct, along with published research, has burgeoned (Salekin, 2006).

Summarizing the sheer volume of research here is difficult, but there is clear evidence from longitudinal and cross sectional studies that adult psychopathy can often be traced back to childhood (Forth and Burke, 1998; Lahey, Loeber, Quay, Frick, and Grimm, 1992; Saltaris, 2002) and that the indices of child psychopathy have structural homogeneity and a similar factor structure to that of adult psychopathy (Salekin, Brannen, Zalot, Leistico, and Neumann, 2006). Apart from some developmental differences, child and adolescent psychopathy is similar to that found in adults (Lynam, Caspi, Moffitt, Loeber, and Stouthamer-Loeber, 2007; Salekin, 2006). According to Barry, Frick, DeShazo, McCoy, Ellis and Loney (2000) it is the presence of Callous and Unemotional traits (C/U) which designate a group of young persons who show characteristics similar to adults with psychopathy. Frick and colleagues further highlighted the presence or absence of C/U traits, coupled with deficits in emotional reactivity as the difference between individuals who are both psychopathic and antisocial, and those who are antisocial but not psychopathic (see Frick, 1998; Frick, Cornell, Loney, Bodin, Dane, and Barry, 2003; Loney, Frick, Clements, Ellis, and Kerlin, 2003; Silverthorn and Frick, 1999). Frick, Cornell et al. (2003) also showed that the presence of C/U traits in mainstream school aged children may designate a distinct, behaviorally dysregulated group of children with conduct problems that may have unique processes underlying their dysregulation that make them more similar to adults with psychopathy. Like adults with psychopathy, children

* Address for Correspondence: Professor Stephen Houghton, Centre for Child and Adolescent Related Disorders, The Graduate School of Education, The University of Western Australia, Crawley 6009. Australia, Tel: ++ 618 6488 2391. Fax: ++ 618 6488 1052. Email: stephen.houghton@uwa.edu.au

and adolescents who display C/U traits show a much more severe and aggressive pattern of behavior (Christian, Frick, Hill, Tyler, and Fazer, 1997).

During adolescence psychopathic traits have also been found to be related to violent offences (Campbell, Porter, and Santor, 2004), serious levels of institutional aggression (Edens, Poythress, and Lilienfeld, 1999), and violent recidivism (Gretton et al., 2000). Moreover, high levels of aggression have been found to be related to psychopathic features in childhood, adolescence and adulthood (Porter and Woodworth, 2006). What is clear therefore is the relationship between psychopathic-like-traits and aggressive behavior (Porter and Woodworth, 2006), but the nature of this relationship appears to not yet have been fully examined. For example, the limited research has suggested that adolescents with psychopathic-like-traits often plan their acts (Pardini, Lochman, and Frick, 2003). That is, they exhibit proactive aggression.

Assessment of Psychopathic-Like-Traits in Children and Adolescents

Although there appears little disagreement among researchers that the interpersonal and affective characteristics central to psychopathy in adults are measurable in children (Forth and Mailloux, 2000; Gresham, Lane, and Lambros, 2000; Lynam, 1997; Salekin, 2006) and adolescents (Murrie and Cornell, 2002; Salekin, Rogers, and Machin, 2001), key concerns pertaining to the construct's downward extension from the adult literature, particularly in terms of potential misapplication or magnified destructive application (Vitacco and Vincent, 2007), the removal or manipulation of key items representative of the construct from instruments, and the conceptual and empirical properties of the childhood instruments (Johnstone and Cooke, 2004; Salekin, 2006) have been raised. Andershed, Kerr, Stattin and Levander (2000) also argued the methodology for assessing psychopathic-like-traits in forensic samples (which takes up to three hours to administer instruments in conjunction with a review of the institutionalized person's files) and the characteristics typical of forensic populations (e.g., promiscuous sexual behavior, short term relationships, recidivism, and criminal versatility) are difficult to apply to mainstream children and adolescents.

Vittacco and Vincent (2007) further commented that previous research has identified numerous shortcomings evident in the downward extension of psychopathy to young persons (particularly centered around developmental complications in assessing youth psychopathy), and also in the downward extensions of psychopathy measures to youth. Thus, additional research is needed if more appropriate measures of psychopathic-like-traits in young persons are to be developed and applied, particularly in non forensic contexts.

The research reported here takes cognizance of the issues and concerns raised and attempts to address these by developing new instruments that measure psychopathic-like-traits and aggression in young persons in mainstream educational settings. Those who know the mainstream school student well (e.g., teachers) should be reliable informants on his or her behavior. Teacher reports are often solicited as part of a diagnostic process and studies point to the value of teachers as reliable sources of information on the behavior of young people (see DuPaul, Power, McGoey, Ikeda, and Anastopoulos, 1998 for a review). Concerns initially raised about the utility of secondary school teachers' ratings of behavior (because of their relative lack of close contact with adolescents compared to elementary school children) (Lahey, Applegate, McHurnett, Biederman, et al., 1994) have long been refuted through empirical evidence demonstrating the criterion-related validity of secondary school teacher ratings of behavior in general (Molina, Smith, and Pelham, 2001).

This research seeks to add to the present day understanding about a disorder, for which there are serious pejorative outcomes for children and their families, and negative connotations for both professionals and the lay public (Frick and Hare, 2001).

METHOD

Phase I: Item Generation

This phase comprised a review of the juvenile psychopathy literature and the instruments most currently used to assess psychopathic-like-traits in children and adolescents. Items were selected from the DSM-IV-TR (19 items) and eight instruments (in some instances items were amended from their original format). Briefly, 20 items were selected from the Antisocial Process Screening Device (APSD: Frick and Hare, 2001), 4 items from the Child Psychopathy Scale (CPS; Lynam, 1997), 5 items from the Psychopathy Checklist: Youth Version (PSL:YV; Forth, Kosson, and Hare, 2003), 5 items from the Psychopathic Personality Inventory (PPI; Lilienfeld and Andrews, 1996), 6 items from the Strengths and Difficulties Questionnaire (SDQ; Goodman, 1997), 3 items from the Millon Adolescent Clinical Inventory (MACI; Millon, 1993), 5 items from the Youth Psychopathic traits Inventory (YPI; Andershed, Kerr, Stattin, and Levander, 2002), and 3 items from the Self-Report Psychopathy-II Scale (SRP-II; Hare, 1990). (A full description of the selection and item amendment can be obtained from the second author.)

To generate new items a series of interviews were also conducted with juvenile detention centre education officers, and mainstream teachers and psychologists responsible for the behavior management of detained persons or challenging students. Specifically, three separate focus group interviews and four individual interviews were conducted with 42 individuals in total. Of the 42, 28 were the entire cohort of education officers from the state's largest juvenile detention centre (19 females and 9 males with 3 to 30 years experience), 4 participants were high school teachers with 6 to 35 years teaching experience, 5 were primary school teachers with between 5 and 30 years experience, and 5 were psychologists resident in behavioral centers. Interviews focused on the interpersonal and behavioral characteristics of detained individuals or students who had been suspended from school for physical and/or verbal assault of teachers and/or peers, and/or property damage.

Phase I: Results

In summary, the consensus among participants in the interviews was that such individuals were: Callous and unfeeling; lacking in remorse and empathy; reactively and proactively verbally and physically aggressive; premeditative in their actions; not bothered about the consequences of their actions on others; highly manipulative; narcissistic; sensation seeking;

highly skilful liars, even to the extent of continuing to lie when confronted with evidence to the contrary; and that they induced a sense of discomfort and fear in others (staff and peers) by invading personal space. (A full version of the interview findings can be obtained from the second author on request.)

The review and interviews resulted in 117 items being generated which described children and adolescents with psychopathic-like-traits. After a review of these items by psychologists and measurement experts for their clarity, readability and congruity with juvenile psychopathy some items were removed. This resulted in 56 items. These items were included in a draft instrument entitled the Child and Adolescent Psychopathy Screening Instrument (CAPSI). Items were preceded by the statement "This student" and participants responded to each item by shading in one of six response options, ranging from definitely true to definitely not true.

During the Phase I interviews participants were also shown current instrumentation and asked to comment on their face and content appropriateness along with the psychological concepts of psychopathy. The consensus was that few instruments provided measures of physical and verbal aggression even though there is a strong link between psychopathy and these variables (see Porter and Woodworth, 2006). Consequently, it was deemed necessary to design an instrument which would also measure various forms of aggression.

Following an analysis of the interview data, and a review of four aggression instruments, and the DSM-IV-TR, and Dodge and Coie research (1987), 63 items were derived, some of which were amended from their original format. Specifically, 13 items were selected from The Revised Teacher Rating Scale (RTRS; Brown, Atkins, Osborne, and Milnamow, 1996), 18 items from the Aggression Questionnaire (AQ; Buss and Warren, 2000), 6 items from The Overt Aggression Scale (OAS; Yodofsky, Silver, Jackson, Endicott, and Williams, 1986), 2 items from The Self-Report Psychopathy Scale-II (SRP-II; Hare, 1990), 6 items from the DSM-IV-TR, and 18 items from Dodge and Coie (1987) for consideration in the new instrument. Again following a review of these items by psychologists and measurement experts for their clarity, readability and congruity with the construct of aggression some items were removed. The remaining 20 items were included in a draft instrument provisionally entitled the Child and Adolescent Scale of Aggression (CASA). This comprised four subscales measuring Proactive Physical Aggression, Proactive Verbal Aggression, Reactive Physical Aggression, and Reactive Verbal Aggression. Items were preceded by the statement "This child" and participants responded by shading in one of four response options, which ranged from definitively true to definitely not true.

Phase II: Initial Testing of the CAPSI and CASA

Participants and Settings

In this phase, 54 participants were involved. Twenty seven teachers (10 primary and 17 secondary, 6 male and 21 female with 3 to 15 years experience) undertaking a Master of Education degree at a University in Western Australia completed the CAPSI. Twenty seven other teachers (6 primary and 21 secondary, 4 male and 23 female with 5 to 35 years experience) completed the CASA. Of these, 21 were undertaking a Master of Education degree and six were recruited through personal communication. Two separate samples were recruited because the CAPSI was constructed prior to the CASA. As the main aim of this initial testing was to examine item functioning of the instruments, having two separate samples was not an issue.

The CAPSI or CASA instruments were administered to all participants either prior to their regular weekly lecture or in their place of employment at a mutually convenient time. Participants were requested to provide data on one student whom they had taught, in any year group, who had been suspended from school for physical and/or verbal assault of teachers and/or peers, and/or property damage.

Phase II: Results

In this section a shortened version of the psychometric properties for both instruments will be presented. A full version is available from the second author on request.

CAPSI Item Affectivity

In this phase of the study item affectivities were selected between the range of .20 and .80. Kline (2000) suggests that items with values "beyond these bounds are not discriminating" (p. 67) and this ensures that items that lack affectivity and those with extreme affectivity (which are unlikely to be endorsed even by those individuals with high levels of psychopathic like traits) are not included as they contribute very little to the measurement. The item affectivity in the sample ranged from .12 to .66 with Item 47 (Justifies their own behavior) being the least affective and Item 22 (Completes certain tasks with meticulous detail) being the most affective. The item discriminations, which represent the strength of the relationship between the individual response pattern and the total response pattern of the sample, ranged from -.05 to .80. Ideally item discriminations should all be positive, similar in value and not too close to 0 or 1.

Based on the item affectivity and discrimination scores eight items were removed from the instrument. It was decided on the basis of the psychopathy research literature to retain item 16 but to reword it as "Does not openly show feelings and emotions" so as to be negatively scored. It was also decided to retain Items 32 (Is not an anxious person) but to reword it as "Is an anxious person" so that it could be negatively rather than positively scored, 35 (Openly admits to unscrupulous and callous acts) and 53 (Has a grandiose sense of self-worth). With a Cronbach's alpha of .93 the remaining 48 items of the CAPSI were considered reliable.

To avoid confusion, Item 30 (Has few friends or is a loner) was separated to form two items and thus the final version of the CAPSI comprised 49 items.

Written and verbal feedback received from participants at this stage suggested that the six response categories in the CAPSI should be reduced to four, ranging from 1 (definitely not true) to 4 (definitely true).

CASA Item Affectivity

The item affectivity for the aggression scale ranged from .12 to .49 with Item 7 (Curses others viciously when provoked) being the least affective and Item 4 (Spreads cruel gossip and rumors about others for no apparent reason) being the most affective. Although one item was outside the range of .20 to .80 as recommended by Kline (2000) it was decided to retain this item because of its theoretical importance to the underlying construct of aggression. The 20 items of the CASA with a Cronbach's alpha of .75 were considered reliable and all were retained. Although there were no suggestions for modifying the CASA, participants suggested that it should remain separate to the CAPSI, but be administered in a single format.

Phase III: Initial Validation of the CAPSI and CASA

Participants and Settings

The new instruments were administered as a single combined instrument to 137 educators who provided data pertaining to 137 students who had been suspended from school for physical and/or verbal assault of teachers or peers, and/or property damage. Of the educators, 96 were female (45 primary school teachers, 34 high school teachers and 17 school psychologists) and 41 were male (8 primary school teachers, 26 high school teachers, 6 school psychologists and 1 student services manager). The 137 participants were from 36 mainstream schools located across a wide range of socio-economic status areas throughout Western Australia. Of the 36 schools, 33 were government schools and 3 were private schools.

Instrumentation

The new combined single format instrument, which is available from the second author on request, comprised 69 randomly ordered items assessing seven dimensions. Dimension 1 (Narcissism) comprised 17 items, Dimension 2 (Callous/Unemotional) 19 items, Dimension 3 (Thrill Seeking) 6 items, Dimension 4 (Proactive Verbal Aggression) 5 items, Dimension 5 (Proactive Physical Aggression) 5 items, Dimension 6 (Reactive Physical Aggression) 5 items, and Dimension 7 (Reactive Physical Aggression) 5 items. Seven items were unable to be classified at this stage.

Procedure

As in previous phases of the research ethics approval was obtained from the Institution's Human Research Ethics Committee. The Student Services Managers or Area Managers in each of the 14 District Education Offices in Western Australia were then contacted to recruit participants. Contact was subsequently made with the principals of schools identified by these managers to request permission to invite teachers to participate. (School psychologists were contacted individually.) An information sheet was given to all teachers in the respective schools and an appointment to meet those interested at their school was then arranged.

During meetings the purpose of the research was explained and teachers were asked to complete each of the instruments with reference to one male or female student in any year group they had taught for at least 3 months, who had been suspended from school during the past 12 months, and with whose behavior they were cognizant. (Students had to have been suspended for physical and/or verbal assault of teachers and/or peers, and/or property damage.) In instances where a meeting was inconvenient, potential participants were sent a detailed description of the research, an information sheet, a consent form, the CAPSI and CASA instruments, and a reply paid envelope.

Phase III: Results

Psychopathic-like-traits in mainstream suspended school students

Data were provided on 111 male students and 26 female students. The mean total CAPSI score for males was 97.99 (SD = 19.72) and 88.96 (SD = 22.31) for females. The mean score for each item is shown in Table 1.

Table 1. Mean and Standard Deviations for the CAPSI Items

	Item Description	M	SD
1.	Blames others for his/her mistakes	2.30	.84
2.	Is geared towards self-gratification	2.25	.83
3.	Is an anxious person ^{R}	1.40	.99
5.	Is quick to make value judgments about others	2.28	.86
6.	Lies easily and skillfully	2.26	.88
10.	Is sarcastic	1.36	1.04
12.	Is desensitised to the consequences of his/her behavior on others	2.48	.75
13.	Has blurred concepts of right and wrong	2.01	1.02
14.	Lacks empathy and compassion	1.96	.95
15.	Has an egocentric view of him/herself	2.23	.88
16.	Manipulates and coerces others to get what they want	2.09	.97
17.	Readily accepts defeat ^{R}	2.09	1.07
18.	Justifies own inappropriate behavior	2.47	.78
19.	Does not openly show feelings or emotions	1.32	1.08
20.	Recklessly disregards the safety of others	2.05	.94
21.	Seems to think that he/she is better than others	1.77	.98
23.	Violates the basic rights of others	2.23	.87
24.	Lacks fear	1.91	.99
25.	Induces a sense of fear or unrest in others	2.13	.98
27.	Sees him/herself as a victim	2.07	.99
30.	Seeks confirmation of status	2.01	.85
31.	Has the ability to present an insincere emotional response	1.91	1.00
32.	Is cunning	2.02	.92
33.	Seeks excitement	2.09	.87
34.	Engages in thrill seeking behavior	1.85	.94
35.	Fulfils commitments to others ^{R}	1.89	.91
36.	Invades the personal space of others	2.09	.95
37.	Is desensitised to consequences of his/her behavior on themselves	2.18	.86
38.	Enjoys teasing and making fun of other people	2.16	.89
41.	Takes responsibility for his/her behavior ^{R}	2.31	.87
43.	Recklessly disregards safety of self	1.93	.98
44.	Is a vengeful person	1.91	.94
47.	Shows respect for those in authority ^{R}	2.07	.94
48.	Continues to lie when confronted with contradictory evidence	2.00	.98
49.	Has few friends	1.64	1.14
50.	Has emotions which seem shallow and not genuine	1.61	1.03

	Item Description	M	SD
51.	Is a loner	1.27	1.09
52.	Avoids risky or dangerous behavior [R]	2.16	.88
53.	Can be charming at times, but in ways that seem superficial or	1.70	1.09
55.	Lacks remorse	1.96	1.02
58.	Has a grandiose sense of self worth	1.55	1.01
59.	Respects school rules [R]	2.31	.90
61.	Openly admits to unscrupulous and callous acts	1.45	1.01
62.	Has limited involvement in social activities within the school	2.04	1.05
63.	Brags excessively about his/her accomplishments	1.47	.99
64.	Feels bad or guilty when he/she does something wrong [R]	2.00	.92
67.	Is indifferent to adult approval or praise	1.47	1.08
68.	Engages in attention seeking behavior	2.10	.95
69.	Is a team player [R]	2.42	.72

[R] Denotes reverse-scored.

A check on item functioning revealed that item affectivity in the sample ranged from .20 to .59 with Item 12 (Is desensitized to the consequences of his/her behavior on others) being the least affective and Item 51 (Is a loner) being the most affective.

Item discrimination values ranged from -.08 (Item 3 Is an anxious person) to .68 (Item 12 Is desensitized to the consequences of his/her behavior on others). Based on these data and the theoretical importance of individual items, Items 3, 17, 19, 27, 51, and 61 were removed, leaving 43 items for further analysis. An internal consistency of $\alpha = .92$ indicated the scale to be reliable.

Factor Analysis

The CAPSI data were subjected to maximum likelihood factor analysis with orthogonal (Varimax) rotation using SPSS version 13.5. A KMO of .78 and Bartlett's Test of Sphericity [$\chi 2 = 3436.34$, df = 1176, p = .00] indicated factor analysis was appropriate. As can be seen in Table 2, four factors describing psychopathic like traits in mainstream school students emerged. The first factor measured *Callous-Unemotional* traits such as a lack of remorse and lack of empathy for others.

The second factor measured *Narcissism* which included a grandiose sense of self-worth, interpersonal exploitativeness and an excessive need of the admiration of others. The third factor measured *Thrill-Seeking Behavior*. The fourth factor consisted of items relating to selfishness and lack of responsibility and was labeled *Moral Detachment of Self.*

The CAPSI had a high degree of internal consistency overall ($\alpha = .92$) and for the 17-item Callous/Unemotional subscale ($\alpha = .81$), the 13-item Narcissism subscale ($\alpha = .86$), the 8-item Thrill-Seeking subscale ($\alpha = .77$), and the 4 item Moral Detachment of Self subscale ($\alpha = .72$). Item 49 (Has few friends) failed to load on any factor and was removed. The correlations for the CAPSI subscales are shown in Table 3.

Table 2. Rotated Factor Loadings for the CAPSI

Item	Item Description	Initial h^2	Factor Loadings			
			1	2	3	4
	Factor 1: Callous/Unemotional					
14.	Lacks empathy and compassion	.71	.769			
55.	Lacks remorse	.71	.698			
64.	Feels bad or guilty when he/she does something wrong [R]	.62	.687			
12.	Is desensitised to the consequences of his/her behavior on others	.65	.685			
67.	Is indifferent to adult approval or praise	.61	.685			
23.	Violates the basic rights of others	.78	.588		.378	
20.	Recklessly disregards safety of others	.71	.541		.479	
59.	Respects school rules [R]	.61	.517			.381
13.	Has blurred concepts of right and wrong	.58	.512			
25.	Induces a sense of fear or unrest in	.67	.507			
41.	Takes responsibility for his/her behavior	.57	.482			.379
47.	Shows respect for those in authority [R]	.54	.473			
62.	Has limited involvement in social activities within the school community	.48	.408			
69.	Is a team player [R]	.50	.390			.364
15.	Has an egocentric view of him/herself	.56	.385			
35.	Fulfils commitments to others [R]	.48	.368			
44.	Is a vengeful person	.51	.353			
	Factor 2: Narcissism					
2.	Is cunning	.62		.652		
31.	Has the ability to present an insincere emotional response	.61		.635		
58.	Has a grandiose sense of self-worth	.68		.596		
21.	Seems to think he/she is better than	.66		.587		
38.	Enjoys teasing and making fun of other	.65		.564		
6.	Lies easily and skillfully	.68		.506		.360
30.	Seeks confirmation of status	.59		.504	.411	
10.	Is sarcastic	.47		.503		
53.	Can be charming at times, but in ways that seem superficial or insincere	.50		.501		
16.	Manipulates and coerces others to get what they want	.62		.482		.320
50.	Has emotions which seem shallow and not genuine	.68	.432	.477		
63.	Brags excessively about his/her	.58		.462		
18.	Justifies own inappropriate behavior	.58		.432		.390

Item	Item Description	Initial h^2	Factor Loadings			
			1	2	3	4
	Factor 3: Thrill Seeking Behavior					
34.	Engages in thrill-seeking behavior	.68			.690	
33.	Seeks excitement	.63			.597	
52.	Avoids risky or dangerous activities [R]	.52			.576	
43.	Recklessly disregards safety of self	.62	.344		.572	
24.	Lacks fear	.59	.354		.498	
37.	Is desensitised to the consequences of his/her behavior on themselves	.56	.361		.426	
36.	Invades the personal space of others	.56		.368	.376	
68.	Engages in attention seeking behavior	.56			.315	
	Factor 4: Moral Detachment of Self					
1.	Blames others for his/her mistakes	.61				.782
48.	Continues to lie when confronted with contradictory evidence	.63		.459		.522
2.	Is geared towards self-gratification	.51				.400
5.	Is quick to make value judgments about	.58				.366

[R] Denotes reverse-scored.

Table 3. Correlations for the CAPSI Subscales

	C/U	NARC	TS	MDS
C/U	1.00	.44**	.48**	.51**
NARC		1.00	.34**	.55**
TS			1.00	.22*
MDS				1.00

** $p < 0.01$ (2-tailed).
*$p < 0.05$ (2-tailed).

Aggression in Mainstream Suspended School Students

The mean CASA score for males was 40.98 (SD = 12.64) and 39.65 (SD = 13.83) for females. The mean score for each item is shown in Table 4.

Further testing of the item affectivity in the sample revealed a range of .18 to .48 with Item 56 (Is inappropriately rude in telling others what he/she thinks of them when provoked) being the most affective and Item 9 (Spreads cruel gossip and rumors about others for no apparent reason) being the least affective. Item discrimination values ranged from .40 to .82. Based on the item affectivity and discrimination values, and the theoretical importance of individual items, all 20 items were retained. An internal consistency of $\alpha = .94$ indicated the scale to be reliable.

Table 4. Mean and standard deviations for the CASA Items

Item	Item Description	M	SD
4.	Uses his/her physical presence to gets others to gang up against a vulnerable individual	1.80	1.14
7.	Becomes angry and breaks things when annoyed or frustrated	2.11	.99
8.	Exaggerates or tells lies about others for no apparent reason	1.72	.98
9.	Spreads cruel gossip and rumors about others for no apparent reason	1.55	1.04
11.	Verbally attacks vulnerable individuals for no apparent reason	1.93	1.04
22.	Uses physical force to dominate	2.04	1.04
26.	Curses others viciously when provoked	2.44	.81
28.	Makes clear verbal threats of violence towards others when provoked	2.36	.94
29.	Premeditates physically aggressive acts against others	1.82	1.03
39.	Verbally encourages others to take part in acts of hostility	2.08	.99
40.	Physically attacks others when threatened	2.23	.93
42.	Physically lashes out at others when very angry or frustrated	2.29	.92
45.	Reacts in an angry physical manner against others when accidents occur	1.96	.92
46.	Initiates physical fights for no reason	1.57	1.05
54.	Verbally attacks a person when there is a difference of opinion	2.17	.84
56.	Is inappropriately rude in telling others what he/she thinks of them when provoked	2.46	.75
57.	Becomes verbally angry when he/she does not get their own way	2.29	.81
60.	Reacts physically when denied what they want	1.81	.95
65.	Uses offensive words to hurt, abuse or insult others for no apparent reason	2.04	.99
66.	Threatens others physically to get what he/she wants	2.07	.96

Factor Analysis

The CASA data were subjected to maximum likelihood factor analysis with orthogonal (Varimax) rotation. A KMO of .92 and Bartlett's Test of Sphericity [$\chi 2 = 1752.432$, df = 190, p = .000] indicated factor analysis was appropriate. As can be seen in Table 5 three factors emerged.

The first factor consisted of items which were physically aggressive in nature and was thus labeled *Physical Aggression*. The second factor was labeled *Reactive Verbal Aggression* and Factor Three, which contained items targeting verbal aggression of a premeditated nature, was labeled *Proactive Verbal Aggression*.

Table 5. Rotated Factor Loadings for the CASA

	Item Description	Initial h^2	Factor Loadings		
			1	2	3
	Factor 1: Physical Aggression				
40.	Physically attacks others when threatened	.75	.855		
22.	Uses physical force to dominate others	.71	.802		
29.	Premeditates physically aggressive acts against others	.68	.779		
42.	Physically lashes out at others when very annoyed or frustrated	.73	.767	.402	
66.	Threatens others physically to get what want	.71	.699	.385	
46.	Initiates fights for no apparent reason	.57	.604		
4.	Uses his/her physical presence to get others to gang up against a vulnerable individual	.60	.599		.458
60.	Reacts physically when denied what they want	.61	.591	.429	
28.	Makes clear verbal threats of violence towards others when provoked	.73	.562	.446	
45.	Reacts in an angry physical manner against others when accidents occur	.59	.551	.415	
	Factor 2: Reactive Verbal Aggression				
57.	Becomes verbally angry when he/she does not get own way	.49		.666	
54.	Verbally attacks a person when there is a difference of opinion	.47		.637	
56.	Is inappropriately rude in telling others what they think of them when provoked	.48		.578	
65.	Uses offensive words to hurt, abuse or insult others for no apparent reason	.60		.548	.463
26.	Curses others viciously when provoked	.61		.517	
7.	Becomes angry and breaks things when annoyed or frustrated	.48	.448	.462	
	Factor 3: Proactive Verbal Aggression				
9.	Spreads cruel gossip and rumors about others for no apparent reason	.57			.756
11.	Verbally attacks vulnerable individuals for no apparent reason	.67		.395	.681
39.	Verbally encourages others to take part in acts of hostility	.66	.495		.633
8.	Exaggerates or tells lies about others for no apparent reason	.48			.545

Cronbach's alpha revealed a high degree of internal consistency for the overall scale (α = .94.) as well as for the 10 item Physical Aggression subscale (α = .93), the 6 item Reactive Verbal Aggression subscale (α = .81), and the 4 item Proactive Verbal Aggression subscale (α = .81). The correlations for the CASA subscales are shown in Table 6.

Table 6. Correlation of the CASA Subscales

	PA	RVA	PVA
PA	1.00	.69**	.53**
RVA		1.00	.53**
PVA			1.00

** p < .01.

DISCUSSION

This research set out to examine psychopathic like traits in mainstream school students suspended from school for physical and/or verbal assault of teachers and/or peers, and/or property damage. Part of the research included developing a new instrument. This was important given some of the criticisms raised about most current instruments utilized in the assessment of juvenile psychopthy (see Andershed et al., 2002; Cook and Michie, 2006; Edens et al., 2001; Vitacco and Vincent, 2007). The process involving an initial review of the literature and instruments, along with the completion of a series of interviews not only confirmed the viability of the construct of psychopathy in young persons, but it also supported Johnstone and Cooke's (2004) assertion that strong measurement instrumentation must be developed. Furthermore, it highlighted the relative absence of aggression items in any current instrumentation. Consequently, it was necessary to develop a second instrument that measured proactive and reactive verbal and physical aggression. Successive phases which involved continued consultations with relevant stakeholders, the use of expert panels, and the application of item affectivity and item discrimination techniques and estimates of internal reliabilities demonstrate a systematic approach to this instrument development.

Research to date has shown the construct of juvenile psychopathy to be underpinned by between two and four factors, with child and adolescent researchers tending towards the traditional two or more recent three factor models (Barry, Barry, Deming and Lochman, 2008). With clinic referred children Johnstone and Cooke (2004) and Frick, O'Brien, Wootton and McBurnett (1994) preferred a two factor structure (Callous-Unemotional and Impulsivity-Conduct Problems). On the other hand, research with both non-diagnosed children and clinic-referred children has used two (Callous-Unemotional and Narcissism-Impulsivity) or three factors (Callous Unemotional, Narcissism, and Impulsivity) (Frick, Bodin, and Barry, 2000; Hoong, Houghton, and Chapman, 2005). However, it has been said that the instruments used in much of this research omitted key Cleckley criteria, for example "superficial charm" was replaced with "impression management" in the PCL: YV. These amendments represent changes in the original construct as expressed by Cleckley (see

Salekin, 2006) and decrease the utility of an instrument for predicting violence and aggression (Cooke, Michie, and Skeem, 2007).

The present research remained close to the original construct while expanding it through the generation of new items. Consequently, a four factor structure comprising Callous-Unemotional traits, Narcissism, Thrill Seeking, and Moral Detachment of Self was observed. While the first three factors are similar to those identified in previous research, the fourth factor "Moral Detachment of Self", which is concerned with young person's deflecting the responsibility of their actions, is new and clearly worthy of further investigation. Case study interview data gathered following this present research (see Cordin, 2008) lends support for the existence of this fourth factor. Specifically, interviews with teachers about children with severe challenging behaviors who had repeated suspensions from school for physical and/or verbal assault of teachers and/or peers revealed that the ability to deflect one's own actions and not accept responsibility was a strong distinguishing characteristic of these individuals.

With reference to aggression, three subscales were identified: Physical Aggression, Reactive Verbal Aggression and Proactive Verbal Aggression. Surprisingly, the distinction between proactive and reactive aggression was only evident with regard to verbal aggression. Given the high number of violent crimes perpetrated throughout the criminal careers of psychopaths and that as adults these individuals are five times more likely to engage in violent recidivism (Porter and Woodworth, 2006) it was anticipated that high levels of physical aggression might similarly characterize these young persons. Indeed, during adolescence, psychopathic traits are associated with convictions for violent offences (Campbell, Porter, and Santor, 2004) and the mainstream sample in the present study had been suspended for physical and/or verbal assault of teachers or peers, and/or property damage. It may be, however, that even more serious types of violent acts differentiate the reactive and proactive aspects of physical aggression and thus this new instrument needs to be administered to forensic populations to confirm this. This may then substantiate the assertion that adolescents with psychopathic-like-traits are often said to plan their aggressive acts (Pardini, Lochman, and Frick, 2003).

Before concluding this chapter a number of points need to be raised. First, why assess mainstream child and adolescent populations? According to Lynam (1997) schools are the best place to conduct research into young persons with psychopathic-like-traits because research on adult psychopaths is confounded by constant substance abuse, physical fighting and multiple incarcerations. Understanding the developmental trajectories to this condition in younger populations less affected by these confounds provides the best opportunities for developing effective treatments. Second, although this research has developed and undertaken preliminary validations of new screening tools to assess psychopathic-like-traits and aggression in mainstream children and adolescents, the question which must be asked is can they be improved? The answer to this is an unequivocal yes. What is now necessary is to examine whether the newly developed instruments demonstrate convergent validity (i.e., they are related to alternate measures of the same construct) and discriminant validity (i.e., they are unrelated to measures of conceptually dissimilar constructs). Finally, was the sample for this present research adequate? While we recognize that 137 is relatively small, all of the sample were mainstream school aged students who had committed physical and/or verbal assault of teachers or peers, and/or property damage. Accessing these individuals is difficult because their attendance at school is limited (due to longer periods of suspension and or repeated suspensions). Future research should seek to recruit larger sample sizes.

In conclusion, Loeber, Farrington and Petechuk (2003) argued that the window for early intervention with the most serious youth is often missed, primarily because they begin their antisocial careers between the ages of seven and 12 years but do not receive intervention from the juvenile justice system until between 10 and 13 years at the earliest. The development of instruments such as presented here, which can be administered as screening instruments with challenging mainstream child and adolescent populations, may assist in addressing this concern. Furthermore, they may also assist in the design of more efficacious interventions for this group of young persons who present with the most frequent, severe, and aggressive behaviors (Caputo, Frick, and Brodsky, 1999), are more likely to reoffend (Forth and Burke, 1998) and resist efforts at rehabilitation (Salekin, Rogers, Ustad, and Sewell, 1998).

ACKNOWLEDGMENTS

This research was partly funded by the Australian Research Council. The authors also acknowledge The Fogarty Foundation for their support.

REFERENCES

Andershed, H., Kerr, M., Stattin, H., and Levander, S. (2002). Psychopathic traits in non-referred youths: A new assessment tool. In E. Blaauw and L. Sheridan (Eds.), *Psychopaths: Current International Perspectives*. The Hague: Elsevier, pp. 131-158.

Barry, T., Barry, C., Deming A., and Lochman, J. (2008). Stability of psychopathic characteristics in childhood: The influence of social relationships. *Criminal Justice and Behavior, 35*, 244-262.

Barry, C.T., Frick, P.J., DeShazo, T.M., McCoy, M., Ellis, M., and Loney, B.R. (2000). The importance of callous-unemotional traits for extending the concept of psychopathy to children. *Journal of Abnormal Psychology, 109*, 335-340.

Brown, K.S., Atkins, M.S., Osborne, M.L., and Milnamow, M. (1996). A revised teacher rating scale for reactive and proactive aggression. *Journal of Abnormal Child Psychology, 24*, 473-480.

Buss, A.H., and Warren, W.L. (2000). *The Aggression Questionnaire*. Los Angeles, CA: Western Psychological Services.

Campbell, M.A., Porter, S., and Santor, S. (2004). Psychopathic traits in adolescent offenders: An evaluation of criminal history, clinical, and psychosocial correlates. *Behavioral Sciences and the Law, 22*, 23-47.

Caputo, A.A., Frick, P.J., and Brodsky, S.L. (1999). Family violence and juvenile sex offending: The potential mediating role of psychopathic traits and negative attitudes toward women. *Criminal Justice and Behavior, 26*, 338-356.

Chauhan, P., Reppucci, N.D., and Burnette, M. (2007). Application and impact of the psychopathy label to juveniles. *International Journal of Forensic Mental Health, 6*(1), 3-14.

Christian, R.E., Frick, P.J., Hill, N.L., Tyler, L., and Frazer, D.R. (1997). Psychopathy and conduct problems in children: II. Implications for subtyping children with conduct problems. *Journal of the American Academy of Child and Adolescent Psychiatry, 36*, 233-241.

Cleckley, H.M. (1976). *The mask of sanity* (5th ed.), St Louis, MO: Mosby.

Cooke, D.J., and Michie, C. (2001). Refining the construct of psychopathy: Towards a hierarchical model. *Psychological Assessment, 13,* 171-188.

Dodge, K., and Coie, J.D. (1987). Social information processing factors in reactive and proactive aggression in children's peer groups. *Journal of Personality and Social Psychology, 53*, 1146-1158.

DuPaul, G., Power, T., McGoey, K., Ikeda, M., and Anastpoulos, A. (1998). Reliability and validity of parent and teacher ratings of attention-deficit/hyperactivity disorder symptoms. *Journal of Psychoeducational Assessment, 16*(1), 55-68.

Edens, J.F., Guy, L.S., and Fernandez, K. (2003). Psychopathic traits predict attitudes towards a juvenile capital murderer. *Behavioral Sciences and the Law, 21*, 807-828.

Edens, J.F., Poythress, N.G., and Lilienfeld, S.O. (1999). Identifying inmates at-risk for disciplinary infractions: A comparison of two measures of psychopathy. *Behavioral Sciences and the Law, 17,* 435-443.

Forth, A.E., and Burke, H.C. (1998). Psychopathy in adolescence: Assessment, violence, and development precursors. In D.J. Cooke, A.E. Forth and R.D. Hare (Eds.), *Psychopathy: Theory, Research, and Implications for Society*, Netherlands: Kluwer Academic Publishing, pp. 205-229.

Forth, A.E., Kosson, D.S., and Hare, R.D. (2003). *Hare Psychopathy Checklist: Youth Version*, Toronto, Ontario: Multi-Health Systems.

Forth, A.E., and Mailloux, D.L. (2000). Psychopathy in youth: What do we know? In C. B. Gacono (Ed.), *The Clinical and Forensic Assessment of Psychopathy: A Practicioner's Guide*, Mahwah, NJ: Erlbaum, pp. 25-54.

Frick, P.J. (1998). Callous-Unemotional traits and conduct problems: Applying the two-factor model of psychopathy to children. In D.J. Cooke, A. E. Forth and R D. Hare (Eds.), *Psychopathy: Theory, Research, and Implications for Society*, Dordrecht, Netherlands: Kluwer Academic Publishing, pp. 161-187.

Frick, P.J., Barry, C.T., and Bodin, S. (2000). Applying the concept of psychopathy to children: Implications for the assessment of antisocial youth. In C.B. Gacono (Ed.), *The Clinical and Forensic Assessment of Psychopathy: A Practitioner's Guide The LEA Series in Personality and Clinical Psychology*, Mahwah, NJ: Lawrence Erlbaum Associates, pp. 3-24.

Frick, P.J., Cornell, A.H., Barry, C.T., Bodin, S., and Dane, H.E. (2003). Callous-unemotional traits and conduct problems in the prediction of conduct problems, severity, aggression, and self-report of delinquency. *Journal of Abnormal Child Psychology, 31*, 457-470.

Frick, P.J., and Hare, R.D. (2001). *The Antisocial Process Screening Device*. Toronto: Multi-Health Systems.

Frick, P.J., O'Brien, B.S., Wootton, J.M., and McBurnett, K. (1994). Psychopathy and conduct problems in children. *Journal of Abnormal Psychology, 103*, 700-707.

Goodman, R. (1997). The strengths and difficulties questionnaire: A research note. *Journal of Child Psychology and Psychiatry and Allied Disciplines, 38*, 581-586.

Gresham, F.M., Lane, K.L., and Lambros, K.M. (2000). Comorbidity of conduct problems and ADHD: Identification of fledgling psychopaths. *Journal of Emotional and Behavioral Disorders, 8*, 83-94.

Gretton, H.M., McBride, M., Hare, R.D., O'Shaughnessy, R., and Kumka, G. (2001). Psychopathy and recidivism in adolescent sex offenders. *Criminal Justice and Behavior, 28*, 427-449.

Hare, R.D. (1990). *The self-report psychopathy scale-II.* Unpublished manuscript, University of British Columbia, Vancouver, Canada, Department of Psychology.

Hare, R.D. (1991). *Manual for The Hare Psychopathy Checklist - Revised (2nd Ed.).* Toronto, Ontario: Multi-Health Systems.

Hare, R.D. (1999). *Without Conscience: The Disturbing World of the Psychopaths Among Us.* Vancouver, BC: University of British Columbia.

Hare, R.D. (2006). Psychopathy: A clinical and forensic overview. *Psychiatric Clinics of North America, 29*, 709-724.

Hinshaw, S.P. (1994). Conduct disorder in childhood: Conceptualization, diagnosis, comorbidity, and risk status for antisocial functioning in adulthood. In D.C. Fowles, P. Sutker, P., and S.H. Goodman (Eds), *Experimental Personality and Psychopathology Research*, New York: Springer, pp. 3-44.

Hoong, W., Houghton, S., and Chapman, E. (2005). Relationships between attention deficit/hyperactivity disorder, conduct disorder, psychopathy, and aggression: The fledgling psychopath hypothesis. In M. Larimer (Ed.), *Attention Deficit Hyperactivity Disorder Research Developments*, New York: Nova Science Publishers Inc., pp. 69-102.

Johnstone, L., and Cooke, D.J. (2004). Psychopathic-like-traits in childhood: Conceptual and measurement concerns. *Behavioral Sciences and the Law, 22*, 103-125.

Lahey, B.B., Applegate, B., McHurnett, K., Biederman, J., Greenhill, L., Hynd, G.W., Barkley, R.A., Newcorn, J., Jensen, P., Richters, J., Garfinkel, B., Kerdyk, L., Frick, P.J., Ollendick, T., Perez, D., Hart, E.L., Waldman, I., and Shaffer, D. (1994). DSM-IV field trials for attention deficit hyperactivity disorder in children and adolescents. *American Journal of Psychiatry, 151*, 1673–1685.

Kline, P. (2000). *Handbook of psychological testing* (2nd Ed). London, UK: Routledge.

Lahey, B.B., Loeber, R., Quay, H.C., Frick, P.J., and Grimm, J. (1992). Oppositional defiant and conduct disorder: Issues to be resolved for DSM-IV. *Journal of the American Academy of Child and Adolescent Psychiatry, 31*, 539-546.

Lilienfeld, S.O., and Andrews, B.P. (1996). Development and preliminary validation of a self-report measure of psychopathic personality traits in non criminal populations. *Journal of Personality Assessment, 66,* 488-524.

Loeber, R., Farrington, D.P., and Petechuk, D. (2003). *Child delinquency: Early intervention and prevention.* Washington, DC: Office of Juvenile Justice and Delinquency Prevention, U.S. Department of Justice.

Loney, B.R., Frick, P.J., Clements, C.B., Ellis, M.L., and Kerlin, K. (2003). Callous-unemotional traits, impulsivity, and emotional processing in adolescents with antisocial behavior problems. *Journal of Clinical Child and Adolescent Psychology, 32*, 66-80.

Lynam, D. (1997). Pursuing the psychopath: Capturing the fledgling psychopath in the nomological net. *Journal of Abnormal Psychology, 106*, 425-438.

Lynam, D., Caspi, A., Moffitt, T., Loeber, R., and Stouthamer-Loeber, M. (2007). Longitudinal evidence that psychopthy scores in early adolescence predict adult psychopathy. *Journal of Abnormal Psychology, 116*, 155-165.

McCord, W., and McCord, J. (1964). *The Psychopath: An Essay on The Criminal Mind.* Princeton, NJ: Van Nostrand.

Millon, T. (1981). *Disorders of Personality: DSM-III Axis II.* New York: Wiley.

Millon, T. (1993). *Millon Adolescent Clinical Inventory Manual.* Minneapolis: National Computer Systems.

Murrie, D.C., and Cornell, D.G. (2002). Psychopathy screening of incarcerated juveniles: A comparison of measures. *Psychological Assessment, 14*, 390-396.

Pardini, D.A., Lochman, J.E., and Frick, P.J. (2003). Callous/Unemotional traits and social-cognitive processes in adjudicated youths. *Journal of the American Academy of Child and Adolescent Psychiatry, 42*(3), 364-371.

Penney, S.R., and Moretti, M. (2007). The relation of psychopathy to concurrent aggression and antisocial behavior in high-risk adolescent girls and boys. *Behavioral Sciences and the Law, 25*, 21-41.

Porter, S., and Woodworth, M. (2006). Psychopathy and Aggression. In C.J. Patrick (Ed.), *Handbook of Psychopathy* New York: Guilford, pp. 481-494.

Salekin, R.T. (2006). Psychopathy in children and adolescents: Key issues in conceptualization and assessment. In C.J. Patrick (Ed.), *Handbook of Psychopathy*, New York: Guilford Press, pp. 389-408.

Salekin, R.T., Brannen, D., Zalot, A.A., Leistico, A., and Neumann, C. (2006). Factor structure of psychopthy in youth: Testing the applicability of the new four factor model. *Criminal Justice and Behavior, 33*, 135-157.

Salekin, R.T. and Lochman, J.E. (2008). Child and adolescent psychopathy: The search for protective factors. *Criminal Justice and Behavior, 35*, 159-172.

Salekin, R.T., Rogers, R., and Sewell, K.W. (1997). Construct validity of psychopathy in female offender sample: A Multi trait – multi method evaluation. *Journal of Abnormal Psychology, 106*, 576-585.

Salekin, R.T., Rogers, R., Ustad, K.L., and Sewell, K.W. (1998). Psychopathy and recidivism among female inmates. *Law and Human Behavior, 22*, 109-128.

Salekin, R.T., Rogers, R., Machin, D. (2001). Psychopathy in youth: Pursuing diagnostic clarity. *Journal of Youth and Adolescence, 30*, 173-195.

Saltaris, C. (2002). Psychopathy in juvenile offenders: Can temperament and attachment be considered as robust developmental precursors? *Clinical Psychology Review, 22*, 729-752.

Silverthorn, P. and Frick, P.J. (1999). Developmental pathways to antisocial behavior: The delayed-onset pathway in girls. *Development and Psychopathology, 11*, 101-126.

Skeem, J.L. and Petrila, J. (2004). Introduction to the special issue on juvenile psychopathy, Vol 2: juvenile psychopathy: Informing the debate. *Behavioral Sciences and the Law, 22*, 1-4.

Vaughn, M.G., and Howard, M.O. (2005). Self-report measures of juvenile psychopathic personality traits: A comparative view. *Journal of Emotional and Behavioral Disorders, 13*, 152-162.

Vitacco, M.J. and Vincent, G.M. (2007). Understanding the downward extension of psychopathy to youth: Implications for risk assessment and juvenile justice. *International Journal of Forensic Mental Health, 5*(1), 29-38.

Yudofsky, S.C., Silver, J.M., Jackson, W., Endicott, J., and Williams, D. (1986). Overt aggression scale for the objective rating of verbal and physical aggression. *American Journal of Psychiatry, 143*, 35-39.

In: Delinquency: Causes, Reduction and Prevention
Editor: Ozan Sahin and Joseph Maier
ISBN 978-1-60741-558-9

Chapter 8

VIOLENT OFFENDING: AN ANALYSIS OF FAMILY, SCHOOL AND COMMUNITY RISK FACTORS

***Estefanía Estévez*[1], *Nicholas Emler*[2] *and Charlotte Wood*[3]**

[1]Universidad Miguel Hernández de Elche, Alicante, Spain
Departamento de Psicología de la Salud, Avda.
Universidad s/n, Edificio Altamira 03203,
Elche (Alicante), Spain.
[2]University of Surrey, Guildford, United Kingdom.
Faculty of Arts and Human Sciences, GU2 7XH,
Guildford, Surrey, United Kingdom
[3]University of Surrey, Guildford, United Kingdom.
Faculty of Arts and Human Sciences, GU2 7XH,
Guildford, Surrey, United Kingdom

ABSTRACT

Violent offending by young people is a visibly growing problem for both society and the particular individuals involved. Recent research conducted in the United Kingdom revealed that over 20% of 10 to 25 year olds report having committed a crime, 59% of which were violent offences (Wilson, Sharp and Patterson, 2006). Prior research has examined particular factors that make children and adolescents more inclined to criminal activities and whether these factors are controllable. This study looks at the interaction of risk factors at the family, social and community levels by testing a causal model in a sample composed of 2528 participants aged 10-16 who were drawn from the 2005 Offending, Crime and Justice Survey dataset.

To begin with, the authors review some data on the prevalence of violent offending among young people in different countries, and continue by discussing some of the main family, school and community factors that have been related to involvement in violent offending and delinquent behaviours in adolescence. Family variables include quality of children-parent relationships and parenting skills such as family communication. School variables refer to attitude to school and whether the child has been suspended or expelled from school. Finally, community variables include the existence of problem behaviours in the local area and degree of trust in local police.

Following this review, the authors analyse the role played by two other direct antecedents of offending that have been highlighted in the scientific literature, namely antisocial behaviour and victimization. Finally, a causal model is tested to examine the interactions among all the aforementioned variables and their joint contribution to the explanation of youth offending. The model tested explained 22% of the variance in violent offending by the young people in the sample. Victimization and anti-social behaviour independently contributed to the amount of variance, while family, community and school contexts had differential effects on these two proximal causes. By jointly considering the influence of the most important social contexts in adolescence, this study provides a fuller picture and clearer understanding of the risks for violent adolescent offending. Implications and future areas of research are discussed.

1. Prevalence of Violent Offending among Young People

Youth violence is a visibly significant problem with extremely negative consequences for both society and the particular individuals involved. Although this is clear enough, it is less clear whether this is a growing or declining problem. The 2006 Offending Crime and Justice Survey (OCJS), conducted by the Home Office, found that 22% of 10 to 25 year olds in England and Wales reported committing a crime in 2006, 59% of which were violent offences (Roe and Ashe, 2008). Meanwhile, in the USA it has been reported that approximately 80% of non-fatal violent offences against young people are committed by juveniles (Baum, 2005). Statistics have indicated that arrests for simple and aggravated assaults have increased in comparison to previous years, in particular for adolescent females (Snyder and Sickmund, 1999), although the prototypical young offender continues to be a male aged between 15 and 17 (Grinberg, Dawkins, Dawkins and Fullilove, 2005). Two of the main sources of crime statistics in the USA are the National Crime Victimization Survey (NCVS) and the Federal Bureau of Investigation's Uniform Crime Reports (UCR). The NCVS, based on a survey of over 77,000 households, has reported that violent crime rates have actually declined since 1994, reaching in 2005 the lowest level ever recorded (Shannon, 2006). Meanwhile the UCR, which looks at crimes recorded by the police, has also painted a positive picture, reporting that although the violent crime rate increased by 1% from 2005 to 2006, the rate had actually fallen 22.5% from 1997 to 2006 (Federal Bureau of Investigation, 2006).

It is an extremely complex task to accurately compare violent crime statistics across countries due to the huge variety of ways that crimes are recorded. However, a survey that has successfully attempted to do this is The International Crime Victimization Survey (ICVS), which has provided evidence on crime rates in 24 industrialised countries since 1989. According to respondents' answers in the ICVS, violent crimes were generally thought to be more serious than, for example, property crimes (Entorf and Spengler, 2002). The ICVS covers ten conventional crimes including contact crimes, which involve robbery, sexual offences and assault and threats. In 2000, rates of contact crimes per 100 inhabitants were found to be well above the average of 10.7 in countries such as England and Wales (20.5) and Australia (20.2) and much lower than average in Japan (3.8), Spain (4.2) and Portugal (4.5). Rather surprisingly the victimization rate for contact crimes in the USA was below average at

9.9 (van Kesteren, Mayhew and Nieuwbeerta, 2001). The most frequent of the three contact crimes were assault and threats. In the 2004/05 findings of the ICVS, 3.1% of respondents were found to be victims of assault and threats. Northern Ireland (6.8), Iceland, (5.9) England and Wales (5.8) and Ireland (4.9) had the highest prevalence of victimization whereas Italy (0.8) Portugal (0.9), Hungary (1.2) and Spain (1.6) had the lowest rates of assault and threats (Dijk, van, Kesteren and Smit, 2008).

In the last few decades, research has focused on analysing the risk factors related to violent offending and crime. We are particularly interested in analysing such behaviour among young people in order to better understand the reasons why some children and adolescents are inclined to criminal activities and whether these factors are controllable. The following section of this chapter will explore some of the more significant risk factors for violent crime among youths, giving particular consideration to social variables related to family, school and locality.

Factors Related to Violent Offending

The term 'risk factor' refers to variables that increase an individual's susceptibility to a certain outcome (Shader, 2001). In recent years the risk factor paradigm has been applied to offending. According to Farrington (2000) the basic idea of this paradigm is to discover the key factors that increase the risk of becoming an offender and then to identify prevention methods to counteract them. The risk factor approach allows practitioners to tailor prevention programmes to the unique needs of individual youths and their communities. Hawkins et al. (2000), among others, stated that it is unlikely that one risk factor can cause violent behaviour, but it is the combination of multiple risk factors that can group together to shape behaviour and heighten the risk of becoming involved in youth violence. They suggested that it is the presence of a combination of certain risk factors that can lead to delinquency.

Three decades ago, Bronfenbrenner (1979) presented the influential ecological paradigm, which explained human development as a function of nested systems of the person, their environment and the interaction of these components. Bronfenbrenner (1979) proposed that it is not just the environment that directly affects the person but there are layers in between that all affect each other. He described four systems that each contain roles and norms shaping development. These include the microsystem constituted by the immediate environment (e.g., family, school, neighbourhood); the mesosystem, which entails connections between immediate environments (e.g., a child's family and neighbourhood, for example); an exosystem of those external environmental settings that affect development indirectly (e.g., a parent's workplace); and the macrosystem of the larger cultural context. Thus, this approach suggests that most human behaviours are multiply determined, and youth offending is not an exception.

A more recent study conducted by Vander Zanden, Crandell and Crandell (2007) applied Bronfenbrenner's theory to the example of an inner-city family who may face many different challenges compared to those of an affluent family in a secure community. For instance, an inner-city family may experience crime and disorders more frequently, whereas an affluent family may lack support from an extended family network. In the next paragraphs we introduce some of the most relevant risk factors related to youth offending, taking into account the importance of interactions among these various social systems and contexts.

2.1. Family Factors

Family environment has been suggested to be extremely important in shaping children's behaviour and attitudes. In particular, the quality of relationship between child and parent, together with parenting skills, are central areas of importance (Dekovic, Janssens, and van As, 2003). Some studies have found that individuals who report having a negative relationship with their parents are more likely to be involved in delinquent behaviour (e.g., Wissink, Dekovic and Meijer, 2006). Others (e.g., Maguin et al., 1995). have suggested that being exposed to high levels of family conflict may increase the likelihood of future violent behaviour in adolescents.

Also poor parenting skills, including failure to set clear expectations, and setting severe or inconsistent discipline parameters, are predictive of violent youth offending (Wells and Rankin, 1988). Studies conducted by Farrington, Loeber, Yin and Anderson (2002) supported these findings and also showed that males who are are frequently involved in family activities are at a higher risk of being involved in delinquency. There may also be a link between family environment and victimization. However, research into this particular relationship is more limited. Bowers, Smith and Binney (1994) studied how bully-victims, people who bully and are bullied, perceive their family environment. They found that bully-victims tend to report poor relationships with their parents, a lack of supervision, inconsistent discipline and a lack of warmth. If children perceive a negative family context they may feel less supported by their parents and could be more vulnerable to becoming a victim of personal crime. Hawkins et al. (2000) noted the importance of caregivers' involvement and communication with their child. In addition children must be shown affection, support and clear boundaries (Lipsey and Derzon, 1998). In summary, previous research indicates that parenting skills and whether the child gets on well with his or her parents are risk factors for delinquent behaviour including violent offending.

2.2. School Factors

Children spend many of their waking hours at school and, after the family, it is one of the most important socialisation contexts in childhood and adolescence. Consequently, school attitudes and behaviours are a key area when exploring possible risk factors. The perception of importance of school is crucial. Thus, Smith (2006) found that negative attitudes towards school was a relevant risk factor indirectly related to criminal activity through misbehaviour at school. Likewise, Hirschi (1969) found that individuals who were committed to school were less likely to be involved in delinquent activities in comparison with those who showed a weak attachment. These findings have been supported by studies carried out in a variety of different cultures (Leblanc, 1994; Moncher and Miller, 1999; Thornberry, Lizotte, Krohn, Farnworth, and Joon Jang, 1991). In fact, Carroll, Houghton, Hattie and Durkin (1999) suggested that educational and delinquent goals can be seen as opposites. Thus, in order to improve children's perceptions of the importance of school, parents and teachers should be encouraged to motivate and inform children about the value of education.

Another important factor closely related to misbehaviour at school and subsequent escalation into serious offending is, as some studies suggest, the fact that in many schools these undesirable behaviours lead to temporary suspension or even expulsion as disciplinary measures. Such action is unlikely to reduce undesirable behaviour (Smith 2006), and what is more, seems to foster involvement in offending behaviour (McAra, 2004). In a study carried out by Bilchik (1999) it was found that boys who had been suspended reported committing many more delinquent acts than those had not been suspended. Bilchik (1999) explained that this may be due to the suspended boys having more time on their hands to get into trouble. Likewise, those who were not attending school committed nearly four times as many delinquent acts compared to those who were attending school. It has been suggested that this link is related to the extra time without supervision that most of these adolescents spend on the streets (Arum and Beattie, 1999). Instead, controlling and preventing misbehaviour within schools may be more effective than using expulsion from school as a punishment measure.

2.3. Community Factors

As well as children's family and school environment, their local area may also influence their attitudes and behaviours. For instance, McCord, Widom and Crowell (2001) found that living in a poor area where there is noticeable crime increased the likelihood of children becoming involved in crime. This association was explained by suggesting that the child learns about people's values through observation of their neighbourhood, which shapes their perceptions of acceptable social behaviour. Therefore, when a child observes frequent delinquent activities occurring in their neighbourhood they may perceive such behaviours as *normal* and acceptable and thus be more likely to commit antisocial behaviour themselves. Some other researchers have also suggested that perception of general neighbourhood conditions influences attitudes towards police and social norms, especially when negative conditions are considered in terms of the functions and control of these formal authorities (Christenson and Taylor, 1983; Weitzer and Tuch, 2004).

One study conducted in the USA by Hurst and Frank (2000), revealed that juveniles who believed that conditions in their communities were worse than in others held the authorities responsible for not engaging in the same enforcement effort in their communities and they generally showed less favourable attitudes towards the police. These findings are of great importance if we take into account the established close association between attitude towards institutional authority and antisocial and offending behaviour in adolescence (Emler and Reicher, 1995, 2005; Tarry and Emler, 2007). Emler and Reicher (2005) argue that a possible explanation for this could be because some young people who do not feel protected by the police decide they have to take the law into their own hands and build up a dangerous reputation in order to protect themselves from victimization. Although lack of trust in the police has previously been linked to antisocial behaviour and delinquency, there may also be a relationship with victimization (Reicher and Emler, 1985). Children may have had negative experiences of the police after being victimized, which could lead to them having lower levels of trust in the police. Another possibility is that the children's lack of trust in the police heightens their vulnerability to victimization because the offender does not think the victim will report the crime and therefore the offender's behaviour is less likely to be punished (Shaffer and Ruback, 2002). Trust in the police is an interesting factor that may show whether children feel safe in their community and further research into this relationship would be useful in order to throroughly understand.these links.

3. Antisocial Behaviour and Victimization as Direct Antecedents of Offending

Together with family, school and community factors, the scientific literature has highlighted two other factors that are closely related to offending among young people, namely antisocial behaviour and victimization. Moreover, it is possible that all the previously mentioned factors are interrelated and jointly explain youth offending. As we suggest in the next section, in which we present a hypothetical structural model, calculated on the basis of a sample composed of more than 2500 adolescents, family, school and community factors may exert significant influences on children's likelihood both of developing antisocial behaviours and of being victims of crime. These two latter, in turn, have been found to be closely linked to offending, as we note in the following paragraphs. Let us start with the relationship between antisocial and offending behaviour.

Although it is well-known that early and middle adolescence are periods of heightened involvement in anti-social activities, it is also true that there are remarkable individual differences in the frequency and stability of such involvement. Thus, and following Moffit's (1993) theory of antisocial behaviour among young people, most adolescents will behave antisocially only temporarily in this period of life; this behaviour will probably not continue into adulthood. However, a minority will show persistent and stable antisocial behaviour which will increase in seriousness and extremity. According to Moffit's (1993) life-course persistent problem behaviour theory, there is a causal sequence beginning very early in life with the formative years dominated by cumulative and negative person-environment interactions, which give little opportunity for adolescents to learn new behavioural repertoires of prosocial alternatives or to practice conventional social skills.

This idea has also been highlighted in a recent longitudinal study conducted by Weisner, Kim and Capaldi (2005), in which the authors suggest that early involvement in antisocial behaviour decreases an individual's opportunities to interact positively with others and conversely fosters the chance of affiliation with deviant peers, trapping the individual in a risky and dangerous lifestyle. Alongside this process, there seems to be an escalating involvement in antisocial behaviours, that is to say, a progression from minor to more serious offending activity (Pudney, 2002). Minor offences are usually antisocial acts, typically defined as acts that disturb the peace and disrupt the social order and that are likely to cause harassment, alarm or distress to members of neighborhood or community (Crime and Disorder Act, 1998, UK). These behaviours, however, may leave the door open for other less *trivial* acts that explicitly entail criminal offending such as shoplifting. In fact, theft (including shoplifting) has been documented as being the most common offence committed by young people, and can be considered as the prototypical *initial* crime for both genders (Barry, 2006; Cunneen and White, 2002; Rutter, Guiller, and Hagell, 1998).

The question of whether or not victimization predicts offending has also been addressed in several studies in the last two decades. In the Offending, Crime and Justice Survey published in 2006 in the United Kingdom, it was found that half (50%) of the youths who had committed a core offence in the last 12 months had also been a victim of crime, compared with 19% of non-offenders (Roe and Ashe, 2008). Previous studies have indicated that young people who have been victimized report greater involvement in delinquent activities (Wiebush, Freitag, and Baird, 2001). Indeed, according to some authors, being a victim of personal crime is one of the most important warning signals for future offending (Shaffer and Ruback, 2002; Smith and Ecob, 2007) and a risk factor even in adulthood (Ford, 2002). More specifically, in the recent study carried out by Shafer and Ruback (2002) with more than 5,000 adolescents from 11 to 17 years old, it was found that prior victimization predicted subsequent violent offending one year later (52% among victims *versus* 17% among non-victims).

Various criminological theories have been developed to interpret the victim-offender link. According to both lifestyle exposure theory (Hinderlang, Gottfredson, and Galofalo, 1978) and routine activities theory (Cohen and Felson, 1979), the risks of criminal victimization principally arise from individuals' lifestyles and routine activities. As Hinderlang et al. (1978) suggest, since individuals are more likely to interact with those who are similar to themselves, the victimization risk is directly proportional to the number of characteristics shared with offenders or to the similarity of their shared lifestyle. This idea implies, on the one hand, that being a victim of crime is linked to exposure or proximity to offender populations or communities and, on the other, that offenders are more likely to become victims of crime because their lifestyles frequently bring them to interact with other offenders (Sampson and Lauritsen, 1990).

The subculture of violence theory, formulated by Wolfgang and Ferracuti (1967), proposes that in certain areas and for certain groups, there is a sub-culturally valued system that supports the use of violence. From this perspective, victims of crime may become offenders because of the existence of 'norms' which justify retaliation, and offenders may become victims because they hold values that endorse the use of violence to resolve conflicts (Singer, 1981, 1986; see also Emler and Ohana, 1992). In these subcultures, harm and violence are seen as legitimate responses and the value system within the group supports this way of resolving disagreements (Deadman and MacDonald, 2004). From a more psychological perspective, social learning theory suggests that experiencing violence as a victim may result in the victim learning violent behaviours (Siegfried, Ko and Kelley, 2004); other researches believe that trauma makes a significant contribution in the explanation of the victim-aggressor link, since victimization and exposure to the feeling of not being safe may develop into a state of chronic threat which in turn leads the young person to get involved in defiant and violent behaviours (Schwab-Stone et al., 1995).

Young people surrounded by a negative environment may become desensitized to violence and hence be more likely to engage in high risk activities (antisocial acts, drug use, offending). Or they may decide to respond to their own experience of victimization through revenge or even protective aggression. Following Emler (in press), some youths turn to antisocial and offending behaviour in the search of protection that they do not find in formal authority (teachers, the criminal justice system); such a traumatic event in the life of a child or adolescent as being a victim of crime may undermine confidence in adults' safety and protection, in turn resulting in 'disappointment' in authority figures and subsequent involvement in misbehaviours, pursued as the best remedy for reducing the risk of being victimized further.

4. A Model of Interactions among Explanatory Variables

On the basis of the findings reviewed in the previous sections, we devised and tested a structural model of interactions with the aim of exploring the ways in which the most relevant social context for young people (family, school and community) and the fact of having been victimized and/or being involved in antisocial behaviour, exert an influence on participation in violent offending.

With this purpose, we used data from the 2005 Offending Crime and Justice Survey (OCJS), which was jointly conducted for the Home Office by the British Market Research Bureau (BMRB) and the National Centre for Social Research (NatCen). The general aim of the 2005 OCJS was to examine the extent of offending across the household population and covered offences against businesses as well as those against individuals and households. The survey also looks at the personal victimization of young people.

This data has been made publicly available through the UK Data Archive (2007). A multi-staged stratified random sample was used to recruit participants and addresses were randomly selected from the postcode address file. The total sample number used in the present study included 2528 youths aged 10 to 16, 53% of whom were males (n=1328) and 47% were females (n=1200), living in households within England and Wales.

We used AMOS version 6.0 (Arbuckle, 2005) Structural Equation Program to test a number of interactions with an outcome of violent youth offending. We grouped variables based on existing measures in the OCJS, obtaining the six following latent factors: (1) Family context: respondents were asked about the quality of their relationships with parents and perceived parental skills (e.g. "my parent(s) usually listen to me when I want to talk"; "my parent(s) usually treat me fairly when I have done something wrong"); (2) School context: respondents were asked about their attitudes to school and studies, as well as whether they had been excluded from school in the previous 12 months; (3) Local context: respondents were asked about the existence of a series of disorder problems in their local area (e.g., teenagers hanging around causing problems, people being drunk or rowdy in public, rubbish or litter lying around) and their degree of trust in the local police; (4) Antisocial behaviour: respondents were asked whether they had been involved in antisocial behaviours in the 12 months prior to interview (e.g., written things or sprayed paint on a building, fence, train or anywhere else where the child should not have, threatened or been rude to someone because of their skin colour, race or religion); (5) Victimization: respondents were asked whether they had been a victim of crime in the 12 months prior to interview (e.g. assault with injury, personal robbery).

Figure 1 shows the structural model calculated. Continuous lines represent significant paths among factors and curved lines represent correlations among latent variables. The model showed a generally good fit with the data as interpreted by the indicators CFI = .97, NFI= .96 and RMSEA = .04. For the CFI and NFI fit indexes, the consensus is that values above .95 or higher are acceptable; for the RMSEA this is the case of values of .05 or less (Batista and Coenders, 2000).

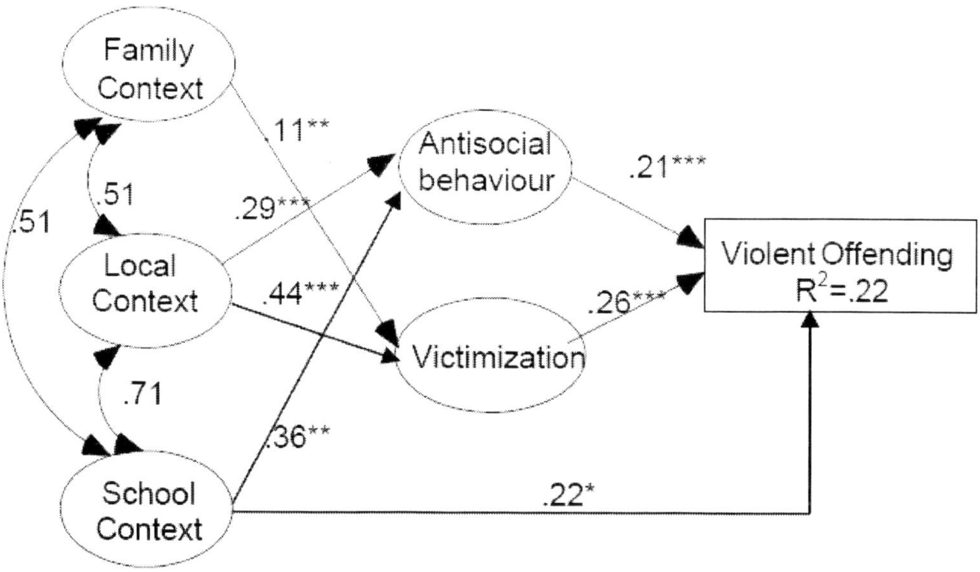

Figure 1. Structural equation model to predict youth violent offending (Significance of the standardized paths is: *p<.05, **p<.01, ***p<.001).

The model accounted for 22% of the variance in youth offending. In the analysis of the direct associations between family, school and local contexts (negatively coded), only the school setting showed a significant direct influence on offending (β =.22, p <.05). Direct associations with violent offending were also found with being involved in anti-social behaviour (β =.21, p <.001) and having been a victim of crime (β =.26, p <.001). Family and community contexts did not show a direct relationship with offending; instead the model suggested an indirect influence of these variables mediated by their impact on antisocial behaviour and victimization. Family context (β =.11, p <.01; the respondent reported not getting on well with their parents and perceived poor parenting skills), and local area (β =.44, p <.001; the respondent perceived higher levels of disorder in their local area and did not trust the local police) were significant predictors of victimization. Meanwhile, school context (β =.36, p <.01; the respondent had been excluded and held a negative attitude towards school and studies) and also local area (β =.29, p<.001) were significant predictors of anti-social behaviour. The robustness of this model was analysed further by testing the measurement and structural invariance across gender groups through multi-group analyses.

Conclusions and Implications for Intervention and for Future Research

The data are cross sectional and correlational, so caution is necessary in making causal inferences. And it would be unwise to treat the structural model tested above uncritically as a description of the relevant causal relations. Moreover, the outcome of the modelling is to some extent bounded by the data available. With these provisos, the findings give grounds for concluding that there are two clear and distinct influences on the emergence of violent offending. One operates through the immediate impact of anti-social behaviour, the other through the immediate impact of victimization. This is potentially an important conclusion for what it rules out, in particular that victimization is merely a side effect of anti-social and violent behaviour. In this section we speculate a little further on the detail that may underlie these two routes, though we seek to root our speculation on what else is known about causes of crime. And we draw out what appear to be the implications for intervention as well as the pointers to areas of uncertainty that would merit further investigation.

The first route to violent offending to which our model points is essentially one of continuity and escalation. A considerable body of research now supports the view that interindividual variations in anti-social inclination are stable over time. Longitudinal research traces these individual differences back into early childhood, and through the course of childhood a feedback loop will have been established between childhood temperament and parental response. Thus the family context is not irrelevant to this route, but its impact lies further in the past.

But what of the two aspects of the microsystem that appear to matter more in the earlier teenage years, the local and school context? Note first of all that these two contexts are very strongly interrelated, and indeed that both are strongly related to the family context. Thus, living in a neighbourhood characterised by disorder is associated with a poor relation with school, while both are also linked to poor relations with parents. There are two obvious ways in which neighbourhood conditions are likely to have amplifying effects on behavioural inclinations. One is through the communication of behavioural norms. Trouble making groups, rowdy drunks, and littered streets all communicate rather different norms to those expressed through their absence. The other is through provision of a like-minded peer group. The close link between delinquency and having delinquent associates is well known and further reinforced by the connection between gang membership and anti-social behaviour. And other work has shown that one factor predicting gang membership is residential instablility (Dupere et al., 2007). One might expect that neighbourhoods characterised by residential instability will lack the informal social control mechanisms that otherwise help to limit delinquency.

The school context encompasses a set of factors that are more likely to be implicated in a feedback relationship with anti-social behaviour. Kids who are disposed to misbehave find the regime of school uncongenial and their relations with school become increasingly abrasive, ultimately leading to exclusion. At the same time the labelling that takes place in the educational setting further reinforces a delinquent reputation (Adams and Evans, 1996), and the more explicit labelling entailed in exclusion further amplifies delinquent activity But the direct link found, in testing the model, between school context and violent offending may more accurately reflect an influence running in the other direction: young people who are violent are in consequence more at risk of exclusion.

This is part of a more general truth, a caution against the the expectation that a simple linear model can fully capture the patterns of cause and effect in which violent of offending is enmeshed. A pattern of individual behaviour can never be only an outcome of environmental forces; it will feed back into the individual's social environment, affecting the way that others, individually, collectively and as institutional actors, respond and react.

The pattern around victimization also embodies this truth. Other work shows that gang membership amplifies criminal activity, but also raises the risk of victimization (Decker et al., 2008). Increased victimization is plausibly an outcome of violent behaviour as gang retaliates against gang. But experience of victimization also feeds into violent offending. The impact of locality could be of two kinds. First a community in which social order is precarious is one whose individual members are exposed to greater risk of victimization. Second, if actual victimization is accompanied by lack of effective police response this would also undermine trust in the police. This could in turn support a resort to violence, whether as a strategic response to the perceived hazard of victimization or as direct action to redress grievances. The strength of the direct path from locality to victimization in the model is striking. We suspect this is in part because the locality variable includes trust/mistrust in the police, which with stronger measures of this attitude would emerge as a joint consequence of victimization and impoverished local context.

The weaker path from family context to victimization may be amenable to a more straightforward interpretation. For some children, treatment at the hands of their parents undoubtedly amounts to victimization, and the route from victim (of child abuse) to offender is well documented (Anderson, 2005; Stouthamer-Loeber et al, 2001).

Turning to the implications for intervention and prevention, the first message must be that there is no single lever to pull, no uniquely effective point of intervention. At the same time some levers are more accessible than others, and some are already very familiar. Thus, we already know that parenting skills matter and the present findings only reinforce the desirability of supporting their enhancement. Likewise the hazards consequent on child abuse are beginning to receive more attention and to attract a stronger response. There is also growing awareness that schools play a critical role in the labelling process and that measures such as exclusion may only exaggerate the effects they are intended to reverse.

What is perhaps newer is the message that action to improve order in communities would pay dividends. And at the heart of this is community policing; community order founded on effective policing should both reduce the risk of victimization and increase confidence in the protection the law should provide. This leads us to our nomination for the most fruitful focus of further research. To untangle the relations between community conditions, victimization, policing and violent offending will require research that is both longitudinal and based on stronger measures of all the relevant variables. In particular the data set available to us could not distinguish sufficiently between neighbourhood conditions and trust in the police. We need to understand better how these are interrelated and how they are different, as well as how they are each connected to the experience of victimization.

REFERENCES

Adams, M. S. and Evans, T. D. (1996). Teacher disapproval, delinquent peers and self reported delinquency: A longitudinal test of labelling theory. *Urban Review*, 28, 199-211.

Anderson, G. (2005). Family relations, adjustment and well-being in a longitudinal study of children in care. *Child and Family Social Work*, 10, 43-56.

Arbuckle, J.L. (2005). *AMOS version 6.0 User's guide.* United States of America: Amos Development Corporation.

Arum, R., & Beattie, I. (1999). High school experience and the risk of adult incarceration. *Criminology, 37,* 515–537.

Barry, M. (2006). *Youth offending in transition: the search for social recognition.* London: Routledge.

Batista, J. M., and Coenders, G. (2000). *Structural Equation Models.* Madrid: La Muralla.

Baum, K. (2005). *Juvenile victimization and offending, 1993–2003.* Bureau of Justice Statistics Special Report. Washington, D.C.: U.S. Department of Justice.

Bilchik, S. (1999). *Violence After School.* Washington, US: Office of Juvenile Justice and Delinquency Prevention.

Bronfenbrenner, U. (1979). *The Ecology of Human Development: Experiments by Nature and Design.* Cambridge: Harvard University Press.

Brook, J., Whiteman, M., Finch, S., and Cohen, P. (1996). Young adult drug use and delinquency: Childhood antecedents and adolescent mediators. *Journal of the American Academy of Child and Adolescent Psychiatry, 35*, 1584-1592.

Carroll, A., Houghton, S., Hattie, J., and Durkin, K. (1999). Adolescent reputation enhancement: differentiating delinquent, nondelinquent, and at-risk youths. *Journal of Child Psychology and Psychiatry, 40,* 593-606.

Chaiken, J. M., and Chaiken M. R. (1990). Drugs and predatory crime. In M. Tonry and J. Q. Wilson (Eds.), *Drugs and crime* (pp. 203-239). Chicago: University of Chicago Press.

Christenson, J., and Taylor, G. S. (1983). The socially constructed and situational context for assessment of police services. *Social Science Quarterly, 63,* 264-274.

Cohen, L., and Felson, M. (1979). Social change and crime rate trends: A routine activities approach. *American Sociological Review, 44,* 588-607.

Copeland, J., Howard, J., Keogh, Y., and Seidler, K. (2003). Patterns and correlates of alcohol and other drug use among juvenile detainees in New South Wales. *Drug Alcohol Review, 22,* 15-20.

Cunneen, C., and White, R. (2002). *Juvenile justice: Youth and crime in Australia.* Oxford: Oxford University Press.

Deadman, D., and MacDonald, Z. (2004). Offenders as victims of crime?: An investigation into the relationship between criminal behaviour and victimization. *Journal of the Royal Statistical Society, 167,* 53-67.

Decker, S. H., Katz, C. M. and Webb, V. J. (2008). Understanding the black box of gang organisation: Implications for involvement in violent crime, drug sales and violent victimizstion. *Crime and Delinquency, 54*, 153-172.

Dekovic, M., Janssens, J. M., and van As, N. M. (2003). Family predictors of antisocial behavior in adolescence. *Family Process, 42*, 223-235.

Dijk, J.J.M., van, Kesteren, J.N. van, and Smit, P. (2008). *Criminal Victimization in International Perspective. Key findings from the 2004-2005 ICVS and EU ICS.* Den Haag: Boom Legal Publishers. (Onderzoek en Beleid, WODC, 257).

Dupere, V., Lacourse, E., Wimms, J. D., Vitaro, F., and Tremblay, R. (2007). Affiliation to youth gangs during adolescence: The interaction between childhood psychopathic tendencies and neighborhood disadvantage. *Journal of Abnromal Child Psychology*, 35, 1035-1045.

Emler, N. (in press). Delinquents as a minority group: Accidental tourists in forbidden territory or voluntary émigrés? In F. Butera and J. Levine (Eds.), *Coping with minority status: Responses to exclusion and inclusion.* Cambridge: Cambridge University Press.

Emler, N., and Reicher, S. (1995). *Adolescence and delinquency.* Oxford: Blackwell.

Emler, N., and Reicher, S. (2005). Delinquency: cause or consequence of social exclusion? In D. Abrams, J. Marques and M. Hogg, (eds). *The social psychology of inclusion and exclusion* (pp 211-241). Philadelphia: Psychology Press.

Entorf, H. and Spengler, H. (2002). Crime in Europe - *Causes and Consequences.* Berlin Heidelberg New York: Springer.

Farrington, D.P. (2000). Explaining and preventing crime: The globalization of knowledge- The American Society of Criminology, 1999 presidential address. *Criminology, 38,* 1-24.

Farrington, D. P., Loeber, R., Yin, Y., and Anderson, S. (2002). Are within-individual causes of delinquency the same as between-individual causes? *Criminal Behavior and Mental Health, 12,* 53–68.

Federal Bureau of Investigation. (2006). *Crime in the United States: Persons arrested (Uniform Crime Report).* Washington, D.C.: U.S. Government Printing Office.

Ford, J. D. (2002). Trauma victimization in childhood and persistent problems with oppositional-defiance. In R. Greenwald (Ed.), *Trauma and Juvenile Delinquency: Theory, Research, and Interventions* (pp. 25-58). New York: Haworth Press.

Goldstein, P. J. (1989). Drugs and crime. In N. A. Weiner and M. E. Wolfgang (Eds.), *Pathways to criminal violence* (pp. 16-48). Newbury Park, CA: Sage.

Grinberg, I., Dawkins, M., Dawkins, M P., and Fullilove, C. (2005). Adolescents at risk for violence: An initial validation of the life challenges questionnaire and risk assessment index. *Journal of Adolescence, 40,* 573–599.

Hawkins, J.D., Herrenkohl, T.I., Farrington, D.P., Brewer, D., Catalano, R.F., Harachi, T.W., and Cothern, L. (2000). *Predictors of Youth Violence.* Washington, US: Office of Juvenile Justice and Delinquency Prevention.

Hirschi, T. (1969). *Causes of delinquency.* Berkeley: University of California Press.

Hurst, Y. G., and Frank, J. (2000). How kids view cops. The nature of juvenile attitudes toward the police. *Journal of Criminal Justice, 28,* 189-202.

Kershaw, C., Nicholas., and Walker, A. (2008). *Crime in England and Wales, 2007/08. Findings from the British Crime Survey and police recorded crime.* Home Office Statistical Bulletin 07/08. London: Home Office.

Kim, H. K., and Capaldi, D. M. (2004). The association of antisocial behaviour and depressive symptoms between partners and risk for aggression in romantic relationships. *Journal of Family Psychology, 18,* 82-96.

Kim, J. Y. S., and Fendrich, M. (2002). Gender differences in juvenile arrestees' drug use, self-reported dependence, and perceived need for treatment. *Psychiatric Services, 53,* 70-75.

Leblanc, M. (1994). Family, school, delinquency and criminality, the predictive power of an elaborated social control theory for males. *Criminal Behaviour and Mental Health, 4,* 101-117.

Lennings, C. J., Copeland, J., and Howard, J. (2003). Substance use patterns of young offenders and violent crime. *Aggressive Behavior, 29,* 414-422.

Lipsey, M.W., and Derzon, J.H. (1998). Predictors of violence or serious delinquency in adolescence and early adulthood. In R. Loeber and D.P. Farrington, (eds). *Serious and Violent Juvenile Offenders: Risk Factors and Successful Interventions.* (pp 86-105). Thousand Oaks, CA: Sage Publications, Inc.

Loeber, R., Stouthamer-Loeber, M., Van Kammen, W., and Farrington, D. P. (1989). Development of a new measure of self-reported antisocial behaviour for young children: Prevalence and reliability. In M. Kleian (Ed.), *Cross-national research in self-reported crime and delinquency* (pp. 203-226). Boston: Kluwer-Nijhoff.

Maguin, E., Hawkins, J.D., Catalano, R.F., Hill, K., Abbott, R., and Herrenkohl, T. (1995). *Risk factors measured at three ages for violence at age 17-18*. Paper presented at the American Society of Criminology, Boston.

McAra, L. (2004). *Truancy, school exclusion and substance misuse*. Edinburgh Study of Youth Transitions and Crime, number 4. Edinburgh: Centre for Law and Society, University of Edinburgh.

McCord, J., Widom. C.S., and Crowell, N.A. (2001) *Juvenile Crime, Juvenile Justice. Panel on Juvenile Crime: Prevention, Treatment, and Control*. Washington, D.C: National Academy Press.

McIvor, G., Murray, C., and Jamieson, J. (2004). Is desistance from crime different for girls?, In S. Maruna and R. Immarigeon (Eds.), *After crime and punishment: Ex-offender reintegration and desistance from crime*. New York: SUNY Press.

Moffitt, T. E. (1993). Adolescence-limited and life course-persistent antisocial behaviour developmental taxonomy. *Psychological Review, 100,* 674-701.

Moffitt, T. E. (2006). Life-course-persistent and adolescent-limited antisocial behaviour. In D. Cicchetti and D. J. Cohen (Eds.), *Developmental Psychopathology, Vol.3: Risk, disorder, and adaptation* (pp. 385-395). New York: Wiley.

Moncher, F. J. and Miller, G. E. (1999). Nondelinquent youth's stealing behaviour and their perceptions of parents, school, and peers. *Adolescence, 34,* 577-591.

Odgers, C. L., Moretti, M. M., Burnette, M. L., Chauhan, P., Waite, D., and Reppucci, D. (2007). A latent variable modelling approach to identifying subtypes of serious and violent female juvenile offenders. *Aggressive Behavior, 33,* 339-352.

Pedersen, W., Mastekaasa, A., and Wichstrom, L. (2001). Conduct problems and early cannabis initiation: A longitudinal study of gender differences. *Addiction*, *96*, 415– 431.

Pettiway, L. E., Dolinsky, S., and Grigoryan, A. (1994). The drug and criminal activity patterns of urban offenders: A Markov chain analysis. *Journal of Quantitative Criminology, 10*, 79-107.

Pudney, S. (2002). *The road to ruin? Sequences of initiation into drug use and offending by young people in Britain*. Home Office Research Study 253, London: Home Office.

Reebye, P., Moretti, M. M., and Lessard, J. C. (1995). Conduct disorder and substance use disorder: Comorbidity in a clinical sample of preadolescent and adolescents. *Canadian Journal of Psychiatry*, *40*, 313–319.

Reicher, S. and *Emler*, N. (*1985*). Delinquent behaviour and attitudes to formal. authority. *British Journal of Social Psychology*, 3, 161-168.

Robins, L. N., and McEvoy, L. (1990). Conduct problems as predictors of substance abuse. In L. R. Robins and M. Rutter (Eds.), *Straight and devious pathways from childhood to adulthood*. New York: Cambridge University Press.

Rodham, K., Hawton, K., Evans, E. and Weatherall, R. (2005). Ethnic and gender differences in drinking, smoking and drug taking among adolescents in England: a self-report school-based survey of 15 and 16 year olds. *Journal of Adolescence*, *28*, 63-73.

Roe, S., and Ashe, J. (2008). *Young people and crime: Findings from the 2006 Offending, Crime and Justice Survey*. Home Office Statistical Bulletin 09/08. London: Home Office.

Rutter, M., Guiller, H., and Hagell, A. (1998). *Antisocial behaviour by young people.* Cambridge: Cambridge University Press.

Sampson, R. J., and Lauritsen, J. L. (1990). Deviant lifestyles, proximity to crime, and the offender-victim link in personal violence. *Journal of Research in Crime and Delinquency, 27,* 110-139.

Schwab-Stone, M. E., Ayers, T. S., Wesley, K., Voyce, C., Barone, C., Shriver, T., and Weissberg, R. P. (1995). No safe haven: A study of violence exposure in an urban community. *Journal of the American Academy of Child and Adolescent Psychiatry, 34,* 1343-1352.

Shader, M. (2001). *Risk factors for delinquency: An overview.* Washington, US: Office of Juvenile Justice and Delinquency Prevention.

Shaffer, J. N. and Ruback, R. B. (2002). Violent victimization as a rick factor for violent offending among juveniles. *OJJDP Juvenile Justice Bulleting.* Washington, D.C.: U.S. Department of Justice, Office of Juvenile Justice and Delinquency Prevention.

Shannon, M. (2006). *Criminal Victimization, 2005* (NCJ 214644): U.S. Bureau of Justice Statistics.

Siegfried, C. B., Ko, S. J., and Kelley, A. (2004). *Victimization and juvenile offending.* California: Publications of the National Child Traumatic Stress Network (www.nctsnet.org).

Singer, S. (1981). Homogeneous victim-offender populations: A review of some research implications. *Journal of Criminal Law and Criminology, 72,* 779-188.

Singer, S. (1986). Victims of serious violence and their criminal behaviour: Subcultural theory and beyond. *Victims and Violence, 1,* 61-69.

Smith, D.J. (2006). *School experience and delinquency at ages 13 to 16.* Edinburgh Study of Youth Transitions and Crime Research Findings No. 13.

Smith, D. J., and Ecob, R. (2007). An investigation into causal links between victimization and offending in adolescents. *The British Journal of Sociology, 58,* 633-659.

Snyder, H. N., and Sickmund, M. (1999). Juvenile offenders and victims: 1999 national report. Washington, D.C.: Office of Juvenile Justice and Delinquency Prevention.

Stouthamer-Loeber. M., Loeber, R., Hornish, D.L., and Wei, E. (2001). Maltreatment of boys and the development of disruptive and delinquent behaviour. *Development and Psychopathology*, 13, 941-955.

Tarry, H., and Emler, N. (2007). Attitudes, values and moral reasoning as predictors of delinquency. *British Journal of Developmental Psychology. 25,* 169-183.

Thornberry, T. P., Lizotte, A. J., Krohn, M. D., Farnworth, M., and Joon Jang, S. (1991). Testing interactional theory: An examination of reciprocal causal relationships among family, school, and delinquency. *The Journal of Criminal Law and Criminology, 82,* 3-35.

Van Kesteren, J., Mayhew, P. and Nieuwbeerta, P. (2001). *Criminal victimization in seventeen industrialised countries: Key findings from the 2000 International Crime Victims Survey.* The Hague: Ministry of Justice.

Vander Zanden, J. W., Crandell, T. L., and Crandell, C. H. (2007). *Human Development.* 8th edition (ed.), New York: McGraw Hill.

Wei, E., Loeber, R., and White, H. R. (2004). Teasing apart developmental associations between alcohol and marijuana use and violence. *Journal of Contemporary Criminal Justice, 20,* 166-183.

Weitzer, R., and Tuch, S. A. (2004). Race and perceptions of police misconduct. *Social Problems, 51,* 305-325.

Wells, L.E., and Rankin, J.H. (1988). Direct parental controls and delinquency. *Criminology, 26,* 263-285.

Wiebush, R., Freitag, R., and Baird, C. (2001). *Preventing delinquency through improved child protective services. OJJDP Juvenile Justice Bulleting.* Washington, D.C.: U.S. Department of Justice, Office of Juvenile Justice and Delinquency Prevention.

Wiesner, M., Kim, H. K., and Capaldi, D. M. (2005). Developmental trajectories of offending: Validation and prediction to young adult alcohol use, drug use, and depressive sumptoms. *Development and Psychopathology, 17,* 251-270.

Wissink, I.B., Dekovic, M., and Meijer, A.M. (2006). Parenting Behaviour, Quality of the Parent-Adolescent Relationship, and Adolescent Functioning in Four Ethnic Groups. *The Journal of Early Adolescence, 26,* 133-159.

Wittebrood, K., and Niewbeerta, P. (1999). Wages of sin?: the link between offending, lifestyle and violent victimization. *European Journal of Criminal Policy and Research, 7,* 63-80.

Wolfang, M., and Ferracuti, F. (1967). *The subculture of violence: Toward an integrated theory in criminology.* London: Tavistock.

Wood, J., Foy, D., Goguen, C., Pynoos, R., and James, C. B. (2002). Violence exposure and PTSD among delinquent girls. *Journal of Aggression, Maltreatment and Trauma, 6,* 109-126.

In: Delinquency: Causes, Reduction and Prevention
Editor: Ozan Sahin and Joseph Maier
ISBN 978-1-60741-558-9

Chapter 9

PEER INTERACTIONS AND DELINQUENCY

Lisabeth F. DiLalla, Kristin Bell, and Sarah S. Long
Southern Illinois University School of Medicine

ABSTRACT

This study aimed to examine the relation between childhood social behaviors and later delinquency. To assess this relation, we used ratings of the level of difficultness and aggression exhibited by 90 5-year-old children during their interactions with an unfamiliar peer and assessed parent ratings of delinquency at age 5 and parent and self-ratings of delinquent activities five to ten years later. Early social behaviors were related to concurrent parent ratings of delinquency but they were not predictive of later delinquency. However, adolescent peers' delinquent behaviors were correlated with adolescent delinquency. Additionally, there was preliminary evidence that youth who began exhibiting delinquent behaviors as young as age 5 were more likely to show interpersonal difficult behaviors at age 5, whereas those who did not report delinquent behaviors until adolescence did not show preschool difficult behaviors but were equally as likely as the early starters to report having delinquent peers. Thus, although early difficult interactions with peers are related to delinquent activities at the same age, peer play behaviors during childhood are neither necessary nor sufficient causes to account for association with deviant peers or engaging in delinquent activities during adolescence.

INTRODUCTION

There has been a considerable amount of research linking early-onset externalizing problems with a variety of poor outcomes, including Conduct Disorder, Attention-Deficit/Hyperactivity Disorder (ADHD), and juvenile delinquency (see Campbell, 2002, for a review). Although for most children early externalizing problems characterized by aggressive and oppositional behaviors decrease dramatically after age 2, for a minority the problems remain stable and lead to more serious outcomes (Campbell, 1995; Campbell, 2002; Hill, Degnan, Calkins, and Keane, 2006). Juvenile delinquency is associated with a significant financial toll from property destruction and accidents, along with potential health risks related to other activities such as drug and alcohol abuse and risky sexual behavior. By studying early childhood to understand the predictors of later delinquency, prevention efforts can be initiated earlier and geared specifically toward those at greatest risk, thus utilizing resources most efficiently.

Trajectory and Development of Delinquent Behaviors

Identifying early-onset delinquency has been a major focus of recent research following the publication of several studies that outlined significant differences between early- and late-starting delinquent youth (DiLalla and Gottesman, 1989; Moffitt, 1993). Specifically, those who begin participating in delinquent activities early, as opposed to later in middle or late adolescence, represent 6-7% of the population but are responsible for nearly half of adolescent crime (Moffitt, 1993; Moffitt and Caspi, 2001; Offord, Boyle, and Racine, 1991; Patterson, Capaldi, and Bank, 1991). Tolan and Thomas (1995) also found that early onset delinquents (before age 12 for males and age 13 for females) showed dramatically increased rates of offending and these increased rates did not decline with time like those who presented with later onset. Late-onset delinquents participated in less serious offenses compared to early starters and their participation was limited to the adolescent years only. Interestingly, Moffitt and Caspi (2001) determined that the sex differences that exist among children classified as life-course persistent offenders (those presenting with stable antisocial behavior problems throughout childhood and adolescence, male to female sex ratio of 10:1) nearly disappears among adolescence-limited delinquents (those with antisocial behavior problems only in adolescence, sex ratio of 1.5:1). DiLalla and Gottesman (1991) and Moffitt (1993) have suggested that there may be a stronger genetic influence on early onset delinquents, whereas adolescent-limited delinquents may be influenced primarily by their delinquent cohorts.

In addition, some early childhood problem behaviors appear to be predictive of later antisocial or delinquent behavior (Caspi, Henry, McGee, Moffitt, and Silva, 1995; Nagin and Tremblay, 2001; Tremblay, 2000; Tremblay and Nagin, 2005). Specifically, Caspi and colleagues determined that at ages 3 and 5, emotional lability, restlessness, short attention span, and negativism were correlated in theoretically consistent ways with behavior problems between ages 9 and 15. These behavior problems include poor concentration, restlessness, fighting, disobedience, destructiveness, lying, and stealing.

Early Childhood Behaviors May Predict Adolescent Delinquency

Adolescent externalizing behaviors often can be traced to problem behaviors observed during early childhood (Burke, Loeber, Lahey, and Rathouz, 2005; Mun, Fitzgerald, Von Eye, Puttler, and Zucker, 2001). For example, behavioral noncompliance from young children is a symptom of aggressive and oppositionally defiant behaviors in adolescence (Campbell, Pierce, March, Ewing, and Szumowski, 1994; Olson, 1992). Commanding, controlling, or bossy behaviors can lead to disagreeableness, aggression, and aversive attempts to influence others' behaviors (Markell and Asher, 1984). In addition, a difficult temperament is often a significant risk factor for aggressive behaviors during the entire childhood period (Guerin, Gottfried, and Thomas, 1997; Windle, 1991). However, it is unknown whether similar behaviors are related to delinquency per se, rather than aggression, in adolescence. Identification of early risk factors for later delinquency would be valuable in terms of intervention. Also, if identification can be made of early behaviors that are related particularly to early-onset delinquency, which is the most severe (DiLalla and Gottesman, 1989; Moffitt, 1993), that would be especially valuable.

THE ROLE OF PEERS IN DELINQUENCY

Peer group characteristics, such as peer rejection and peer delinquency, frequently are examined as both predictors of delinquency and concurrent related factors. Barnow, Lucht, and Freyberger (2005) tested a model for aggressive and delinquent conduct problems in 12- to 18-year-old male and female adolescents and examined peer group characteristics, including both peer rejection and participation in deviant peer groups. Barnow and colleagues found that peer rejection in adolescence was strongly associated with aggressive behavior and only moderately linked to delinquency. Because these findings were not longitudinal, it cannot be determined which came first – aggressive behavior, delinquency, or peer rejection. However, it is somewhat intuitive that adolescents who are rejected by peers might engage in less delinquent behavior because they have fewer peer relationships and, thus, more limited opportunities in which to engage with peers in delinquent activities.

Peer rejection in fifth grade has also been shown to predict nonspecific negative outcomes, such as academic problems, school suspension, truancy, or police contact (specifically for nonstatus offenses) in later adolescence (Kupersmidt and Coie, 1990). The authors also found that early aggression significantly predicted later police contacts specifically, along with other nonspecific negative outcomes as noted above. Thus, although being rejected by peers may indicate that some children and adolescents participate in less delinquent behavior because they do not have a peer group to participate with, for others this rejection actually may provide the impetus for beginning to engage with more deviant peers, thus leading to delinquent behaviors.

These studies suggest that peer rejection has a moderate effect on later delinquency. Other factors such as peer deviance must also be considered. Barnow et al. (2005) examined peer deviance using a three item questionnaire, inquiring about drug and alcohol use among peers, use of fighting to solve problems, and presence of peers who have committed crime or have had police contacts. In this study, participation in deviant peer groups was positively related to both self- and mother-reported delinquency. Similarly, Tolan and Thomas (1995) found that involvement in deviant peer groups best explained delinquent behavior in boys. Among girls in their sample, school and family variables such as delinquent peers, the belief that others hold a negative view towards her in the family, school, or peer group, and beliefs that it is necessary to violate conventional norms to obtain family, peer, or school goals, best explained delinquent behavior. Fergusson and Horwood (1996) found that 14- and 16-year-old adolescents who had conduct problems at age 8 were more likely to associate with deviant peers and thus participate in more deviant behavior. In a later study (Fergusson and Horwood, 1999), they also found that children who showed early onset conduct problems and had several negative psychosocial factors, including dysfunctional families and disadvantaged socioeconomic status, were more likely to associate with deviant peers in adolescence. The previous two studies suggest that delinquent individuals are more likely to associate with deviant peers, and also speak to the continuity of early-onset delinquent behavior. Thus, childhood problems can predict association with deviant peers, and deviant peers may predict increased delinquent behavior.

Although deviant peers are important for predicting deviant behaviors in adolescence, the role of deviant siblings is also critical. Several studies (Criss and Shaw, 2005; Garcia, Shaw, Winslow, and Yaggi, 2000; Rowe, 1985; Snyder, Bank, and Burraston, 2005) have shown that deviant siblings have significant influence on delinquency in younger siblings through a variety of pathways. Although siblings share genes, which may account for some of the correlation between siblings, there appears to be a strong shared environmental component (Rowe, 1985). Thus, having a delinquent sibling may provide deviancy training, rewarding of deviant behavior, and opportunities to associate with older, deviant peers.

Hypotheses

Based on previous research, we hypothesized that aggression during a peer interaction at age 5 would be predictive of delinquency in adolescence. Difficult behaviors at age 5 were also expected to be predictive of delinquency, but perhaps not as directly as aggression. Although difficult temperament should put children at greater risk for peer rejection, which tends to predict problems other than delinquency, a behavioral measure of difficult interactive behaviors that includes some aggressive behaviors may indeed be related to delinquency in adolescence. In addition, parent ratings of delinquency at age 5 were expected to be predictive of parent and self-ratings of delinquency at follow-up. Finally, association with delinquent peers and siblings at follow-up was expected to be associated with higher levels of delinquent behavior.

Method

Participants

Children in this study were part of a larger project, the Southern Illinois Twins and Siblings Study (SITSS; DiLalla, 2002). The 90 youth in this study comprised children who originally were tested at age 5 and then participated in a follow-up study in early adolescence. All children initially were tested within two months of their fifth birthday. These data were collected over a period of 5 years. Five years later, families of youth now aged 10 to 15 years were contacted by mail and invited to participate in a follow-up study that involved mailed questionnaires for both parents and children as well as a telephone interview for the children. 254 families had children who were old enough for the follow-up study. 108 families were able to be contacted, and 90 agreed to participate. 146 families apparently had moved and could not be located. A MANOVA examining whether the families who did and did not participate in the follow-up study differed in terms of early delinquent behaviors (parent-rated and peer play, as described below) was non-significant ($F(3,212) = 2.42$, p = ns). However, univariate results showed that the families who participated in the follow-up study had children who were rated by their parents as significantly more delinquent at age 5 ($F(1,214) = 6.92$, $p < .01$).

Of the 90 families in the final sample, 96% were Caucasian, 1% were African American, 3% were classified as "other." At the time of the 5-year-old study, all but one set of parents were married and mothers' ages ranged from 24 to 46 (mean = 34.8, sd = 4.3). Family incomes ranged from "$15,000-$20,000" to "more than $35,000", with the median being "more than $35,000." Parent education ranged from completed high school to having an advanced degree, with the median for both mothers and fathers being completion of a college degree. The mean number of children in the home was 2.8 (sd = 1.8). There was not a significant difference between the families who participated in the follow-up study and those who did not on these SES variables ($F(3,215) = 1.67$, p = ns).

Procedure and Materials

Prior to coming to the lab, parents completed a series of questionnaires about their children, including questionnaires about family demographics and child behaviors. At the time of testing, children were brought to a laboratory playroom and were paired with a same-age, same-sex, unfamiliar singleton child. One twin and one singleton were allowed to enter the playroom and play freely, by themselves, for 20 minutes. The room was equipped with puppets, a toy tool set, kitchen toys, checkers, and posters. There were two one-way mirrors, one through which to videotape and the other for parents to watch through if they chose. Children's play was videotaped for later behavioral coding and two behaviors were used for the present study: Difficultness and Aggression. The children were rated twice, following the first and second ten minutes of play. "Difficultness" was a rating of how difficult a child was during the peer play session, including such behaviors as complaining, ignoring the other child, and/or being aggressive, unpleasant, or unfriendly. This was rated on a 5-point scale, from 1 = not at all difficult, a real pleasure to interact with, to 5 = very difficult, highly aggressive. Inter-rater reliabilities were calculated using Cohen's weighted kappa (Cohen, 1968) which takes into account the fact that response rates for each option were not equally likely. Inter-rater reliability across coders was .78. "Aggression" was used to rate all negative behaviors and activities. These behaviors included negative grabs, rejections, toy struggles, physical abuse toward an object or the other child in anger, verbal abuse, or other behaviors exhibited in a "nasty" manner. "Aggression" was rated on a 5-point scale, from 1 = no aggressive behaviors, to 5 = six or more aggressive behaviors. Inter-rater reliability across coders was .80.

At the age 5 testing, parents completed a series of questionnaires, including the Child Behavior Checklist (CBCL; Achenbach and Rescorla, 2001). The CBCL is a parent rating of 113 different problem behaviors in which a child may or may not engage. One of the syndrome scales is the Delinquency subscale, with test-retest reliabilities of .86 (Achenbach and Rescorla, 2001). This scale includes items such as child lies or cheats, child steals at home, and child doesn't feel guilty if she or he misbehaves. This was the scale used for the study analyses. Raw scores were used rather than T scores due to the non-clinical nature of the sample.

For the follow-up study, families were sent packets of questionnaires and asked to mail them back. Youth also were asked to participate in a telephone interview, during which time they were asked to complete a questionnaire assessing frequency of delinquent behaviors engaged in by their friends and siblings. This was measured using a modification of the Self Report Delinquency Scale (Resnick et al., 1997) with youths answering the questions about their siblings and friends rather than about themselves. They also were asked to complete the Youth Self Report (YSR; Achenbach, 1991), which is a youth self-report questionnaire that parallels the CBCL. Children rate the degree to which they engage in 113 behaviors. The items form 2 superfactors, Introversion and Extraversion, and 8 first order factors, including the Delinquency subscale that was used for the present study. Test-retest reliability for this factor is approximately .90 (Achenbach, 1991).

Also during the follow-up study, parents completed the CBCL again, as described above, providing current delinquency and aggression ratings.

RESULTS

Variables that were included in analyses were first examined for sex effects to determine whether there were significant differences between boys and girls. Multivariate analysis of variance (MANOVA) demonstrated a significant effect of sex ($F(6,83) = 4.49$, $p < .001$). Boys scored higher on all variables, although the difference was not significant for parent ratings of delinquency (see Table 1).

Table 1. Descriptive statistics

	Total sample		Boys		Girls	
Variable	Mean (sd)	Range	Mean (sd)	Range	Mean (sd)	Range
Peer Play Difficult	2.17 (0.64)	1-4	2.37 (0.69)	1-4	1.99 (0.54)	1-3
Peer Play Aggressive	1.51 (0.53)	1-3.5	1.66 (0.59)	1-3.5	1.36 (0.43)	1-2.5
CBCL Delinquency age 5	1.28 (1.23)	0-6	1.53 (1.39)	0-6	1.04 (1.02)	0-4
CBCL Delinquency follow-up[a]	0.84 (1.10)	0-5	1.00 (1.25)	0-5	0.70 (0.93)	0-3
YSR Delinquency[b]	1.76 (1.74)	0-8	2.33 (1.80)	0-8	1.23 (1.54)	0-8
Peer/Sibling Delinquency	4.31 (4.91)	0-24	5.86 (5.67)	0-24	2.89 (3.61)	0-15

Note: Boys scored significantly higher ($p < .01$) than girls on variables except CBCL Delinquency age 5 ($p < .06$) and CBCL Delinquency follow-up ($p = .20$).

[a] Significantly less than CBCL Delinquency age 5 and YSR Delinquency for total sample and for boys.

[b] Significantly greater than CBCL Delinquency age 5 for total sample as well as both boy and girl subsamples.

Parent ratings of delinquency. We first examined whether early peer interactions during the peer play were related to delinquent behaviors reported by parents at age 5. Pearson correlations demonstrated a significant relation between early difficult behaviors with peers and 5-year-old parent ratings of delinquent behaviors ($r(90) = .21, p < .05$), but not between aggressive behaviors exhibited with peers and parent ratings of delinquency ($r(90) = .06, p =$ ns). However, when the correlations were repeated separately for boys and girls, the relation between difficult behaviors and delinquency was no longer significant (for boys: $r(43) = .17$, $p =$ ns; for girls: $r(47) = .14, p =$ ns).

Regression analysis then was used to determine whether 5-year-old play behaviors were predictive of parent-rated delinquency at follow-up, and the overall model was significant ($F(2,87) = 3.28, p < .05$), accounting for 11% of the variance (see Table 2). Again, difficult behaviors during the peer play situation were significantly related to parent ratings of delinquency (*beta* = .25, $p < .05$), but aggressive behaviors were not. When parent ratings of 5-year-old delinquency were added to the regression equation in step 2, the final model was significant ($F(3,86) = 4.51, p < .01$; , R^2 change = .07, $p < .05$). Delinquency ratings at age 5 were significantly predictive of parent delinquency ratings at follow-up (*beta* = .26, $p < .05$), and difficult peer play behaviors were still marginally significant (*beta* = .20, $p < .06$).

Finally, a third step was added to the regression model to determine whether adolescents' reports of delinquent behaviors among their siblings and peers were related to parent ratings of delinquency. This step accounted for a significant amount of variance ($F(5,84) = 4.96, p < .001$, R^2 change = .09, $p < .01$). With the peer and sibling behaviors in the model, 5-year-old difficult play behaviors were no longer predictive, but peer delinquency was (*beta* = .37, $p < .01$), as were age 5 delinquency ratings.

Table 2. Summary of hierarchical regressions of adolescent delinquency at follow-up on peer play behaviors, CBCL Delinquency at age 5, and peer delinquency at follow-up

	Parent Reported Delinquency			Youth Reported Delinquency		
	B	S.E.*B*	Beta	*B*	S.E.*B*	Beta
Step 1: Peer Play Behaviors						
Difficult	.44	.18	.25*	.47	.29	.17
Aggressive	.09	.22	.04	.20	.35	.06
Step 2: Age 5 CBCL						
Delinquency	.24	.09	.26*	.18	.15	.12
Step 3: Adolescence						
Peer Delinquency	.12	.05	.27**	.31	.07	.59***
Sibling Delinquency	.07	.08	.11	-.07	.11	-.08

Note: For Parent report: R^2=.07* for step 1, ΔR^2 = .07* for step 2, ΔR^2 = .09** for step 3.
For Youth report: R^2 = .04 for step 1, ΔR^2 = .02 for step 2, ΔR^2 = .28*** for step 3.
* $p < .05$, ** $p < .01$, *** $p < .001$

This regression was repeated separately for boys and girls. For boys, the full model was again significant ($F(5,37) = 4.43, p < .01$) and explained 29% of the variance. Both early difficult behaviors (*beta* = .33, $p < .05$) and 5-year-old CBCL delinquency (*beta* = .33, $p < .05$) were significant predictors at step 2, but in step 3 peer delinquency was added to the model and was a significant predictor (*beta* = .48, $p < .05$) and 5-year-old difficult behaviors were no long predictive. However, for girls, the model was not significant ($F(5,41) = 0.33$, p = ns) and none of the variables predicted later CBCL delinquency score. Thus, preschool difficult interpersonal behaviors were related to parent ratings of delinquency in adolescence for boys but not for girls.

Youth self-reports of delinquency. Predictors of youth self-reports of delinquency in adolescence were examined also to determine whether the same variables were related to self-report measures. Again, a three-step regression was run, with 5-year-old peer play behaviors entered in step 1, parent ratings of delinquency at age 5 entered in step 2, and peer and sibling delinquency entered in step 3. Interestingly, although the full model was significant ($F(5,84) = 8.44$, $p < .001$), the only significant predictor of self-reported delinquency was peer delinquency (*beta* = .59, $p < .001$). Neither earlier peer play behaviors nor early parent reports of delinquency were predictive of self-reported delinquency in adolescence. Additionally, when this was repeated separately for boys ($F(5,37) = 3.30$, $p < .05$, Adjusted $R^2 = .22$, $p < .01$) and girls ($F(5,41) = 2.83$, $p < .05$, Adjusted $R^2 = .17$, $p < .01$), similar results were found for both, with both boys and girls reporting an increase in delinquent behaviors when they reported that their peers engaged in more delinquent behaviors.

Peer relationships for early versus late starters. In order to determine whether early or late starters differed in terms of peer relationships at age 5 and delinquent behaviors among peers in adolescence, children were divided into 4 groups: early starters, who had a score of 2 or greater on CBCL Delinquency at age 5 and a score of 3 or greater on YSR Rule-Breaking at adolescence (N = 9); late starters, who had a score of 0 or 1 at age 5 and a score of 3 or greater at adolescence (N = 12); early only, who had a score of 2 or greater at age 5 and less than 3 at adolescence (N = 24); and never delinquent (N = 45). Because the groups were small, these analyses should be considered exploratory.

A MANOVA was run using delinquency group as the independent variable and peer play difficultness, peer play aggression, and adolescent peer delinquency as the dependent variables. The MANOVA was significant ($F(9,258) = 4.77$, $p < .001$), and univariate tests showed that group differences were significant for all dependent variables (see Table 3). Bonferroni post hoc tests showed that early starters exhibited significantly greater difficult behaviors during the age 5 peer play compared to late starters and non-delinquents. Bonferroni post hoc tests also showed that early starters showed more aggressive behaviors during the 5-year-old peer play compared to late starters and the early-only group, but not compared to the non-delinquents. Finally, Bonferroni post hoc tests showed that both early and late starters had significantly more delinquent friends than did nondelinquents and early-only children. Early and late starters, both of whom were delinquent in adolescence, did not differ in number of delinquent behaviors of their peers, and early-only and non-delinquents, who were not delinquent in adolescence, did not differ on this variable.

Finally, parent ratings of 5-year-old delinquent behaviors were compared with both parent and youth reports in adolescence to assess whether they were related to later behaviors and whether the delinquent behaviors increased or decreased over time. Youth self-reports yielded higher rates of delinquency in adolescence compared to both the 5-year-old parent reports ($t(89) = 2.30$, $p < .05$) and the parent reports at follow-up ($t(89) = 4.93$, $p < .001$). However, parent reports yielded a significant decrease in number of delinquent behaviors from preschool to adolescence ($t(89) = -2.99$, $p < .01$). This was interesting because although delinquent behaviors appear to decrease over time according to parent reports, they actually are increasing according to youth self-reports.

Table 3. MANOVA results comparing early starters, late starters, early only, and nondelinquents

Variable by Group	Mean (sd)	Univariate *F* (df)
Peer Play Difficultness		3.34 (3,86)*
Early Onset (N = 9)[a,b]	2.72 (0.97)	
Late Onset (N = 12)[a]	1.92 (0.47)	
Early Only (N = 24)	2.23 (0.68)	
Non-Delinquents (N = 45)[b]	2.10 (0.53)	
Peer Play Aggression		3.78 (3,86)*
Early Onset (N = 9)[c]	1.94 (0.73)	
Late Onset (N = 12)[c]	1.21 (0.33)	
Early Only (N = 24)	1.44 (0.52)	
Non-Delinquents (N = 45)	1.43 (0.49)	
Adolescent Peer Delinquency		8.74 (3,86)**
Early Onset (N = 9)[d,e]	5.44 (4.03)	
Late Onset (N = 12)[f,g]	5.83 (4.73)	
Early Only (N = 24)[d,f]	1.63 (1.69)	
Non-Delinquents (N = 45)[e,g]	2.07 (2.67)	

Note: Same superscripts mean that the two groups differ significantly, Bonferroni posthoc test $p < .05$.
* $p < .05$, ** $p < .001$.

DISCUSSION

Difficulty in engaging in positive, friendly interactions with unfamiliar peers at age 5 was related to delinquent behaviors contemporaneously, although it did not predict to adolescent behavior. Overall, there was no correlation between preschool peer interactions and later reports of delinquent behaviors. However, at adolescence there was a significant relation between association with deviant peers and engagement in delinquent activities. Youth who reported spending time with friends and siblings who participate in delinquent activities also reported increased delinquent behaviors themselves. In this study, age of onset of delinquency (i.e., early versus late starting delinquent youth) did not impact severity of delinquency of peers. Both early and late starting delinquent youth reported associating with delinquent friends and siblings who engaged in similar levels of antisocial activities. Regarding stability of delinquency ratings, parents' reports of their children's delinquent behaviors decreased from age 5 to adolescence. This is in contrast to adolescent self-report ratings of delinquency, which show greater incidence of delinquent behaviors in comparison to parent reports at age 5 and adolescence.

The concurrent relation between difficulty interacting with peers (i.e., complaining, being unpleasant or unfriendly, ignoring the other child in the room) and delinquency at age 5 is consistent with prior research elucidating a relation between problematic play behaviors and behavioral difficulties among school-aged children (Gagnon and Nagle, 2004; Mendez and Fogle, 2002). Throughout the developmental literature, peer play among young children has been viewed as an important means through which children develop the social competencies that are necessary to establish relationships and understand social norms (Gagnon and Nagle, 2004; Guralnick, 1993; Ladd and Hart, 1992). Thus, finding a relation between difficult peer play behaviors and delinquent behaviors at age 5 suggests that delayed or maladaptive development of social competencies, such as emotion regulation and conflict resolution, may be contributing to both behaviors.

Previous research supporting a link between delinquent behaviors in adolescence and the earlier expression of poor social skills (difficultness) or aggressive behaviors with peers during childhood (Coie, Terry, Zakriski, and Lochman, 1995; Garnier and Stein, 2002) was not replicated with this sample. Among the children within this study, association with delinquent peers during adolescence was a more robust correlate of delinquency than was childhood peer play behaviors. One reason for the failure to find a longitudinal relation between early peer play behaviors and adolescent delinquency could be that across development, the expression of difficult or antisocial behaviors during early childhood peer interactions may lead to other problematic behaviors that themselves are more directly related to adolescent delinquency, such as peer rejection (Dishion, Patterson, Stoolmiller, and Skinner, 1991). Others have shown that children who engage in greater problematic or negative peer interactions were rated several years later as having fewer friends and lower peer acceptance (Henricsson and Rydell, 2006; National Institute of Child Health and Human Development Early Child Care Research Network, 2008). Peer rejection during childhood has been shown to be related to both association with deviant peers (Brendgen, Vitaro, and Bukowski, 1998; Dishion et al., 1991) and delinquency in adolescence (Barnow et al., 2005; Laird, Jordan, Dodge, Pettit, and Bates, 2001). Therefore, it may be that peer rejection mediates the relation between early peer play behaviors and adolescent delinquency.

It is also the case that our sample includes more late-starter delinquents than children who began their delinquent behaviors earlier in life, thereby restricting the opportunity to find a relation between early childhood peer play behaviors and adolescent delinquency. This was expected, as only about 6-7% of children tend to be early-starter delinquents (Moffitt and Caspi, 2001), and in our sample a comparable 10% of the children fell into the early-starter category. Among adolescent-limited delinquents, it has been proposed that engagement in delinquent activities is primarily the result of influence by deviant peers (DiLalla and Gottesman, 1991; Moffitt, 1993). These teenagers generally do not evidence a protracted history of behavior difficulties and, thus, a relation between childhood peer play behaviors and adolescent delinquency would not necessarily exist. In contrast, a correlation between childhood peer play and adolescent delinquent behaviors would be expected among early-starter delinquents, who display a chronic and stable pattern of aggressive and delinquent activities across childhood and adolescence. This was demonstrated by our analyses showing that children who were rated as delinquent both at age 5 and in adolescence showed more aggression and difficult behaviors during the 5-year-old peer play situation than did the late-starters.

This study did find a significant positive association between engagement with delinquent peers and siblings and the frequency of adolescent delinquent activities. This has been confirmed across many studies (Barnow et al., 2005; Criss and Shaw, 2005; Fergusson and Horwood, 1996; Garcia et al., 2000; Rowe, 1985; Snyder et al., 2005; Tolan and Thomas, 1995). However, this study adds further information to this knowledge base by illustrating that peer associations in adolescence appear to be stronger predictors of adolescent delinquency than are early problematic peer interactional styles.

Interestingly, we also found that adolescent ratings of delinquency showed more delinquent activities than did parent ratings. In fact, parents' ratings of their children's delinquent behaviors actually decreased over time from age 5 to adolescence. This difference may be explained by studies showing that from the period of childhood to early adolescence, the number of youth participating in overt delinquent or antisocial behaviors (e.g., physical aggression, arguing with adults) significantly declines, whereas engagement in covert delinquent activities (e.g., shoplifting, vandalism, drug abuse) increases (Loeber, 1982; Patterson, Shaw, Snyder, and Yoerger, 2005). Thus, parents in our study may be rating their children as engaging in greater delinquency at age 5 because their children's delinquent actions are more salient, or overt. Also, parents are usually more directly involved in the activities of younger children, who often rely on parents to provide them with peer opportunities. Adolescence is a period of emerging independence. Parents often give their teenagers greater liberties regarding activities and peer group affiliations than are afforded during early childhood. As a result, recent research has suggested that most of what parents know about an adolescent's peer group and activities away from home come from the adolescent him- or herself, rather than from direct monitoring of the youth's behaviors (Kerr and Stattin, 2000; Soenens, Vansteenkiste, Luyckx, and Goossens, 2006). Therefore, it seems plausible that children engaging in delinquent activities would neglect to share that information with their parents. Taken together, previous research suggests that parents' ratings of their children's delinquency is decreasing over time due to more limited knowledge about their children's activities and may not reflect true events.

There are several possible limitations to this study. First, the relatively small sample size may have provided us with limited power with which to identify smaller effects that may exist between variables in this study. Second, the majority of children participating in this study are from middle-class, Caucasian families. Therefore, the results of this study may not generalize to ethnically diverse populations. Third, our outcome measure of delinquency included a composite score of a variety of delinquent behaviors. There is evidence to suggest that early childhood peer behaviors may relate differently to various types of delinquent activities (Vitaro, Pedersen, and Brendgen, 2007). Thus, we may have found different results if we had separated our outcome measure into more cohesive categories of delinquency, such as property crimes versus crimes against persons. This should be explored further in future studies. Lastly, there was considerable time between assessment of delinquency at age 5 and follow-up measures of delinquent activities. More frequent data collection might have revealed longitudinal associations between peer play behaviors and subsequent delinquency measured at younger ages, as well as helped us to identify the age at which play behaviors are no longer predictive of delinquent activities. However, it is important to note that this time interval is not uncommon and several other longitudinal studies in the area of delinquency have similar or longer time lags (e.g., Caspi and Silva, 1995; Mesman and Koot, 2001; Sourander et al., 2007).

In light of these limitations, our study evidences notable strengths. This study is longitudinal, which allows us to make causal inferences and assess the relation between behaviors during peer interactions in childhood and delinquent activities in adolescence. Another strength is the use of a variety of methodologies (e.g., peer play observations, parent ratings, youth self-reports) and informants (i.e., parents and youth) to assess the relation between peer behaviors and delinquency. This methodology allowed us to gather more information about the variables of interest in this study, while improving the reliability of findings.

Future research should focus on more frequent assessments of the association between peer play behaviors and delinquency to determine the scope of negative peer behaviors on development. Additionally, future studies should directly examine the relation between difficult or aggressive behaviors during peer interactions in early childhood and the development of particular social skills difficulties contributing to peer rejection and/or deviant peer relations, and subsequent delinquency.

Conclusion

We have demonstrated that difficult behaviors exhibited by preschoolers during interactions with their peers was related to engagement in delinquent activities at the same age. However, this difficult interactional style was not directly related to later delinquency. Delinquent activities in adolescence were better accounted for by association with deviant siblings and peers rather than by early aggressive or difficult behaviors with peers during childhood. It is possible, however, that difficult behaviors with peers during early childhood contribute to future behaviors that are themselves more directly related to delinquency in adolescence, such as peer rejection and association with deviant peers. These findings suggest that although difficult or aggressive behaviors with one's peers during early childhood may signal contemporaneous antisocial or delinquent behaviors, they are not the best predictors of adolescent delinquency. Rather, research should focus on identifying the developmental progression of difficult or aggressive peer behaviors over time to determine their relation to delinquency.

References

Achenbach, T.M. (1991). *Manual for the Child Behavior Checklist and 1991 profile.* Burlington, VT: University of Vermont, Department of Psychiatry.

Achenbach, T.M., and Rescorla, L.A. (2001). *Manual for ASEBA School-Age Forms and Profiles.* Burlington, VT: University of Vermont, Research Center for Children, Youth, and Families.

Barnow, S., Lucht, M., and Freyberger, H-J. (2005). Correlates of aggressive and delinquent conduct problems in adolescence. *Aggressive Behavior, 31,* 24-39.

Brendgen, M., Vitaro, F., and Bukowski, W.M. (1998). Affiliation with delinquent friends: Contribution of parents, self-esteem, delinquent behavior, and peer rejection. *Journal of Early Adolescence, 18*, 244-265.

Burke, J.D., Loeber, R., Lahey, B.B., and Rathouz, P.J. (2005). Developmental transitions among affective and behavioral disorders in adolescent boys. *Journal of Child Psychology and Psychiatry, 46,* 1200-1210.

Campbell, S.B. (1995). Behavior problems in preschool children: A review of recent research. *Journal of Child Psychology and Psychiatry, 36,* 113-149.

Campbell, S.B. (2002). *Behavior problems in preschool children: Clinical and developmental issues* (2nd ed.). New York: Guilford Press.

Campbell, S.B., Pierce, E.W., March, C.L., Ewing, L.J., and Szumowski, E.K. (1994). Hard to-manage preschool boys: Symptomatic behavior across contexts and time. *Child Development, 65*, 836-851.

Caspi, A., Henry, B., McGee, R., Moffitt, T., and Silva, P. (1995). Temperamental origins of child and adolescent behavior problems: From age three to age fifteen. *Child Development, 66,* 55-68.

Caspi, A., and Silva, P.A. (1995). Temperamental qualities at age three predict personality traits in young adulthood: Longitudinal evidence from a birth cohort. *Child Development, 66,* 486-498.

Criss, M.M., and Shaw, D.S. (2005). Sibling relationships as contexts for delinquency training in low-income families. *Journal of Family Psychology, 19,* 592-600.

Cohen, J. (1968). Weighted kappa: Nominal scale agreement provision for scaled disagreement or partial credit. *Psychological Bulletin, 70,* 213-220.

Coie, J.D., Terry, R., Zakriski, A., and Lochman, J. (1995). Early adolescent social influences on delinquent behavior. In J. McCord (Ed.), *Coercion and punishment in long-term perspectives* (pp. 229-244). New York: Cambridge University Press.

DiLalla, L.F. (2002). Preschool social and cognitive behaviors: The Southern Illinois Twins. *Twin Research, 5*, 468-471.

DiLalla, L.F., and Gottesman, I.I. (1991). Biological and genetic contributors to violence – Widom's untold tale. *Psychological Bulletin, 109,* 125-129.

Dishion, T.J., Patterson, G.R., Stoolmiller, M., and Skinner, M.L. (1991). Family, school, and behavioral antecedents to early adolescent involvement with antisocial peers. *Developmental Psychology, 27*, 172-180.

Fergusson, D.M., and Horwood, L.J. (1996). The role of adolescent peer affiliations in the continuity between childhood behavioral adjustment and juvenile offending. *Journal of Abnormal Child Psychology, 24,* 205-221.

Fergusson, D.M., and Horwood, L.J. (1999). Prospective childhood predictors of deviant peer affiliations in adolescence. *Journal of Child Psychology and Psychiatry, 40,* 581-592.

Gagnon, S.G., and Nagle, R.J. (2004). Relationships between peer interactive play and social competence in at-risk preschool children. *Psychology in the Schools, 41*, 173-189.

Garcia, M.M., Shaw, D.S., Winslow, E.B., and Yaggi, K.E. (2000). Destructive sibling conflict and the development of conduct problems in young boys. *Developmental Psychology, 36,* 44-53.

Garnier, H.E., and Stein, J.A. (2002). An 18-year model of family and peer effects on adolescent drug use and delinquency. *Journal of Youth and Adolescence, 31*, 45-56.

Guerin, D.W., Gottfried, A.W., and Thomas, C.W. (1997). Difficult temperament and behavior problems: A longitudinal study from 1.5 to 12 years. *International Journal of Behavior Development, 21*, 71-90.

Guralnick, M.J. (1993). Developmentally appropriate practice in the assessment and intervention of children's peer relations. *Topics in Early Childhood Education, 13*, 344-371.

Henricsson, L., and Rydell, A-M. (2006). Children with behavior problems: The influence of social competence and social relations on problem stability, school achievement and peer acceptance across the first six years of school. *Infant and Child Development, 15*, 347-366.

Hill, A.L., Degnan, K.A., Calkins, S.D., and Keane, S.P. (2006). Profiles of externalizing behavior problems for boys and girls across preschool: The roles of emotion regulation and inattention. *Developmental Psychology, 42,* 913-928.

Kerr, M., and Stattin, H. (2000). What parents know, how they know it, and several forms of adolescent adjustment: Further support for a reinterpretation of monitoring. *Developmental Psychology, 36*, 366-380.

Kupersmidt, J.B., and Coie, J.D. (1990). Preadolescent peer status, aggression, and school adjustment as predictors of externalizing problems in adolescence. *Child Development, 61,* 1350-1362.

Ladd, G.W., and Hart, C.H. (1992). Creating informal play opportunities: Are parents' and preschoolers' initiations related to children's competence with peers? *Developmental Psychology, 28*, 1179-1187.

Laird, R.D., Jordan, K.Y., Dodge, K.A., Pettit, G.S., and Bates, J.E. (2001). Peer rejection in childhood, involvement with antisocial peers in early adolescence, and the development of externalizing behavior problems. *Development and Psychopathology, 13*, 337-354.

Loeber, R. (1982). The stability of antisocial and delinquent child behavior: A review. *Child Development, 53*, 1431-1446.

Markell, R.A., and Asher, S.R. (1984). Children's interactions in dyads: Interpersonal influence and sociometric status. *Child Development, 55*, 1412-1424.

Mendez, J.L., and Fogle, L.M. (2002). Parental reports of preschool children's social behavior: Relations among peer play, language competence, and problem behavior. *Journal of Psychoeducational Assessment, 20*, 370-385.

Mesman, J., and Koot, H.M. (2001). Early preschool predictors of preadolescent internalizing and externalizing *DSM-IV* diagnoses. *Journal of the American Academy of Child and Adolescent Psychiatry, 40,* 1029-1036.

Moffitt, T.E. (1993). Adolescence-limited and life-course-persistent antisocial behavior: A developmental taxonomy. *Psychological Review, 100,* 674-701.

Moffitt, T.E., and Caspi, A. (2001). Childhood predictors differentiate life-course persistent and adolescence-onset antisocial pathways among males and females. *Development and Psychopathology, 13,* 355-375.

Mun, E.Y., Fitzgerald, H.E., Von Eye, A., Puttler, L.I., and Zucker, R.A. (2001). Temperamental characteristics as predictors of externalizing and internalizing child behavior problems in the contexts of high and low parental psychopathology. *Infant Mental Health Journal, 22*, 393-415.

Nagin, D.S., and Tremblay, R.E. (2001). Parental and early childhood predictors of persistent physical aggression in boys from kindergarten to high school. *Archives of General Psychiatry, 58,* 389-394.

National Institute of Child Health and Human Development Early Child Care Research Network. (2008). Social competence with peers in third grade: Associations with earlier peer experiences in childcare. *Social Development, 17*, 419-453.

Offord, D.R., Boyle, M.H., and Racine, Y.A. (1991). The epidemiology of antisocial behavior in childhood and adolescence. In D.J. Pepler and K.H. Rubin (Eds.), *The Development and Treatment of Childhood Aggression* (pp. 31-54). Hillsdale, NJ: Lawrence Erlbaum Associates.

Olson, S.L. (1992). Development of conduct problems and peer rejection in preschool children: A social systems analysis. *Journal of Abnormal Child Psychology, 20*, 327-350.

Owens, E.B., and Shaw, D.S. (2003). Predicting growth curves of externalizing behavior across the preschool years. *Journal of Abnormal Child Psychology, 31,* 575-590.

Patterson, G.R., Capaldi, D.M., and Bank, L. (1991). An early starter model for predicting delinquency. In D.J. Pepler and K.H. Rubin (Eds.), *The development and treatment of childhood aggression* (pp. 139-168). Hillsdale, NJ: Lawrence Erlbaum Associates.

Patterson, G.R., Shaw, D.S., Snyder, J.J., and Yoerger, K. (2005). Changes in maternal ratings of children's overt and covert antisocial behavior. *Aggressive Behavior, 31*, 473-484.

Resnick, M.D., Bearman, P.S., Blum, R.W., Bauman, K.E., Harris, K.M., Jones, J., Tabor, J., Beuhring, T., Sieving, R.E., Shew, M., Ireland, M., Bearinger L.H., and Udry, J.R. (1997). Protecting adolescents from harm: Findings from The National Longitudinal Study on Adolescent Health. *Journal of the American Medical Association, 278*, 823-832.

Rowe, D.C. (1985). Sibling interaction and self-reported delinquent behavior: A study of 265 twin pairs. *Criminology, 23,* 223-240.

Snyder, J., Bank, L., and Burraston, B. (2005). The consequences of antisocial behavior in older male siblings for younger brothers and sisters. *Journal of Family Psychology, 19,* 643-653.

Soenens, B., Vansteenkiste, M., Luyckx, K., and Goossens, L. (2006). Parenting and adolescent problem behavior: An integrated model with adolescent self-disclosure and perceived parental knowledge as intervening variables. *Developmental Psychology, 42,* 305-318.

Sourander, A., Jensen, P., Davies, M., Niemela, S., Elonheimo, H., Ristkari, T., Helenius, H., Sillanmaki, L., Piha, J., Kumpulainen, K., Tamminen, T., Noilanen, I., and Almqvist, F. (2007). Who is at greatest risk of adverse long-term outcomes? The Finnish from a boy to a man study. *Journal of the American Academy of Child and Adolescent Psychiatry, 46,* 1148-1161.

Tolan, P.H., and Thomas, P. (1995). The implications of age of onset for delinquency risk II: Longitudinal data. *Journal of Abnormal Child Psychology, 23,* 157-181.

Tremblay, R.E. (2000). The development of aggressive behaviour during childhood: What have we learned in the past century? *International Journal of Behavioral Development, 24,* 129-141.

Tremblay, R., and Nagin, D. (2005). The developmental origins of physical aggression in humans. In R.E. Tremblay, W.W. Hartup, and J. Archer (Eds.), *Developmental origins of aggression* (pp. 83-106). New York: Guilford Press.

Vitaro, F., Pedersen, S., and Brendgen, M. (2007). Children's disruptiveness, peer rejection, friends' deviancy, and delinquency: A process-oriented approach. *Development and Psychopathology*, *19*, 433-453.

Windle, M. (1991). The difficult temperament in adolescence: Associations with substance use, family support, and problem behaviors. *Journal of Clinical Psychology, 47*, 310-315.

In: Delinquency: Causes, Reduction and Prevention
Editor: Ozan Sahin and Joseph Maier
ISBN 978-1-60741-558-9

Chapter 10

THE BIOSOCIAL FOUNDATIONS TO ANTISOCIAL BEHAVIOR

Kevin M. Beaver*[*], *J. C. Barnes*[*], *Brian B. Boutwell*[*] and *Jonathon A. Cooper*[**]

[*]Florida State University
[**]Arizona State University

ABSTRACT

The discipline of criminology has a long history of focusing narrowly on the environmental correlates to antisocial behaviors, while simultaneously ignoring the possibility that genetic factors are important. With the mapping of the human genome and with the advent of complex brain imaging machines, researchers have been able to study the genetic basis to all types of human behaviors. The results of these studies have unequivocally shown that virtually all antisocial outcomes are the result of genetic *and* environmental factors working independently and interactively. An emerging perspective—known as biosocial criminology—has recently been advanced as a way of incorporating these findings from the biological sciences into criminology. In the current chapter, we provide an overview of the biosocial criminological perspective. In doing so, we pay particular attention to explaining gene X environment interactions, gene X environment correlations, and epigenetic processes, and how they affect the development of antisocial behaviors.

INTRODUCTION

Virtually every contemporary criminological theory explains crime and delinquency through social factors, such as neighborhoods, peers, subcultures, and parents. Empirical-based research has provided some evidence linking these and other environmental conditions to criminal and delinquent involvement. What is missing from these theories, however, is any mention of genetic factors. Criminologists and other social scientists have historically been opposed to genetic research, especially genetic research relating to crime and delinquency.

Part of the reason for this trepidation stems from the erroneous thinking that if criminal behavior is genetically influenced, then it would be possible to identify all criminals at birth by examining their genetic profile. The oppressive and inhumane policy implications that would result, according to critics, are immediately obvious: criminals would be locked up at birth, they would be subjected to forced sterilization, and a new eugenics movement would swing into full force. Against this backdrop, genetic research has been effectively purged from mainstream criminology.

Recently, however, there has been a growing line of research that has begun to map out the complex ways in which genes and the environment work in tandem to produce antisocial behaviors. This emerging perspective—known as biosocial criminology—has demolished the antiquated view that only the environment produces criminal behavior. At the same time, the biosocial perspective has also revealed that genetic influences are dependent on the presence of environments. Genes and the environment, in short, are mutually interdependent on each other and studying one at the expense of the other is completely misguided. The biosocial perspective recognizes this and seeks to study antisocial behavior by focusing on both environmental and genetic factors. Given that biosocial criminology is still relatively new to most criminologists and to most students of criminology, this chapter will provide an overview of some of the most salient biosocial issues.

Behavioral Genetic Research

Some opponents of biosocial research argue that the reason that genetic research has been censored from criminology is because there simply is not any empirical evidence linking genes to antisocial conduct. This argument, although widely employed, is vacuous. Researchers from fields outside of criminology have employed samples of twin pairs to explore genetic influences on virtually every imaginable trait and behavior. Twins represent a naturally occurring experiment, where the similarity of monozygotic (MZ) twins can be compared to the similarity of dizyogtic (DZ) twins. If MZ twins are more similar to each other than are DZ twins on the behavior being studied, then genes are thought to influence that particular behavior. The reason for this conclusion is due to the fact that MZ twins share 100 percent of their DNA, while DZ twins share, on average, about 50 percent of their genetic material. MZ and DZ twins, however, are equally influenced by the environment. As a result, the only reason that MZ twins should be more similar to each other than DZ twins is because they share about twice as much DNA. If genes are not influential on the behavior being studied, meaning that only the environment is involved, then MZ twins and DZ twins should be just as similar to each other.

At this point it is also important to note the distinction between two types of environments: shared environments and nonshared environments. Shared environments are environments that are the same between two siblings from the same household. Typically shared environments are equated with environments that are found within the family, such as socioeconomic status and parental socialization. Shared environments work to make siblings more similar to each other on behaviors and personality traits. Nonshared environments, in contrast, are environments that are different between two siblings from the same household. Although nonshared environments can be found within the family, such as when parents favor one child over the other, they are usually equated with environments that are found outside the household, such as each child's unique peer group. Nonshared environments affect human development by making siblings dissimilar from each other. Importantly, in behavioral genetics research, environment (both shared and nonshared environments) refers to anything that is nongenetic.

A wealth of research—known broadly as behavioral genetic research—has analyzed samples of twin pairs to examine the effects of genes, the shared environment, and the nonshared environment on antisocial behaviors. The results of these studies, which have been summarized by three recent meta-analyses (Mason and Frick, 1994; Miles and Carey, 1997; Rhee and Waldman, 2002) and a number of literature reviews (Moffitt, 2005), have converged to show that about 50 percent of the variance in antisocial phenotypes is due to genetic factors, about 40 percent of the variance is attributable to the nonshared environment, and approximately 10 percent of the variance is accounted for by the shared environment. These findings provide compelling evidence that antisocial behavior is largely influenced by genetic factors.

Although twin-based research provides an initial step in studying the genetic correlates to antisocial behaviors, it is host to one main shortcoming: it does not provide any information about which specific genes are involved. Stated differently, all that twin-based studies can reveal is the percentage of variance accounted for by genetic factors. Methodologies that move beyond analyzing twin pairs are needed to uncover the particular genes implicated in the etiology of criminal behavior. With the mapping of the human genome, researchers have been presented with a vast amount of information about genes—known as candidate genes—that might be associated with antisocial conduct. A growing number of criminologists are beginning to use this information to determine which genes might confer a risk to aggressive, violent, and antisocial behaviors.

It is still too early in the genetic game to say with any degree of certainty which genes are implicated in the etiology of antisocial behavior, but what has become apparent in recent years is that genes and the environment do not work independently, but instead are intimately intertwined. Studying only genetic factors or only environmental factors produces an incomplete view of the causes and correlates to antisocial conduct. As a direct result, most cutting-edge biosocial criminological research seeks to examine the interplay between genes and the environment. Below we explain three different types of gene-environment interplay—gene X environment interactions, gene X environment correlations, and epigenetics—and discuss how they can be applied to the study of criminal and delinquent behaviors.

Gene X Environment Interactions

The first type of gene-environment interplay is known as a gene X environment interaction (GxE). GxEs are often defined in the following way: the effect of the environment depends on the presence of certain genetic factors and the effect of genetic factors depends on the presence of certain environments. To help clarify the meaning of GxEs, it is first necessary to draw attention to the fact that people who are exposed to the exact same environments often turn out quite differently. For example, being reared in a disadvantaged environment is a risk factor for delinquency, but most children living in disadvantaged environments do not become delinquent. According to the logic of GxEs, people react to the same environments differently because each person has their own unique suite of genetic factors. Persons with one set of genetic factors may respond to environments in one way, while persons with a different set of genetic factors may respond to that same environment in a completely different way.

It is also true that environmental factors work to moderate the effects of genetic factors. A medical example will help to make this point clear. A sizeable portion of the population is genetically at-risk for heart disease—that is, heart disease runs in their family and is passed on from generation-to-generation via the transmission of genetic material. Whether or not heart disease actually emerges depends, in part, on environmental factors. Suppose, for instance, that two people have the exact same genetic vulnerability to heart disease. Pretend that one person exercises regularly, eats a healthy diet, and visits the doctor annually. Their environment would probably be able to curtail the genetic susceptibility to heart disease. Contrast this person with another person who is also genetically predisposed to heart disease, but smokes, eats fatty foods, does not exercise, and rarely visits the doctor. For this person, their environment would exacerbate their predisposition for heart disease, making it highly likely that they will suffer a heart attack. Clearly the environments within which people are embedded can either dampen or intensify genetic predispositions. This same logic can be applied to the study of antisocial behavior, where genetic vulnerabilities to violence and aggression only materialize when they are paired to criminogenic environments.

During the past 10 years a rapidly growing pool of empirical research has examined GxEs as they relate to a wide array of criminal and delinquent outcomes. The results of these studies, while far from conclusive, have provided a considerable amount of evidence revealing that GxEs are implicated in the etiology of antisocial behaviors. Perhaps the most influential study to detect a GxE was carried out by Caspi and his colleagues (2002). This team of researchers was interested in examining whether variants of a gene called MAOA were associated with different measures of violence, aggression, and criminal activity. Rather than hypothesizing that the MAOA gene would have an independent effect on antisocial behaviors, they employed the logic of GxEs and posited that the MAOA gene would only have an effect for males who were maltreated as children; the MAOA gene was not hypothesized to have an effect on antisocial outcomes for males who were not maltreated as children. To examine this hypothesis, they analyzed male respondents from the Dunedin Multidisciplinary Health and Development Study. The results of their analysis indicated that the MAOA gene was unrelated to antisocial behaviors for males who had not been maltreated. For males who had been subjected to maltreatment as children, the MAOA gene was associated with a range of antisocial outcomes. The effect size was quite drastic: although only 12 percent of the sample had been maltreated and had the MAOA risk allele (i.e., the variant of the gene that confers an increased likelihood of engaging in antisocial conduct), they accounted for 44 percent of the cohort's violent convictions and 85 percent of them displayed at least some form of antisocial behavior. This study provided the first evidence showing that a measured gene (i.e., MAOA) interacted with a measured environment (i.e., childhood maltreatment) to predict a behavioral phenotype (i.e., antisocial behaviors).

Since the publication of Caspi et al.'s (2002) study, a number of researchers have attempted to replicate this GxE in different samples. Some of these studies have failed to detect the GxE between MAOA and maltreatment (e.g., Haberstick, et al., 2005; Prichard, et al., 2008), while other studies have produced evidence substantiating this GxE (e.g., Foley, et al., 2004; Oreland, et al., 2007). A recent meta-analysis was conducted to help sort out whether the interaction between the MAOA gene and maltreatment is more of a methodological artifact or a relatively accurate representation of reality (Kim-Cohen et al., 2006). The results of this meta-analysis revealed that the MAOA X maltreatment interaction was a significant predictor of various psychopathologies, thereby providing some strong empirical evidence implicating GxEs in the etiology of antisocial behaviors.

The pool of studies that revealed a GxE between MAOA and maltreatment in the prediction of antisocial conduct set the stage for researchers to examine whether other genes (beyond MAOA) and other environments (beyond childhood maltreatment) may be involved in maladaptive outcomes. Genes from the dopaminergic system, for example, have been found to interact with various environmental conditions to predict crime and delinquency (Guo, Roettger, and Cai, 2008). Antisocial behaviors have also been found to be predicted by GxEs between genetic factors and sexual abuse (Beaver, 2008), between genetic factors and neighborhood socioeconomic status (Tuvblad, Grann, and Lichtenstein, 2006), and between genetic factors and adverse home environments (Cadoret et al., 1995; DeLisi et al., 2008). During a relatively short period of time, an accumulating line of research has underscored the likelihood that GxEs are involved in the etiology of antisocial behaviors.

What is also of interest is that GxEs have been detected on behaviors that have typically been thought to be due purely to social factors. To illustrate, Beaver and associates (2007) were interested in examining whether variants of a dopamine receptor gene—DRD2—were associated with the odds of being victimized in adolescence. Given that a substantial amount of research had indicated that exposure to delinquent peers was associated with adolescent victimization, Beaver et al. hypothesized that the effect of DRD2 would be conditioned by the degree of contact with antisocial friends. The results of their study were quite revealing: DRD2 was associated with victimization among those adolescents with relatively few delinquent peers, but DRD2 was not associated with victimization among adolescents with a high concentration of antisocial friends. At first glance this GxE between DRD2 and delinquent peers might seem somewhat counterintuitive. After all, much of the GxE literature has shown that genetic effects only emerge when paired with a criminogenic environment. This study revealed the opposite pattern, which Beaver and associates explained cogently. According to the authors of the study, adolescents who are in close contact with delinquent peers are likely to be victimized simply because of the company they keep. But, for those youths who have relatively little exposure to antisocial friends, other factors, including genetic factors, may play at least some role in the odds of victimization. The important point to garner from this study, however, is that genetic factors are likely at play in a range of outcomes that are typically assumed to be due mainly to environmental factors and are thought to be insulated from genetic effects.

SUMMARY AND FUTURE DIRECTIONS

Criminological theory and research has underscored the saliency of environmental conditions in the development of crime, delinquency, drug abuse, and other forms of antisocial behaviors. And while an impressive amount of research has provided some empirical support for these social explanations, there remains a tantalizing paradox: Although environmental factors, such as disadvantaged neighborhoods, are risk factors for antisocial behaviors, most persons who are exposed to these types of criminogenic environments do not become criminals. The precise factors that are responsible for producing this heterogeneity to environments have not been fully explored among criminologists. However, with the recent wave of molecular genetic studies revealing that genes and the environment interact, there is good reason to suspect that genetic factors may be one cause of this heterogeneity. Unfortunately mainstream criminological scholarship has been slow to explore the ways in which GxEs may be involved in the development of criminal and delinquent conduct.

We recommend that future criminological research incorporate GxEs in at least three different ways. First, criminological theories could be enriched if they directly discussed the ways in which particular genetic factors may moderate the effects of environments, such as parental socialization, neighborhood disadvantage, and antisocial peer groups. By integrating genetic research in this way, criminological theories would become much more accurate when explaining who will become criminals and under what conditions. Second, criminologists need to follow the lead of researchers from other disciplines and begin to examine empirically the interaction between specific genetic markers and criminogenic environments. By doing so, criminologists will provide a much richer knowledge base about the correlates and potential causes of antisocial conduct. Third, criminologists need to collect genotypic information from respondents in their samples. This has already been done in some large longitudinal samples, such as the National Longitudinal Study of Adolescent Health (Add Health), but a much more concerted effort needs to be undertaken. Until data are readily available, criminologists will be handcuffed in their ability to develop and test theories that implicate GxEs in the etiology of antisocial conduct.

Gene X Environment Correlations

The second type of gene-environment interplay is known as gene X environment correlation (rGE). To understand what is meant by rGE, it is necessary to revisit twin-based research designs. Remember that behavioral geneticists analyze samples of twin pairs to decompose the variance in antisocial behavior into a genetic component, a shared environmental component, and a nonshared environmental component. Some researchers have also employed certain environmental measures as dependent variables and estimated the proportion of variance in that environmental measure that is due to genetic, shared environmental, and nonshared environmental effects. An impressive amount of empirical research has revealed, moreover, that virtually every environment from peer groups to parental socialization is due, in part, to genetic factors (Kendler and Baker, 2007). At first glance, it might seem somewhat odd to think that an environment—something that is usually assumed to be purely social—could be affected by genetic factors. rGEs have been advanced, however, as a way of explaining why and how genes may have an effect on environments (DiLalla, 2002; Jaffee and Price, 2007). In order to explain the logic of rGE, we discuss and provide examples of three types of rGEs: passive rGE, evocative rGE, and active rGE.

The first type of rGE is passive rGE. Passive rGEs refer to the fact that parents pass along two main elements to their offspring: an environment and genes. Since the child's environment and the child's genes both originate from the same source (i.e., their parents) the two should thus be correlated. To explain the logic of passive rGEs in a little greater detail let's turn our attention to a non-criminological example. Imagine two mates, both of whom are professional golfers. Assuming that the ability to play golf is at least partially heritable, it is likely that their offspring will be born with the skills to excel as a golfer. These parents, moreover, are also likely to provide their offspring with environments that promote golf skills, such as practicing golf on a regular basis and belonging to prestigious country clubs with top-notch golf courses. It takes no stretch of the imagination to see that these children are not only born with the genetic tendencies to be proficient golfers, but they are also born into environments that will help them reach their potential as a golfer. Passive rGEs thus capture the fact that children passively receive genes and environments from their parents, both of which are likely to be correlated.

Passive rGEs also can be applied to the study of crime and delinquency. Take, for example, two parents who are chronically violent criminals. Their children are at-risk, genetically speaking, for becoming violent and aggressive as well. There is also evidence indicating that criminals, in comparison to non-criminals, engage in more ineffective rearing techniques and are more likely to abuse and neglect their children (Farrington and Welsh, 2006). What this means is that children born to violent criminals are hit with a "double whammy," where they are genetically predisposed to become aggressive and they also are born into criminogenic family environments that promote the use of aggression and violence. Passive rGEs thus have the potential to partially explain why antisocial behavior concentrates in certain families.

The second type of rGE is known as evocative rGE. The logic of evocative rGE is relatively straightforward: people, based on their genetic propensities, elicit differential responses from their environments. For instance, a person with the genetic tendency to have an explosive temper is likely to elicit negative reactions from their environments, while another person with the genetic tendency to be outgoing and friendly is less likely to elicit negative reactions from their environments. The person with the bad temper is likely to have difficulties forging long-term, stable relationships with others, while the person who is friendly and outgoing will have no trouble developing a large and supportive peer network.

It is important to point out that in the above examples genes do not directly evoke environmental responses. Instead, and as should have been made clear by now, genes exert their influence on environments by affecting personality traits and temperaments. It is these personality traits, in turn, that are ultimately responsible for evoking differential reactions from the environment.

The third and final type of rGE is referred to as an active rGE. Active rGEs capture the process by which persons actively seek out and pursue environments that are compatible with their genetic tendencies (Scarr, 1992; Scarr and McCartney, 1983). To illustrate, singers are likely to join choirs and other musical groups, while those who are athletically inclined are likely to try out for sporting teams. The key point with active rGEs is that our interests and talents are partially genetically influenced and it is these interests and talents that push us into certain environments.

Active rGEs have a clear application to the field of criminology. Among criminologists there is widespread debate over whether some of the more important criminogenic environments are true causes of antisocial behavior or whether they are spurious relationships (Warr, 2002). One of the more heated discussions where this debate exists is for delinquent peers. For some criminologists, especially those working from a social learning perspective, delinquent peers are thought to be extremely potent causes of delinquency and other forms of misconduct (Akers, 1998; Akers and Jensen, 2006). This is known as the social causation perspective. For other criminologists, however, the nexus between delinquent peers and delinquency is not as clear cut. Instead of viewing delinquent peers as causal factors of delinquency, some critics argue that youths are delinquent before they join antisocial peer networks. Seen from this perspective, contact with delinquent peers does not have a causal effect on delinquent involvement because it is delinquents who befriend antisocial peers. This is known as the self-selection perspective (Gottfredson and Hirschi, 1990).

A handful of studies have provided some evidence indicating that part of the reason for why youths self-select into delinquent peer groups is due to genetic factors. Beaver and colleagues (2009) analyzed data from the Add Health and reported that between 37 to 62 percent of the variance in contact with delinquent peers was attributable to genetic factors. Other researchers have found very similar results (Cleveland, Wiebe, and Rowe, 2005; Iervolino et al., 2002; Kendler et al., 2007). In another recent study, Beaver et al. (2008) were interested in determining whether variants of a specific gene—known as the dopamine transporter gene (DAT1)—were associated with delinquent peer group formation. Their analysis of the Add Health data indicated that variants of the DAT1 gene were associated with delinquent peers, but only for males from high-risk environments; the effect of DAT1 on delinquent peers was nonexistent for males from low-risk environments. Taken together, these studies provide some evidence that selection into antisocial peer groups is partially governed by genetic factors, findings that are supportive of an active rGE.

SUMMARY AND FUTURE DIRECTIONS

Genetic research has begun to move beyond the question of whether genes matter in the creation of behaviors and has recently begun to examine the genetic underpinnings to various environments. The results of these studies have provided compelling evidence indicating that virtually every known environment, including environments that are typically studied by criminologists, is partially the result of genetic factors. This phenomenon has been termed gene X environment correlation (rGE) and researchers have delineated three different ways that genes and the environment are correlated. Specifically, genes and the environment may be correlated because individuals passively receive genetic material and an environment from their parents, (i.e., a passive rGE), because individuals evoke certain responses from their environments based on their genetic propensities (i.e., an evocative rGE), and because individuals actively seek out environments based on their genetic propensities (i.e., an active rGE).

Criminological research has placed a heavy emphasis on the environmental contributors to criminal and delinquent behaviors. The overriding assumption among criminologists is that environmental factors, such as delinquent peers, are free from genetic influence. However, as the discussion of rGEs has made clear, this simply is not the case. Environments and genes cannot be neatly bifurcated because environments are dependent on genes and because genes are dependent on environments. Future criminological research needs to begin to explore in greater detail the role that rGEs play in the development of serious, violent offending because as DiLalla (2002, p. 598) has noted, rGEs "probably occur with most of the behaviors that we study." rGEs represent a simple concept that criminologists can use to unpack the complex ways in which genes and the environment work together to produce antisocial behaviors.

EPIGENETICS

Thus far we have discussed two main types of gene-environment interplay: gene X environment interactions (GxE) and gene X environment correlations (rGE). The last type of gene-environment interplay that will be discussed is epigenetics. Epigenetics is on the cutting-edge of science and is revolutionizing the way that genes are viewed. Before moving into a discussion of epigenetics, including what it is and how it applies to criminal behavior, it is first necessary to provide some basic background information. All cells, except red blood cells, contain the same DNA. For instance, the genetic material found in heart cells is the same genetic material that is found in pancreatic cells. The question that comes to bear then is: What factors are responsible for separating heart cells from pancreatic cells and what separates all other cells from each other? The answer to this question appears to be found in genetic expression—more specifically, only those genes that are needed for the functioning of the particular cell are expressed and all other cells are silenced. In the current example, only those genes that are involved in the functioning of the heart are expressed in heart cells, while all the other genes, including the genes that are involved in the functioning of the pancreas, are silenced.

So now the question becomes: What are the factors that are responsible for turning genes "on" and for turning genes "off." This is obviously a complex question, but emerging evidence has converged to show that epigenetic factors govern which genes are "on" and which genes are "off" and when, during development, these genes are switched "on" and "off." Genes are turned "on" and "off" by chemical markers that are situated along what has become known as the epigenome. Two of the more well-known epigenetic processes are DNA methylation and histone acetylation. Although the underlying biology of epigenetics will not be discussed here, it is important to note that DNA methylation works to make the expression of genes less likely (i.e., turns genes "off"), while histone acetylation works to make the expression of genes more likely (i.e., turns genes "on").

Each person not only has a unique genome, but they also have a unique epigenome that controls the expression of genes located on the genome. So the reason that cells are different from each other is not due to DNA (because DNA is identical in all cells) but rather is due to the epigenome. In the current example, the epigenome would direct one set of genes in the heart to be expressed and others to be silenced, while the epigenome would direct a different set of genes in the pancreas to be expressed and others to be silenced. Of particular interest is that two people could, hypothetically speaking, have the exact same set of genes (e.g., MZ twins), but have a different epigenome. The difference in the epigenome could lead to an array of disparities not only in physical characteristics, but also in the development of disorders, diseases, behaviors, and personality traits (Walsh, 2009).

One of the most fascinating findings to emerge from epigenetics is that unlike the genome that is immutable, the epigenome changes in response to environmental stimuli. Environments, such as prenatal exposure to toxins, nutrition, and use of tobacco, are all thought to result in epigenetic modifications. One environmental influence in particular—early life rearing conditions—has also been identified as a potentially important source of epigenetic modifications. This is of utmost importance to criminologists because almost every single criminological theory implicates parental socialization as a causal factor in the etiology of antisocial behavior. Evidence supporting the role of parents in the structuring of epigenetic modifications was garnered in a groundbreaking study conducted by Weaver and his colleagues (2004). These researchers examined maternal nurturing techniques in rats and their effects on stress reaction in newborn rat pups. (As a side note, criminologists often view research conducted on non-human subjects as irrelevant. However, non-human animal research provides some of the richest information when it comes to examining the biological and genetic basis to human phenotypes [Fishbein, 2001].) The mothers of the rat pups were placed into two groups based on their nurturing strategy. One group consisted of high-nurturing mothers who consistently licked and groomed their offspring and nursed with an arched back. The other consisted of low-nurturing mothers who largely neglected their pups. Initially, the researchers were interested in how the rat pups would react to stressful events based on the type of nurturing that they had received from the mother. Not surprisingly, the findings revealed that rat pups reared by low-nurturing mothers reacted poorly to stressful conditions when compared to the pups raised by high-nurturing mothers.

Weaver and his associates were also curious about whether these findings reflected genetic factors or environmental factors. For instance, perhaps low-nurturing mothers passed along genetic material that caused their rat pups to react poorly to stressful situations or perhaps it was the low-nurturing rearing conditions (i.e., the environment) that caused the rat pups to react poorly. To tease apart genetic and environmental effects, the rat pups were cross-fostered, meaning that the rat pups born to low-nurturing mothers were reared by high-nurturing mothers, while the rat pups born to high-nurturing mothers were reared by low-nurturing mothers. After the cross-fostering was completed, the rat pups were once again examined. What these researchers found was quite revealing: the rat pups resembled their "adoptive" mother more so than they resembled their "biological" mother. These findings are very much in line with social science explanations, where the environment (e.g., rearing conditions) is thought to trump the effects of genetic factors. Weaver et al., however, took their analysis a step further and examined epigenetic patterns in the rat pups. What they found was groundbreaking: low-nurtured rat pups, in comparison with high-nurtured rat pups, had fewer methylation markers on glucocorticoid receptor genes, which are genes that are partially responsible for responding to stress. Taken together, these findings indicated that the effect of rearing conditions on response to stress is not a purely environmental effect, but rather an epigenetic effect, where the environment alters the epigenome.

Studies are also beginning to emerge showing the saliency of epigenetic processes using samples of human subjects. For example, Petronis and his research team (2003) were interested in studying the epigenetic underpinnings to schizophrenia. To do so, they examined one MZ twin pair that was discordant for schizophrenia—that is, one twin had been diagnosed with schizophrenia and the other twin had not—and one MZ twin pair that was concordant for schizophrenia—that is, both twins had been diagnosed with schizophrenia. They then compared the epigenomes of all the twins. The results of their analysis revealed that the twin (from the discordant twin pair) who was diagnosed with schizophrenia was more similar, epigenetically, to the twins from the concordant twin pair then they were to their own co-twin.

Perhaps even more intriguing is that epigenetic modifications can be passed from generation-to-generation. What this means is that each person's epigenome reflects epigenetic modifications that were inherited from their parents, their grandparents, their great grandparents and so on and so forth. Against this backdrop, it is easy to see that the field of epigenetics is casting a whole new light on the way that genes, genetic expression, and genetic effects are being viewed. Epigenetic research, however, remains in its infancy and much of the epigenetic research has been conducted on non-human subjects. What role do epigenetic modifications play in the development of antisocial behaviors? Walsh (2009, p. 45), a leading biosocial criminologist, shed some light on this question when he stated: "It is too early in the epigenetic game to go much beyond speculation, but for my money the possibilities are about as exciting and intriguing as anything that has come along in the behavioral sciences in the past 50 years."

SUMMARY AND FUTURE DIRECTIONS

Criminologists have expended a considerable amount of time and energy examining the environmental correlates to criminal and delinquent behaviors. Typically, criminologists assume that any significant association between an environmental measure (e.g., ineffective parenting) and an antisocial outcome (e.g., drug use) is evidence of the power of socialization in shaping human development. With recent epigenetic research, however, a new twist is being put on both genetic and environmental research. Epigenetic research has revealed, for instance, that epigenetic modifications that occur in response to the environment can alter genetic expression. Moreover, epigenetic research has also indicated that part of the effect that environments have are indirectly operating via epigenetic modifications. Criminological theories could begin to entertain the possibility that epigenetic modifications are important contributors in the etiology of antisocial outcomes.

An additional point that may have application to criminology in the future is that epigenetic modifications have been found to be reversible. Recall the study discussed previously that examined epigenetic patterns in rat pups reared by high-nurturing mothers and rat pups reared by low-nurturing mothers. This same study found that the epigenetic modifications that characterized rat pups that were reared by low-nurturing mothers could be altered through the administration of a drug known as trichostatin. Just as important was that after the epigenetic modifications were reversed, the behaviors of the rat pups changed and became more in line with the rat pups that were reared by high-nurturing mothers. Whether these types of epigenetic interventions could ever be used to change human behavior remains an open empirical and ethical issue.

CONCLUSION

During the past ten to twenty years, there have been monumental scientific breakthroughs, including the successful mapping of the human genome. With the information provided by this daunting endeavor, a wealth of research has been undertaken attempting to link certain genetic markers to diseases, personality traits, and behaviors. The findings flowing from these studies have provided a great deal of insight into the potential causes to an array of human phenotypes. But perhaps the most important discovery to emerge has been research showing that all human phenotypes are the result of genetic *and* environmental factors working independently and synergistically. Even in the face of this research, criminologists have continued to pretend as though only the environment matters and have failed to take seriously the role that genes play in the development of antisocial behaviors. The end result is that criminologists have created a mythical knowledge base grounded in ideology and political correctness.

The biosocial perspective represents a welcome alternative to conventional criminological theories that focus only on the environment. This chapter was designed to provide an overview to some of the topics and concepts that are germane to the biosocial perspective. Toward this end, we discussed gene X environment interactions (GxEs), gene X environment correlations (rGEs), and epigenetics, and showed how each of these could guide and inform criminological scholarship. Although the biosocial perspective is still relatively new, it has already provided a great deal of information about the genetic and biological foundations to antisocial behaviors (Beaver, 2009). There can be little doubt, however, that as the biosocial perspective gains more and more traction, what we know about the causes and correlates of criminal behavior will grow exponentially.

REFERENCES

Akers, R. L. (1998). *Social learning and social structure: A general theory of crime and deviance.* Boston: Northeastern University Press.

Akers, R. L., and Jensen, G. F. (2006). The empirical status of social learning theory of crime and deviance: The past, present, and future. In F. T. Cullen, J. P. Wright, and K. R. Blevins (Eds.), *Taking stock: The status of criminological theory* (pp. 37-76). New Brunswick, NJ: Transaction Publishers.

Beaver, K. M. (2009). *Biosocial criminology: A primer.* Dubuque, IA: Kendall/Hunt.

Beaver, K. M. (2008). The interaction between genetic risk and childhood sexual abuse in the prediction of adolescent violent behavior. *Sexual Abuse: A Journal of Research and Treatment,* 20(4), 426-443.

Beaver, K. M., Shutt, J. E., Boutwell, B. B., Ratchford, M., Roberts, K., and Barnes, J. C. (2009). Genetic and environmental influences on levels of self-control and delinquent peer affiliation: Results from a longitudinal sample of adolescent twins. *Criminal Justice and Behavior*, 36(1), 41-60.

Beaver, K. M., Wright, J. P., DeLisi, M. (2008). Delinquent peer group formation: Evidence of a gene X environment correlation. *The Journal of Genetic Psychology*, 169(3), 227-244.

Beaver, K. M., Wright, J. P., DeLisi, M., Daigle, L. E., Swatt, M. L., and Gibson, C. L. (2007). Evidence of a gene X environment interaction in the creation of victimization: Results from a longitudinal sample of adolescents. *International Journal of Offender Therapy and Comparative Criminology*, 51(6), 620-645.

Cadoret, R. J., Yates, W. R., Troughton, E., Woodworth, G., and Stewart, M. A. (1995). Genetic-environmental interaction in the genesis of aggressivity and conduct disorders. *Archives of General Psychiatry*, 52(11), 916-924.

Caspi, A., McClay, J., Moffitt, T. E., Mill, J., Martin, J., Craig, I. W., et al. (2002). Role of genotype in the cycle of violence in maltreated children. *Science*, 297(2), 851-854.

Cleveland, H. H., Wiebe, R. P., and Rowe, D. C. (2005). Sources of exposure to smoking and drinking friends among adolescents: A behavioral-genetic evaluation. *Journal of Genetic Psychology*, 166(2), 153-169.

DeLisi, M., Beaver, K. M., Wright, J. P., and Vaughn, M. G. (2008). The etiology of criminal onset: The enduring salience of nature and nurture. *Journal of Criminal Justice*, 36(3), 217-223.

DiLalla, L. F. (2002). Behavior genetics of aggression in children: Review and future directions. *Developmental Review*, 22, 593-622.

Farrington, D. P., and Welsh, B. C. (2006). *Saving children from a life of crime: Early risk factors and effective interventions*. New York: Oxford.

Fishbein, D. (2001). Biobehavioral perspectives in criminology. Belmont, CA: Wadsworth.

Foley, D. L., Eaves, L. J., Wormley, B., Silberg, J. L., Maes, H. H., Kuhn, J., et al. (2004). Childhood adversity, monoamine oxidase: A genotype, and risk for conduct disorder. *Archives of General Psychiatry*, 61(7), 738-744.

Gottfredson, M., and Hirschi, T. (1990). *A general theory of crime*. Palo Alto, CA: Stanford University Press.

Guo, G., Roettger, M., and Cai, T. (2008). The integration of genetic propensities into social control models of delinquency and violence among male youths. *American Sociological Review*, 73(4), 543-568.

Haberstick, B. C., Lessem, J. M., Hopfer, C. J., Smolen, A., Ehringer, M. A., Timberlake, D., et al. (2005). Monoamine oxidase A (MAOA) and antisocial behaviors in the presence of childhood and adolescent maltreatment. *American Journal of Medical Genetics Part B-Neuropsychiatric Genetics*, 135B(1), 59-64.

Iervolino, A. C., Pike, A., Manke, B., Reiss, D., Hetherington, E. M., and Plomin, R. (2002). Genetic and environmental influences in adolescent peer socialization: Evidence from two genetically sensitive designs. *Child Development*, 73(1), 162-174.

Jaffee, S. R., and Price, T. S. (2007). Gene-environment correlations: A review of the evidence and implications for prevention of mental illness. *Molecular Psychiatry*, 12, 432-442.

Kendler, K. S., and Baker, J. H. (2007). Genetic influences on measures of the environment: A systematic review. *Psychological Medicine*, 37(5), 615-626.

Kendler, K. S., Jacobson, K. C., Gardner, C. O., Gillespie, N., Aggen, S. A., and Prescott, C. A. (2007). Creating a social world: A developmental twin study of peer-group deviance. *Archives of General Psychiatry*, 64(8), 958-965.

Kim-Cohen, J., Caspi, A., Taylor, A., Williams, B., Newcombe, R., Craig, I. W., et al. (2006). MAOA, maltreatment, and gene-environment interaction predicting children's mental health: New evidence and a meta-analysis. *Molecular Psychiatry*, 11(10), 903-913.

Mason, D. A., and Frick, P. J. (1994). The heritability of antisocial behavior: A meta-analysis of twin and adoption studies. *Journal of Psychopathology and Behavioral Assessment*, 16(4), 301-323.

Miles, D. R., and Carey, G. (1997). Genetic and environmental architecture of human aggression. *Journal of Personality and Social Psychology*, 72(1), 207-217.

Moffitt, T. E. (2005). The new look of behavioral genetics in developmental psychopathology: Gene-environment interplay in antisocial behaviors. *Psychological Bulletin*, 131(4), 533-554.

Oreland, L., Nilsson, K., Damberg, M., and Hallman, J. (2007). Monoamine oxidases - activities, genotypes and the shaping of behaviour. *Journal of Neural Transmission*, 114(6), 817-822.

Petronis, A., Gottesman, I. I., Kan, P., Kennedy, J. L., Basile, V. S., Paterson, A. D., and Popendikyte, V. (2003). Monozygotic twins exhibit numerous epigenetic differences: Clues to twin discordance? *Schizophrenia Bulletin*, 29(1), 169-178.

Prichard, Z., Mackinnon, A., Jorm, A. F., and Easteal, S. (2008). No evidence for interaction between MAOA and childhood adversity for antisocial behavior. *American Journal of Medical Genetics Part B-Neuropsychiatric Genetics,* 147B(2), 228-232.

Rhee, S. H., and Waldman, I. D. (2002). Genetic and environmental influences on antisocial behavior: A meta-analysis of twin and adoption studies. *Psychological Bulletin*, 128(3), 490-529.

Scarr, S. (1992). Developmental theories for the 1990s: Developmental and individual differences. *Child Development*, 63(1), 1-19.

Scarr, S., and McCartney, K. (1983). How people make their own environments: A theory of genotype (leading to) environment effects. *Child Development*, 54(2), 424-435.

Tuvblad, C., Grann, M., and Lichtenstein, P. (2006). Heritability for adolescent antisocial behavior differs with socioeconomic status: Gene-environment interaction. *Journal of Child Psychology and Psychiatry*, 47(7), 734-743.

Warr, M. (2002). *Companions in crime: The social aspects of criminal conduct*. New York City: Cambridge University Press.

Walsh, A. (2009). Criminal behavior from heritability to epigenetics: How genetics clarifies the role of the environment. In A. Walsh, and K. M. Beaver (Eds.), *Biosocial criminology: New directions in theory and research* (pp. 29-49). London: Routledge.

Weaver, I. C., Cervoni, N., Champagne, F. A., D'Alessio, A. C., Sharma, S., Seckl, J. R., Dymov, S., Szyf, M., and Meaney, M. J. (2004). Epigenetic programming by maternal behavior. *Nature Neuroscience*, 7(8), 847–854.

In: Delinquency: Causes, Reduction and Prevention
Editor: Ozan Sahin and Joseph Maier
ISBN 978-1-60741-558-9

Chapter 11

MODEL AND METHOD FOR CLINICAL EVALUATION OF NARCISSISTIC IDENTITY VULNERABILITY. UNDERSTANDING AND PREVENTING MALADJUSTED BEHAVIOUR IN ADOLESCENTS

Nathalie Bardouil[1], Anne- Marie Favard[2] and Nicolas Combalbert*[3]

[1]CERPP -Université de Toulouse II,
5 allées Antonio Machado TOULOUSE Cedex 31058 France
[2]UMR 5193 -Université de Toulouse II
5 allées Antonio Machado, 31058 Toulouse Cedex, France
[3]Université de Paris X –Laboratoire IPSé
200 avenue de la République, 92001 Nanterre, France

ABSTRACT

This research work focuses on twenty-five male adolescents who have been placed in a children's French community home. We have developed a theoretical model to deal with the specific identity disorders of adolescents by developing *the concept of narcissistic identity vulnerability* and making it operational. The clinical protocol used and more particularly the hypothetic-deductive methodology applied to case studies constitute a *clinical evaluation method* of narcissistic identity vulnerability that can be transposed, in situations of clinical practice, to problem adolescents with a view to assessing and guiding personalized projects. This concept enables us to offer a *dynamic-economic analysis of maladjusted behaviour* in adolescents.

We suggest a clinical battery of investigation that can be applied to clinical practice. This battery including *Wechsler's Intelligence Test, Rorschach's Projective Test, Life Line and Genogram, The Family Test « FAST »* (developed by Gehring and Debry in Belgium), enables us to analyse the adolescent's representation of his family and to grasp

* Corresponding author: 34 boulevard Carnot 31000 Toulouse France, *E-mail address:* bardouil.nath@orange.fr

the intra-family dynamics and an adaptation to an analysis of adolescents' representation of the institution *The institutional FAST.*

As concerns the suggested model, its results confirm the clinical interest of the concept of narcissistic identity vulnerability which is operational, particularly as we can integrate the physical, cognitive and behavioural dimensions, making it possible to take *the complexity of the bio-psychosocial functioning of the subject* into account.

As for the suggested clinical evaluation method; its results reveal that no index is pertinent in itself and that only a dynamic reading which links the various indicators is meaningful.

The progressive hypothetic-deductive approach used for case studies constitutes *a clinical method* that can be applied in clinical practice.

The etiological, structural and risk diagnosis opens up interesting possibilities for *clinical expertise* which could be *an interesting tool for magistrates* when they have to make decisions as to the socio-judicial answers to be found as concerns notably *juvenile offenders.*

Keywords: adolescent, narcissistic identity vulnerability, maladjusted behaviours, delinquency, risk.

1. Introduction

The following paper is an attempt to describe a method of clinical evaluation of narcissistic identity disorders specific to adolescence by suggesting the theoretical concept of Narcissistic Identity Structure and its corollary, Narcissistic Identity Vulnerability.

It is mostly a psychodynamic approach to the complexity of the subject. That's why we have taken ideas from the theory of complex systems, the working concepts of a *problematic anda systematic approach* (?), to which we have added the concept of reactivity.

These different concepts have finally been made operational thanks to a diversified clinical battery. We are giving details of it further on in this article.

2. Three Concepts

We will start with a definition of the three concepts problematic, systematic approach and reactivity, in a global approach, before getting into a psychodynamic development.

The problematic approach of a system indicates the opening of a system to information of a high degree, i.e. information which requires costly work for the system, especially because it requires a reorganization of the latter.

The systematic approach shows the ability of the system to be transformed, i.e. its ability to adapt in different ways according to different situations, while maintaining its inner coherence.

Finally, *reactivity* shows the orientation and the carrying out of the systems' answers.

It's the externalized consequence of the inner dynamics, its observable form.

These three working concepts are indicators of clinical evaluation of the structuring quality of narcissistic identity.

3. From Narcissism to the Narcissistic Identity Structure

We will now develop the way we put forward the hypothesis of a narcissistic identity structure from the Freudian concept of narcissism.

Freudian Model of Narcissism

In the Freudian model and in its post-Freudian variants (……, among the main ones), narcissism is always considered as a mode of directing the libido to the Ego

Indeed, in a first period of development, there is an absence of differentiation between the Ego and the others, leading the subject to invest his own body as love object. This is what we call primary narcissism, when the libido is directed to the Ego.

With the process of separation-individuation, the Ego is going to differentiate from what is outside of it and is thus going to be able to invest an external object. This directing the libido to the object is called object relation or object investment.

Finally, secondary narcissism is when the object libido withdraws from the object to be directed to the Ego.

Narcissistic and object investment are thus constantly under tension, placing as a result secondary narcissism as not directed to the object. It is the case, for example, in the McGill object relations Scale, or MORS, which makes it possible to evaluate narcissistic and object investments.

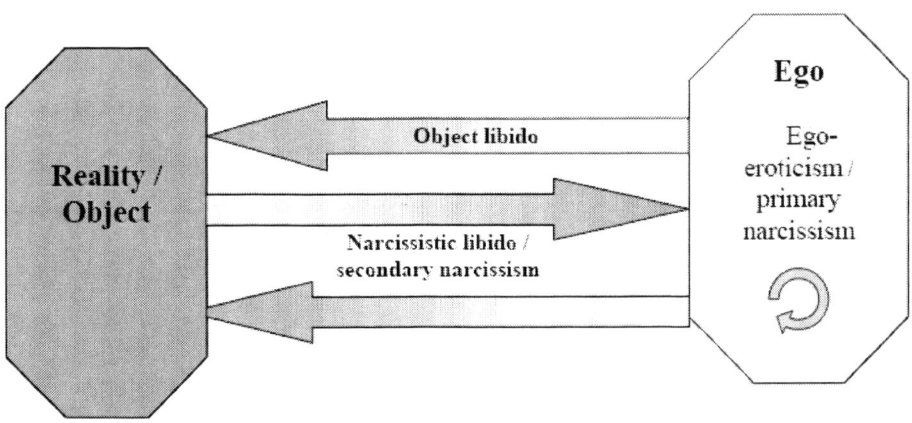

Figure 1. Freudian model of Narcissism.

We have three main observations to make regarding this Freudian concept of narcissism and its post-Freudian variants.

First, much has been written over the years about narcissism which remains one of the most debated concepts, a kind of stumbling block both in psychoanalysis and in psychopathology.

Second, narcissism is seen as part of a pejorative conception of egocentrism, always seen as being to the detriment of the relationship to the other outside often seen as an ideal. Besides, narcissism is most often considered in the context of a psychopathological approach:

personality disorders are dealt with in terms of narcissistic pathology or even narcissistic personality, (DSM…)

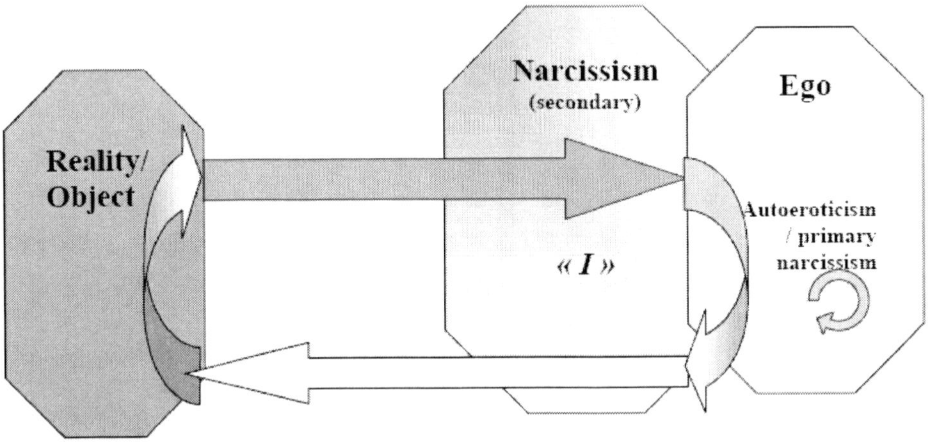

Figure 2. Narcissism as leading libidinal regulation.

Narcissism is but rarely approached as normal, necessary and structuring libido cathexis.

Most of all and to finish with, it is not considered as a close relation between the Ego and the object, in an enriching interaction, whether it is for the Ego or for the object.

That's why, our purpose is to get out of this dualistic approach between narcissism and object relation.

We suggest the assumption that narcissism is an intrapsychic structure with an interface between the Ego and reality. This structure is the foundation of the subject's identity: the Ego, referring to the Ego as defined by Lacan in the Mirror Stage.

This structure's function is to regulate the double libidinal investment of the I and the object. The aim of this regulation is to maintain both the quality of the link between the Ego and reality and the ability of the Ego to maintain the inner regulation of the psychic system.

4. Regulating the Double Libidinal Cathexis

We have defined the narcissistic identity structure's function as one of regulation of the double libidinal investment. We are now going to develop this function.

First we must identify the various interacting realities.

To begin with, there is external reality. It is in itself a complex system including School, Peers, Family, and other social subsystems. The host institution can be one of these subsystems.

Then we find the psychic system in internal reality. It includes the Ego, but also the Superego and the Id, according to the second Freudian topography.

Still within internal reality, we have somatic reality or body reality.

At the interface between external reality and internal reality there is an envelope which can be divided into two complementary sub-envelopes: the body envelope and the cognitive envelope.

Stimulations coming from external reality are first grasped by both envelopes which have a screening function helping the psychic system and somatic reality understand them. These envelopes are more or less permeable and process stimulations with various degrees of transformation. We are dealing here with the problematic analysis, assessing the degree of openness of internal reality, notably of psychic reality, to information coming from external reality.

Once they have entered psychic reality, stimulations have to be metabolized by the psychic system. We are dealing with the drive binding work, notably through symbolic elaboration. This corresponds to the level of system evaluation, i.e. the psychic system's capacity to change so as to be able to metabolize this new element, this outside body which represents the external object within the psychic reality.

This psychically –bound energy also goes through the body which does its metabolic work as well. This aspect is not developed.

The subject does not receive outside stimulations in a passive way. He or she is the creator and actor of this three-dimensional reality. Reactivity shows both the orientation and the implementation of the subject's response. The subject's potential emotions, cognitions, behaviors as well as somatic expressions must be grasped in their relationship and reciprocal interactions, as suggested by the functional analysis developed in cognitive and behavioral therapy.

The subject's reactivity has an impact on external reality (which, in turn, will have to achieve the same sort of filtering and metabolic work of the subject's response to remain a social body), but also on the subject's own body and psychic system, just like the return of a boomerang.

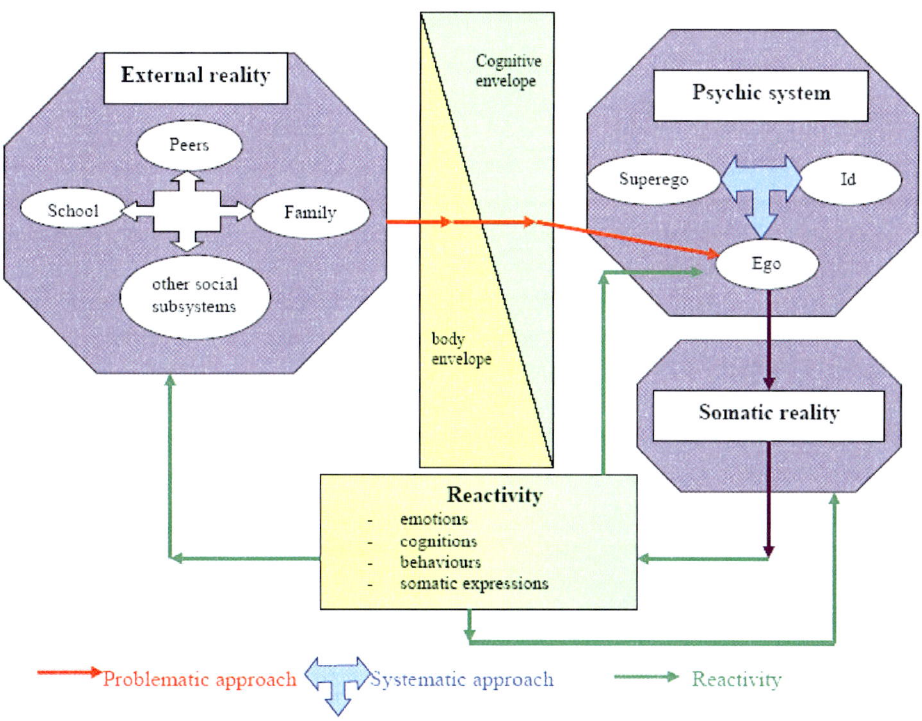

5. Narcissistic Identity Vulnerability

We can now define the concept of narcissistic identity vulnerability. Since the structuring quality of narcissistic identity vulnerability tells us about the quality of its double libidinal investment regulation function, then narcissistic identity vulnerability indicates a lack of regulation of the double libidinal investment. It can be a defect either in the problematic, systematic or/ and reactivity systems.

Thus the concept of narcissistic identity vulnerability is essentially economic and dynamic.

6. Triple Identity Inscription and Points of Vulnerabilization

The following diagram describes the various layers which take part in the developing of narcissistic identity. Identity depends on the quality of the socializing and humanizing inscription which is given by the family group, in which the individual takes a specific place, and in the various social groups, thus giving the way the individual takes his place in the social fabric.

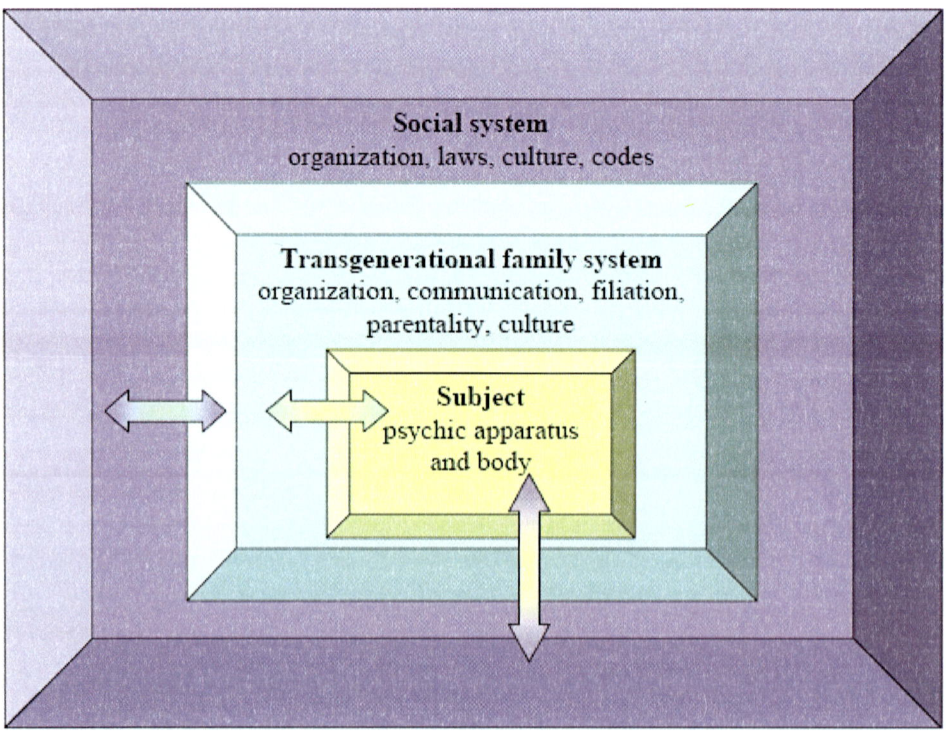

Diagram 3. The three layers of identity development.

7. Operationalization

The table below gives a detailed description of the tools and some indications used for each evaluation stage:

Problematic approach/ cognitive envelope	Wechsler's intelligence test Rorschach's psychogram with the projective technique
Problematic approach/ body envelope	Fisher and Cleveland' barrier and penetration index with Rorschach's projective test
Systematic approach	Cassiers's symbolic elaboration index completed with a drive activation index (Bardouil 2002) with Rorschach's projective test Dynamic analysis of responses to Rorschach in relation to the symbolism of plates (anxiety, defense mechanisms…)
Inscription in transgenerational family dynamic (across generations)	Genogram and Life line (graphic representation of individual and family anamnesis, N. Bardouil) Family test (FAST,T. Gehring, Zurich university)
Inscription in social group	Adaptation of the Family test into an institution Test
Reactivity	Criminological behavioral analysis of maladjusted behaviors + dynamic and economic analysis from the economic typology of maladjusted behaviors (Bardouil, 2002)

For the problematic approach, as concerns the cognitive envelope, we use Wechsler's intelligence test and the psychogram with Rorschach's test. As concerns the body envelope, we use Fischer and Cleveland's Barrier and Penetration index, calculated from a specific rating of the responses to Rorschach's test. For the systematic approach, we use Cassiers's symbolic elaboration of sexual and aggressive drives, improved with a drive activation index which allows us to nuance Cassiers's index. We also do a dynamic analysis of the responses to Rorschach' test by focusing particularly on response contents, referring to the symbolism of plates, to defense mechanisms, and to the nature and intensity of anxiety.

As concerns the place in the transgenerational family dynamic, we use the genogram and the Life Line, as well as T. Gehring's family test. (From Zurich university)

As for the place in the social group, we suggest an adaptation of the family test, changed into an institution test, inviting the teenager to speak about the institution, adults, and the peers he lives with during his or her placement.

Finally, as concerns reactivity, we use a behavioral and criminological approach of maladjusted behaviors. It is completed by an economic-dynamic analysis of maladjusted behaviors, with notably a new typology for the analysis of maladjusted behaviors.

8. Analysis of Maladjusted Behaviors

Maladjusted Behaviors and Acting Out

In order to explain this notion of economic-dynamic analysis of maladjusted behaviors, we have to redefine it in relation to the acting-out concept.

Acting out is not a behavior; It is a psychic process which shows the failure of drive binding and a break in internal coherence, which results in a major destructive, Ego or hetero-centered act. This concept has a serious limit, because it does not enable us to take into account all adolescent maladjusted behaviors. Indeed, a number of maladjusted behaviors cannot be considered as acting out. For example, a teenager smoking hashish every night before going to sleep is not part of it.

André Green, in his work on anxiety and narcissism, mentions a frequent defense strategy to fight against psychic pain; he calls it "unsettled space limits".

He mentions wandering and traveling as examples of this. These defenses' distinctive feature is that they are acted out.

This suggestion offers us a new opening, which is the possibility to consider the behavior itself as a defense strategy and no longer only as the enacted result of the failure of defense mechanisms.

Thus we develop a model of analysis of the dynamics and the economy of maladjusted behaviors, by putting forward a typology.

Typology of the Dynamics and the Economy of Maladjusted Behaviors

This typology aims at differentiating three types of maladjusted behaviors: defensive, destructive and borderline ones.

Defensive behaviors' characteristic feature is that they are meant to test the reality, the permanence and the strength of boundaries. They have a defensive function in the sense that the psychic apparatus wants to move external boundaries whereas it is not or no longer possible to move, to adapt internal boundaries. They make it possible, then, to achieve in externalizing and acting, the metabolic work which is normally supposed to take place internally. We make a difference between minor and major defensive behaviors, according to their seriousness and intensity.

Destructive behaviors consist of destructing or attempting to destruct the external object causing the derangement and thus the pain. They can emerge either suddenly, because at one point the psychic apparatus is suddenly invaded, which means that it was severely vulnerable. Or else they appear after one or several defensive behaviors which were not strong enough to cope with the perturbations caused by the external object. Here again we distinguish minor from major destructive behaviors according to their seriousness and intensity. The acting out essentially corresponds to destructive behaviors.

Finally, we put forward the notion of borderline behaviors. We are dealing with behaviors which are neither defensive, in the sense of moving or testing the permanence and strength of boundaries, nor destructive,, in the sense that the object is not likely to be attacked. These behaviors stand in between these two types, as it's the boundary itself which is attacked, crossed. This is not done in order to test reality, but to size up the consequence of going beyond the limit, cross the boundary, like in the myth of the Rubicon, the river that must not be crossed at all if you did not want to be excluded from human life and world, but that some did cross without anything happening to them.

Minor defensive Rated 1	major defensive Rated 2	Boundary Rated 3	minor destructive Rated 4	major destructive Rated 5
Behavior disorders School problems Absenteeism Repeating a school year Petty offence	delinquency linked to substance abuse Substance abuse Running away Stealing a vehicle shoplifting Common theft	Ego- mutilation Housebreaking Some suicide attempts	Robbing someone Aggravated theft Suicide attempt vandalism	Major physical violence Sexual offence Assault on someone Suicide

The graphic illustration is built from the rating of all the listed maladjusted behaviors according to this typology, presented in chronological order of appearance. It makes up a psycho-criminological profile (PPC- teenage)

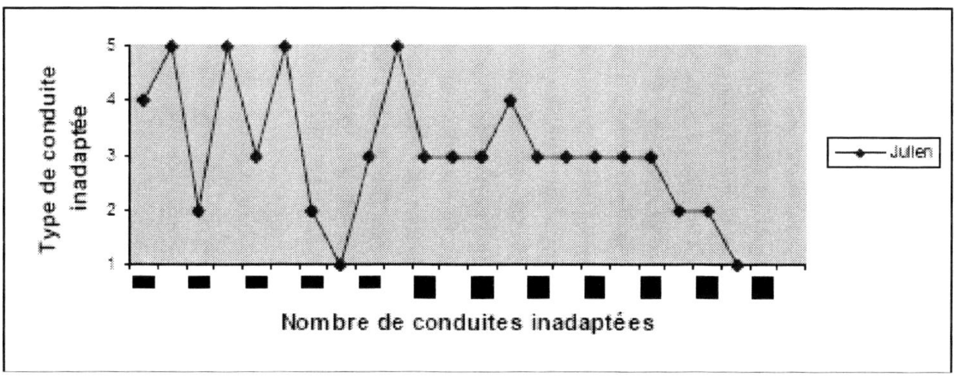

We can then proceed to the spotting of stages, cycles, breaks, questioning. This analysis is always done by taking into account the anamnestic context of the emergence of maladjusted behaviors (see Life Line below)

In Julien's case, which is used as an illustration, we can see how, after a very eventful stage, alternating defensive and destructive behaviors, we reach a borderline plateau. The anamnesis tells us that at the end of this limit cycle, society's response is imprisonment.

This socio-judiciary decision answers the question of the consequence of crossing the border, into anomie. This answer makes Julien give up the destructive dynamics to take up a more defensive one. Indeed he is still an offender, but he is no longer into a destructive attitude.

An example of a Life Line

The Life Line is a graphic illustration of the teenager's individual and family anamnesis.

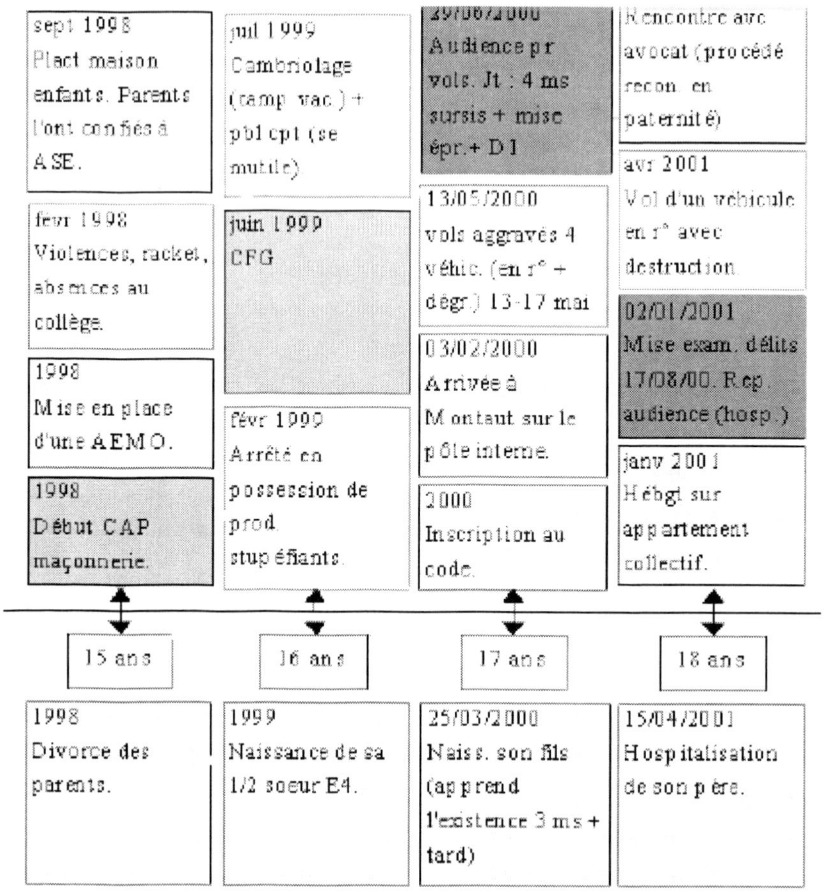

An example of a Life Line.

A color codification allows us to differentiate life events (yellow), school record (blue), institution record (green), criminal record (red border), court record (red).

The time line is punctuated by all the ages of the teenager's life and not only the dates when events happen. This presentation makes it easier to analyze the impact of events on the teenager's development. It also makes it easier to see the links between life events and the appearance of maladjusted behaviors. In the extract shown here, it can be noticed that significant family life events are present when offences are committed..

9. Example of a Genogram

The here shown genogram has been set up from elements known to the multidisciplinary team at the institution where the adolescent is placed. This graphic illustration allows us to take account simultaneously of the family composition, various family members' individual problematics and relationships between family members.

The analysis is then made from the notions and concepts of a family system: family secrets, transgenerational repetition.

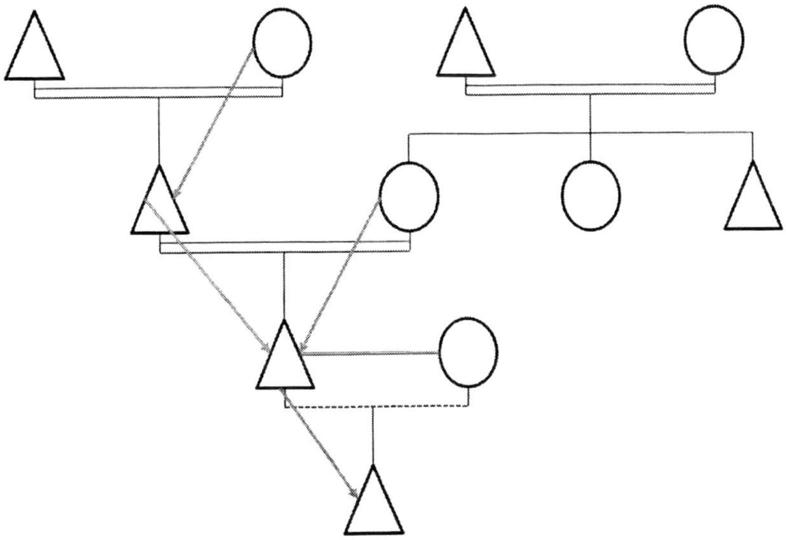

10. Clinical Case : Remy, 18 Years Old

Problemati approach	Cognitive envelope	strong normal intellectual efficiency Non-significant.VIQ < PIQ difference < 12 points Thought invaded/overrun by affects Skills inhibition when confronted with conventionality constraints Good norms and social codes internalization Defensive intellectual rigidity Poor Ego representation. Dangerous identification figure Paranoid-like real-life experiences. Global apprehension
	Body envelope	lack of differentiation of the ego and the non-ego Strong malleability Intrusive life experiences
Systematic approach	Symbolic elaboration	Good capacities for symbolic elaboration
	Inner resonance	introversive participation of imaginary life
	Anxiety	fear of castration fear of death
	Sexual identity	failure of sexuation process (androgyny)
	Mood	depressive elements
	Relationship to others:	dependence and search for affection
Family dynamics	relation to parental imagoes	Paranoid functioning rooted as relationship model. Access to autonomy goes through breaking with parental imagoes

	Relationship to the mother	indifferentiation, lack of triangulation
	Relationship to the father:	emotional deprivation. Search for affection provocation
	Identification	impossible identification to the father. Identification with a deviant model Search for the abolition of intergenerational difference
	Family differentiation	Double
Social integration	sociocultural	no intercultural integration
Reactivity	defensive behaviors	consumption of cannabis, provocation, call for father's help Risk behaviors during a depressive phase
	Destructive behaviors	destruction of the subject's double

11. Conclusions and Applications for a Preventive and Therapeutic Practice

The suggested modeling technique and the concept of narcissistic identity vulnerability lead to a triple psychodynamic analysis: etiological, structural and functional. It opens up new perspectives for a preventive and therapeutic practice with adolescents displaying maladjusted behaviors.

Etiological Analysis

As concerns the etiological analysis, we are more precisely dealing with transgenerational developmental psychic etiology of narcissistic identity vulnerability. The level of this analysis permits to answer such questions as:

What is the origin of narcissistic identity vulnerability?

What are the points of break, failure in the identity development of the adolescent?

What are the intrapsychic and family deprivations that need working on to help the adolescent get over the teenage identity crisis, i.e. to recover an I adapted to the Ego and to social reality?

Structural Analysis

The structural analysis consists in an economic analysis of the structuring quality of narcissistic identity, regulating quality of the double libidinal investment. It notably consists in an evaluation of anxieties, defense mechanisms and their adaptive nature.

The level of this analysis allows us to bring some answers to such questions as: How did the adolescent structure his identity to ensure at least a psychic adaptation and at best a social adaptation? What do the failures of these adaptations entail on the behavioral level?

Functional Analysis

Finally, the functional analysis is not the functional analysis of behavioral and cognitive (though it includes the latter) therapies, but an analysis which questions the economic function of maladjusted behaviors.

It combines an economic and criminological-behavioral analysis of maladjusted behaviors.

This analysis allows us to answer such questions as: What meaning should be given to maladjusted behaviors? In what psychic economy do they take their place? What risk of new maladjusted behaviors appearing is there? What living conditions increase the risk?

This directly answers magistrates' questions on the possibility of re-offending and on measures to be taken to avoid these behaviors.

What Institutional Plan for a Shelter for Teenage Offenders?

We had assumed that the analysis of the adolescent's representation of the institution would enable us to evaluate his social inscription in continuity with his family inscription, the Community Home offering a socializing space with psycho-affective care inspired from the family environment.

Our findings show that, for these adolescents, the institution appears to be a place of mere projection of their family problematics much more than to be a place of socialization and this in spite of a contrary explicit request for vocational training, social integration and an initial and obvious refusal to mention family history.

Family therapeutic work thus appears to be a prerequisite for any socio-professional training and integration work, otherwise the social space, in its turn, is likely to become or become again a place of projection of the problematics, and as a result a place favoring maladjusted behaviors.

References

J. LACAN, Le stade du miroir comme formateur de la fonction du Je (1949), in *Les Ecrits*, Seuil (1966), p. 90.

GEHRING T.M., DEBRY M. (1992). *L'évaluation du système familial:* le FAST. ATM : Braine-Le-Château.

A. GREEN, Narcissisme de vie, narcissisme de mort, chapitre 3 : l'angoisse et le narcissisme (1979), *Editions de minuit*, p.152.

In: Delinquency: Causes, Reduction and Prevention
Editor: Ozan Sahin and Joseph Maier
ISBN 978-1-60741-558-9

Chapter 12

PSYCHOSOCIAL BACKGROUND AND MOTIVATIONS IN HOMICIDE WITH AND WITHOUT PREMEDITATION

Nicolas Combalbert[1]*, Hélène Bazex[2], Dorothée Lazorthes[3] and Anne Andronikof[1]

[1]Université de Paris X –Laboratoire IPSé
(Psychopathologie de l'Identité, de la Pensée et Processus de Santé).
200 avenue de la République 92001 Nanterre, France
[2]Ecole Nationale d'Administration Pénitentiaire,
440 avenue Michel Serres BP28, 47916 Agen Cedex 9, France
[3]Université Paris V –Département de psychologie, 71 avenue Edouard Vaillant,
92774 Boulogne Cedex France

ABSTRACT

Premeditation in homicide is defined as the clear intention to kill someone preceding the act. There is little research on the personal and social context and the psychological and pathological variables associated with premeditation.

Our study compares two groups of inmates, all convicted of homicide, through 210 penal and prison files of the male homicide inmates of the Muret Detention Centre (South West region of France).

The groups were constituted on the basis of the penal conviction label: 94 were labelled "premeditated murder" (group 1) and 116 "unpremeditated murder" (group 2).

The results revealed socio-demographic, psychiatric and forensic differences between the groups.

In the logistic regression model, a higher risk of committing a first degree murder (*vs.* second degree) was related to being socially isolated during the days preceding the homicide (OR 2.86). Furthermore, jealousy motives (OR 5.80) and revenge motives (OR 8.33) were the most significant risk factors in committing premeditated murder.

Finally, we discuss these results and propose two distinct criminological profiles for the individuals in the two groups.

* Corresponding author: 35 rue de la Gaîté 75014 PARIS – France. *E-mail address:* ncombalbert@hotmail.com

Keywords: homicide, premeditation, psychological background, motivations, criminological profiles.

1. Introduction

Various criteria for classifying homicides are used in the world [1]. In France, in the category of intentional homicide (as opposed to manslaughter), the penal code distinguishes between "murder" and "assassination", the latter describing a murder with premeditation (articles 221-1 and 221-3 of the penal code) [2]. Corresponding terms in American Law would be "second degree murder" for murder and "first degree murder" for assassination. Premeditation is defined as the clear intention to kill someone preceding the act. A conviction for murder is punished by up to 30 years of imprisonment whereas assassination leads to life imprisonment.

The notion of premeditation therefore has a crucial importance for the Law and consequently for the indicted person but it has seldom been studied in its psychological and/or psycho-pathological dimensions, i.e. what type of personal and social context breeds premeditation and whether there is a psychological counterpart to the distinction between "murder" and "assassination" [3].

This study is an initial approach to the question and compares two groups of inmates convicted of homicide, according to several socio-demographic, psychiatric and forensic characteristics.

2. Material and Methods

The Ministry of Justice and the Penitentiary Board granted us access to some penal files and authorized us to collect data.

All the legal and prison files of the male homicide inmates of the Muret Detention Centre (South West region of France) were screened and the groups were constituted on the basis of the penal conviction label, i.e. "premeditated murder" *vs.* "unpremeditated murder".

Certain subjects had been convicted on several charges. In such cases, we only admitted the first charge mentioned in the court order, which entailed the longest imprisonment sentence.

Excluding the persons who had been in prison for less than 5 years, 210 files were retrieved of which 94 were labelled "premeditated murder" (group 1) and 116 "unpremeditated murder" (group 2). We selected subjects who had spent at least five years in jail so as to monitor the evolution of their behavior while incarcerated.

The data were collected by two psychologists between September 2002 and September 2003. Information was then computed following the 161 item questionnaire developed from the violent crimes kinetic model which explores the history of the subject, the criminal pattern and their feelings, moods and thoughts before, during and after the homicidal act [4]. Information was drawn from all the available legal material kept at the penal records department of the detention centre, including penal file, decisions of the Parole Commission, legal extracts of the Court decision, forensic psychiatric and psychological assessments (both pre-trial and during detention), recommendations to the court when conditional release had been filed, evaluation of the social environment, behavioural reports during detention, and the report from the National Observation Centre in Fresnes where the newly convicted are examined and observed for several months before being sent to their detention centre (psychosocial, psychological and psychiatric assessments performed by health professionals).

Most variables studied in the research such as "motives" or the "risk of antisocial behavior" were assessed by expert psychologists and psychiatrists as requested by the judge prior to the trial. Therefore, we didn't interpret or analyze these variables, we only gave them a code (yes/no). Every single penal file was simultaneously studied by two psychologists. Hence, the presence or the absence of the elements necessary for the study was systematically double-checked while collecting the data.

It should be indicated that for each subject we only admitted one type of motivation, the one that led to committing murder, whether premeditated or not. The motivation type was specified in the bill of indictment and/or during the psychiatric and/or psychological assessment.

We hypothesized that there are socio-demographic, psychiatric and forensic differences between the groups.

3. Results

The average age in group 1 (n=94) was 43.92 years (23-76, SD = 13.98), in group 2 (n=116) it was 42.15 years (23-74, SD = 11.97). The socio-demographic characteristics (age, nationality, education background, professional status, military and penal situation, children), of the groups were similar except for marital status, with more single people in group 2 (60.3% *vs.* 43.6% in group 1; $p < .05$). The familial characteristics (familial penal background, siblings, familial difficulties, abuses, and relations) of the groups were similar.

Diagnostics screening (structural and intelligence), impulsivity (physical and verbal behaviour and suicide...) and medical characteristics obtained no difference between the groups. The main items about the global modus operandi (prior, during and after the crime) such as the characteristics of the context, offender's affect (except culpability), the crime itself, and victim's characteristics did not differ between the groups; nor did medical treatment in jail. Table 1. presents the main differences between the groups

Among the 161 variables studied, only 11 present significant differences between the groups. Motives in group 1 were more frequently jealousy (42.5% *vs.* 24.1%) or revenge (37.3% vs. 25.8%); in group 2 they were of a sexual (18.9% *vs.* 7.4% in group 1) or financial nature (19.8% *vs.* 10.6%). Group 2 revealed a higher percentage of non motivated crimes (11.3% *vs.* 2.2%).

To summarize, people in group 1 (murder with premeditation) were more frequently social outcasts and had more obvious criminal motives than people from group 2; they also experienced guilt feelings after committing their acts and were aware of their seriousness.

Frequently, people in group 2 (murder without premeditation) had a criminal history and addiction to toxic substances, and they were more often deemed dangerous by psychiatrists. During detention, they were punished with disciplinary confinement and according to the psychiatrists, a proportion of offenders in both groups was qualified as being at risk developing antisocial behaviour upon their release from prison, but group 2 more frequently than group 1.

Table 1. The main differences between group 1 and group 2 (χ^2 test)

Characteristics	Group 1 ($N = 94$) (%)	Group 2 ($N = 116$) (%)
	$p < .001$	
Apparent motives	97.8	88.7
	$p < .01$	
Criminal record	37.2	53.4
Social isolation	65.9	44.8
Drug use	44.6	64.6
Guilt feelings	29.8	15.5
	$p < .05$	
Marital status (single)	43.6	60.3
Drug addiction record	41.5	58.6
Dangerousness	11.7	23.2
Awareness of seriousness of act	64.9	50
Disciplinary measures	40.4	54.3
Risk of antisocial behaviour upon release	35.1	51.7

The logistic regression was estimated using a backward stepwise regression. The level of significance for entering variables was set at 0.05. Three variables were chosen in the final model. The estimated model appears to have good predictive power (82%).

Hence, a higher risk of committing first degree murder (*vs.* second degree) was related to being socially isolated in the days preceding the homicide (OR 2.86, $p<.01$, IC 1.46-5.61). Furthermore, jealousy motives (OR 5.80, $p<.05$, IC 1.12-29.86) and revenge motives (OR 8.33, $p<.01$, IC 1.66-44.28) were the most significant risk factors for committing a murder with intent.

4. Discussion

Among the variables that failed at distinguishing the groups are those which describe the family histories and relationships. Most of the individuals from both groups reported family disturbances during childhood and school failure. This finding is well documented in international literature [5,6,7].

Statistically significant differences between the groups describe two criminological profiles for persons convicted of murder. Second degree murderers appear to act under the influence of a substance. In our study, it was the case for 64.6% of the group. The relation between substance abuse and second-degree murder is well known [8,9].

Behaviour during detention is consistent with the profiles so described. Considering the fact that first-degree murderers are more inclined to recognize their guilt and more aware of the seriousness of their crime.

Conversely, second-degree murderers appear to have less insight, to be less aware of the seriousness of their act and they tend to experience difficulties in adjusting to social life and/or in abiding by prison rules in detention. The criminological profiles of the persons in the two groups stand in contrast: the persons incarcerated for second degree murder have a history of poor social adjustment (their history of delinquency is much more frequent and they undergo more disciplinary sanctions) and of substance abuse [10]. Psychiatrists tend to consider them as dangerous and at risk of delinquent behaviour on release from prison.

People incarcerated for first-degree murder present a more specific pre-homicide pattern (as evidenced in the logistics regression analysis): they have jealousy and/or revenge feelings and become socially isolated. This type is evocative of what Pinatel (1975) described as "pseudo dispenser of justice" crimes [11].

The results also showed the impact of social isolation on an unpremeditated acting out (group 2). Little literature is available on the quality of the murderers' social relations the days preceding the acting out. The relation between social variables and homicide was dealt at a « macro – criminological » level, showing that the indicators of social aids are inversely and significantly associated to the frequency of violent crimes [12]. At an individual level, the theoretic modelisation « General Strain Theory » grants the immediate social environment as well as the different levels of social aids an influence on the way individuals respond to tension [13]. The relations between the social aid (perceived social aid, « objectivized » social aid and immediate social aid), tension, and situational anger were examined with the intention to commit a crime (Proposals of criminal scénarii) [14]. However, the sampling and the methodology used prevent any comparison with the results of our research.

The influence of social isolation on the type of homicide (premeditated or not) deserves a development through a conceptual and methodological survey of the social aid and on a population of criminals and offenders.

The results obtained on the specific motivations of group 1 show the impact of the feeling of revenge and jealousy through the premeditated murder acting out. We found no survey on the motivations for homicides according to the dichotomy of premeditation.

However, the study of the motivations for homicide were the subject of empirical research centred around specific group, such as spouse [15], family [16], serial killer [17], homicides as well as suicide [18].

It appears difficult to find a specific motivation concerning homicides committed by serial killers: some say they are « wanton crimes », « apparently motiveless » [17], others think it is a will to express a power on the victim [19]. Concerning the homicides committed in the family circle, the authors mentioned report a predominancy of jealousy and possessive feelings expressed within the scope of a couple's relation towards the spouse [15] or transferred on the child [16]. The jealousy and revenge feelings were also found within the scope of homicide – suicide [18].

Our results are in accordance with the current literature in the sense of a predominancy of jealousy and revenge motivations within the scope of homicides committed mainly within a family context. Indeed, 80% of the group 1 population have killed a family member. The jealousy and revenge feeling invades the processes of thought and inhibits all other aspects of mental and emotional life [20,21]. As emotion becomes central in the person's life, so does the building of plans [22] to retaliate, to bring justice or simply to eliminate the culprit. Social withdrawal induces a blurring of the real world and increases self-focus and introspection

[23,24]. In the absence of external criteria of judgment, the sense of grievance turns into paranoia and the persecutor is seen as the perfect victim-target.

Conclusion

This study shows that from a criminological viewpoint, differences between the people who commit homicides (first degree *vs.* second degree murder) exist. However, the main limit to this study lies in the experts' subjectivity and in their methodology to assess and determine the subjects' motivations or the risks of antisocial behavior. Thus, it now appears necessary to explore these characteristics through a standardized protocol based on objective criteria. This could explain why in France very few studies have had criminal motivations as their main topic [25,26].

Motivational aspects of homicide need to be further explored, in particular jealousy [27] and revenge [28,29]. Criminal motivations are difficult to study insofar as they probably involve complex mental processes and different levels of consciousness, and are complicated by toxic states, cautiousness and concealment in the indicted person [30]. Social isolation is known to be a risk factor of homicide in general but its precise role in and degree of influence on the genesis of crime remains to be understood.

Further comparisons between different types of murder (here fist-degree *vs.* second-degree) are needed for advancing our understanding of the exact nature of premeditation and motives [31].

References

[1] M.J. Mohanty, Variants of homicides: a review. *Journal of Clinical Medicine* 11 (2004) 214-18.

[2] Code pénal, Livre II, Titre II, Dalloz, Paris, 2005.

[3] E. Green, R. Wakefield, Patterns of middle and upper class homicide. *Journal of Criminal Law and Criminology* 70(2) (1979)172-81.

[4] N. Combalbert, A.M. Favard, S. Bourdet-Loubere, Un nouveau modèle criminologique : la cinétique du crime. *Revue Française Psychiatrie et Psychologie Médicale* 70 (2003) 37-43.

[5] R. Block, *Homicide in Chicago*, Loyola University Press, Chicago, 1986.

[6] L. Mucchielli, Approche sociologique de l'homicide. *Etude exploratoire*, CESDIP : Etudes et données pénales, Guyancourt, 2002.

[7] T. Laajasalo, H. Häkkänen, Background characteristics of mentally ill homicide offenders – a comparison of five diagnostic groups. *Journal of Forensic Psychiatry and Psychology* 15(3) (2004) 451-74.

[8] E.C. Senay, R. Wettstein, Drugs and homicide: A theory. *Drug and Alcohol Dependence* 12(2) (1983) 157-66.

[9] K. Tardiff, P. M. Marzuk, K. Lowell, L. Portera and A. C. Leon, A study of drug abuse and other causes of homicide in New-York. *Journal of Criminal Justice* 30(4) (2002) 317-25.

[10] C.G. Salfati and DV. Canter, Differentiating stranger murders: profiling offender characteristics from behavioural styles. *Behavioral Sciences and the Law* 17(3) (1999) 391-406.

[11] J. Pinatel, *Traité de droit pénal et de criminologie*, Dalloz, Paris, 1975.

[12] T.C. Pratt, Godsey T.W., Social support and homicide: a cross-national test of an emerging criminological theory. *Journal of criminal Justice* 30 (2002) 589-601.

[13] R. Agnew, A revised strain theory of delinquency. *Social Forces* 64 (1992) 151-167.

[14] G.E. Capowich, P. Mazerolle, A. Piquero, General strain theory, situational anger, and social networks. An assessment of conditioning influences. *Journal of criminal Justice* 29 (2001) 445-461.

[15] G. Serran, P. Firestone, Intimate partner homicide: a review of the male proprietariness and the self defense theories. *Aggression and violent behaviour* 9 (2004) 1-15.

[16] K. Cavanagh, E.R. Dobash, R.P. Dobash, The murder of children by father in the context of child abuse. *Child Abuse and Neglect* 31 (2007) 731-746.

[17] J.L. Senninger, E. Hiegel, J.P. Kahn, Le Tueur en série, *Annales Médico-Psychologiques* 162 (2004) 634-644.

[18] C.M. Milroy, The epidemiology of homicide-suicide. *Forensic Science International* 71 (1995) 117-122.

[19] C.J. Ferguson, D.E. White, S. Cherry, M. Lorenz, Z. Bhimani, Defining and classifying serial murder in the context of perpetrator motivation. *Journal of Criminal Justice* 31(3) (2003) 287-292.

[20] W.C. Myers, K. Scott, A.W. Burgess, A.G. Burgess, Psychopathology, biopsychosocial factors, crime characteristics, and classification of 25 homicidal youths. *J. Am. Acad. Child Adolesc. Psychiatry* 34(11) (1995) 1483-9.

[21] W.A. Pridemore, What we know about social structure and homicide: a review of the theoretical and empirical literature. *Violence and victims* 17(2) (2002) 127-56.

[22] A. Andronikof, Le passage à l'acte comme réalisation d'un scénario privé. *L'Evolution Psychiatrique* 66 (2001) 632-9.

[23] W.H. Martens, G.B. Palermo, Loneliness and associated violent antisocial behaviour: analysis of the case reports of Jeffrey Dahmer and Dennis Nilsen. *Int. J. Offender Ther Comp. Criminol.* 49(3) (2005) 298-307.

[24] J.R. Meloy, A.G. Hempel, K. Mohandie, A.A. Shiva, B.T. Gray, Offender and offence characteristics of a non-random sample of adolescent mass murderers. *J. Am. Acad. Child Adolesc. Psychiatry* 40(6) (2001) 719-28.

[25] P. Le Bihan, M. Bénézech, Degré d'organisation du crime de parricide pathologique : mode opératoire, profil criminologique. A propos de 42 observations. *Annales Médico-psychologiques* 162(8) (2004) 615-25.

[26] M. Bénézech, Le passage à l'acte homicide en milieu médical et carcéral. *Annales Médico-psychologiques* 163(8) (2005) 632-41.

[27] L. Muzinic, M. Goreta, V. Jukiv, V. Dordevic, E. Koic and M. Herceg, Forensic importance of jealousy. *Coll. Antropol.* 27(1) (2003) 293-300.

[28] C.M. Parkes, Psychiatric problems following bereavement by murder or manslaughter. *British Journal of Psychiatry* 162 (1993) 49-54.

[29] C.M. Milroy, The epidemiology of suicide homicide-suicide (dyadic death). *Forensic Science International* 71 (1995) 117-22.

[30] C.J. Ferguson, D.E. White, S. Cherry, M. Lorenz and Z. Bhimani, Defining and classifying serial murder in the context of perpetrator motivation. *Journal of Criminal Justice* 31 (2003) 287-92.

[31] PH. Schmidt, SA. Padosch, MA. Rotschild and B. Madea, Forensic case profiling aspects on multiple homicides from the Cologne-Bonn Metropolita, Area 1985-2000. *Forensic Science International* 153 (2005) 168-173.

In: Delinquency: Causes, Reduction and Prevention
Editor: Ozan Sahin and Joseph Maier

ISBN 978-1-60741-558-9

Chapter 13

SHYNESS *AND* SOCIABILITY: A DANGEROUS COMBINATION FOR ANTISOCIAL AND DELINQUENT BEHAVIOR?◊

Louis A. Schmidt*
Department of Psychology, Neuroscience and Behaviour
McMaster University

ABSTRACT

The search for the origins of antisocial and delinquent behavior has a long and rich history in the fields of personality and abnormal psychology. Current thinking suggests that a combination of two orthogonal personality traits, shyness *and* sociability, may play an important role in understanding antisocial and delinquent behavior. The author argues that an interaction of these two traits results in a "socially conflicted" personality style. Socially conflicted individuals exhibit distinct patterns of brain and autonomic activity at rest and in response to social challenge and are at risk for antisocial and delinquent behaviors. These individuals may engage in risky and antisocial behaviors as a means of coping with their conflict.

The search for personality predictors of risky and antisocial behavior has a long and rich history in personality theory and abnormal psychology. This work can be traced to noted personality theorists such as Gordon Allport (1937), Henry Murray (1938), and Hans Eysenck (1967). However, recent research on the topic suggests that a combination of two orthogonal personality traits, in particular, may play an important role in understanding antisocial and delinquent behaviors. These two traits are shyness *and* sociability.

◊ Much of this chapter appeared in two earlier newsletters: *Mental Notes Magazine*, 26-27, Fall, 2008, and the *International Society for the Study of Behavioural Development Newsletter*, *27*(3), 6-8, 2003.

* Address correspondence to: Louis A. Schmidt, Department of Psychology, Neuroscience and Behaviour, McMaster University, Hamilton, Ontario L8S 4K1 Canada. Email: schmidtl@mcmaster.ca

Three decades ago, Cheek and Buss (1981) suggested that some people appear quiet and reserved in social situations but probably for different reasons. Cheek and Buss asked: Are these people shy and reserved because they feel anxious and inhibited in social situations (i.e., they are shy). Or are these people quiet and reserved because they have little need to affiliate with others (i.e., they are introverted)? Cheek and Buss found that there were indeed people who varied in both shyness and sociability. These investigators then selected participants who were shy *and* social and observed them in a social interaction. The shy *and* social participants appeared conflicted in their interactions, displaying more overt anxiety than other combinations of shy and social participants. It was if the participants who were shy *and* social wished to interact, but felt inhibited and restrained in doing so.

Are Socially Conflicted Individuals at Risk for Antisocial and Delinquent Behaviors?

It turns out that socially conflicted individuals are in fact at risk for a range of behavior problems. Research has shown that adolescents and young adults who are shy *and* social (i.e., socially conflicted) are likely to engage in risky and antisocial behaviors. For instance, adolescents (Page, 1990) and young adults (Santesso, Schmidt, and Fox, 2004) who are shy *and* social are more likely than shy and low social and nonshy people to engage in illicit drug use and are likely to use and abuse alcohol, possibly leading to increased delinquency. Other recent studies have implicated a combination of shyness and sociability in other forms of psychopathology, including depression and anxiety (Schmidt and Fox, 1995) and, most recently, disordered eating in non-clinical samples of young adult women (Miller, Schmidt, and Vaillancourt, 2006, 2008). We have speculated that engaging in risky and controlled behaviors (perhaps in the case of disordered eating) in socially conflicted individuals is presumably their attempt to cope with the ongoing psychological conflict that they experience in social situations or anticipation of social interactions. These coping behaviors, however, may often be problematic and may lead to antisocial and delinquent behaviors and psychopathology.

What Are the Origins of Socially Conflicted Behavior?

The origins of socially conflicted behavior are undoubtedly multiply-determined, including environmental and biological influences and their interactions. Evidence from our laboratory, however, suggests that the frontal cortical brain and forebrain limbic areas involved in the regulation of emotion and autonomic output may play key roles. There appear two be distinct neural systems underlying shyness and sociability. For example, in a recent study (Beaton, Schmidt et al., 2008), we collected brain scans on shy and socially outgoing adults using fMRI measures while they were presented with personally familiar and stranger faces. We found that shy adults exhibited more amygdala (an area of the brain involved in threat detection) activation when presented with stranger faces, while social adults displayed more activity in the nucleus accumbens (an area of the brain involved in reward and pleasure). We have also noted distinct patterns of psychophysiological responses during baseline and in response to social stress in people who are shy *and* social. For example, adults who are shy exhibit greater relative frontal brain electrical (EEG) activity at baseline, while social adults display greater relative left frontal EEG activity at baseline (Schmidt, 1999). Interestingly, those adults who were shy *and* social exhibited greater relative right frontal EEG activity that was characterized by increased activity in both the left and right frontal brain regions during baseline compared with adults self-reporting other combinations of shyness and sociability. We have also found that shy *and* social people exhibit a distinct pattern of autonomic activity in response to social challenge (Schmidt and Fox, 1994). The socially conflicted individuals exhibited a higher and more stable heart rate in response to an anticipated social interaction. We speculated that the pattern of heightened activity in both the left and right frontal region and high and stable heart rate may reflect a predisposition to experience heightened positive and negative affect, resulting in an approach-avoidance conflict (i.e., a conflict between an individual's desire to affiliate with others, but also the experience of fear in doing so).

What Is Next?

Shyness and sociability represent two of the most salient temperamental features that are conserved across mammals and whose neural substrates underlying their expression are beginning to be well-mapped. Extreme shyness has been a consistent predictor of internalizing-related problems (e.g., anxiety, depression, withdrawal), while extreme sociability has been a robust predictor of externalizing-related problems (e.g., aggression, hyperactivity, delinquency). An interaction of these two traits may serve as a dangerous combination for the development of internalizing- and externalizing-related problems in adolescents and young adults above and beyond manifesting one trait. Given that the two traits manifest and express themselves in early infancy and childhood, identifying and tracking preschool children who exhibit a high degree of shyness *and* sociability is of critical importance to possibly offsetting a developmental course of antisocial and delinquent behaviors and psychopathology.

References

Allport, G.W. (1937). *Personality: A psychological interpretation.* New York: H. Holt, Rinehart and Winston.

Beaton, E.A., Schmidt, L.A., Schulkin, J., Antony, M.M., Swinson, R.P., and Hall, G.B. (2008). Different neural responses to stranger and personally familiar faces in shy and bold adults. *Behavioral Neuroscience, 122*, 704-709.

Cheek, J.M., and Buss, A.H. (1981). Shyness and sociability. *Journal of Personality and Social Psychology, 41*, 330-339.

Eysenck, H.J. (1967). *The biological basis of personality*. Springfield, IL: Thomas.

Miller, J.L., Schmidt, L.A., Vaillancourt, T., McDougall, P., and Laliberte, M. (2006). Neuroticism *and* introversion: A risky combination for disordered eating among a non-clinical sample of undergraduate women. *Eating Behaviors, 7*, 69-78.

Miller, J.L., Schmidt, L.A., and Vaillancourt, T. (2008). Shyness, sociability, and eating problems in a non-clinical sample of female undergraduates. *Eating Behaviors*, *9*, 352-359.

Murray, H.A. (1938). *Explorations in personality*. New York: Oxford University Press.

Page, R.M. (1990). Shyness and sociability: A dangerous combination for illicit substance use in adolescent males? *Adolescence*, *25*, 803-806.

Santesso, D.L., Schmidt, L.A., and Fox, N.A. (2004). Are shyness *and* sociability still a dangerous combination for substance use? Evidence from a U.S. and Canadian sample. *Personality and Individual Differences*, *37,* 5-17.

Schmidt, L.A. (1999). Frontal brain electrical activity in shyness and sociability. *Psychological Science*, *10*, 316-320.

Schmidt, L.A., and Fox, N.A. (1994). Patterns of cortical electrophysiology and autonomic activity in adults' shyness and sociability. *Biological Psychology*, *38*, 183-198.

Schmidt, L.A., and Fox, N.A. (1995). Individual differences in young adults' shyness and sociability: Personality and health correlates. *Personality and Individual Differences, 19*, 455-462.

INDEX

A

B

C

D

E

F

G

H

I

J

K

L

M

N

O

P

Q

R

S

T

U

V

W

Y